An Uncommon Man

Also by

G. WAYNE MILLER

BOOKS

Thunder Rise, 1989

The Work of Human Hands, 1993

Coming of Age, 1995

Toy Wars, 1998

King of Hearts, 2000

Men and Speed, 2002

The Xeno Chronicles, 2005

FILMS

On The Lake: Life and Love in a Distant Place,
    writer and producer, 2009

Behind the Hedgerow: Eileen Slocum
    and the Meaning of Newport Society,
    writer and producer, 2010

AN UNCOMMON MAN

G. WAYNE MILLER

The Life & Times

of Senator Claiborne Pell

University Press of New England

Hanover and London

UNIVERSITY PRESS OF NEW ENGLAND

www.upne.com

© 2011 G. Wayne Miller

All rights reserved

Manufactured in the United States of America

Designed by Eric M. Brooks

Typeset in Arno Pro and Ultra Condensed Sans

by Passumpsic Publishing

University Press of New England is a member of the
Green Press Initiative. The paper used in this book meets
their minimum requirement for recycled paper.

For permission to reproduce any of the material in this
book, contact Permissions, University Press of New England,
One Court Street, Suite 250, Lebanon NH 03766;
or visit www.upne.com

Library of Congress Cataloging-in-Publication Data

Miller, G. Wayne.

An uncommon man: the life and times of Senator Claiborne
Pell / G. Wayne Miller.

   p. cm.

Includes bibliographical references and index.

ISBN 978-1-61168-186-4 (cloth : alk. paper) —

ISBN 978-1-61168-187-1 (e-book)

1. Pell, Claiborne, 1918–2009. 2. Legislators — United States —
Biography. 3. United States. Congress. Senate — Biography.
4. United States — Politics and government — 1945–1989.
5. United States — Politics and government — 1989–
I. Title. II. Title: Life and times of Claiborne Pell.

E840.8.P36M55   2011

328.73'092 — dc23   2011021267

[B]

5 4 3 2 1

For Yolanda Gabrielle

My dearest and bestest

CONTENTS

Illustrations follow page 182

An Uncommon Man

PROLOGUE ▫ A Cold Winter Day

Dawn had barely broken when the crowd began to build outside Trinity Episcopal Church in Newport, Rhode Island. A frigid wind blew and snow frosted the ground. Police had restricted vehicular traffic to allow passage of the motorcade, soon to arrive, carrying a former president, the vice president-elect, and dozens of U.S. senators, representatives, and other dignitaries. Men in sunglasses with bomb-sniffing dogs patrolled the church grounds, where flags flew at half-mast.

It was January 5, 2009, the day of Senator Claiborne deBorda Pell's funeral.

Some of those waiting to get inside Trinity Church were members of Newport society, to which Pell and Nuala, his wife of sixty-four years, had belonged since birth. Some were working-class people who knew Pell as a tall, thin, bespectacled man who once regularly jogged along Bellevue Avenue, greeting strangers and friends that he passed. Some knew him only from the media, where he was sometimes portrayed, not inaccurately, as the capitol's most eccentric character, as interested in the afterlife and the paranormal as the federal budget. Some knew him mostly from the ballot booth or from programs and policies he'd been instrumental in establishing. First elected in 1960, the year his friend John F. Kennedy captured the White House, Pell served thirty-six years in the U.S. Senate, the fourteenth longest term in history as of that January day. His accomplishments from those six terms touched untold millions of lives.

Pell died at a few minutes past midnight on January 1, five weeks after his ninetieth birthday and more than a decade after the first symptoms of Parkinson's disease, which slowly stole all movement and speech, leaving him a prisoner in his own body. He died, his family with him, at his oceanfront home — a shingled, single-story house that he personally designed and which stood in modest contrast to Bellevue Avenue mansions and Bailey's Beach, the exclusive members-only club that has been synonymous with East Coast wealth since the Gilded Age. Pell, whose colonial-era ancestors established enduring wealth from tobacco and land, and Nuala, an heiress to the A&P fortune, belonged to Bailey's. But the Pells were unflinchingly liberal and Democratic. In the old manufacturing state of Rhode Island, where the American Industrial Revolution was born, blue-collar voters embraced their aristocratic senator with the unconventional mind.

The motorcades passed the waiting crowd, which by 9 a.m. was more than a block long. Former President Bill Clinton stepped out of an SUV and went into the parish hall to await the procession to the church. Vice President-elect Joe Biden and Sen. Edward M. Kennedy, whose brain cancer would claim him that summer, followed Clinton. A bus that met a jet from Washington brought more senators, including Majority Leader Harry Reid and Republicans Richard Lugar and Orrin Hatch. Pell's civility and even temper during his decades in the Senate had earned him the respect of his colleagues. "I always try to let the other fellow have my way," is how Pell liked to explain his Congressional style. It was the best means, he maintained, to "translate ideas into actions and help people." He had learned these philosophies from his father, a minor diplomat and one-term Congressman who had cast an inordinate influence on his only child even after his death in the first months of Kennedy's presidency.

The doors to Trinity opened and the crowd went in, filling seats in the loft that had been reserved for the public. The overflow went into the parish hall, to watch the live-broadcast TV feed. Led by their mother, Nuala and Claiborne's children, grandchildren, and great-grandchildren took seats near the pulpit. The politicians settled in pews across the aisle. The organ played, the choir sang, and six Coast Guardsmen wheeled a mahogany casket draped in white to the front of the church.

From early childhood, Pell had loved the sea, an affection he captured in sailboat drawings and grade-school essays about the joys of being on the water. When he was nine, he took an ocean journey that would influence him in ways a young boy could not have predicted: traveling by luxury liner with his mother and stepfather, he went to Cuba and on through the Panama Canal to California and Hawaii. "It was the most interesting voyage I have ever taken," he wrote, when he was twelve, in an essay entitled *The Story of My Life*. After graduating from college in 1940, more than a year before Pearl Harbor, he enlisted in the Coast Guard, pointedly remaining in the reserves until mandatory retirement at age sixty, when he was nearing the end of his third Senate term.

In the many stories that had accompanied his retirement from the Senate, Pell had named the 1972 Seabed Arms Control treaty, which kept the Cold War nuclear arms race from spreading to the ocean floor by prohibiting the testing or storage of weapons deep undersea, as among his favorite achievements. He pointed also to his National Sea Grant College and Program Act of 1966, which provided unprecedented federal funding of university-based oceanography. And one of his deepest regrets, he said 1996, was in failing to achieve U.S. ratification of the international Law of the Sea Treaty, which establishes ocean boundaries and protects global maritime resources.

In planning his funeral, Pell requested a ceremonial honor guard from his beloved service. The Coast Guard granted his wish — and added meaning when selecting Pell's pallbearers. Two of the six had graduated college with the help of Pell Grants, the tuition-assistance program for lower- and middle-income students that Pell called his greatest achievement. Since their inception in 1972, the grants by 2009 had been awarded to more than 115 million recipients. Without them, many could not have earned a college degree.

▫ ▫ ▫ Kennedy left his wife, Vicki, in their pew and walked slowly to the pulpit.

In his nearly eight-minute eulogy, the last substantial speech the final Kennedy brother would make, Ted talked of Pell's fortitude when he and Nuala lost two of their grown children. His hands trembling but his voice strong, he spoke of his family's long relationship with Pell, which began before the Second World War — and of his own friendship with Pell and their thirty-four years together in the Senate. He spoke of Pell's political support for his president brother and his support for his own son, Patrick Kennedy, representative from Rhode Island's First Congressional District, which includes Newport. He recalled the summer tradition of sailing with Vicki on his sailboat, *Maya*, from Long Island to Newport, en route to their home in Hyannis Port on Cape Cod. During their overnight visits with the Pells, Claiborne, who owned no yacht, relished sailing on Ted's boat, even after Parkinson's disease left him in a wheelchair and unable to speak. "The quiet joy of the wind on his face was a sight to behold," Kennedy said.

Kennedy closed with tribute.

"During his brilliant career, he amassed a treasure trove of accomplishments that few will ever match," Kennedy said, citing the Pell Grants, Pell's 1965 legislation that established the National Endowment for the Arts and the National Endowment for the Humanities, and the Seabed Treaty. "It was Claiborne Pell who advocated the power of diplomacy before resorting to the power of military might. And it was Claiborne Pell who was an environmentalist long before that was cool. Claiborne Pell was a senator of high character, great decency and fundamental honesty. And that's why he became the longest serving senator in the history of Rhode Island. He was a senator for our time and for all time. He was an original. He was my friend and I will miss him very much."

Kennedy returned to his pew and Clinton took the pulpit of the historic old church, which has overlooked Newport Harbor since 1726. Drawing laughter, the former president told of first seeing Pell: in 1964, when he was a freshman at Georgetown University living in a dorm that overlooked the backyard of the Pells' Washington home.

"I was this goggle-eyed kid from Arkansas. I had never been anywhere or seen anything and here I was in Washington, D.C., and I got to be a voyeur looking down on all the dinner parties of this elegant man. So I got very interested in the Pell family. And I read up on them, you know. And I realized that they were a form of American royalty. I knew that because it took me twenty-nine years and six months to get in the front door of that house I'd been staring at. When I became president, Senator and Mrs. Pell, who had supported my campaign, invited me in the front door. I received one of Claiborne Pell's courtly tours of his home, which was like getting a tour of the family history. There were all these relatives he had with wigs on. Where I came from only people who were bald wore wigs. And they weren't white and curled. It was amazing.

"And even after all those years, I still felt as I did when I was a boy: that there was something almost magical about this man who was born to aristocracy but cared about people like the people I grew up with."

He cared, too, Clinton said, for the citizens of the world. Clinton spoke of Pell's belief that together, nations can solve the planet's problems — a belief that took root in his childhood travels and solidified in 1945 in San Francisco, where delegates of fifty countries drafted the U.N. Charter. Pell served as an assistant for the American delegation.

"Every time I saw him — every single time — he would pull out this dog-eared copy of the U.N. Charter," Clinton said. "It was light blue, frayed around the edges. I was so intimidated. There I was in the White House and I actually went home one night and read it all again to make sure I could pass a test in case Senator Pell asked me any questions. But I got the message and so did everybody else that ever came in contact with him: that America could not go forward in a world that had only a global economy without a sense of global politics and social responsibility."

The ex-president ended with a reference to ancestors.

"The Pell family's wealth began with a royal grant of land in Westchester County where Hillary and I now live," he said. "It occurred to me that if we had met 300 years ago, he would be my lord and I would be his serf. All I can tell you is: I would have been proud to serve him. He was the right kind of aristocrat: a champion by choice, not circumstance, of the common good and our common future and our common dreams, in a long life of grace, generous spirit, kind heart, and determination, right to the very end. That life is his last true Pell Grant."

Despite the work of transitioning from the Bush to the Obama administration, Biden had taken the morning off to eulogize the man who befriended him when he arrived in Washington in 1972 as a twenty-nine-year-old senator-elect.

Biden had just lost his wife and baby daughter in a car accident. "You made your home my own," Biden said, turning to Nuala. In the Senate, Pell became Biden's mentor.

The Vice-President-elect, who served with Pell on the Senate Foreign Relations Committee, enumerated more of Pell's accomplishments, including legislation that helped build Amtrak and a lesser-publicized campaign against drunk driving—a cause Pell embraced when two of his staff members, including one central in the fight for Pell Grants, were killed by drunk drivers. In these efforts and in all of his Congressional dealings as well as all of his campaigns, none of which he ever lost, Biden noted that Pell brought a gentlemanly sensibility that seemed outdated in an era of hot tempers and slinging mud.

"I'm told, Ted," Biden said, "that your brother, President Kennedy, once said Claiborne Pell was the least electable man in America—a view that, I suppose, was shared by at least six of his opponents when he ran for the United States Senate over the course of thirty-six years."

Laughter filled Trinity Church.

"I understand how people could think that," Biden continued. Here was a graduate of an exclusive college-preparatory school and Princeton, who later earned an advanced degree from another Ivy League school, Columbia—a man born into wealth who married into more and had traveled the world many times over before ever seeking office.

"He didn't have a great deal in common, I suspect, with many of his constituents in terms of background, except this: I think Claiborne realized that many of the traits he learned in his upbringing—honesty, integrity, fair play—they didn't only belong to those who could afford to embrace the sense of *noblesse oblige*. He understood, in my view, that nobility lives in the heart of every man and woman regardless of their situation in life. He understood that the aspirations of the mother living on Bellevue Avenue here in Newport were no more lofty, no more considerable, than the dream of a mother living in an apartment in Bedford-Stuyvesant . . . each of those mothers wanted their children to have the opportunity to make the most of their gifts and the most of their lives."

Biden told some favorite stories, drawing laughter with the one about Pell going for a jog during a trip to Rome dressed in an Oxford-cloth button-down shirt, Bermuda shorts, black socks, and leather shoes—an image of Pell that his friends and family knew well. Sweatsuits and Nikes were not Pell's style.

"To be honest, he was a quirky guy, Nuala," Biden said.

The mourners laughed—Nuala most appreciatively, for she understood best what Biden meant. For two-thirds of a century, she had experienced his odd dress, his obsession with ancestors, his bad driving, his frugality, his fascination with ESP and the possibility of life after death, his manner of speaking, as if he had indeed traveled forward in time from the 1600s, when Thomas Pell was named First Lord of the Manor of Pelham. These traits were all part of his charm, which sometimes annoyed but often amused his wife. This and his handsome looks and ever-curious mind were why Nuala had fallen in love when they met in the summer of 1944, when she was twenty, and why she married him four months later. Claiborne Pell was different. Unlike most other young men of her circle, he aspired to be something more than a rich guy who threw parties.

Biden's eulogy was nearing a half hour, but he had one more story.

"One day, I was sitting in the Foreign Relations Committee room waiting for a head of state to come in." Pell was there.

"He took his jacket off, which was rare — I can't remember why — and I noticed his belt went all the way around the back and it went all the way to the back loop. I looked at him and I said, 'Claiborne, that's an interesting belt.'

"He said, 'it was my father's.' And his father was a big man.

"I looked at him and I said, 'Well, Claiborne, why don't you just have it cut off?'

"He unleashed the whole belt and held it up and said, 'Joe, this is genuine rawhide.' I'll never forget that: 'This is genuine rawhide.' I thought, *God bless me!*"

◻ ◻ ◻ Almost a half-century before, Pell's father, Herbert Claiborne Pell, Jr., had been remembered here in Trinity Church after dying of a heart attack in Munich, Germany, on July 17, 1961. A plaque bearing Herbert's name hung on the wall behind the pulpit from which distinguished men now eulogized his son. "Lay Reader in this Church," the plaque read. "Kind and beloved Public Servant & Scholar. Member 66th United States Congress. United States Minister to Portugal and to Hungary."

Elected from Manhattan's Silk Stocking District, Herbert served one term, from 1919 to 1921, in the U.S. House of Representatives. Losing reelection, he became chairman of New York's Democratic State Committee, remaining until 1926. His friend President Franklin Delano Roosevelt named him Minister to Portugal in 1937, and then, in 1941, Minister to Hungary. When Hitler's war forced Herbert to return home, Roosevelt named him a delegate to the United Nations War Crimes Commission.

Herbert was more an intellectual than a politician — a bibliophile, art collector, and writer whose inheritance allowed him to do whatever he desired. Herbert owned properties in Manhattan, New York state, and Newport, and kept a staff that included a chauffeur and a personal secretary. He traveled extensively, preferring to stay at the many European and American men's clubs to which he belonged. But of all his passions, none rivaled the interest he took in his only child.

Herbert made the decisive decisions about Claiborne's education. He critiqued the young boy's penmanship and tennis serve and brought Claiborne along with him on his world adventures. He used his considerable influence in attempting to place the young man in the military and, after the war, in public service. He advised Claiborne on matters of business, politics, ethics, and love. He responded at length when Claiborne sought his counsel, as Claiborne regularly did. He established the trust fund that would free his son, as his parents had freed him, from the concerns of earning the daily bread. He taught his son that the family had maintained its wealth since the seventeenth century not with the sort of obscene extravagance that had eroded many a Gilded-Age fortune, but by living a refined life without want, but with limits that protected the base for subsequent generations.

"Financial independence, even the humblest, is not a necessity but it is a most desirable concomitant of spiritual and intellectual freedom," he wrote to his son in 1939, the year Claiborne turned twenty-one and Herbert, fifty-five, gave him control of the trust. With the money came words of fatherly wisdom. "I strongly advise you not to make the mistake I made: Do not accumulate possessions. I do not say that if I had my life to live over again I would own nothing except my clothes, but I would give a lot of heart to following that drastic course than to doing what I did."

Claiborne was six months into his first Senate term when Herbert died, without warning or goodbye, 4,000 miles away. Claiborne flew to Germany to oversee his cremation, returning with his father's ashes, which were scattered in the ocean off Jamestown, an island next to Newport. Already obsessive about Pell family ancestry, as Herbert had been, Claiborne decorated his Washington and Newport homes with paintings and mementoes of his father. He began wearing his clothes, much too big for him. Herbert stood six feet and five inches tall and weighed nearly 250 pounds; at six-foot-two and 156 pounds, Claiborne was physically slight by comparison.

But it was not the only measure by which Pell likened himself to his father—and in which he saw himself falling short. This senator who would draw many of the nation's political elite to his funeral was never convinced that he was the man his father had been. It was a judgment that would both drive and haunt Pell, in his legislative career and personal life. It was central to the fascination he developed with the paranormal and his largely unpublicized but obsessive quest to learn what, if anything, lay beyond death—and whether it was possible to communicate to those who were departed.

If it was, perhaps he could reach his father, who had not lived to see what his son had become. Perhaps he could receive Herbert's approval.

▫ ▫ ▫ Senator Jack Reed, who had received Pell's endorsement and succeeded him in the Senate, joined the other eulogists in praising his predecessor's accomplishments. Like Biden, Reed had a funny story related to Pell's forbears. It took place in 1992, when Reed, a freshman member of the House, was waiting with Pell for President George H. W. Bush to sign the reauthorization of the Higher Education Act, which provides the funding for Pell Grants. Reed, the son of a janitor and a housewife, had grown up admiring Pell.

"Now, Claiborne was a master of many things, but small talk was not one of them," Reed told the mourners. "We got through the weather and the traffic pretty quickly and we were rapidly moving into the area of awkward silence. But I was sitting next to one of my heroes and felt compelled to keep talking so I blurted out:

"'Are you going up to Rhode Island this weekend, senator?'

"Claiborne perked up noticeably and said: 'Well, no, Jack, I'm going up to Fort Ticonderoga for a family reunion.'

"I was a bit thrown by the response, so I said: 'Why would you ever go up there for a family reunion?'

"'Well, Jack, you see, we own it.'"

Laughter filled the church.

"For a moment, I thought he was pulling my leg," Reed continued. "But that was not Claiborne Pell. As President Bush entered, we stood up and I realized one more reason why Claiborne Pell was so unique and so deserving of trust: he owned his own fort."

The last to speak was Nick Pell, thirty-one, Claiborne's oldest grandson. Tall and slim like his grandfather, Nick listed the qualities he would remember best about him: his stubborn resolve, his patriotism, and his generosity to his family and constituents, though not in the ordinary sense to himself. Pell could have bought many things, but he had heeded his father's 1939 admonition about possessions.

"My grandfather will be remembered by those who loved him for his extreme frugality," Nick said. "For some, this may be a negative trait, but in true New England WASP form, my grandfather was actually quite proud of his ability to conserve resources. He served famously bad cigars and wine. He jogged in actual business suits that had been reluctantly retired. He drove a Chrysler LeBaron convertible, which was outfitted with tattered red upholstery, a roof held together with duct tape, and an accelerator that was so old it required calf-strengthening exercises just to depress the pedal. When it finally fell apart, he replaced it with a Dodge Spirit which he had purchased used from Thrifty Rental Car. I guess Hertz was too expensive.

"When my sister lived with him in Washington for the summer, he used to make her gather hors d'oeuvres from cocktail parties as he'd just as soon not pay for dinner. He used to say 'food is fuel' and 'never turn down a meal, as you never know when your next one will come.' He was able to strike the perfect balance between a gentleman and a man in tattered suits living from meal to meal."

Nick did not repeat his grandfather's Congressional achievements, some of which came after years of work. What he would remember with deepest respect was his grandfather's inner strength as his Parkinson's advanced and freedom slipped away.

"He won some impressive battles during his time on the Hill," the grandson said, "but in my mind, his greatest show of strength was his battle with his failing health. He had been sick for well over ten years and while his body gave out long ago, his will to live was of mythic proportions. He showcased what we in the family call 'warrior spirit'—and his resolve to live and enjoy time with the people he loved most, his family, his friends, and his constituents. It's as if God had told him years ago that his time was up and he just said, 'Not until I'm ready.'"

ONE ▫ THE MOST UNLIKELY CANDIDATE

CLAIBORNE PELL OF NEWPORT

On April 9, 1960, Rhode Islanders learned that a memorable primary election was likely to unfold later that year. Congressman John E. Fogarty announced he would not seek the Senate seat that would open upon the retirement of Theodore F. Green, the ninety-two-year-old patriarch of Rhode Island politics who had served in Washington since 1936. The popular Fogarty said he would instead seek an eleventh term in the House of Representatives.

With Fogarty out of contention, former governor J. Howard McGrath announced he was running. A Democrat like Fogarty and Green, McGrath, fifty-six, enjoyed the favor of some party insiders. He had been governor three times, and a U.S. Senator already, from 1947 to 1949, when he resigned to become Attorney General under President Truman. McGrath would be a credible, if unspectacular, candidate.

Another prominent Democrat, four-term ex-governor Dennis J. Roberts, fifty-seven, was coy when asked if he also intended to get into the race, but many who had followed his long career assumed — correctly, as it developed — that he eventually would. Like McGrath, Roberts was a force within the Democratic Party, having served as state party chairman and a delegate three times to the Democratic National Convention. He had been a state senator and mayor for ten years of Providence, Rhode Island's capital and largest city. Like McGrath, Roberts enjoyed widespread voter recognition.

A third person mentioned in the front-page story in *The Providence Journal*, Rhode Island's dominant newspaper, enjoyed no such visibility.

Claiborne deBorda Pell had never even sought elective office.

"I submit my candidacy to the Democratic Party and to the people of Rhode Island with confidence in my experience, and in the belief that they will consider me qualified to occupy the seat which has been so ably held by Senator Theodore Francis Green," Pell said in a prepared statement. If the candidate felt excitement about his announcement, his words failed to reflect it. This did not seem to be a man given to emotional excess.

State Democratic insiders knew "Claiborne Pell of Newport," as the reporter called him, from his successful fundraising activities, his own considerable contributions, and the midlevel posts he had held with the state and national parties. But to most Rhode Islanders — especially those in the northern metropolitan areas that decided statewide elections—Pell was no household name. Voters may have read about his involvement in refugee-resettlement causes, a topic of the occasional newspaper piece about him or letter to the editor he had written in the 1950s. But it was equally likely that they'd heard stories about an independently wealthy, Ivy League–educated man who spoke with an odd accent and who didn't live in the state full time. This boded poorly for a candidate in Rhode Island, where manufacturing remained the dominant economic force in 1960. People of Pell's class owned factories and did not toil in them; the self-made man, not the one to the manor born, was the sort to find favor with blue-collar voters.

Pell, forty-one, was betting on his innovative ideas for campaigning, the financial resources he and his wealthy wife Nuala would bring to the fight, his status as a World War II veteran, and his time as a Foreign Service officer, which might play well to Rhode Island's large immigrant population. He was betting that his relative youth, like newly announced presidential candidate John F. Kennedy, would be an asset. He thought that voters might see in him the promise of a fresh face and fresh ideas, his wealth notwithstanding.

Whatever the outcome, he was tired of waiting.

For years, Pell had longed to follow his father to Congress—an ambition supported by Herbert, who served one undistinguished term in the House of Representatives, 1919 to 1921, from Manhattan's Silk Stocking District. Even as he embarked on what could have been a lifelong career in international diplomacy, which had been another of Herbert's avocations, Pell was pondering the best route to Washington.

In 1946, his first year in the Foreign Service, Pell, a new vice consul at the American embassy in Prague, Czechoslovakia, had sought advice from his father. Should he resign from the service and move to New York, where Herbert lived, to seek some office there? Or should he try his luck in Rhode Island, where he had spent much of his childhood and where Nuala's mother owned a Newport mansion? New York, Herbert advised, offered limited possibilities. "A residence in Newport would be immensely better for you from a political point of view," he wrote to his son on September 4, 1946. "The possibility of election is immeasurably greater, and I believe that the combined difficulties and chances of nomination/election would be less."

Pell did not leave the Foreign Service then, for he still found satisfaction in his European assignments, which evoked pleasant memories of childhood travels. But as the 1940s ended, Pell had become increasingly restless. In 1951, Nuala's mother gave an acre of her spectacular oceanfront property near the end of Bellevue Avenue to her daughter and son-in-law. Pell designed and built the house he would die in, making Newport his legal residence. He bought a second home in Washington, resigned from the government in 1952, and as the 1950s progressed, took a variety of positions in business, for which he had little passion. Politics pulled at him. With the help of his father's connections and his own relationships with influential Democrats, notably the Kennedys, whom he had known since before the Second World War, Pell established a reputation as an informed and hard-working party lieutenant who someday might run for some office himself—though not U.S. Senate on the first try, or so insiders believed. State representative or senator seemed a wiser start for this man who was, as he would describe himself in a speech to a gathering of fellow Princeton graduates, as "about as improbable, impossible and implausible a candidate that could have turned up in many a moon."

But Pell had rarely been comfortable with conventional wisdom of any sort. As 1959 dawned and he looked toward the 1960 elections, only two possibilities appealed to him: the House seat that included Newport, held by Democrat Aime J. Forand, who was in his eleventh term; or a more challenging yet more appealing possibility, the Senate seat held by Green, who had not yet confirmed a decision but was expected to retire. Either route would require a good right-hand man.

John L. Lewis, a former labor leader who had served in the Rhode Island Assembly, had never run a statewide campaign, but Pell liked what he'd heard about him. Something of an icon in his hometown, blue-collar East Providence, Lewis knew the political landscape intimately and he had friends on town and city Democratic Committees throughout the state who might help build the local organizations Pell believed he would need to win. In fall 1959, Pell introduced himself at a Women's Democratic Club dance. Lewis was impressed.

"In those days," Lewis would recall, "guys with a lot of money wouldn't spit on you."

Pell was not the ordinary sort of fellow with a lot of money. He had aristocratic manners and an old-fashioned way of speaking, as if he had dropped in from another century—but he spoke earnestly, without arrogance or bluster, or seemingly even ego. He had intriguing ideas both for campaigning and for the policies he would pursue if elected to national office. Despite his wealth, he came across on a one-on-one level as a good guy who was on your side. And while he made no public show of his and his wife's considerable wealth, Pell let Lewis know that he would be willing to tap deeply into it to further his ambition. When Pell asked him to sign on, Lewis agreed.

"My friends thought I was crazy," Lewis recalled. They believed aristocrat Pell, as opponents surely would paint him, could never win.

On January 11, 1960, Green confirmed that he would retire at the end of his term. Pell decided that if the seemingly unbeatable Fogarty decided not to seek Green's Senate seat, he would run for it. With Lewis, he continued refining the blueprint for a race that would present Pell as a man for the people.

Pell's father, who was in Paris, approved of what was taking shape.

"I think your plans are very intelligently made," Herbert wrote on February 19. "Naturally, I have every hope of your success," he wrote a week later, "and would not encourage you if I did not think you had a good chance and that in the long run, this campaign will do you a lot of good."

ROUGH AND TUMBLE

Not long after Fogarty declared he would seek reelection to the House, Pell bought an advertisement in Rhode Island newspapers.

In "An Open Letter to the People of Rhode Island," Pell presented what he called his biography. Illustrated with a photograph of Nuala and Claiborne, their four young children, and their dog Dizzy, the copy was a mix of the substantial and the esoteric. Certainly, primary voters would be impressed by his work, mostly behind the scenes, for the Democratic Party. Some would agree that his time in the Coast Guard and Foreign Service, as well as his father's lessons in diplomacy, would be assets to a senator. And some would appreciate that Nuala and he spoke Italian and French ("he has a French grandmother") and Claiborne was "familiar with Portuguese." But would any Rhode Islander in 1960 really care that he was "secretary-treasurer of the Fort Ticonderoga Museum" and that "his grand uncle, Duncan Pell, ran for office in Rhode Island as a Democrat prior to the Civil War and was elected lieutenant governor in 1865"? But this was Pell, who was proud to publicize his obsession with his ancestors. It spoke to tradition and family, both of paramount importance to him virtually since birth.

The ad listed Pell's residence as Ledge Road in Newport, but he wasn't living there in April. As readers could see from the address at the top of the letter, Pell and his family had moved to the Sheraton-Biltmore Hotel in Providence, to a suite of rooms on the twelfth floor that would be their home and campaign headquarters through the primary — and general election, if Pell won. The move had practical value: Newport, at the southern end of Rhode Island, was distant from the more heavily populated communities that would decide the election and where Pell would need to concentrate his efforts. But there was important symbolic value, too. The Biltmore was in the heart of the capital city — next door to City Hall, a block from *The Providence Journal* and *Evening Bulletin*, and a short walk from the State House, where McGrath and Roberts had held office.

Even just coming and going, Pell would attract attention. Providence was that kind of city: folks knew who you were, and if they didn't, they made an effort to find out. It mirrored Rhode Island, which is sometimes described as America's city-state.

Pell's Open Letter was the first manifestation of a media campaign that, in scope and cost, would be unlike any Rhode Island had seen. With Lewis and Ray Nelson, a *Journal* reporter who had quit his job to become press secretary, and who was soon an integral voice in campaign strategy, Pell began to buy radio and television spots, and advertisements in Rhode Island's daily, weekly, and specialty newspapers — *The Visitor*, for example, the official publication of the Diocese of Providence, which reached tens of thousands of the faithful in the heavily Catholic state. And some of the radio spots even featured Claiborne and Nuala speaking in French, Italian, and Portuguese. With the latest data from the state Board of Elections estimating that 17 percent of the names on voting lists were French and 16 percent Italian, Pell taped some of his radio commercials in those languages. A smaller percentage of voters were Portuguese, but Pell believed his father's years as minister to Portugal would count heavily with this group and some of his commercials were in that language.

Listeners would also regularly hear Nuala on the radio with Pell, not by accident: a warm woman who spoke easily, Nuala would balance her husband's more formal demeanor. Nuala would accompany Pell on the campaign trail, and not just occasionally; she embraced Pell's ideals and ambition and was willing to work for them on a daily basis. She was also the mother of the Pells' young children, two boys and two girls, a family image with significant appeal to many voters. As the campaign progressed, photographs of the attractive Nuala with the handsome Pell, often with their four children and dog, would appear in newspapers and campaign literature. Nuala charmed, much as Jackie Kennedy did. She had a sense of humor and could poke fun at her husband, as journalists who came to know her learned. To use a more modern term, she was real.

Behind the scenes, Nuala was also a partner in her husband's campaign; Pell made few major decisions without her input. And she brought something else, also largely unpublicized: generous financing. Great-granddaughter of George Huntington Hartford, founder of the Great Atlantic & Pacific Tea Company, a relationship the Pell campaign did not trumpet, Nuala contributed $50,000 of her own money to the race — the equivalent of nearly $380,000 in 2011 dollars. Pell contributed $50,000 of his own, with his father adding another $50,000. With the exception of a 1940 van-turned-mobile-headquarters donated by a friend of Pell and a few other contributions, this $150,000 war chest financed the campaign. Most would be spent on media.

□ □ □ Near the end of April, friends of Roberts commissioned a poll that showed the former governor and Providence mayor with a substantial lead in a Democratic primary — and also in a general election against the likely Republican nominee, Raoul Archambault, Jr., a federal bureaucrat. "There can be no doubt that as of late April, the strongest candidate for United States Senator from Rhode Island that could be submitted to the voters by either party this November is Dennis J. Roberts," *The Providence Journal* reported. Pell's own early polling confirmed his disadvantage.

"I have a good deal of hard work in front of me in the ensuing months, which I look forward to doing," Pell told a reporter, whose story noted that Pell "has moved around the state to attend local party affairs, testimonials, and to talk with leaders and rank-and-file members." With their many friends and acquaintances, Lewis and Nelson helped with introductions. Broadcast commercials were airing and billboard space had been rented.

As he himself acknowledged, Pell was not a naturally gifted speaker, despite his father's frequent admonitions when he was in school that he develop the skill, whatever career path he decided to follow. Pell's accent and the rigid way he often constructed his sentences, evocative of an earlier time, did not enhance his performance in front of a crowd. But speaking individually with voters, Pell connected, as Lewis had discovered when they first met. "A most important factor," Pell would explain to fellow Princeton graduates in a June 1961 address, "is a willingness to go directly to the people, to talk with the people — never up, down or at the people, but to the people — and to do a great deal of listening, which is particularly difficult for a politician."

Pell also mingled, walking for hours at a stretch accompanied by only an aide or two — and sometimes alone — through neighborhoods and business and industrial districts, greeting people on the street, and walking into workplaces, stores, restaurants, and homes, if invited. Pell genuinely enjoyed meeting people of all kinds, as if his privileged childhood had created some pent-up desire to discover how the other half — or 99 percent — lived. What staff would later call Pell's "walkabouts" became a staple of his style as candidate and Senator through six terms and five reelection campaigns. But there was political currency as well. The fact that millionaires Kennedy and senior Senator Leverett Saltonstall held office in neighboring Massachusetts, and the even wealthier Nelson Rockefeller was governor of nearby New York, might indicate that the "silver-spoon" factor, as Pell called it, might be less significant in his race — but this was gritty Rhode Island, a city-state of factories and mills and neighborhood bars. Pell understood that his opponents would seek to exploit his wealth. Images of Pell among blue-collar people, not bluebloods, would help counter that. And so the campaign photographs showed the candidate in places like Central Falls and Pawtucket, not along Bellevue Avenue in Newport.

"Sheer hard work is an unduplicated recipe for success," Pell said in his talk to Princeton graduates in 1961. "Tenacity is another necessary ingredient. Speaking in a less complimentary term, tenacity might be called obstinacy. But no matter what it is called, I felt particularly the need for tenacity, or obstinacy, when I was going into a primary election realizing that no unendorsed candidate had ever won such an election in the history of my state; where my party's Executive Committee had turned me down 30 to 1; and where a poll, for which I had engaged Lewis Harris, showed me being beaten three-and-a-half to one."

▫ ▫ ▫ Image and money alone were not likely to win such an underdog the election. Voters had to believe Pell would do something for them on issues that mattered.

Concerns about the economy and the Cold War were the issues preoccupying many voters in 1960 — and Pell's campaign slogan, "Jobs and Peace," reflected that. With the state's manufacturing base beginning to erode as textile jobs migrated to the south and overseas, Pell promised economic revitalization, diversification of industries, and a minimum wage — $1.25 an hour, which he incorporated in his platform as his eighth plank, "Right To Live." He promised no new taxes, and he promised aid to workers over the age of forty who had lost their jobs. He supported a strong defense against enemies that might threaten war, including Fidel Castro's Cuba — and legislation that would build "a real home and industrial fallout shelter program." Fears of nuclear attack by the Soviet Union were heightened that spring by the May 1 downing of an American U-2 spy plane, an incident that prompted Soviet Premier Nikita Khrushchev to pull out of a scheduled Paris summit. Pell advocated negotiations with the Soviets from a foundation of strength, as some other Democrats did; this was the proper path, he maintained, toward eventual nuclear disarmament. Pell proposed creating a "Bureau of Peace Affairs" within the Department of State that would have "jurisdiction over disarmament negotiations, weapon limitations and all the related facets of diplomacy connected with the control of weapons in this nuclear age."

But unlike many other politicians, Pell did not believe the March of Communism, as the headline writers called it, would necessarily claim more nations beyond the Iron Curtain — or that military force alone would stop the spread.

In a foreshadowing of his position on the bloody U.S. attempt to prevent another domino from falling, the Vietnam War, Pell urged a balanced policy that would present the American system as an attractive alternative that people around the world would sooner or later adopt. For nations said to be threatened by Communism, Pell, in the second plank of his platform, said: "Our hope—and their best hope—lies in raising the living standards of their people, giving them moral support and helping them to help themselves attain economic self-sufficiency and self-respect. Communism breeds on poverty, ignorance and despair. Military aid does not cure these ills." With his Foreign Service background and the wisdom he had learned from his diplomat father, Pell spoke with an authority that Roberts and McGrath could not match. They were old-school Democrats who had prevailed, Roberts especially, with the politics of favors and friendships—the politics of the machine. Pell had no machine, only ideas, money, and a growing group of volunteers excited by this new face.

Incorporated under the campaign slogan of "forward thinking Democrat," Pell's platform presaged other Great Society issues he would play a significant role in shaping. Pell pledged better health care for all and universal coverage. "I believe that all our people, without regard to their financial condition or age, must be sure of decent medical care, particularly in the event of major or mortal illness," he wrote. His tenth plank, Civil Rights, committed him to pursuing "the fullest possible realization of the rights of all our citizens as set forth in our Constitution."

Pell's commitment to improving education for every student, public or private, belied his own privileged schooling. The candidate supported increasing teachers' salaries "to assure adequate and competent instruction for our youth at all school levels." He supported public libraries, which, he said, should "stimulate the opportunities for home education for all our people." And his belief that a college education should be available to all who wanted one, regardless of income, would be incorporated into the 1965 Higher Education Act, origin of the Pell Grants. Pell would be instrumental in passage of the legislation, which President Lyndon Johnson would sign into law.

"A nation is only as strong as the sum total of its people, their character and their education," Pell wrote. "It can remain strong only if the leadership of each generation has the opportunity to develop its maximum potential. We cannot afford to waste this great resource. Yet only about half of those qualified and desirous of doing so can expect to obtain a college education unless some help is given to them. It is my conviction that every American is entitled to the opportunity to obtain all the education he desires and can assimilate. Moreover, the broadest practical development of the talents and intellectual gifts of our youth is essential to the welfare of our nation and all its people."

◻ ◻ ◻ On June 22, Roberts joined McGrath and Pell as confirmed candidates. In a letter to state Democratic Party chairman John G. McWeeney, Roberts stressed that he had "always lived in Rhode Island" and "always worked in the best interests of Rhode Island" — shots at Pell. As the summer wore on, Roberts would attempt to paint Pell as a wealthy carpetbagger (and an oddball, at that) who perhaps knew a lot about the world but little about the state he hoped to represent. Indeed, most of Roberts' letter, excerpts of which were widely published, seemed aimed at Pell and not McGrath, whose realistic chances of winning were fading. Roberts' instincts were sound.

"Through a long and thorough experience in governmental affairs, I have acquired a comprehensive knowledge of government at all levels and in all fields," Roberts wrote. "This, together with my long and active association with civic and community affairs outside of government, has provided me with a broad and complete understanding of our people and our state . . . Mine has not been a vicarious participation in endeavors to meet and resolve our economic and civic problems; my participation has been constant, direct and tangible. Such experience and qualifications are essential today to the man who is to represent the people of Rhode Island in the United States Senate during the coming six years. In the hands of that man in that august body lie the very destiny of not only the people of Rhode Island but of our entire country as well."

It was a grandiose contrast to Pell's own announcement, and it commanded immediate attention, particularly within the party, whose endorsement Roberts, McGrath, and Pell all sought. Roberts gave no hint of the tenor of the campaign he would run, but it would turn ugly as September approached and the race developed into a two-way battle, with Pell's popularity climbing. Lost in the heat would be Roberts' appreciation for the hours Pell and Nuala had invested in Democratic campaigns, including his own successful 1956 gubernatorial reelection bid.

In reacting to Roberts' formal announcement, Pell pledged not to attack character — a pledge he would keep in every campaign through 1990, his last. Pell told *The Journal* that he hoped that the campaigns of Roberts and McGrath "will be fought on as high and lofty a plane as is reflected by the dignity of the offices they have occupied . . . I know that my own campaign, while aggressive, will be aimed at the development of issues and ideas, and not at personalities." This was Pell's personal philosophy, one he would carry into his many Senate debates. But it also reflected respect and a degree of gratitude to Roberts, who had helped, in a minor way, build Pell's stature within the state and national parties during the 1950s.

With Roberts' entry into the race, party insiders loyal to him began to activate the old city-hall levers. Pell did not enjoy that option. Along with the work of organizing town and city committees, he looked for ways to keep himself in the news; ideas and issues alone, he had concluded, would not give him the visibility he wanted. And so Pell reached into his imagination to come up with novel tactics—what in a later age would have been dismissed as attention-seeking stunts, but which many voters in 1960 found a refreshing change from the politics of smoke-filled rooms his opponents typified. Though dismissed by detractors as out of touch, Pell had an appreciation for how the emerging power of the media was transforming elections.

Six days after Roberts formally entered the race, Pell and Nuala left the Biltmore Hotel. The sun was just rising. Trailing the campaign's mobile headquarters, the 1940 van, the Pells set off in a Ford convertible on a tour of every one of Rhode Island's thirty-nine cities and towns. Reporters and photographers, including a crew from NBC News, followed. Press secretary Nelson had done his advance work well.

Accompanied by one of their sons, the Pells headed north into the state, and then west and back south toward the coast. They visited restaurants, a bus stop, factories, a farm, a State Police barracks, a shoeshine shop, city and town halls, an airport, a gas station, and a beach (where Nuala "walked barefoot through the sand," a newspaper reported), among other places. They walked Main Streets, knocked on neighborhood doors and, after riding a ferry to Newport, joined their other son for more photos. They flew to Block Island, the town of New Shoreham. They handed out balloons, flyers, and "bells for Pell." A mandolin-playing barber serenaded them with a song:

If you wish Rhode Island well, come on and vote for Claiborne Pell. Claiborne Pell, we can tell; about you we have no doubt, that our foes you'll quickly rout.

The coverage of what one reporter described as "a unique drive to reach every nook and cranny of the smallest state in the union in a fast-paced, one-day tour" was largely complimentary, with quotes from potential voters expressing their support for Pell—or at least their interest in learning more about this new guy who wanted them to send him to Washington. Here was a candidate—"the six-foot, one-inch Pell, his black hair showing light touches of gray," one newspaper said—who was an approachable, if sometimes shy, man who liked meeting people. Here was a man journalists liked, in part because he gave them colorful copy. "The tour was almost over before Mr. Pell found a pipe he had been looking for during most of the trip," wrote a reporter. "He discovered he had been sitting on it. The tour yesterday was a long way from Mr. Pell's college days at Princeton, but maybe not so far at that. In 1940, it so happens, he got his letter there in cross-country."

Four weeks after the statewide tour, on the eve of the party meeting that would decide the Democratic endorsement, Pell and Nuala and their children made another unusual trip — on a fifty-foot boat on Narragansett Bay, which divides the land mass of Rhode Island in two. Joined again by reporters, the Pells made several stops on both sides of the bay, winding up at Warwick's Rocky Point, home of the state's most popular amusement park. "The excursion, described as a combination outing and campaign trip, was reported a success by all hands," *The Journal* reported.

Serving as chief delegation tally clerk, a post he had held at the 1956 Democratic National Convention, Pell attended the mid-July national-party gathering in Los Angeles, where Massachusetts Senator John F. Kennedy was nominated for president. Pell returned to Rhode Island still seeking his state party's nomination for Senate — but vowing to continue his campaign if he did not. It was a bold statement. No unendorsed Democrat had ever won a statewide election in Rhode Island.

In a letter to each of the 200 members of the party's State Central Committee, Pell made a final bid for the endorsement, which by late July was certain to be Roberts'.

"I do not seek to go into a primary contest," Pell wrote. "But I am sure you understand that both under our democratic system of government and our Democratic Party operations, the people themselves are sovereign and theirs should be the ultimate decision . . . I ask you to be guided with all your heart in your decision by one consideration and only one consideration, and that is what is best for the Democratic Party and our state, which candidate is more likely to add strength to the ticket and win. Vote according to your convictions and to the people who elected you.

"Do what *you* think is right."

◻ ◻ ◻ With 137 votes for Roberts and 54 for Pell, the party voted on August 1 to endorse the former governor and Providence mayor. The AFL-CIO had also endorsed Roberts, noting its "long and friendly relationship with him" — though also implying that in the unlikely event of an upset, they could support Pell, whom they found appealing for his "knowledge of foreign affairs, integrity and sincerity." McGrath stayed in the race, with little realistic chance of winning. But his dislike of Roberts would benefit Pell. McGrath would remind voters that after winning a bruising Democratic primary in 1958, Roberts had gone on to lose the governorship to a Republican in the general election. History could repeat itself, McGrath suggested.

Endorsements in hand, Roberts immediately made Pell's wealth a central issue, one he would raise repeatedly in the nearly two months until the September 28 primary.

Pell had already been criticized for using his own money to finance a campaign, notably on the eve of the endorsement vote in a much-publicized letter to the editor by a John Carney of Pawtucket, evidently a Roberts supporter, who claimed inside knowledge of "how a millionaire runs a political campaign"—with thousands of dollars a month for media, staff, billboards, and a suite at the Biltmore, a claim that was essentially correct. "If the boy millionaire is spreading around this kind of cash before a primary election, imagine how he will spend it for the general election if he manages to buy the nomination," Carney wrote. "I consider it a scandal to be spending such an amount of money in an effort to win political office." Pell responded with a statement that compared himself to another wealthy man—popular in Rhode Island—who was seeking high office. "Mr. Carney's criticism reminds me of the type of exaggerated criticisms leveled at Senator Kennedy's primary campaign," Pell said. Like Kennedy, Pell sought to turn financial independence to advantage. "I believe the people of Rhode Island do not object to having a candidate spend of his own resources, which then means he is under no obligation to any special interest group," Pell said. Unlike Roberts, the unendorsed candidate was not beholden to a machine.

As the campaign progressed, Roberts accused Pell of "trying to buy the voters of Rhode Island with his Proctor and Gamble advertising methods," as he described his opponent's considerable media expenditures on one occasion. McGrath joined in, calling Pell "this man with all the money who wants to go to Washington to extend his social acquaintances." Lawyer Edward J. Gnys, another Democrat who disliked Pell, went on TV to attack him. Said Gnys: "The moral question remains: Should a man be allowed to buy an election?" Roberts and McGrath also repeatedly knocked Pell's supposedly thin ties to Rhode Island and his unquestioned inexperience in governing, with Roberts, at one of his receptions, calling their opponent "naïve and immature."

Pell responded by again comparing himself to Kennedy, who would face Richard M. Nixon in the general election.

"I notice that both my veteran opponents are spending a good deal of their time criticizing me along the same querulous lines that Harry Truman and others criticized John Kennedy: young, less experienced, too traveled and independently wealthy," Pell said. "I believe that this line of criticism will have the same effect on my candidacy as it did on Jack Kennedy's candidacy: none."

Pell emphasized the simple ranch-style Newport home he had designed and built (though not its proximity to Bellevue Avenue, with its Vanderbilt and Astor mansions), the Newport-area homes his divorced parents owned and where he lived when he was growing up, and the fact that he had enlisted in the service while in Newport. "It was from Rhode Island that I joined the Coast Guard and it was to Rhode Island that I was to be sent, were I killed," Pell said morosely, if effectively. "It is my home." Photographs of the candidate with his family at their house on Pelican Ledge illustrated the point. He said that his Foreign Service years, his business ventures, and his work with the Democratic Party qualified him to serve in the Senate, where larger issues were decided.

Pell believed that those issues, bundled into the campaign slogan of "Jobs and Peace," mattered to voters, not whether he had arrived on the scene by an ordinary route.

▫ ▫ ▫ Seventy-six years old now and long into retirement, Herbert Pell had decided not to return from his latest European travels to witness at first hand his son's campaign.

"I am so far removed from any practical knowledge of the way things are run today that anything beyond the merest suggestions are worthless," he wrote to Pell in one letter during the summer. But he had many suggestions in his letters — and answers to all of the questions his son posed in their correspondence. "Take every chance you get to make a speech on any known subject, whenever you are asked," Herbert advised. Ask supporters to write letters to newspapers, including the small weeklies. Use luminous ink for signs and consult with a professional when choosing the colors. Capitalize on the "natural gift" of a last name with just four letters, which lent itself to large type. Provide no great details about the source of his campaign financing or how he was using it.

"Spend what you find necessary and desirable," Herbert wrote on July 26 from Lucerne's Grand Hotel National, "but I think it would be better not to give the effect of using too much money . . . I want you to be an honored member of the Senate and a respected member of the upper circle of the State Organization. To achieve this, you must play down the apparent and visible signs of expenditure." Pell's inspiration, the father said, should be the late Senator Nelson Aldrich, a Republican of Rhode Island, whom Herbert had admired when he was a young man. A man of considerable wealth from a prominent New England family, Aldrich served two decades with distinction, holding chairmanships of the Senate Finance and Rules Committees.

Herbert urged Pell not to worry that his contributions to the campaign would affect him or his wife, Olive, Claiborne's stepmother. Herbert had sold or donated most of his properties by now, and had little interest in possessions.

"It all means nothing to me now. I shall continue to live comfortably and do what I want without much regard to cost. I am making no sacrifice in giving you what you need — in fact, and very glad to be able to do so — but I can only do it because my father and mother, my grandparents, my great-grandparents and their predecessors pretty well avoided any great waste, although they all indulged in reasonable, pleasant and intelligent expenditure. It is for you, not for me, to judge the intelligence of your course. The stake is obviously large and I do not want the ship to be lost for a ha'p'orth of tar. Take what you need firmly and use it as you think best. I mean this with all sincerity."

The father closed with affection for his daughter-in-law, a favorite since meeting her in 1944, when she became a Pell by marriage.

"You are certainly lucky to have Nuala associated with you and helping you and really interested in what you are doing. Give her my best love and genuine respect. Go ahead and good luck, and remember that you are now carrying the flag which is that of your children as my flag was yours and the one carried by my ancestors was mine."

▫ ▫ ▫ Labor Day passed and the primary entered its final weeks. By now, Pell's full-time paid staff included Lewis, Nelson, three secretaries, and the mobile headquarters driver. Their work was supplemented by volunteers, whose numbers had grown over the summer as excitement built over what some people (and two of Pell's internal polls) were predicting would be a dramatic upset on September 28. Lewis had opened 20 local People for Pell headquarters around the state. A Youth for Pell group was in operation. Risking repercussions if Roberts won, several city and town committees had thrown their support behind Pell.

Pell increased his media presence, spending $31,533 in the final two weeks of campaign, an amount that pushed total primary sending past $44,000, almost certainly more than his opponents — or any Rhode Island primary candidate ever. He bought spots on the Providence market's three major TV stations and virtually every Rhode Island radio station. He invested heavily in advertisements in nearly all of the state's newspapers, but his focus was *The Providence Journal*, paper of record.

On Sept. 18, *Journal* readers found a twelve-page supplement in their Sunday paper. It had cost $7,311.73 — more than $55,000 in 2011 dollars. The expenditure drew fire from Pell's opponents, and in an appearance with Franklin Delano Roosevelt, Jr., Pell answered them with barbed humor. "They used to say 'who was Pell?'" Pell said. "Now that they've found out, they claim I use Madison Avenue techniques to become too well known. Unfortunately, most of the money spent has been my own . . . One thing's certain: A political career is not going to make me any richer and I daresay it's a different situation with both of my opponents."

"The Claiborne Pell Story" presented the candidate as a good husband and father of four fine children: Herbert Claiborne Pell III, "Bertie," fifteen, named for Claiborne's father; Christopher Thomas Hartford Pell, "Toby," twelve, who bore the name of Nuala's great-grandfather, the founder of A&P; Nuala Dallas Pell, ten; and Julia Lorillard Wampage Pell, "Julie," seven, named for two of Claiborne's ancestors. Public service, the supplement proclaimed, had been a Pell family tradition for decades. Herbert was pictured with Franklin Delano Roosevelt and Alfred E. Smith. Grand-uncle Duncan Pell, elected lieutenant governor in 1865, was mentioned. A photograph of Pell, Nuala, and their children outside their modest Newport home deliberately did not show its oceanfront location or proximity to the exclusive Bailey's Beach Club, to which the Pells belonged — but the caption suggested the importance Pell placed on Democratic ancestors. Dallas, it read, was "named for a forebear, George Mifflin Dallas, a Democratic United States Senator and Vice President of the United States from 1845 to 1849," serving under President James K. Polk. Dallas was Claiborne Pell's great-granduncle. He was a Princeton graduate, like Pell, and had gone on to be Treasury Secretary for President James Madison (and also, briefly, Secretary of War for Madison). He was mayor of Philadelphia in 1828, Russian ambassador from 1837 to 1839, and ambassador to England after his term as vice president, from 1856 until 1861.

Pell listed his wartime years in the Coast Guard, his Foreign Service duty, and his business experience, which included a partnership in the investment firm Auchincloss, Parker and Redpath, and a directorship with the North American Newspaper Alliance, a wire service. The supplement included his ten-plank platform and a column of "Pellets," vignettes about the campaign and the candidate. It retold the previously published story of Coast Guardsman Pell donating blood in the 1940s to "an ailing Negro minister," which broke a taboo against whites giving blood to African-Americans. The image of Pell as a man for the people was emphasized on one full page of "testimonials" signed by a car salesman, a laborer, an artisan, a sign poster, a retired pharmacist, a bartender, and two housewives. "There's no shilly-shallying with Pell," said one of the housewives, Dorothy Bianco of Cranston. "He's 100 percent honest." Bianco ended her endorsement with the same message all eight people had: "I hope he wins the Democratic Primary in September. I'm voting for him. Are you?" Thirty-six photographs illustrated the supplement. Eleven featured Nuala, including one in which she posed with Jackie Kennedy, taken when the two were campaigning for JFK in West Virginia.

The Kennedy connection was made also in a quote from the presidential candidate on the back cover: "It is time, in short, for a new generation of leadership — new men to cope with new problems and new opportunities," a line from Kennedy's acceptance speech at the Democratic National Convention. Pell stressed Kennedy once more in a press release sent to weekly newspapers days before the election.

The release provided Pell a final opportunity to reach voters who might not subscribe to *The Providence Journal* or pay attention to TV or radio ads. "In person," the release said, Pell

> is above average in height, trim physically — he was a cross-country runner in college and has kept in shape playing tennis and sailing boats. His movements are quick and without wasted motion. His voice is quiet and natural. There is evidence of determination but personal warmth and complete lack of artificiality. He says what he deems right with a sincerity and candor most politicians consider highly impolitic. He admits his mistakes, rejects untruth and refuses to disseminate even within commonly accepted political bounds. He seems to like people and appears at home with those he meets of all backgrounds of life. He detests long-winded formal speeches and won't make one himself. He prefers to answer questions and does so with forthrightness and patience.

Pell hoped that in contrast to Roberts and McGrath, he would be seen as young and refreshing, in the mold of Kennedy, who was just two years older.

Written by press secretary Nelson, the release described a "primary campaign which took him to every city, town, village and hamlet in the state." In his line-by-line hand-written edit, in which he corrected spelling and grammar, Pell replaced "primary" with "Kennedy-like." He knew well the power of the name.

And he made another change, in a sentence about how Roberts and McGrath, who were not named, were reacting to his candidacy. Where Nelson had written that Pell's opponents were "running scared," Pell wrote that they were "feeling the effects of his campaign." He had scrupulously kept his vow not to go negative.

In the week leading up to the primary, Pell stepped up his presence on radio and TV. He visited rural areas of Rhode Island, but concentrated his appearances on the cities of Woonsocket, Pawtucket, Cranston, and especially Providence, Democratic strongholds. He tracked the final week in a small calendar, crossing off each day in pencil when it was done. He wrote a single entry for September 28: "Pelection Day."

◻ ◻ ◻ The mood was turning electric on the seventeenth floor of Providence's Biltmore Hotel the evening of September 28. Democratic Party workers were writing early returns on chalkboards in the hotel ballroom, where winners of the primary elections for governor, lieutenant governor, attorney general, U.S. representative, and U.S. senator would be celebrated. The Senate chalkboard showed Pell with a widening lead.

At 10 p.m., an hour after the polls closed, results from Burrillville were posted: 779 votes for Pell, 227 for Roberts, and just 35 for McGrath. A Pell victory was all but assured.

"It looks like an anti-machine election this time," someone in the crowd said.

"It looks like the kid is really giving them the business," a middle-aged man added.

Five floors down, Pell was sequestered in his suite with Nuala, his children, mother, mother-in-law, brother-in-law, and the Pell's housekeeper; only Herbert, who had remained in Europe, where he would not be tempted to meddle in his son's campaign, was missing. Staff set up tables outside the door to keep the growing crowd away. Police manned another post to keep control.

At 10:15 p.m., the phone rang inside Pell's suite. Roberts was calling to concede.

A few minutes later, he appeared in the corridor outside Pell's door.

Pell emerged and shook hands with his opponent. He was smiling, but his eyes were tearing.

"I have had the opportunity of congratulating Mr. Pell on his tremendous victory and I wish him good luck, good health and success," Roberts said.

Pell stood, unsmiling. An emotionally contained man, he had never been prone to exuberance.

"Come on, look happy," Roberts said.

Pell thanked Roberts and predicted success in his race against Republican nominee Raoul Archambault, Jr. "I look forward to a clean campaign, fought on issues," Pell said. "I believe that the Democratic Party will beat his."

The lopsided nature of Pell's primary victory stunned Rhode Island. The count showed him receiving 83,184 votes out of 135,905 cast — 61 percent of the total. Pell's tally was nearly double that of Roberts, who received 45,196 votes. The former governor carried just eight small, mostly rural municipalities that would not be decisive in a general election: Exeter, Foster, Jamestown, Narragansett, New Shoreham (Block Island), South Kingstown, Westerly, and West Greenwich. He did not even take Providence, base of his machine. McGrath carried no city or town; with 7,525 votes, less than 6 percent, his political career was over. So, essentially, was that of Roberts.

Pell cabled his father, who was staying at the Ritz Hotel in London. Herbert wrote back to his son immediately.

"When your cable came, I broke out in a yell and danced a jig," Herbert wrote. "I have never been so delighted in my life — at least I can't remember any such happy occasion. You have shown courage and intelligence and as I have suggested proved to me that my recollections are past history. I'm very glad I wasn't over there with you. I know that I would have interfered and protested much that you have proved. You have the highest post that has been held by any member of the family; you are the Top Pell for three hundred years. It really is magnificent."

Herbert also wrote immediately to his daughter-in-law, for whom he had held great affection since first meeting her, shortly before the Pells' wedding, when any thought of winning elections was a distant dream. He understood that without Nuala, her husband's campaign would have been deficient. She completed his son. She possessed sound political instincts of her own.

"Dear Nuala," he wrote, "There are hundreds of congratulatory messages coming in to you both, let me send a special tribute of admiration and gratitude to you. I have heard of your work, which has been hard, and of your tact, which has been continuous. You will be one of the most valuable senatresses in Washington . . . I thank you with all my heart."

THE LARGEST PLURALITY

With the assistance of a national clipping service, Pell filled a scrapbook with accounts of his victory. The Boston and Rhode Island newspapers published original stories, and dozens of other papers around the country used stories originating with the Associated Press and United Press International. Out-of-town headline writers were not quite sure what this never-before-elected man was. Several headlines described him as a "blueblood" and "socialite." The Flint (Michigan) *Journal* saw Pell as a "businessman," while the Columbus (Ohio) *Dispatch* viewed him as both: "socialite-businessman." He was a "rookie," a "novice," an "unknown," and an "amateur." He was a "newcomer," the most common description in the headlines.

In its October 10 issue, *Time* magazine brought Pell to a national readership. Its headline, "Odd Man In," created a precedent for future unflattering nicknames, some with a sharper edge. The body of the story foreshadowed Pell's future senatorial conduct, which even his political adversaries would praise for its civility.

"In Rhode Island's Democratic primary to choose a successor for retiring patriarchal U.S. Senator Theodore Francis Green," the magazine wrote,

no one figured that Claiborne deBorda Pell, 41, had much of a chance. No one, that is, except Newcomer Claiborne Pell. So while the statehouse pros snickered, and while his opponents — former Governor Dennis Roberts and former U.S. Attorney General J. Howard McGrath — sniped at each other, pipe-smoking Princetonian Pell put together an energetic campaign. Last week, in a state that is 58 percent Roman Catholic, Episcopalian Pell carried the primary with a walloping 83,000 votes to Roberts' 45,000 and McGrath's 7,500.

Pell, though running for office for the first time, was born to the political purple. His family, down through the generations, counts five Congressmen and one Rhode Island lieutenant governor. Young Pell himself had put in a tour in the U.S. Foreign Service (Czechoslovakia, Italy) and dabbled in state politics, mostly as a fund raiser. But in this campaign it was his fat checkbook, his patrician manners and his softly spoken determination to get to Washington that counted most. Billboards and statewide TV wrote his name large across the summer. He traveled tirelessly, talking to Rhode Island's immigrant minorities in French, Italian or Portuguese. He promised relief for Rhode Island's failing industries, and he tied himself firmly to the coattails of Jack Kennedy.

When his family's longtime friend Theodore Green heard of his doubts about beating Republican Nominee Raoul Archambault, Jr., 39, former assistant director of the U.S. budget, the old patriarch (93) set Claiborne straight: "Tush, young man, you don't have to worry in this state."

◻ ◻ ◻ Archambault, thirty-nine, was a decorated Marine Corps combat veteran of the Second World War who had spent eight years in the federal government, most recently with the Bureau of the Budget. He modeled himself after Arizona Senator Barry Goldwater, whose philosophy of minimal government taxing and spending had gained him national attention. Archambault's last race had been for governor in 1951. He lost — but won 47 percent of the vote, a respectable result that indicated promise for another race. Archambault acknowledged the historic nature of Pell's primary victory, but he maintained that the Democrat could be defeated — albeit narrowly.

"It won't be by much," Archambault said in a radio interview. He foresaw a margin of 15,000 to 25,000 votes, a prediction that would prove laughably wrong.

The Republican began his campaign by attempting to depict Pell as a free-spending, high-taxing liberal who would be accommodating to Communists, putting the nation at risk. But Archambault did not confine his rhetoric to issues. He understood, as Roberts had come to, that while Pell was indeed a newcomer, he ran a sophisticated campaign. "He very cleverly sold the image of himself as a political neophyte and a new, fresh face," a Republican insider told a *Providence Journal* reporter, "where actually he is a cool, calculating politician in this image similar to the candidates he defeated."

Countering that, Archambault concluded, would require some hardball tactics. Borrowing from Roberts' election strategy — a questionable decision, given Roberts' lopsided loss — Archambault sought to depict Pell as a man who bought elections.

The campaign was young when Archambault attacked Pell for his campaign expenditures, calling them "vulgar" and "extravagant" in a radio interview. He continued that theme at a Republican rally in Woonsocket, a manufacturing city north of Providence. "Mr. Pell came from obscurity to prominence in one expensive step," Archambault said. "He buried his opponents in a mountain of gold . . . Mr. Pell can probably afford to spend it, but we can't afford to send another left-wing, free-spending liberal to the Senate." Republican Governor Christopher Del Sesto, who was seeking reelection, carried on the theme — with a touch of humor.

"We can't be too harsh on Mr. Pell because our object is to get more jobs for the people of Rhode Island and Mr. Pell has certainly done that," the governor said. "There is no unemployment problem among former newspaper reporters nor among public relations men. They all work for Mr. Pell."

Republicans were irritated that former *Journal* reporter Nelson had resigned to become Pell's press secretary. During a television interview, Raoul Archambault accused the *Journal* of conspiring with Pell to keep his name a "secret" in its coverage of the election. "You can't read about me in that paper," Archambault said.

But readers could when the paper published its choices in the election.

"We differ strongly with Mr. Pell's Kennedy-like approach to economic problems, and we disagree just as strongly with Mr. Archambault's ultra-conservative views as a self-styled 'Goldwater Republican with some exceptions.' For us, therefore, it boils down to a choice between Mr. Pell's sincerity, intelligence and capacity for growth and Mr. Archambault's experience and capability in government. On balance, we are inclined to take a chance on Mr. Pell." It was hardly a ringing endorsement — but for the ordinarily conservative *Journal* editorial board, it was a bold statement that drew attention. And this was in an era when newspaper endorsements still mattered.

As Election Day neared and a Pell victory seemed likely, Archambault turned ugly, accusing his Episcopalian opponent of orchestrating an award in an effort to win Catholic votes in heavily Catholic Rhode Island. In awarding Pell its Cross of Merit, the Rhode Island chapter of the Knights of Malta, a Catholic charitable group based in Rome, had recognized the Democrat's work as vice president of the New York–based International Rescue Committee's help in resettling refugees from the 1956 Hungarian Revolution. The Knights denied that the timing of the award, presented to Pell at his Biltmore Hotel suite, was intended to influence the election — but Archambault believed otherwise. He was similarly disturbed by Pell's revelation during a radio interview that the Ku Klux Klan had threatened to kidnap him when he was a six-year-old boy, a claim confirmed in press reports at the time. The threat came in response to Pell's father's support for New York Governor Alfred E. Smith, a Catholic who was seeking the Democratic nomination for president. Herbert, chairman of the state party, publicly despised the KKK.

"The Democrats have left nothing undone to stir up racial and religious prejudice in a search for votes," Archambault, himself a Catholic, said in a statement. "Mr. Pell has been just as guilty of this as anyone and more guilty than most."

Archambault said he had initially refrained from making anything of Pell's award and mention of the kidnapping threat. "When I first read this news story in which my opponent was clearly dragging religion into the campaign, I was inclined to keep silent about it. I am a Catholic, but above all I am an American and I deeply deplore any reference to religion in politics. After careful consideration of the matter, however, I decided that Mr. Pell should be called to account for this statement, which is so clearly an attempt to gain votes by a religious appeal. A number of my friends, many of them of my own and other faiths, were deeply incensed at Mr. Pell's statement."

Pell had indeed courted the Catholic vote, beginning during the primary election, when his September 18 Sunday newspaper supplement had drawn his connection to Kennedy, whose Catholicism was controversial nationally — but an asset in Rhode Island. The supplement had noted, prominently on the inside front cover, that the Catholic Church had benefited when Herbert, in 1940, decided he no longer wanted a house in Newport. "The Pell home in Newport was on Bellevue Avenue in a house which since has been established as St. Catherine Academy — a gift from Pell's father to the Catholic Diocese of Providence," the supplement said. Four pages further in, a photograph of Pell with Nuala's Catholic half-sister appeared. "Sibilla Tomacelli O'Donnell, originally of Naples, Italy, and Mr. Pell's sister-in-law, gave him a willing hand when he fastened a Pell-for-Senator bumper strip to the family car," the caption read.

Pell had kept to his themes of jobs and peace, but Archambault's claims, he said, were irresponsible. They warranted rebuttal.

"Apparently," Pell said, "my opponent has not signed the code of fair campaign practice or he would not engage in such reckless, extravagant statements against the Democratic Party and me." Pell in a later statement expanded Archambault's Knights of Malta allegation. "I challenge my opponent to document his charge," Pell said. "He knows he cannot do so and therefore it will remain what it is — a reckless, last-minute accusation typical of a candidate about to be beaten. It is unfortunate that his action at this time contributes nothing to the campaign but rather is a disservice to the people of Rhode Island and detracts from the dignity of the office we seek."

◌ ◌ ◌ At 2 a.m. on November 7, the day before the election, Kennedy flew into Rhode Island from Lewiston, Maine, on the two-day tour of New England that would complete his campaign for president. A small crowd greeted him at the airport and a larger crowd awaited at the Biltmore Hotel, where Kennedy slept a few hours and then walked to the plaza in front of City Hall. Providence schoolchildren had been let out of class to see the candidate, and they helped swell the crowd to an estimated 30,000 — largest in the city since President Truman had campaigned there in 1948. Pell stood with Kennedy and the crowd let out "an ear-splitting shout" when Kennedy mentioned his name.

Bound for his next stop in Springfield, Mass., Kennedy's motorcade departed the plaza. "Screaming, jumping teenagers and adults broke through police lines on narrow Washington Street as Mr. Kennedy left the mall," *The New York Times* reported. "A forest of groping arms threatened to pull him from his convertible. Finally, after some leapers fell in front of the press bus, the police managed to open a line." With thousands lining the route, the motorcade progressed to the airport.

Pell headed south to a rally in Newport, where he called Archambault's latest charge that he was a "carpetbagger" another example of his opponent's "gutter tactics." Speaking in Warwick, Archambault played on fears.

"A vote for my opponent, Claiborne Pell," the Republican said, "is a vote for Democratic promises of reckless spending which will lead to inflation and chaos, coupled with strong hints of appeasement of the Reds in Russia and China — a policy which can only expose us to the danger of nuclear war."

On Election Day, Pell voted in Newport and headed north for the final day of campaigning. Early reports revealed an unusually heavy turnout, with lines that had formed before voting opened at many polling places. Most observers were predicting Pell would win, but he was not taking victory for granted. He continued to campaign until about an hour before the polls closed, and then returned to the Biltmore to join his wife, children, mother, stepmother and father, who had arrived from Europe.

By 10 p.m., returns all but confirmed a Pell victory, but Pell remained cautious.

"It's too early to tell," he said.

Half an hour later, Archambault conceded.

"My heart is so big it feels like it is going to expand through my skin," Pell said.

He hugged Nuala.

"Isn't it wonderful?" he said.

Pell posed with his family, and alone with his father. Herbert's presence was commanding, journalists said.

"Pell headquarters came to a boil when Mr. Pell's father, Herbert Claiborne Pell, former minister to Portugal and Hungary, arrived after traveling from London with his wife," the *Journal* wrote. "Almost a half foot taller than his tall son, the now-retired diplomat said 'I have run for public office and I have handled campaigns but no campaign in which I was interested has given me anything like the pleasure and happiness I have now.'"

Although most observers were agreeing with Pell that Archambault would be beaten, they were astonished by the margin.

Excluding a few thousand absentee ballots, Pell took 275,010 votes to Archambault's 121,014—nearly 70 percent of the vote, the largest plurality in any statewide election in Rhode Island history. Pell won each of the state's eight cities and twenty-three of its towns. Archambault took only eight small rural communities—losing even West Warwick, where he lived, by a better than two-to-one margin. A later analysis by the state Board of Elections estimated that Pell had won up to 17,443 Republican votes—roughly the number of votes by which Archambault had predicted he would win.

Asked the next day to explain his margin of victory, Pell at first seemed puzzled.

"Those are questions you ought to ask the people," he said. "I don't know the answer."

Pressed by a journalist, Pell said voters must have found him believable.

"Apparently, I've struck some kind of chord," he said. "The people trust me. They have faith in me. I secured my nomination completely independently. There was no more improbable candidate than I was. Most groups, including labor, endorsed my opponent in the primary. Essentially, the people feel there is nobody between me and them."

Pell listed another likely factor: a campaign in which "he never deprecated an opponent," as one reporter wrote. "Some have told me," Pell said, "'We voted for you because you never got dirty.'"

Other explanations were offered shortly before the election by one of New England's most prominent labor leaders. Speaking to a reporter after a rally of more than 500 Pell supporters at Woonsocket's Italian Workingmen's Club, Joseph A. Salerno, vice president of the Amalgamated Clothing Workers of America, said Pell seemed something more than just another Democrat that organized labor was obligated to endorse. The garment workers had joined the AFL-CIO in backing Pell.

"I remember 40 years ago, the fights I used to have with the Marxists who said leadership of the working class has to come from the proletariat," Salerno declared. "I always said that some of our best leadership would come from the intellectuals and the aristocrats. Second, our people are status-seekers like everyone else. They like to shake hands with someone from the right side of the tracks. But third, there is something in this aristocrat, something in the heart, that our people know by intuition."

◻ ◻ ◻ Not long after the election, a reporter for the *Newport Daily News* went to Pelican Ledge, where Herbert was visiting with his son. The father spoke of his son's long interest with politics, which began, he said, when Claiborne was a child. "Claiborne was always interested in politics and from his earliest days, was fascinated by the senators and congressmen who visited our home from time to time," Herbert said.

Herbert had sustained a leg injury when walking on rocks on the coast outside the Pells' house — but he vowed to be in Washington in early January, when Claiborne would be sworn in to succeed Senator Green. He predicted exemplary things from his son.

"Claiborne never gave me a moment's worry in my life and he won't give any to his home state," Herbert said. "The Senate seat is in good hands and he'll do a fine job."

Herbert had lived to see this only child in whom he had invested so much — and so much in addition to money — become the first Pell elected to the Senate. But he would die before his son left his mark, something that would haunt Claiborne for decades.

TWO □ ONLY CHILD

LORDS AND LADIES

More than one hundred people gathered the morning of November 3, 1915, at the Episcopal Church of the Heavenly Rest on New York City's Upper East Side to celebrate the wedding of a woman and a man who, like them, stood prominently in American society. An account of the ceremony and the reception that followed at the St. Regis New York hotel, built by John Jacob Astor IV, who had gone down with the Titanic three years before, was published the next day in *The New York Times*.

Matilda Bigelow, twenty, was the daughter of Nelson Pendleton Bigelow, who had made a fortune in lumber, and Bigelow's ex-wife, the former Sophia Dallas deBorda, a demanding and sometimes disagreeable woman whose family included a former vice president and U.S. senator. Matilda was a shy woman who had completed eighth grade in America, followed by four years of art school in Italy, passing all of her young life in cocooned privilege. She had long dark hair, pale skin and brown eyes that hinted of sadness. She was beautiful, despite fragile health.

Herbert Claiborne Pell, Jr., ten years older than his bride, was the son of Katherine Lorillard Kernochan, whose family's riches originated in tobacco, and Herbert Claiborne Pell, a direct descendant of the second Lord of the Manor John Pell, a wealthy seventeenth-century landowner. Herbert possessed a keen mind, an interest in politics, and insatiable wanderlust. At six-foot-five and nearly 250 pounds, he physically overwhelmed Matilda, who was a full foot shorter and thin almost to the extreme.

And that was not the only difference. Matilda's emotional warmth stood in contrast to Herbert's cool intellect, which ruled him.

They had met a year before, after Herbert had returned from almost a decade in Europe. Asked to a dance by a suitor, Matilda had replied that her mother would not permit her to go alone — to which the suitor had replied that he would bring his own mother and a friend, Herbert Pell. Pell was smitten, and the next day, he sent Matilda an orchid and a copy of *Anna Karenina*, not the sort of book she ordinarily read. Their engagement was among the highlights of the 1915 summer season in Newport, Rhode Island, where Herbert's maternal grandmother, a Lorillard, hosted a tea for her grandson and fiancée at her summer home, which was run with a staff of eighteen.

Pink chrysanthemums and autumn leaves decorated The Church of the Heavenly Rest. Matilda's brother, Anson, a midshipman at the U.S. Naval Academy, gave her away; Herbert's best man was his brother, Clarence, his only sibling. Dressed exquisitely, Matilda captured the fancy of *The New York Times*. "She wore a frock of white satin having a short skirt over a many-tiered underskirt of white chiffon, touched with silver," the paper reported. "The corsage was draped with tulle, and straps of silver cloth going over the shoulders held the tremendously long plain train of silver cloth in place. Clusters of orange blossoms were fastened at one corner of the square end. The long tulle sleeves were loose and the veil of old family point, an heirloom of many generations, was banded flat on her dark hair just above the forehead with orange flowers and the veil fell in mantle effect over the long train. She wore a plastron of emeralds and diamonds, the gift of the bridegroom, and carried a sheaf bouquet of white orchids with valley lilies."

The Times society writer provided scant details of the reception beyond where the bridal party received their guests, in the Louis XVI suite. But more was revealed in the gift book that Matilda kept. Among others, it listed members of the Fish, Saltonstall, Roosevelt, and Pyne families—people with primary residences in Philadelphia, Chicago, Washington, Manhattan, and the exclusive community of Tuxedo Park, New York, founded in 1885 as an alternative resort to Newport by Pierre Lorillard IV, Herbert's great-uncle. Matilda received a gold bracelet with sapphires and diamonds, a jewelry box, fine linen, clocks and mirrors, but silver gifts predominated. Mrs. Newell Tilton of 63 East 82nd Street, New York, presented a bronze box.

Mrs. Tilton was the former Mildred Bigelow, a friend and distant cousin of Herbert's new wife. She was closer in age to Herbert, and her eccentric personality and developing reputation as an artist impressed him. She seemed more the sort who would appreciate a Tolstoy novel and a man who gifted it.

▫ ▫ ▫ On June 27, 1654, a well-to-do colonialist by the name of Thomas Pell gathered with Siwanoy Indians under the shade of an oak tree to conclude a treaty for the purchase of more than 9,000 acres of land in the vicinity of what would be known as New Rochelle, Pelham, and the Bronx borough of New York City. Brother of the noted English linguist and mathematician John Pell, Thomas had arrived in America in 1635 at the age of twenty-two. An Algonquin-speaking tribe, the Siwanoys accepted "trou valew & just Satisfaction" for their land, according to the treaty. No price was listed, although a historian would later assert that the Indians received "sundry hogshead of Jamaica rum."

Named first Lord of the Manor, Pell left his property to his nephew John when he died, childless, in 1669. John prospered, as evidenced by his ship, in which he was cruising when he drowned off City Island in 1700. John's son, Thomas, third Lord of the Manor, born in 1675, married Anna, who was said to be a daughter of Wampage, one of the five Siwanoy Indian signatories to the 1654 treaty. Thomas and Anna had four daughters and six sons, among whom they divided their land. The wealth had been diluted, and the American Revolution, which fractured the family and destroyed the manorial system, further diminished the Pells' prominence.

But Joshua, one of Thomas and Anna's ten children, gave birth to a son with entrepreneurial ambition. Raised on the Pelham Manor, Benjamin Pell opened a business in Burlington, Vermont, after the Revolution — and then returned to New York, where by the end of the eighteenth century he had a thriving import company at 286 Pearl Street, on the shoreline of lower Manhattan. Benjamin's son William Ferris Pell, born in 1779, increased the family wealth with imports of wood, Italian marble, and wine. William bought a square mile of land in upstate New York that overlooked the south end of Lake Champlain — land that included the abandoned Fort Ticonderoga, instrumental in the Revolutionary War. William built a country estate, Beaumont, on the property. The family wealth had been firmly reestablished — and by practicing thrift and wise investment management, his son Clarence, born in 1820, maintained it.

Clarence's son Herbert Claiborne Pell, born in 1853, did more than protect the base: in marrying Katherine Lorillard Kernochan, he expanded it. Katherine was the daughter of James P. Kernochan, whose father was a wealthy Louisiana sugar farmer, and Catherine Lorillard — the great-granddaughter of the founder of the Lorillard Tobacco Company. Catherine, Herbert's maternal grandmother, had two brothers: Jacob Lorillard and Pierre Lorillard IV, who had owned The Breakers, one of Newport's most opulent mansions, before selling it to a Vanderbilt when developing Tuxedo Park.

First of Herbert and Katherine Pell's two children, Herbert Claiborne, Jr., was born on February 16, 1884, and grew up in the Gilded-Age comfort of Tuxedo Park and Newport, where he visited with his maternal grandmother in summer. The Pells traveled to Europe frequently, beginning with Herbert's first overseas trip at age eleven, on a crossing that took them to the Portuguese Madeira Islands, Gibraltar, Italy, and France. Herbert attended St. Bartholomew's School in Morristown, New Jersey, and then the Pomfret School, in Pomfret, Connecticut, graduating in 1902. He enrolled in Harvard College that fall, but was soon disillusioned by what he perceived as a culture in which preparation for making money was all that mattered. Students like himself who wanted to grow intellectually or pursue nonbusiness passions, he believed, were discounted.

"Those boys who were studying architecture were looked on as deserters," he later recalled. "Those who were studying painting were supposed to be merely devoting themselves to immorality — whereas the possibility of going into public life was never even considered."

During his sophomore year, Herbert fell ill, left Harvard, and never returned. For a while, he took courses in European history and American politics at Columbia and New York University and passed hours reading in the library at the Union Club, one of New York's oldest men's organizations, to which he had been elected. It was at about this time that his Lorillard uncle died young, leaving his mother the sole heir to his grandmother's tobacco fortune. "This of course totally changed my prospects," Herbert would recall many years later in a letter to his son. Herbert's prospects were further enhanced a few years later when his grandmother gave him and his brother the building she owned at 384 Fifth Avenue, a prime property in the heart of the richest city in America, whose land alone would have great increasing value. "I then decided I would rather live with little magnificence but freely and without occupation," he would write to his son. "There seemed to be the absolute certainty of decent lodgings, clothes and three meals everyday for the rest of my life, so I decided to stand on the cards in my hand." Freed from the ordinary concerns, Herbert headed to Europe, where he lived on his own, returning periodically to Newport, Tuxedo Park, and Manhattan, for the better part of a decade.

The year 1912 found Herbert back in Tuxedo Park. He was twenty-seven years old and interested in the Progressive Party of former President Teddy Roosevelt, who had split from the Republicans to seek the presidency again on an anti–big business platform that also included women's suffrage and social-welfare programs for children. "To destroy this invisible Government, to dissolve the unholy alliance between corrupt business and corrupt politics, is the first task of the statesmanship of the day," Roosevelt proclaimed in the party's platform. "This country belongs to the people. Its resources, its business, its laws, its institutions, should be utilized, maintained, or altered in whatever manner will best promote the general interest." The Bull Moose Party, as it was popularly known, enjoyed no support among Tuxedo's residents — but many of the community's workers, some of them immigrants, quietly backed it. So did Pell — and not quietly. He had developed an appreciation for the working person. Knowing he would earn ridicule from Tuxedo's residents, he joined the Bull Moose Party's local County Committee, which organized support for Roosevelt. Roosevelt lost, but Herbert had found his calling.

Like inherited wealth, public service seemed to be in the blood. Herbert had grown up hearing stories of members of both branches of the family who had served their country or their state. On the paternal side, grandfather John Frances Claiborne had belonged to the Mississippi State House of Representatives from 1830 to 1834, then served as U.S. Representative from 1835 to 1888. Grand-uncle Duncan C. Pell had been lieutenant governor of Rhode Island. More distant relatives Thomas B. Claiborne, Thomas B. Claiborne, Jr., and John Claiborne had served in the House of Representatives from Virginia and Tennessee. On his mother's side, Herbert's grand-uncle George M. Dallas had been vice president, U.S. Senator, and mayor of Philadelphia.

In 1914, Herbert was nominated by both the Progressive and Democratic Parties to New York's state constitutional convention. He lost. After marrying the next year, Herbert traveled with Matilda and spent time with a growing circle of politicians — among them Franklin D. Roosevelt. He wanted to enlist in the military when the United States entered the war in April 1917, but his poor eyesight disqualified him. He considered asking his friend FDR, who had been with him at Harvard, to help him into a job with the Navy Pay Corps. Roosevelt, former New York state senator, was assistant secretary of the Navy. "Although my eyes were not good enough to distinguish a submarine two or three miles at sea," Herbert later said, "they were amply good enough to tell a one-dollar bill from a two." But he did not seek the favor — although he would ask a similar one for his son when Roosevelt was president.

In the summer of 1918, Herbert decided to run for Congress from the Seventeeth District, the so-called Silk Stocking District, which included the Upper East Side of Manhattan. He and Matilda, who was expecting their first child, were living on East 94th Street.

Pell's opponent was lawyer Frederick C. Tanner, former chairman of the state Republican Party. Tanner made residency a central issue of the campaign, calling Pell a carpetbagger for never having voted in the Seventeenth District. Pell acknowledged that he had only voted in Orange County, where Tuxedo Park was located — but his family's long history in New York, he said, qualified him to represent a New York district Congress, perhaps more so than Tanner, who, hypocritically, was originally from Illinois. Then he went after Tanner for his supposed role in redrawing the lines of the Seventeenth District to include more Republicans, as Democrats claimed. In an open letter to Tanner published in *The New York Times* on October 23, Herbert wrote:

> May I also, even if I descend to personalities, ask you what part you had in forming the boundaries of this seventeenth Congressional District, eighty-five blocks long and never more than five blocks wide, so that it looks like a tuning fork and comes out as expert a piece of gerrymandering as has hap-

pened in our day and generation? Apparently my worthy opponent, who has come to our state comparatively recently, is teaching some of us old New Yorkers more than we ever knew before. I am yours very sincerely, Herbert C. Pell Jr.

On November 5, Pell narrowly defeated Tanner.

Seventeen days later, on November 22, Matilda gave birth to a boy. The Pells gave him names from each of their families: Claiborne, Herbert's maternal grandmother's maiden name; deBorda, Matilda's mother's maiden name.

COMING OF AGE

Claiborne deBorda Pell began life in a world where nannies, nurses, governesses, and tutors helped with the children, and chauffeurs drove the children to their private schools. Claiborne's first was the Buckley School, some twenty blocks from the Pell home at 20 East 94th Street. His teachers and parents impressed on him the need to excel at reading and writing, but even before he had mastered them, he learned to anticipate the mailman. The mailman brought postcards and letters, often the only way the family stayed connected.

Claiborne was a newborn when his father departed for Washington, where he would spend much of his time as Congressman the next two years. Losing reelection in 1920, Herbert became chairman of the state Democratic Party, a position requiring frequent travel that he kept until early 1926. Matilda mostly remained with their son in New York City or, in good weather, Newport.

"Dear Claiborne," Herbert wrote to his son from Boston on November 21, 1925, the day before his son's seventh birthday. "I saw the new house in Newport. It looks fine. There will be lots of lawn where you and your friends can play. I miss you a great deal and wish you many happy returns of your birthday. I hope that you enjoy next year. My seventh birthday was in 1891. I look forward to seeing you on Thanksgiving Day and I am very sorry that I shall not be able to hear you recite. Affectionately, Daddy."

"Dear Daddy," Claiborne wrote to Herbert from Newport the following June 13. "The party yesterday was lovely, I got a gun at the end of a spider-web. My garden is fine & the two trees are living. I want you to come here, all you have to do is fold yourself up & get in an envelope, then post yourself here. There! Love."

Claiborne was apart from his mother less frequently than Herbert, but he wrote to her when he was. "Dear Mummy," he wrote on September 11, 1926, in pencil between neat lines he'd drawn, "Mr. Young and Mr. Stoke helped me fly my kite. Mary Lee came over to play with me yesterday. Send my love to daddy.

Love from Bomba and Clay." Bomba was his nickname for his grandmother Padelford.

Claiborne was a happy child, if frequently sick, as his mother also frequently was. He enjoyed fishing and sailing and drawing pictures of sailboats and airplanes. He played tennis. He had a home chemistry set and a motion-picture camera. He collected coins and stamps—and carefully organized his collections. The typewritten catalogue of his coins when he was about nine years old listed, in alphabetical order, 315 coins from thirty-three countries, including eighteen from ancient Rome, nineteen from Russia and Bulgaria, and one from Monaco. The catalogue indicated the location of each coin in their box.

He read books from a growing library that his father helped select for him. When he was eight, his nanny compiled a two-page list of the books, thirty in all, that he had read during the previous two years. History, religion, and classical literature predominated. Claiborne had read *The Story of the Bible*, *The Life of Christ*, *The Story of Mankind*, and *The Story of Rome*, his nanny recorded. He'd read *Tales of Shakespeare*, the *Iliad*, and the *Odyssey*. He had read *Oliver Twist*, *David Copperfield*, and *Alice in Wonderland*, and books about Robin Hood and King Arthur. He'd read *Little People Who Became Great: Stories of the Lives of Those Whom Every Child Should Know*, published in 1920.

▫ ▫ ▫ Claiborne's parents' frequent time apart provided opportunity to develop romantic interests in others, if desire was there.

For both Matilda and Herbert, there was.

By the mid-1920s, Matilda had fallen in love with Hugo William Koehler, a handsome Navy officer nine years her senior whom she and Herbert, whom friends called Bertie, had met in 1921. Kohler's background—notably his mission in post-Revolutionary Russia, where some believed (based entirely on rumor and hearsay) that he had helped Czar Nicholas II and his family escape the Bolsheviks—lent an air of mystery to him, and his military adventures fascinated Matilda and Bertie, to whom he wrote when he was abroad. "Dear familie Pell," began a 25-page single-spaced, typed letter Koehler sent to Matilda on July 5, 1922, from Warsaw. "You have been very much in the conversation lately, for I have just come back from Berlin, where I saw a good deal of our new ambassador and we discussed all your Bertie's virtues." Koehler ended: "I wish I could expect to see you soon, but I suspect if I really want to see you in a hurry I had better make myself plans to head for New York. In the meantime, my very best to the family and yourself, and blessings on the heir-apparent, who, I take it, should be about half the size of his Pa by now."

Koehler was a lady's man—charming, worldly, passionate, an entertaining storyteller. "I have much sympathy for women — a great deal more than I have for men," he wrote to his mother from China in 1913. "The more I know of women, the more I believe in their innate goodness and unselfishness . . . with my temperament, the wildness of it, my love of excitement and adventure, which excitement and adventure only made the wilder — well, you can imagine I have learned about women." These were romantic sentiments the analytical Herbert would have found difficult to express, if he even experienced them.

Koehler was assigned to the Naval War College in Newport in April 1926 and he was openly seeing Matilda that summer, when he was living in a house he rented near the commercial end of Bellevue Avenue. That fall, Matilda fell sick, perhaps from stress, as she prepared to divorce Herbert, who had become involved with another woman.

Herbert's new interest was the former Mildred Bigelow. Since her attendance at Matilda and Herbert's wedding, she and her husband had divorced.

Olive Bigelow, as she now called herself, had made a name for herself as an artist, with exhibitions of her work in New York and London. Like Herbert, Olive's forbears had served their country with distinction: her grandfather, John Bigelow, an owner of the *New York Post*, had been President Lincoln's minister to France, and an uncle, West Point graduate Poultney Bigelow, was a decorated veteran of the Spanish-American War. Like Herbert, Olive possessed an expansive mind — but unlike him, she had an eccentric streak that manifested itself in oddly creative ways. Later in life, she would rewrite the Bible, condensing it to a fifth of its original length by eliminating "the endless histories of kings," as she called them, and other passages she considered extraneous. "This labor of love was not accomplished in a few days or even in a few weeks," she would write in the preface to her Bible, published in 1952. "It was the work of twelve years. I prayed without ceasing that I might be led always to that which was the most spiritual." Olive was talented and well-intentioned, but quite strange.

As 1926 neared its end, lawyers for both Pells began to draw up divorce papers. Separated now, Matilda and Herbert began to quietly plan second weddings.

On February 26, 1927, Matilda filed for a petition to divorce in a court in Paris, where she and Claiborne were staying with her mother, Mrs. Edward M. Padelford, as the former Sophia Dallas deBorda was known in the society pages. A month later, the divorce was granted, with Matilda receiving legal custody of Claiborne. Three months after that, readers of *The New York Times* learned more about the story behind the headlines.

"Mrs. Matilda Bigelow Pell of 1060 Park Avenue, who won a divorce last March in Paris from Herbert Claiborne Pell, was married yesterday afternoon in the Madison Baptist Church, 30 East Thirty-first Street, to Lieut. Commander

Hugo W. Koehler, U.S.N., who is stationed at Newport, R.I.," the paper reported on June 3. "Although they had been acquaintances for several years, their marriage yesterday came as a surprise to many of their friends. When a rumor circulated a week ago that Mrs. Pell would marry a naval officer, she forcefully denied it. The couple obtained their marriage license at the Municipal Building only a few hours before the ceremony. The only others present at the wedding, at which Rev. George C. Moor, pastor of the church, officiated were the bride's brother, Anson Bigelow, and Mrs. Bigelow. Following their honeymoon, Commander and Mrs. Koehler will live in Newport."

An account of Herbert's wedding, in Paris on June 25, was published two days later in *The Times*.

"Relatives of Mrs. Bigelow Tilton and Herbert Claiborne Pell have been informed by cable of their marriage in Paris last Saturday," the paper reported. "No previous announcement had been made of the wedding plans of the couple." The story included a summary of Herbert's political career and Olive's art. "The present Mrs. Pell is the granddaughter of the late John Bigelow, Minister to France under Lincoln and Johnson. Recently, she has been making her home at 44 Gloucestershire Square, London. She is a niece of Mrs. Guest, the wife of the Hon. Lionel G. Guest of that city. She has two daughters. Miss Mildred Tilton, the elder, was presented at Buckingham Palace last summer and later made her debut in London. She spent the winter studying music in France. The other daughter is Pyrma Tilton."

Olive's quirky but sophisticated intellectualism suited Herbert, and he would remain married to her for thirty-three years, until his death. Matilda also seemed to have found peace, for a spell. On July 16, 1927, Koehler wrote about his new wife from Newport, where the newlyweds were staying. "She looks younger, healthier and happier than I have ever seen her in five years, and she is continuing to improve still more!" Koehler declared. "Her general appearance, her renewed interest in things, the sparkle in her eye, the eagerness that is not a burning nervousness as of old, but a calm and quietly growing interest—all these, I think, tell much more about her health" than the five pounds Koehler wrote that she had gained since the wedding.

But the renewal was short-lived. That September, Matilda fell sick and required surgery. Koehler was forced to borrow money from a bank to pay for Matilda's operation and long hospital stay, a portent of money difficulties that would sadden her son, moving him to help her financially, beginning when he was a young adult.

▫ ▫ ▫ Over the next several years, Claiborne would lead a comfortable but nomadic existence, traveling regularly and living with one or the other of his parents in Paris, London, Manhattan, Newport, and his father's country estate, Pellbridge, located in Hopewell Junction, New York, near Herbert's friend Franklin Roosevelt's Hyde Park home.

Claiborne's first foreign travel had been when he was four and he crossed with his mother to France, where he stayed with Bomba in one of the Paris hotels that she fancied. A longer journey began on March 10, 1928, when he departed with his mother and stepfather, whom he (and his father) usually called "the commander," on a journey that took him to Cuba and through the Panama Canal to California and on to Hawaii and back, finishing with a railroad trek across the continental United States. Claiborne was nine, and his diary reflects a sense of intelligent wonder that would remain with him, influencing his world-view and politics, into adulthood.

"Our cabin number was I 44," he wrote on March 13. "Mummy sleeps below me and the commander sleeps besides Mummy. We sighted an island today. I have seen flying fish by the hundred. It is very good weather. Mummy is feeling better. I have my meals at the children's table." After passaging the Canal, he wrote: "I went on deck as the ship went through the locks. The ship did not go through of its own power. Powerful engines called 'mules' pull it. They are on tracks. They can go up and down steep hills. I then had breakfast. I took three pictures. The scenery was very pretty. It was a jungle. It would be the best place on earth to explore in a motor boat. I saw lots of drowned trees in a lake. The ship passed through them. This is how it happened. There was a small lake with a jungle on each side. When the United States Government dug the canal they made the little lake much bigger. The water went over the lake and drowned it. I saw about a dozen Indians in three canoes. They are made of a single tree hollowed out and shaped."

In February 1929, Koehler retired from the Navy. That September 3, Matilda gave birth to their only child, Hugh Gladstone Koehler. Early 1930 found the three Koehlers and Claiborne in Dane End, Hertfordshire, England, where Lord Herbert John Gladstone, former British Home Secretary, seventy-six, was dying. Koehler had known Gladstone since the First World War, and the two had become more than friends: before Koehler married Matilda, Gladstone had countenanced the commander's affair with his wife Dolly, more than twenty years younger than her husband. Koehler honored him with his son's middle name.

The Koehlers had hired a tutor for Claiborne, who had finished his studies at Manhattan's Buckley School. Matilda and Herbert had so far agreed with their son's schooling, but come fall, Herbert wanted his son to attend St. George's

School in Middletown, Rhode Island, a short distance from the Bellevue Avenue mansion that Herbert had bought and where he lived part of the time now with Olive. Years later, as Claiborne was about to graduate from college and his father had tired of Newport society, Claiborne would donate the property to the Catholic Diocese of Providence.

On February 5, Matilda wrote Herbert a long letter. Lord Gladstone's health was precarious, she said, forcing postponement of a trip the Koehlers had planned to the south of France. The report on Claiborne, who was prone to respiratory infections and other illnesses, was more promising. "So far we have had no real winter weather and Claiborne has been able to be out every day for a great part of the time," Matilda wrote. "He looks fine and has a huge appetite. He is getting on well with his lessons, too, and accomplishing a great deal more than he does at the same time in school."

Matilda did not agree with Herbert's newly stated desire for Claiborne's further education. Uncharacteristically for Matilda, this February 5 letter was typed, which suggested Koehler's input, if not authorship — as did the language, which was uncharacteristically harsh. Matilda and Herbert had remained civil after their divorce, but she wanted Claiborne to remain in London.

"About St. George's — as you know," the letter continued, "you have always said you would never send Claiborne to a boarding school, so I cannot understand your sudden change of view. Of course I realize you would like to have him near you but even so I can't believe you would now want to do something you have for years disapproved of on the ground it would be the worst possible thing for Claiborne, just because it happens to be convenient for you at this time. All of the reasons which you have always advanced against a boarding school still exist in full force.

"I admit that Claiborne has shown improvement this last year, but as you know, he has not a strong constitution and all experience of having him at school indicates that he needs painstaking and personal attention. He cannot be treated as one of a group; he needs individual care and nothing less than constant watching and instant attention can prevent these illnesses that start with slight colds from taking a sudden turn into really dangerous conditions. As you know, we have experienced this again and again. Surely you have not forgotten the trouble we have with him every winter, particularly the tendency of his colds to develop into serious ear trouble. You know I don't approve of coddling and you know, too, how very important I consider games and association with other boys, but as you have so often agreed, his health is the first consideration and we must conduct his education on such a plan that his health may not suffer, no matter what sacrifice and personal inconvenience for us it may demand.

I appreciate very much your offer to pay his expenses at St. George's and of course it would help, but even so, feeling as I do about it, I couldn't agree to sending him."

Matilda wrote of her long stay in the autumn of 1926 at Newport Hospital, and how, she said, nurses there talked of the many St. George's students who had been hospitalized with pneumonia. "Then also there was a boy there when I was from St. George's who had lost his memory and the doctor from the school was there and we thought him disgracefully inadequate and incompetent."

Matilda closed on a cordial note, acknowledging Olive's latest paintings, which included one of Herbert with Claiborne's dog, Yankee, a wirehaired fox terrier. "Claiborne was so pleased with the catalogue of Olive's pictures," Matilda wrote. "We all thought her pictures lovely. I liked the one of you with Yankee best. It is really splendid. Please give her my congratulations and love. Affectionately, Matilda."

Herbert agreed to Matilda's wishes, and Claiborne was enrolled in London's Gibbs School, on Sloane Street, an all-boys academy that the young brothers Robert F. and Edward M. Kennedy would also attend later in the 1930s after their father, Joseph, had been named ambassador to England by President Roosevelt. Claiborne was a good but not outstanding student during the two years (punctuated by visits with his father at Newport and Hopewell Junction) that he attended Gibbs. Claiborne struggled with Latin, Bible Studies, and English Grammar. His penmanship, one teacher wrote, "has a lot of character in it" — a euphemistic way of saying it needed improvement — and his spelling was only fair. But he was a decent French student, and was strong in math and geography. Perhaps not surprisingly, given his travels and his father, history and English composition — writing — were his strongest subjects. The overall impression he made with the Gibbs faculty was of an unusually smart, intellectually curious, and fun-loving student — not the ordinary pupil at Gibbs, which specialized in privileged boys who did not necessarily possess a superior mind. "He has an extensive knowledge of general history and has interesting views," one teacher wrote. "A promising pupil, possesses splendid reasoning power," wrote his arithmetic, algebra and geometry teacher.

As Claiborne prepared to leave the school, in July 1932, headmaster and school founder Charles Herbert Gibbs praised the boy and predicted a successful future. "He takes interest in all his work and is well-informed for his age," Gibbs wrote on Claiborne's final report card. "A light-hearted yet thoughtful boy for whom I predict a useful career. He is absolutely frank and fearless." Gibbs concluded his assessment in the September 1932 School Notes: "During his short two years with us," the headmaster wrote, "he has won the regard of all with whom he came in contact: a keen scout, always cheery and at the same time a thoughtful person and reader."

Claiborne's years in pre-war London marked the beginning of an intense letter (and telegram) correspondence between the Pells. Wherever he and Olive went — whether traveling or during stays at their residences in Manhattan, Newport, and Hopewell Junction — Herbert wrote incessantly, sometimes daily, dictating his letters to his secretary, who typed them (with carbon paper, saving copies for Pell's archives) and mailed them to his son. Herbert's single-spaced letters, which often ran to several pages, were filled with accounts of life in Depression-era America, when even he, always mindful of protecting the Pell base, was forced to curtail his expenses. Herbert shared his political views with Claiborne and offered advice on his son's studies, his penmanship, his typing, his attire, his sports activities (swimming and cricket). He sent clippings from American newspapers. He sent a regular allowance and gave Claiborne a few shares of General Electric and U.S. Steel stock, a $50 Liberty Bond, a personal bond of $75, and $175 in bank deposits — along with guidance on managing these assets. He instructed his young son on making a last will and testament.

In his will of April 10, 1932, Claiborne, thirteen, "canceling all wills made before this one," left his gold watch, gold ring, "antiques and curios," and silver to his father. His stepfather was to receive "all my furniture," and his stepbrother, who would turn three that year, was to get his books, his gold tie pin, his clothes and "all my toys." Claiborne wanted his mother, whose relative poverty he observed, to receive "all my money, including stocks and bonds," with the provision that "ten percent must go to a suitable American charity." The thirteen-year-old Claiborne ended his will with instructions for miscellaneous possessions. "My odds and ends (including my collections of different things)," he wrote, "to be given by my mother to those who loved me during my life. They must be given mainly to my family. Signed, Claiborne deBorda Pell."

Along with worldly guidance, Herbert wrote frequently of his longings for his son — of how empty his homes sometimes seemed with only Olive and Yankee. They were tender sentiments from a man whose core was intellect and logic.

"We are going down to New York today to spend Christmas in town," he wrote to his son from Newport on December 22, 1931. "I shall miss you very much and I hope that you will have a jolly Christmas . . . Newport seems very quiet without you. I have no roughhouses in the morning, no fleaus, no cold water dashed on me in the shower and my rings left on the table where I left them the night before. It is an easy but unexciting existence and I also miss the shooting and the occasional frights from the driving lessons. I have done very little in the shop except to make a better stand for your big boat, which I have set

up in your room on top of the chest of drawers, where it looks very well indeed
. . . The Christmas tree this year is at Pyrma's house and I shall be very glad
indeed to see the family gathered there, as I always enjoy being with them.

"But I am very sorry that the one I most want to be with will be so far away.
Bad bank reports, past dividends and lowered rents will, I am afraid, make it
quite impossible for me to get abroad during this spring, much as I would like
to do it.

"I am looking forward to hearing from you all the time. Let me know if there
is anything that I can do for you here.

"Most affectionately, HCP."

▫ ▫ ▫ In return for allowing his son to remain with his mother and stepfather
in London, Herbert insisted on a change in the January 29, 1927, agreement
governing custody, visitation, and education of Claiborne. Matilda signed the
amended agreement, which required her to return to America by early September 1932 and enroll their son in a New York City school. Matilda chose The
Browning School, three blocks from the apartment at 502 Park Avenue that she
and Koehler had taken. But come the fall semester of 1933, Herbert would have
"absolute discretion" about Claiborne's schooling.

The amended agreement named St. George's as Herbert's first choice for
Claiborne. But should he be declined admission, nine other private schools
were listed in descending order of acceptability: St. Andrew's, in Delaware;
Lawrenceville, New Jersey; Exeter, New Hampshire; St. Marks, Massachusetts;
Kent, Connecticut; Hotchkiss, Connecticut; Hill, in Pottstown, Pennsylvania;
Morristown, New Jersey; and Pomfret, Herbert's alma mater, in Connecticut.
Herbert would pay for all of his son's expenses while at boarding school, and
would make provision in his will for payment should he die before Claiborne
graduated. The agreement also specified Herbert's choices for his son's college,
although it gave Claiborne the right to decide among them: Harvard, Princeton, Yale, the Massachusetts Institute of Technology and the U.S. Naval Academy. It was a privileged schooling Herbert foresaw for his son, one that seemed
unlikely to produce a man who one day would champion the philosophy that
anyone wanting a college education should be able to receive one, regardless of
ability to pay.

Herbert greeted Claiborne when he arrived with the Koehlers in New York
on September 2, 1932. After several days in Newport with his father and Olive,
Claiborne went back to New York to begin his year at The Browning School.
He was a teenager now, beginning to ponder his future. His father, of course,
had advice.

On November 21, the day before his son's fourteenth birthday, Herbert sent a letter from Newport, where he and Olive would celebrate with him on November 23. "It seems almost unbelievable to me that you are already fourteen years old and no longer a little boy," Herbert wrote. "I've always tried to do as well for you as I can and to put you in at least as good a position in the world as I was placed by my parents. It is possible that I have made mistakes, but I do not believe that on the whole you will be badly fitted when you grow up." The grown-up Claiborne, Herbert said, would find things greatly changed.

"In seven years, you will be your own master, so you are now two-thirds along the road to legal maturity. The world, as you will face it, will be very different from that which was presented to me when I first took my place in it. Reminiscences of that time are interesting and may give profitable suggestions, but I do not believe that at this time a young man should be too much controlled by the experiences of a past generation. Things have changed too much. Institutions which we believed to be fixed foundations of the world have disappeared; principles, purposes and standards have been changed; people, especially young people, seem today to demand things quite different from those which satisfied the early desires of my contemporaries. I can not say that I believe the present point of view to be worse, but it is unquestionably different.

"You must always remember, however, that in spite of changes in the popular appraisal of qualities, there remains one thing the same: honor, honesty and truth do not follow fashions, even though a worried generation may believe they have gone out of fashion. Successfully to practice truth and honesty in your dealings with the world, you must first manage the extremely difficult task of never deceiving yourself, and to do this, you must keep yourself as independent as possible.

"An old Westerner once said that the only really happy man was he who could look any damn galoot in the eye and tell him to go to Hell! Such a person may be very much poorer than the majority of his fellow citizens. There may be other things lacking for him, but in the long run, he will lead a fuller life and a happier one than can possibly be achieved by the most successful man who is overwhelmed by the world . . .

"I have tried to lead my life in such a way as to be every man's friend and no man's client. I can commend this to you as a permanent principle that will survive even the tremendous outward changes that have taken place in the world since my time.

"I look forward to seeing you on Wednesday, and send my love to Mommy.

"Most affectionately, HCP."

ᵒ ᵒ ᵒ After a summer in Europe, during which he stayed (separately) with his mother and his father, Claiborne sailed back to America in early September 1933. Matilda brought him to St. George's, reluctantly. "Mummy didn't much like leaving me behind," Claiborne wrote on September 20 to his father, who was in Paris. But Claiborne liked his new school. "It is very great fun here," he wrote. "My room is quite big and has two windows looking out over Newport . . . I am starting German and have already written a short German translation with the help of a dictionary. I have to close now, as lunch is ready."

Almost fifteen years old now, Claiborne had a more mature understanding of the balance required in trying to accommodate divorced parents who shared their child's custody. He wanted to please both and also please himself, all the while avoiding conflict, which he seemed innately to dislike. Negotiating between his parents required a degree of persistent but polite teenaged diplomacy — the sort that would characterize his handling of potentially contentious issues as an adult. As his father would say after he won election to the U.S. Senate, the boy was not a "problem."

"Dear Dad," Claiborne wrote to his father a month into St. George's, "Thank you very much for your letter and four postcards. I am enjoying myself exceedingly here. About my holidays, don't you remember that at my first year at boarding school (if Mummy let me go) I told her I would spend all my Xmas and Easter holidays with her and you yourself this summer said you thought it was a good idea to spend them in New York with her? But I also have some good news for you. I can spend every other Saturday and Saturday night with you in Newport. I also can be with you every Sunday from 11:15 a.m. to 5:30 p.m. Also during the week, you can spend some time with me at school so I am sure you don't mind letting me spend Xmas holidays and Easter holidays with Mom (which you yourself said was a good idea). I miss Mom very much and we are already making plans what we will do in New York during Xmas holidays. I think you overestimate Thanksgiving, it amounts to just 18 hours holiday and I am not allowed to invite boys out for the one night. I was also hoping that Mommy would come down for Thanksgiving."

In his first semester, Claiborne ranked first of twenty-three students in his English class, third of seventeen in geometry and sixth of fourteen in French. He fared poorly in biology, where he barely passed, and in German, where he flunked his final exam and ranked twenty-sixth of thirty-two students. But he earned an A or B for effort in every discipline, and the teacher who signed his report card was satisfied with his performance and prospects: "A good start with promise of future improvement. Claiborne is settling in very well." The teacher's confidence was rewarded. Claiborne ended the spring 1934 semester having raised his ranking in German and biology, and remaining first in English.

During his three years at St. George's, Claiborne played tennis and soccer, and belonged to the Stamp Club and Library Association. He was president of the Friday Night Club, an informal social group whose central activity was cooking dinner on a rock overlooking the ocean. Tall and handsome, he began to date, at chaperoned parties and dances. He was frequently sick, as he had been as a younger child. A case of measles in the winter of 1935 kept him from classes and sports — but did not deter him from thinking of his social life, which his mother was helping manage from New York. "Feel pretty miserable but will probably feel better tomorrow," he wrote on February 4 in a telegram to Matilda. "If you have not already accepted Lesley Ripley's invitation to April Seconds dance and since I have been invited to the same dance by Barbara Pell, whom do you think I should go with? I should prefer going with Barbara since I don't like Leslie Ripley's dinner hostess as much. Love, Claiborne."

Influenced by his father, whose regular Sunday-afternoon dinners for his son and friends at his Newport estate served as discussion roundtables (that the son himself would later emulate with his children at his own dinner table), Claiborne continued to refine his political views: they were, like those of his father, Democratic. Since leaving the chairmanship of the New York State Democratic Party, in early 1926, Herbert had lectured and written journal articles and letters to the editor. A published letter was a succinct way to formulate a thought and express an opinion — and a way for someone who enjoyed or aspired to prominence to build or maintain visibility. Herbert encouraged Claiborne to attempt a letter to the editor of his own, and he did, in 1934, writing from St. George's to *The New York Times*, a favorite paper of Herbert's. The three-paragraph letter criticized the U.S. government as corrupt and unaccountable to the people. Claiborne suggested that a better system would be a form of dictatorship headed by one man of superior merit who would give heed to, and answer to, his countrymen, not politicians. The best candidate, he said, was his father's friend Roosevelt, who was in his first term as president. *The Times* published the letter in its books section on May 10, 1934:

> This country of ours is neither ruled by one man nor by the community at large, so, as with all mediocre things, the present method of government is a failure.
>
> Some conservatisms say that, through the medium of Congress and the Senate, this government is in reality one of the people, by the people and for the people. If these persons should only cast aside their prejudices, they

would realize that the man in the street is but a pawn, his sole value being that he has the doubtful privilege of voting, wavering between two corrupt politicians, each of whom is trying to convince him that his party is the lesser of two unavoidable evils.

Surely the best government of all would be that conducted by a single intelligent, honest and strong-willed man, who would be virtually a dictator while in office and would be appointed for a very much longer term of office than is the present case. Instead of having an independent Congress and Senate, there would be different advisory committees, every one of which would be subordinate to the dictator. In the present instance, it can easily be seen that the man best suited for the job is Franklin Delano Roosevelt.

Claiborne's admiration for FDR, his father's good friend, seemed to have perverted his understanding of the Constitution, such as it was at the age of fifteen.

Herbert savored publication of the letter, if not the form of government it advocated.

"I was very pleased indeed to see the letter in *The New York Times*," he wrote from his Newport home to his son, a few miles away at St. George's, a few days later. "I don't agree with your idea of government, but I am glad to see you expressing it." Predictably, and hardly for the first time, Herbert offered guidance on his son's writing. He urged Claiborne to avoid "hack phrases" and the use of uncommon words when simpler ones would do: "Odd words," he wrote, "are as bad a habit as strong drink, and in the long run, as weakening." His broad advice was for Claiborne to keep at it. "Writing is not a thing that can be taught," he asserted. "You will have to learn by practice how to express yourself and it will only be by trial and error that you will find out what manner best expresses your way of thinking. The only fixed rule that I can give you is to remember the old Harvard triplets: Clearness, Force and Ease. These are important in the order named. Never sacrifice clearness for force or force for beauty of diction . . . Olive joins me in congratulating you and we both look forward to seeing you on Sunday."

Claiborne's school essays as a younger child reflected his love of adventure and the sea, and his St. George's writings continued with those themes. One, "An Imaginary Light Yacht Cruise," told the story of a boy who leaves Newport in the misty dawn on a forty-foot sloop bound for Block Island. The sloop passes various fishermen and men of the sea, and the narrator and his unnamed companions stay out for two weeks, until a terrible storm drives them back home "with some very pleasant memories." But his letter to *The Times* marked the start of his transition to more substantial interests. In his final English essay for the spring

1935 semester, Claiborne was critical of the narrow college-preparatory focus of his school, which, he asserted, did not provide a comprehensive education. His father, who had left Harvard before graduating, would have understood, but it was a contrarian view for a prep school boy, who was not supposed to challenge the traditional route to status — nor have an affinity, however nascent, with the working classes. Claiborne began with a diplomatic nod to his school:

"St George's offers more educational opportunities beyond college require-ments than any other school of its type. By the word type, I mean that limited group of private schools whose objective is the securing of a boy's entrance into college rather than a rounded education — the high school's goal.

"Let us examine the extra-curricular activities offered to a boy here. I will dwell particularly on the Fifth Form, with which I am the most familiar. There is a social studies class, formerly called the economics class; a navigation class, and a mechanical drawing class. Then, again, we have the different organizations such as the Civics Club, the Radio and Science Club, and the Library Associ-ation, all of which are certainly mentally beneficial to us. Most of these classes have started fairly recently and show that the depression has at least one good point — it makes these boys, who come from families with an independent income, take the utmost advantage of their opportunities. Though beating other schools in this respect, there is still plenty of room for improvement as St. George's is still a school that is essentially for the boy who intends to go to college."

But shouldn't even a college-bound student find lessons outside of a class-room? And shouldn't there be room for teenage rebellion?

"A gentleman can still be a gentleman and not go to college," Claiborne con-tinued. "In fact, a college education is only needed if a student is going to follow a very specialized career in later life. Parents, whether financially straitened or not, are adopting the point of view that instead of letting their boy go to college for four years, during which time he will learn to act like a gentleman, hold his liquor and perhaps absorb a certain amount of learning, it is more practical to let him have a year in town to enjoy himself and then to embark on his career. In time to come, I am certain that St. George's will break away from the rigid rule of the omnipotent College Board and will offer a more rounded and interesting education. Mr. Christie had already got a course completely mapped out for the boy who is more interested in reading French fluently than in the irregular verbs and other points of French grammar."

As his son's high school years neared their end, Herbert turned his atten-tion to Claiborne's future, which unquestionably would include college, and Claiborne agreeing (as he would) to attend one of the five schools named in the amended custody agreement. Discussion of a career path was also now appropriate, and in keeping with what had become the custom of a birthday letter, Herbert on November 14, 1935, wrote from Newport to his son at Middletown. Claiborne was in his final year at St. George's.

"Your birthday is coming next year," he began. "Whenever this day comes around I try to think of myself at the same age. I was seventeen in February 1901. I was six feet high—overgrown in bulk. I do not think I was too tall for that age but I was undoubtedly too big for my strength. I was short-winded and halfway through the Fifth Form at Pomfret and editor of the paper. I had begun practicing public speaking in the school and was rather given to reading. I was not a popular boy. I was much too vigorous in upholding my own conclusions and too contentious and intolerant. I was also too lazy.

"The world at large was very different than what it is today. We were still rubbing our eyes at the thought that there was no longer a Queen Victoria. She had been a great world figure since the time my grandmother was a girl. The Austrian Empire was one of the great facts of Europe stretching back with intermissions but with substantial continuity until the time of Charlemagne. The new German Empire, then only thirty years old, had proved itself a new but permanent and firmly founded thing on which the structure of the world could rest. Russia was solid background, penetrable but impassable like a huge sand bank. Further east there was the unchanging Empire of China, recently beaten in a skirmish with Japan . . .

"I, alas, am too old to change and will go with my civilization and, I hope, before. You will have an entirely new world to face. Your generation will probably have an easier time than would the average of mine in your efforts to do for yourself, but you can be quite sure there will be no one for whom things will be done as lavishly as they were for me. Thirty-five years from now, men will not be working to keep you comfortable; you will not have people at your command to keep your house in order.

"You will have to find some serious occupation for yourself and I think you should give this question the most serious consideration. You must not think only of immediate gain or opportunity. I have suggested not for you to go into general business, particularly into banking or stock broking, [which] would be as stupid as it would have been for a boy in my time in 1905 to have gone into an inherited livery stable. At that time, there were several livery stables going full blast in Newport and there was one small garage.

"I think you should seriously consider a profession which will be of value at all times. Scientists are today honored and valued citizens both in fascist and communist states. Chemists, engineers, dietitians, teachers will always be sure of their food, clothes and lodging under any regime. Your future, provided you look at it from all angles and with consideration of the new standards of social obligation, of comfort and of taste, need not be any less pleasant than my life has been but there can be no doubt in the world that it will be very different in so many ways that I hesitate to give you detailed advice knowing I am speaking from a point of view and with prejudices which do not at all fit and which prevent me from having a proper understanding and appreciation of the changes that have occurred.

"As you get older, you must submit to your own judgments since nothing in the world can substitute for them, but I hope that you will always remember that you can count on my love and affection. Though I may treat you as a man, I still think of you as my little boy and I hope you will always think of me as one who loves you and is proud of you, as I hope you will always love me and at least not be shamed of what I have done.

"I am not as widely known as I had hoped to be when I was your age, but I think I have achieved the respect of my acquaintances and the affection of my friends.

"I am yours very affectionately, HCP."

◻ ◻ ◻ Claiborne graduated from St. George's in June 1936, and during the early summer—when he was staying in Portsmouth, near Newport, with his mother, stepfather, and half brother at the villa called Eastover—he pondered his choice for college.

Of the schools suggested by Herbert, Harvard and Princeton appealed to him most—but he worried that if he chose Harvard, his father, who had left before graduating, would disapprove. Herbert reassured him. "There is no reason in the world that you should not go to Harvard if you want to," he wrote. "It is a great university and you will be able to get a very good education there. My own experience suggested that there is more tendency to loaf at Harvard than at other places, but I may be doing it an injustice. I realize that you are making the choice with the serious desire to learn and for that reason I shall not interfere in the least." Claiborne leaned toward Princeton, but worried that if he were accepted, his father would use his considerable stature to improve his son's chances for admission to certain advanced courses, as he had done for his son at St. George's. "Perhaps the best course at present would be to wait till I hear whether I am even accepted at Princeton or not," Claiborne wrote. "I always think it is a mistake to make a special application, as it is likely to prejudice the faculty against you. At least, this was true at St. George's." On the contrary, Herbert maintained, "a man giving a course is always pleased at having a student try to take it and would feel no special resentment at being asked to give particular consideration to a particular individual."

Claiborne was looking to the fall—but pleasure was his goal for the summer. He was about to experience the freedom of his first car. With the approval of Herbert, who was with Olive at Pellbridge, he went shopping with his stepfather. After discovering that cars sold in Newport were more expensive than those for sale in Fall River, Massachusetts, just across the Rhode Island border, he purchased a 1931 Chrysler sports roadster there. It cost $210.

Pell's car troubles began almost immediately—and they would continue for decades, until the aging senator, experiencing the early symptoms of Parkinson's disease, which may have been caused by an accident while he was riding in a taxi, stopped driving for good. Claiborne was terrible behind the wheel—easily distracted, his thoughts often anywhere but on the road, often not heeding (or seeing) stop signs, red lights, and posted speed limits. And his cars seemed to disagree with him.

In late June, Claiborne left Portsmouth on his first road trip, to visit a friend in New Jersey; he arrived without incident, but had difficulty navigating. "I got here perfectly safely and the car went very well indeed," he wrote to Herbert from his friend's house. "I got slightly befuddled in the district around Newark, but otherwise found my way easily. Had lunch enroute at the Raritan Country Club."

The return trip proved a disaster, with his machine refusing to oblige him.

"After leaving," he wrote to his father on July 5 from Eastover, "I had *five* separate blowouts. I also managed to miss the last ferry at Saunderstown, and started to spend the night in my car. Fortunately, a lady who lived near there sent her son down to wake me up and spend the night at her house. Next morning, I arrived in Newport with exactly 35 cents and the gas register at zero." The troubles continued that fall, when the state Division of Motor Vehicles suspended his registration and ordered him to return his license plates for failing to have insurance. Herbert returned them, and took his son's car off the road until the next summer.

During that last summer before college, Claiborne played tennis and passed afternoons with friends at Bailey's Beach, where he bought, for five dollars, a share of a sailing canoe. "I took Mom out in it yesterday," he wrote to Herbert on July 10, "and the whole thing tipped over, considerably damping Mom." He was sick briefly—developing a boil on his left arm that stopped him from swimming. He took girls to dances, parties and the movies—and brought one girl with him in his car on a visit to Olive and Herbert at Pellbridge. Herbert enjoyed meeting Claiborne's friend. "Please give my best regards to Lucy and tell her that we enjoyed having her here so much," he wrote when Claiborne had left. "She is a nice girl."

Claiborne played tennis on the Pellbridge courts, and Herbert was pleased by his son's performance, but not fully satisfied. "Your lawn tennis is a good deal better than it was," he wrote on July 24, "but I think you will find the greatest improvement will come from the better use of your feet. When you watch a good player, you will find he is very rarely standing still while the ball is in play. I know a great deal more about doubles that I ever did about singles and, although I have never been a good player, I understand the game." Herbert continued on, filling half of the first page and spilling over onto the second. He never lacked for an opinion on anything.

INTERNATIONAL INTRIGUE

Claiborne chose Princeton, and his father approved. He approved also of the courses his son selected: physics, economics, English, public speaking and English history. "If you want any assistance, books or suggestions for theses and treatments," he wrote, "of course you know you have only to apply to me." Claiborne joined the Franklin Delano Roosevelt Club. He was sick with pneumonia that fall, and required hospitalization at the Princeton infirmary. His mother visited three times. His father, who was himself sick with a cold and sequestered at Pellbridge, paid the infirmary bill, and urged Claiborne to rest. "I know that after pneumonia, it is necessary to take pretty good care of yourself for some time and probably most of the winter," he wrote shortly after Claiborne's eighteenth birthday. "A relapse in your present condition would be really dangerous and would certainly prevent you from continuing in your present class."

The freshman Pell recuperated over the Christmas holiday, but was back in the infirmary in mid-January 1937 — and considering transferring to another college, where, he hoped, a better climate would improve his health. Perhaps a university out west, or abroad. His father discouraged this: western colleges, he maintained, were inferior, and the growing threat of war in Europe boded poorly for study in England or France, where Herbert believed a suitable education might be obtained. Herbert paid for a tutor to help Claiborne with his studies and his son remained at Princeton. By the end of February, his grades and his health had both improved.

One morning that spring, the telephone rang at Pellbridge, which Herbert and Olive were preparing to leave on a trip to England, where they would attend the coronation of King George VI. A representative of President Roosevelt was on the phone; the president, he said, wanted his friend to become minister to Portugal. Herbert accepted, and on May 20, the Senate confirmed the nomination.

Claiborne visited his father in Lisbon that summer, and when he returned to America for his sophomore year at Princeton, Herbert wrote of how deeply he missed him. He was also concerned for his son's health. "I do not understand why it is you get sick so often," he wrote on August 10 to Claiborne, who was at Eastover. "I have never seen anyone, not recognized as an athlete, who was as careful about regular exercise as you. You do not drink nor do you smoke to excess. You have more than the average physical strength. Your tendency toward sickness is a mystery to me and I am inclined to charge it to coincidence rather than to any inherent weakness." Claiborne did indeed exercise regularly, notably jogging, which would remain a passion until disease stilled him. He would continue to eat a fastidiously healthy diet, in hope that would prevent a recurrence of his many illnesses in childhood.

During his son's visit, Herbert observed a new trait Claiborne had developed during his freshman year at Princeton, and it was not one he believed would serve the previously mannered eighteen-year-old well.

"In your social intercourse, you must remember that a wise-crack or an epigram may readily undo the good effects of a great many genuinely kind and thoughtful deeds," the father wrote. "I have no recollection of you ever having done anything deliberately unkind, but you occasionally say things which hurt people. As a rule, it does not pay to enter into unimportant arguments and it is certainly unwise to try and set people down. In the first place, somebody else will always volunteer for the job, and in the second, if the person you are criticizing is worthless, he will pull himself down more surely than you can do it for him. I do not mean to suggest that there is no place in the world for proper indignation. As a matter of fact, I have often felt that there is too little righteous wrath in our country. I have sometimes thought that the reason for this may be that too much indignation is wasted on unimportant matters."

As Claiborne passed the halfway point of his sophomore year, he was finally enjoying good health — and coming into his own as a man about campus. He played rugby, traveling in April 1938 with the Princeton team for a game in Bermuda. He had joined the Colonial Club of Princeton University and the Princeton Anti-War Society — and the Veterans of Future Wars, an indication that if America joined the large-scale conflict that many were predicting was coming, he would want to serve his country. *The New York Times* had published another letter, supporting statehood for Hawaii, and *The Daily Princetonian* was regularly publishing his ruminations on topics including one he knew from personal experience: divorce, which, he hoped, the Social Hygiene curriculum could explore. "The majority of divorces," he wrote, "are caused by ignorance of various psychological and physical factors which this course would eliminate.

Only by a full and sympathetic understanding of both the physical and mental makeup of his wife can a man remain happily married and it is far better to teach this understanding by means of a college course than by experience." Perhaps, he seemed to imply, his parents would have fared better with such instruction; perhaps if they had understood each other better before walking down the aisle, they would have remained married.

And he was writing essays and poems for *The Princeton Tiger,* the university's venerable humor magazine, founded in 1882. One concerned the so-called Glamour Girls: a group of wealthy young women — many of whom he knew and some of whom he had dated — who appeared regularly in the society pages of the major newspapers, which chronicled their debuts, visits to Bailey's Beach and Manhattan opera houses, engagement announcements and weddings as fanatically as TV and the Internet would chronicle a later generation of the pampered and privileged. In his "Lamentation of a Glamour Girl," Claiborne wrote wryly of the shallow essence of youthful celebrity — and with a mature prescience of the fate that awaited some of these women as they aged and their beauty faded. It seemed none was a woman he'd ever want to marry.

I am a glamour girl.
You may doubt it,
But Cholly says it.
My hair so long, my eyes so wide
And my so-o-o sophisticated line
Just does things to the stag line.
I am frightfully busy.
Up at eleven for a photo,
Lunch at the Stork,
Only a dollar for *us,* you know.
A movie, a tea, a this and a that
Just makes the day one hectic rush.
Then home to change for Betty S———,
Never saw her before, but still,
And on to the Blinks' and the Blanks' and the Blahs.'
Hank, Bill and Francis may take me,
But home I go with Serge,
So different and so you know what I mean!
Day in, day out I do the same
But as the months go by
The columns give me less.

My glamour is on the wane.
I became last year's most photogenic deb,
And this year's forgotten maiden.
(Accompanied by beating of the breast, groans and wails.)
I've got to get a man or,
Dear God, don't say it, be on the shelf.
Serge? No.
Hank, Bill or Francis? Already plucked.
What shall I do?
A convent, Dorothy Dix, or, aha, the Persian Room?

A history major, Claiborne in more serious moments explored weightier topics — and not simply to fulfill course requirements, but with an eye toward outside publication. He succeeded with a six-page essay comparing whites and African-Americans that was published in the October 1939 edition of Howard University's *Journal of Negro Education*, founded in 1932 as the first scholarly publication to examine issues of race in education. Claiborne's essay, "Anthropological Differences Between Whites and Negroes," attempted to answer the question of whether the races are different by nature — or whether whites and blacks are essentially the same, their prospects determined by environmental factors (including the quality of schooling) as they grew up in what the Princeton student described as "a country ridden with racial prejudice as we are." It was a progressive attitude for a white teenaged child of privilege, attending an Ivy League school. It spoke of a sense of social justice.

In his conclusion, Claiborne stated: "Distinctions between the races are purely artificial and arbitrary. Professor Bunch put it very aptly when he said: 'Modern racial classifications are based on man-made distinctions; the resultant groupings are thus purely arbitrary. If we could include in our problem the education of racial tolerance, there would soon be no anthropological differences, since racial prejudice would disappear and we would have complete miscegenation,'" or integration.

▢ ▢ ▢ Claiborne spent part of the summer of 1938 again with his father in Lisbon and the remainder with his mother and the Koehlers at Eastover, then returned to Princeton for his junior year. For the summer of 1939, he wanted to visit Europe again and his father proposed a schedule that would include three weeks in Lisbon, followed by a month in Italy and France. "Olive will meet us in Paris," he wrote, "and then you will have a few days there before you sail." Claiborne would return to America in September 1939, to begin his senior year.

But in June 1939, Claiborne decided he wanted to visit his father earlier and return to America that August. And he wanted to visit other countries than his father proposed. He sent his desires in a June 10 letter that included the latest chapter in his continuing car troubles. "My car was eating up so much oil and chugging so," he wrote, "that it had to have a new engine." Claiborne also noted that his father owed him $17.85 for tutoring.

Not long after sending the letter, Claiborne sailed from the U.S. on a Polish ship to Copenhagen, where he stayed for a couple of days, and then made his way to Danzig, as the Polish city of Gdansk was known in 1939. Under terms of the Versailles Treaty that ended World War I, Danzig had been declared the Free City of Danzig, a semi-independent state under the auspices of the League of Nations. In the summer of 1939, German forces in Danzing were staging for war. The Jewish population was fleeing.

The young American took many photographs, including one of a synagogue being torn down, and he kept careful notes, with the idea that American newspapers would publish his firsthand observations of the contested city when he returned to the U.S. They would, after Claiborne was detained by the Nazis and questioned at a police station after trying to visit Bishopsberg, a hill overlooking Danzig where the Germans were preparing a garrison under the guise of a youth hostel. It made for a dramatic account that newspapers, hungry for firsthand chronicles of Europe on the edge of war, were pleased to publish.

"When I was inquiring my way to Bishopsberg," Claiborne wrote in a lengthy letter to the *Newport Herald* that was published on August 30, after his return to America, "a rather burly individual with a swastika in his buttonhole came up to me and said he would take me to the Tourists headquarters, where I could get all the information I wished. A little suspicious of this sudden manna from heaven, I nevertheless accepted. My surprise was complete when I found myself on the fourth floor of the Poliziduim behind a locked grill instead of the hoped-for Tourist Bureau. When I said that I was an American, they decided I was quite harmless and probably mad. Then, when I said I thought Bishopsberg was a museum or monument or something of the sort, they grew positively friendly towards me and the happy climax was when I lunched the next day with the Gestapo official who had questioned me."

It was the young Pell's first foray into diplomacy, his father's business now, and it ended peacefully. Peaceful endings would be Pell's goal throughout his life.

But the situation in Danzig, Claiborne wrote, was a grim prelude to almost-certain war. "There are two Danzigs," he explained to *Newport Herald* readers. "A walk through the little side streets, bordered by gabled houses, crisscrossed by canals and filled with women carrying market bags and children with bathing suits gives no hint that here is the sore spot of Europe. But when you happen upon one of the main streets, then it is a different story. Uniforms are everywhere — the black shirts of Hitler's Elite guards, the brown of the Storm Troopers, the green of the Danzig police and the gray of the regular German Army. There is a continual procession of armored trucks, cars and anti-tank guns trundling backwards and forwards. This is the Danzig that is of such interest to Europe now. What are the effects of the Nazi penetration and all of these activities? That was the first question I asked of myself when I arrived there. The answer is two-fold.

"There has been a change in the social life of the people and a general fortification and arming of the place. Perhaps the most self-evident sign of the social change is the tearing down of the synagogue. Most of the social changes have taken a negative rather than positive side. There is not to be found one of those orthodox Jews, who, in their skull caps and long black coats, abound in the nearby Polish towns. Not only are the Jews the more noticeable because of their absence, but so are the Poles. Though there are some eight thousand Polish women left in Danzig, there is scarcely a Polish man. And what Polish men there are concentrated either in the Polish-owned Continental Hotel, the railroad station, or the garrison at Westerplatte."

On July 21, Claiborne reached Warsaw, where he wrote of his adventures to his father, whom he would soon join.

"This was reported by the press, AP," he wrote, "so I would be much obliged if you could save any clippings for me since it is about impossible to get U.S. papers here." Claiborne also wrote, to his father and later for the Newport papers, of setting off after dark for an all-night row around an island off Danzig where the German military was preparing for attack. It was a risky adventure that an ordinary Ivy League kid would have been unlikely to undertake — and one that surely would have resulted in Claiborne's arrest, perhaps with a charge of espionage that would have embarrassed his diplomat father and country, if he had been caught. "Since there was no moon, and we weren't carrying a light," the *Newport Herald* account related, "we were able to slip along in the dark without being spotted by either the sentries on the shore or the police boats. First, we passed a couple of military depots and then next came to Kaiserhaven, where the railroad ferry that carries the heavy guns was at anchor. As we went on a little further, we passed the actual entrance to the Harbour of Kolm, where most of the ammunitions came to. Every Saturday night at around ten o'clock the river is closed to all regular activities and then there is a tremendous bustle as the railroad ferry shuttles backwards and forwards with its shipments from East Prussia and there is a stream of ships from Germany . . . This is not the only time that the river is closed. Kolm is also used as a submarine base and whenever the arrival of one of these underseas crafts is scheduled, the police boats scurry around and clear the river . . . At present, there are three submarines that are being made shipshape by the machinists and workers on the island and an unknown number of submarines there temporarily."

Claiborne's newspaper account did not include his exercise of patriotic duty. "I put any information I had at the disposal of the military attaché" at the American embassy, he wrote to his father on July 21.

Claiborne left Warsaw to meet up with his father and the two went to Naples, and then traveled at a leisurely pace by car north through Italy, which Herbert knew well from the years he had spent in Europe before he married and his travels with Matilda and then Olive. "Italy was much changed since I had last seen it," Herbert wrote to President Roosevelt, who looked to his Portuguese ambassador for insight into the deteriorating situation on the continent. "The gaiety and noise to which I was accustomed were entirely absent. There were no excited groups talking vigorously and no singing . . . belligerent phrases extracted from Mussolini's speeches are displayed in enormous letters and it is a rare thing to be out of sight of at least one: 'Believe, obey, fight.' 'Italy fears no one.' 'The plough opens the land but the sword defends it.'" Herbert was disheartened, for he could see that the civilization he savored would soon be lost to war. The father and son continued to Paris, and then to London, and in August sailed back to the U.S.

At 4:45 a.m. on September 1, German Luftwaffe bombers began dropping bombs on Poland. Minutes later, the German battleship *Schleswig-Holstein*, which had sailed to Danzig under the pretext of a "courtesy visit," began to shell the Polish garrison of Westerplatte, a peninsula off the Polish city that Claiborne had visited. With Blitzkreig forces advancing deeper into Poland, France and Great Britain declared war on Germany two days later. World War II had begun.

▫ ▫ ▫ Herbert made his way back to Lisbon and Claiborne entered his senior year at Princeton, where he took up bodybuilding and ran cross-country. Claiborne was a member of the National Anti-Syphilis Committee of the American Social Hygiene Association. He continued work on his thesis, about Thomas Babington Macaulay, the nineteenth-century British historian, poet, and politician who served in Parliament and was Secretary of War — a worthy subject, Herbert decreed.

And he dated young women, including Anne Grosvenor, who had attended the Foxcroft School while Claiborne was at St. George's and who was now at

Vassar College—located in Poughkeepsie, New York, near Pellbridge, which Herbert had left available to his son. Daughter of New York lawyer Edwin P. Grosvenor (whose brother, Gilbert H. Grosvenor, was the longtime editor of *National Geographic Magazine*), and Thelma Cudlipp, a socially ambitious illustrator for *Harper's*, *Vanity Fair*, and other magazines, Anne was a year younger than Claiborne. They met in Newport in about 1930, when her father died of pneumonia at the age of 55. An attractive dark-haired girl, Anne found kindness and comfort in Claiborne, her daughter Kip Greenthal would recall, at a difficult period of her life. They would remain friends after each married.

Herbert approved of his son's interest in women. "You seem to be having a pretty good time and are seeing a lot of girls," he wrote from Lisbon. "When I was your age, I did exactly the same thing." But in securing his son's financial future, Herbert urged caution regarding suitors and family money.

His concern was evident in late September, when he decided to hand his son control of the trust he had established for him; waiting five more years, as Herbert had once considered, no longer made sense. "You will be twenty-one very soon," he wrote on September 29, "and you should get accustomed to handling capital as soon as possible . . . There are no conditions attached to this trust at all; my only advice is that you say nothing about it. If you do, you will find yourself a mark for salesmen who will try to get you to shift your investments and give you immature advice, and as a rule, you will do better to consider the opinions of stupid old men than of silly young ones." Certain women who got wind of Pell money would also come calling, Herbert said; many had ties to Newport, which had lost any appeal to Herbert after his son had graduated from high school. He judged the endless social events and Glamour Girl mystique as empty, and he wanted no part of the scene anymore.

"Although the amount involved is not enormous," Herbert wrote, "it is at least sufficiently large to make you an object of interest to some of the young adventuresses around Newport who may very well make the mistaken inference that their charms will extract large sums from me. As a matter of fact, they will not . . . However charming a girl may be and whatever real qualities she may have, I cannot say that I relish the prospect of having grandchildren who are likely to resemble the cousins and brothers of some very delightful young women whom we both know." When Claiborne finally found the woman he wanted to marry, he knew that his father would not be easy to please.

The principal of the trust was sufficient to produce about $4,000 a year in interest (about $65,000 in 2011 dollars). It was no pot of gold—but managed properly, it could support Claiborne for life, even if he never made more money, from his own work or through further investments, as was unlikely. And it did not, of course, include what Herbert would leave his son — his sole heir — in his will, nor any other gifts or continuing support Herbert would offer while still alive. Pells took care of their own.

"You will find that the law of Diminishing Returns applies to money as it does to many other things in life," Herbert wrote on November 27, five days after Claiborne turned twenty-one. "The difference between having three thousand dollars a year and having nothing at all is far greater than the difference between three and thirty thousand . . . I very strongly advise you to hang on to your capital. Live, if necessary, uncomfortably on your income, but do not dig into your principal. This is in no sense a question of honor, it is entirely one of worldly wisdom and long-run advantage."

Claiborne spent part of his winter holiday in Washington and part at Pellbridge, where he worked on his thesis in his father's library, skied, and entertained Anne Grosvenor and friends. As 1940 began, he was looking past graduation. He considered buying a Caribbean island as an investment — the first of several esoteric investment schemes over the next several years, none ever realized, that suggested high finance was not his forte. A job in an overseas embassy, his father's perhaps, also appealed to him, as did journalism, but his father strongly opposed it. "I do not think much of newspaper work or of newspaper men," Herbert wrote. "They seldom get any real literary faculties, and when they do, their work is always hurried and a habit of speed destroys any quality they may have had. A daily theme at college is one thing, but a daily article in a newspaper will ruin the most honest and conscientious writer. It's like spitting in the flour mill."

A superior career, Herbert maintained, would be a position in the State Department — stateside. "I do not think you would like the Foreign Service," he wrote. "The life is very uncertain, the competition is severe, and the bouncing about must be unpleasant." His words would prove prophetic.

The war in Europe would prevent Herbert and Olive from attending Claiborne's graduation. "I am only sorry that I shall not be able to get over on June 11th for your commencement exercises," Herbert wrote. "The situation in Europe is very bad and it is practically impossible for me to leave Lisbon." But he was pleased with the finish to his son's college years. "You have worked hard and honestly and spent practically nothing on tutoring. I must say that my ambitions as far as you are concerned are pretty well satisfied at the present time."

Still, Claiborne's future remained uncertain. As he pondered his prospects, he thought of his father's term in Congress, the many politicians he had met through Herbert, and his own enjoyable visit to Washington over the previous winter. He began to think that elective politics might be for him. Herbert urged him to consider it, if other career options lost their appeal—and to take steps soon that would start him down the road, if that was his choice.

With roots in two states, Claiborne's possibilities were double those of most potential candidates, Herbert noted. A call on Senator Theodore Francis Green would be worthwhile for any eventual run in Rhode Island, Herbert advised; for his New York chances, Herbert suggested calling on his friend Jeremiah T. Mahoney, recent candidate for New York mayor and a well-connected Democrat in the city and the state. Regardless of where Claiborne established residence, Herbert recommended contacting Jim Farley, eight-year chairman of the Democratic National Committee and Roosevelt's Postmaster General. But politics provided no guarantees, as Herbert knew well; should he decide on seeking office, Herbert urged his son to have something to fall back on.

"I cannot, however, too strongly advise you against a career of elective office without resources," he wrote. "A university professor as a rule could get leave without pay to attend the legislature or Congress, and this would not interfere with the security of the position. This would not be true of other occupations. Writing is a doubtful livelihood, but seems to be attractive to those who are in it. A term in the Assembly or State Senate would be a good thing, however, as it would give you an understanding of how things are run which you can really get in no other way."

Start small. It was a good piece of advice—and one of the few from the father that the son, when he finally decided to seek office, would completely ignore.

A TIME OF DISCONTENT

On June 11, 1940, Claiborne graduated from Princeton with an honors degree in history; his twenty-two-page Macaulay thesis earned high honors. Leaving Princeton, he visited a friend on Long Island, then went to Manhattan, where he stayed at the Racquet & Tennis Club on Park Avenue. He was planning a cross-country trip with a friend that would consume much of the summer, but come fall, he wanted to be in Europe. On June 28, he wrote from the club to his father, looking for employment. "Can you get me some sort of job—you know my tastes as well as I do—in Europe starting approximately October 10th. It could be in Lisbon or any other part of Europe."

And he was weighing another option.

With America's entrance into the war increasingly likely, Claiborne was considering the military—on his terms. With the Selective Training and Service Act of 1940 now before the Senate, Claiborne did not want to be drafted; he wanted to serve his country, but not in the infantry. Serving at sea, which he so loved, seemed ideal. "What do you think of my joining the Navy reserve?"

he wrote to his father. "First you take a month's cruise, then an exam, then a three month's intensive shore course in naval science. You end up with a reserve officer's commission in the Navy which I should much prefer to have as against a buck private's slot in the Army if there should be trouble."

Herbert approved of the plan. "As you say, it is far better than the Army," he wrote back. Herbert's only concern was that his son's poor eyesight might disqualify him, as it had disqualified Herbert himself.

After visiting his mother, stepfather and half-brother at Eastover, Claiborne headed west across America with a friend on an end-of-college road trip. His car kept overheating, requiring him to stop constantly to fill the radiator — but eventually he made it to Oklahoma, where the commander's brother had arranged for him and his friend to work as roustabouts on an oil rig, the only time in his life he would be able to call himself a laborer. After two weeks on the rig, he drove to Texas, then to Wyoming, and then to Davenport, Iowa, where his stepfather's family had lived. He bought a pair of glasses to replace one he had lost. The loss drew a mild rebuke from his father, who urged him to be more careful.

In late August, Claiborne was back in Newport. He was anxious. The Senate had passed its conscription bill and Roosevelt was planning to sign it into law. Claiborne's application to the Navy had been rejected because of his eyesight, and his request for a waiver was pending, a process that could be lengthy. In hopes of expediting approval, he had enlisted the help of Koehler, a Navy veteran — and the help of his diplomat father, a friend of the president. Koehler wrote letters on Claiborne's behalf, and Herbert began a campaign that would last nearly a full year and reach directly to Roosevelt in the White House.

Herbert's efforts began in early September, when he wrote to two old friends from his Washington days: Senator Carl Vinson, chairman of the Senate Committee on Naval Affairs, and Peter Gerry, Senator from Rhode Island. "My son, Claiborne Pell, passed the examinations for the Naval Reserve in Rhode Island except for the eye test," Herbert wrote to Vinson. "I should be very grateful indeed if you could do something to have this waived."

Claiborne was increasingly frustrated. "At the moment," he wrote to his father as fall approached, "I am getting very tired of waiting to hear from this Navy scheme. You don't know how restless I feel with no set plans and, even more, with [the] world collapsing all around. As I have said, if I hear negatively r.e. the Navy, I shall probably telegraph you about coming to Europe."

Pell wrote his letter on September 15. The next day, Roosevelt signed the Selective Training and Service Act into law — and Claiborne learned the Navy would not grant him a waiver. "The Bureau of Medicine and Surgery of the Navy recommended that the defect of eyesight not be granted," Senator Gerry explained in a letter to Herbert. "I am told by the Department, and this is consistent with the action taken in previous cases of which I know, that waivers have been given only where the defect concerned such things as the height of the applicant. Your son also wrote me, and I am transmitting this information to him."

Claiborne sent a telegram to Herbert from Newport. "Definitely unacceptable by Navy," it read. "Would like come Lisbon now." He made arrangements for the Atlantic crossing.

When he arrived in Portugal, his father offered him a job. Claiborne would assist in the war effort by delivering Christmas gifts to British soldiers held prisoner in Germany. He would drive an ambulance flying a Red Cross flag from Lisbon through Spain and France to Geneva, where the Red Cross would accept the presents for delivery to the prisoners. The journey would be much in the spirit of his adventures in Danzig the year before, and Claiborne was enthused—even if, as he suspected, his bad luck with motor vehicles would continue to haunt him. With a Red Cross mechanic—and notebooks to chronicle his trip for newspaper accounts he planned to write—he left Lisbon on December 12. The Pells had alerted the Associated Press about his arrival, and a story with a photo moved that day over the wires.

Back in Newport in February 1941, Claiborne wrote about his experience for several publications and he granted several interviews, including to *The Providence Journal*, whose good favor, he knew, would prove useful in any Rhode Island political ambitions. Published accounts would be proof of the daring humanitarian effort, which might speak to Claiborne's character in an appeal to voters.

"Securing an old ambulance, which he converted into a truck, and hiring a Portuguese chauffeur, with whom he could talk only by signs, since neither knew the other's language, Pell loaded 263 prisoners' bundles aboard and started out," *The Journal* reported in its February 12 editions. The bundles, according to the earlier AP account, contained 10,000 cigarettes, 150 plum puddings, more than 400 pounds of wool clothing, 70 pairs of shoes and 70 pairs of clippers, and "half a ton of foodstuff" collected by the wife of a British prisoner of war.

"There really wasn't anything to it," Pell told *The Journal*, "as we passed through the war zones. We broke down a couple of times, but my chauffeur made quick repairs and it took us three weeks to make the round trip. Motoring over there is quite different from this country. They have no snow plows, the roads are rough and often we found bridges under water but passable. The distance was about 1200 miles, the same as Newport To Tulsa, Oklahoma, which I made in three days last summer, but French and Spanish roads are different and this trip took us more than a week."

In this and other published accounts, Claiborne described, in engaging detail, the people he met and places he passed through on his way to Geneva and back. But his accounts were more than a travelogue by one of the few Americans on his own on the continent as Hitler's forces solidified their occupation of France and moved toward war with America. They were informed by a sense of geopolitics and history.

"Everyone in Europe is talking about the war and preparing for a long war, but there is no hysteria involved," he told *The Journal*. "Over here, everyone seems to be talking about it, judging by the press, yet at the same time, seems to be going around in circles wondering just what it is all about. I believe the United States must do two things quickly. First, they must decide if they are willing to go to war, and if that decision is made, to assume leadership in the war and back it up heart and soul. Apparently, the United States is half-hearted about the war. They do not realize that if the war is to be fought successfully, they must be prepared to give up automobiles and their money, as England has done, and sacrifice all towards war production. You can't win a war with half-measures. We must send over our entire merchant marine and half our fleet to help England. She will win the war, if we in this country help to the utmost."

❑ ❑ ❑ Claiborne drew a high number in the draft, and did not, he told *The Journal*, expect to be conscripted until the spring of 1942 at the earliest. His mother expected it would be even longer — and she urged her son not to enlist, on the belief the war would end before he was called. "I don't know why it should be necessary for you to try to get into the Naval Militia either here or in New York," she wrote from Eastover before Claiborne returned from Lisbon. "You tried to enter the Navy this autumn, and now that your draft no. doesn't come up for so long, [and] we will hope the war will be over before it does, I see no reason to rush into the service."

Intent on serving, though not through conscription, Claiborne applied for acceptance into the Office of Naval Intelligence, a translation and information-gathering branch where it seemed eyesight would be less critical than in any combat-related assignment. Claiborne traveled to Washington in the spring of 1941 to personally make his case and Herbert, whom Roosevelt had reassigned to Hungary, renewed his efforts from overseas.

At Eastover, meanwhile, a crisis was unfolding.

Claiborne's stepfather was seriously ill with kidney disease, complicated by high blood pressure and what one doctor diagnosed as hardening of the arteries. He was fifty-four.

"Mom thought it best not to tell the commander how serious his condition was, as he could then lose heart," Claiborne wrote to his father. "The doctors agree to this, so we are trying to make things as normal as possible for him." The Koehlers returned to their apartment on Manhattan's Park Avenue, where he could be close to skilled doctors. But they could not save Koehler.

On June 17, the commander died and was buried at the cemetery at Saint Columba's Chapel in Middletown, not far from Eastover.

Claiborne cabled his father, who responded with a letter asking his son to help with Matilda and Claiborne's half-brother Hugh, Koehler's only child, who was eleven. "I have just received your cable and have written Mommy," Herbert wrote. "Look out for her and be as considerate as you can. She is in great trouble. I am only sorry that I cannot be present to help in some way." Herbert foresaw difficulty if Matilda moved in with Bomba, his former mother-in-law, a cold and disagreeable woman who still dominated her daughter — and he asked Claiborne to use his influence to prevent that from happening. "I need not tell you that I am writing confidentially when I tell you to do what you can to prevent Mommy from setting up housekeeping with her mother. It would be a bad thing for her and for Hugh. Look out for her as much as possible. I think it would be a good thing for her to sell the place at Newport to Lord Camoys and take a house in town with Hugh. She has lots of friends there and can find a certain amount of interesting work to do. See that she is occupied and does not work too hard."

With the nation emerging from the Great Depression, Herbert's investments were increasing his wealth. With the death of Koehler, Claiborne's mother's financial situation, already deteriorating, continued to decline. Claiborne would be there for Matilda until she died many years later — and her diminished means (and diminishing health) would give the son an unusual appreciation for those less fortunate that would be a hallmark of his long Senate career.

THREE ▫ LAND AND SEA

On the evening of August 2, 1941, the American embassy in Budapest, Hungary, attempted to reach the president of the United States by telephone. It was midday in Washington. For a moment, the connection was made; Herbert Pell, minister to Hungary, heard Roosevelt's voice. The president was saying he couldn't hear who was calling. Then the connection was lost. The next day, Herbert sent Roosevelt a cable:

> HAVE FAILED TELEPHONE YOU. PLEASE HELP MY BOY CLAIBORNE. DISAPPROVED APPLICATION INTELLIGENCE THIRD NAVAL DISTRICT. HE WANTS PUBLIC RELATIONS SAME DISTRICT. PLEASE ADVISE HIM. I AM FAR AWAY AND WORRIED. HAVE CABLED HIM CONTACT WATSON. PLEASE ANSWER. PELL.

Herbert was becoming frantic, and the president and Edwin M. Watson, Roosevelt's appointments secretary, were not the only ones he attempted to influence that summer in his campaign, now almost a year long, to get his son into the navy: in the days before telephoning Roosevelt, he had contacted Rear Admiral Adolphus Andrews, commandant of the Third Naval District, whose headquarters were in New York City. Herbert was trying to help his son obtain a public relations position or get into the Navy Supply Corps, from which he might later transfer into Intelligence. He continued to fear that his son would be drafted into the Army, which, he believed, would foreclose any chance of Claiborne becoming an officer — with or without his connections.

"If you become a private in a draft army," the father wrote the son, "it will be almost impossible to transfer you to any other service and promotion will be extremely difficult."

By the first week of August, the young Pell had tired of his father seeking favors. He'd wearied of the visits he himself had made, with his father's encouragement, to Navy officers in Washington and New York. On August 8, he was on the verge of a decision that he knew his father might not like — but it would be a decision all his own. He cabled Herbert: AM TRYING WORK OUT COUPLE OTHER ANGLES DO NOTHING FURTHER UNTIL CABLED. STOP.

Ten days later, Pell enlisted in the Coast Guard.

"I feel quite happy about it because I have gotten in entirely on my own," he wrote to Bomba from Eastover, where he was visiting his newly widowed mother and young half-brother. "In fact, they wanted me so much that they gave me a waiver for my poor eyesight without any urging on my part. I am starting out as a second-class seaman and leave this Monday to report for duty."

Pell elaborated on his decision in a longer letter to his father. "It seemed to me better to be in an organization that was genuinely desirous of my services and where the eyesight waiver was granted without any question of outside influence whatsoever. That I shall be starting out from scratch and not with the strikes against me of an adverse report and any individual hostility I might have incurred. Finally, I shall get a chance for sea duty. I am enlisting in this as a seaman instead of a yeoman's petty officer with officer duty that was offered to me for this same reason — so that I can get out in the open air. I know this will be no picnic, but the next few years are going to be tough all around." Pell explained that the Coast Guard wanted to eventually bring him to Washington for an assignment in public relations, once he had become an officer. That, too, pleased him. Pell continued his letter with an uncharacteristic slap at his father.

"I was really damn sick of going around to a bunch of naval officers and trying to push myself in on them by straight drag or of trying to sell myself. This way, I just happened to walk in on the Coast Guard on my own hook and hit it off right away with the people there before they had any idea of who I was or that I was your son."

Moreover, Pell wrote, he was joining a group that, while pressed into war duty, had a peacetime humanitarian mission. "When this shindig is all over, I shall be an accomplished sailor and navigator," he wrote. "I shall be in an organization devoted to saving lives instead of exterminating them — and they are definite human ones, since I am not yet convinced that all Britons are Gods and all Germans are devils . . . All told, I am very happy and enthusiastic about what I am doing and hope that you are, too."

Herbert was not enthusiastic, nor was he overtly critical. He sent Pell a telegram stating his respect for his son's judgment, following it with a letter in which he expressed the hope that Pell would indeed be commissioned an officer — and he offered his help in that, cause, too. "Never hesitate to ask me to telephone to anybody from here," he wrote. He seemingly had not grasped the significance of Pell's initiative.

Herbert did, however, have a pressing concern — for his wine collection, nearly 2,000 bottles with a value he estimated at nearly $20,000, left when he departed for Hungary in the cellar of his Hopewell Junction estate, to which he planned someday to return. Now that Pell was entering the service, he hoped another relative would arrange for transfer of the collection to storage in

Manhattan. "I am very much afraid that local gossip will exaggerate the amount of beverages in the house," he wrote, "which will incite local thieves to break into the house and might even bring professional ones from New York who might set it on fire to cover their traces. This would be such a calamity which would alter my entire life. I should not attempt another collection, but would probably spend the rest of my life with headquarters at a New York hotel."

As it would happen, Herbert's wine would remain safe. He would return to Hopewell Junction, but with a postwar perspective in which the accoutrements of wealth would matter less to him. In his letter, he already sensed it.

"Europe seems condemned to a shattered destruction, and to a hiatus in its civilization such as we see in Germany between the great medieval survival of Maximillian and Bismarck's empire," he wrote. "It is hard to see what will happen, but neither plague nor tyranny nor starvation are pleasant prospects. The repercussions of the war will be less severe in America, but we must prepare ourselves for great material changes. I have been fortunate. I am among the last who have been able to enjoy practically complete independence and the control of my work and leisure. Now that I am getting old, I am very glad indeed that I made the choice I did. At the worst, I can always haunt a public library, and at best go on with the simpler comforts which in later life replace the expensive pleasures of youth. I have led a conspicuously happy life and I see no reason that I will be unable to adapt myself to the future, and to continue to get something out of each day as it goes by."

◻ ◻ ◻ August 1940 neared its end. Newport's annual Tennis Week brought the usual partying, and Pell, who had been in Europe the previous several summers, unable to attend, made the rounds.

"It has been more than fun, to put it mildly," he wrote to his father. "Perhaps the reason I enjoyed it so much was that my immediate future was settled." But the festive abandon of Tennis Week, like much else of Newport Society, was soon to be lost to war, which would draw so many young men like Claiborne. The Gilded Age of Herbert's youth would remain only in memories and the once-opulent mansions that families would abandon or sell at a fraction of their earlier worth.

Tennis Week ended and Pell reported for duty, as seaman second class, at Chelsea Depot in Boston, on August 18. He was assigned short-term duty on a picket boat, a small patrol vessel, and two weeks later, he was placed on the cutter *Duane*, part of a force that Roosevelt had ordered to North Atlantic duty. Pell advanced quickly. On October 31, he was made seaman first class. On November 6, he stood quartermaster watch on the cutter *Argo*. After a visit with her son, the recently widowed Matilda wrote to him of how she and his half-brother rejoiced in his success.

"I am so very proud of you, passing the navigation section of your exams first! I do think it is really splendid and you taught it all to yourself, too. You really are a very clever boy. Hughie was terribly impressed and I think it may do much to show him what one can do by one's own effort and work. We are just delighted and send you lots of love and congratulations. I'm glad you got the duty you wanted on the *Argo*, but won't be too happy at the thought of you living at sea these days. However, I'll be hoping it won't be far from this coast and know you will enjoy Newport as a base. Only heard about Navy taking over Coast Guard the evening you left. Don't you suppose it means war is more imminent than we think?"

Matilda closed on an emotional note.

"Take good care of yourself and again congratulations on your fine exam. I will tell Bomba today and know she will be very excited, she has been asking a lot about you. How pleased the commander would have been with you! Perhaps he does know . . . Lots of love, dear, Your devoted Mom."

Pell liked Coast Guard life, which brought him for the first time into daily contact with working-class people who were officially his peers, not the hired help — an experience that would further refine his views of those less privileged. "All the fellow sailors here are very nice indeed to me and I really do look forward to the next few months," he wrote to Herbert. "It should be interesting, if not a picnic."

Pell was no snob but neither did he present himself as someone other than a son of wealth: one of his first activities in Boston, on the very day he reported for duty, was to visit a rare-books store, where the dealer, learning his name, told him of nineteenth-century Pell family engravings he had once sold. The new Coast Guardsman bought his first new car: a blue 1942 Studebaker Skyway Commander. He added a radio, red leather upholstery, a Climatizer heating and ventilation system, and a Pell family coat of arms custom-painted on the door, bringing the total cost to $1,500.70, a fair sum.

Pell was about to be named ensign when, on December 7, the Japanese attacked Pearl Harbor, bringing America into the war. Five days later, Hungary declared war on the United States. Herbert closed the American legation, and with Olive, left Budapest on a train, first leg of a long journey back to America that would end when the Swedish American liner *Drottningholm* docked in Jersey City on June 1, 1942. Herbert and his wife made their way to their New York City apartment, and then to Pellbridge, where they would spend nearly two years, until Roosevelt found a new position for him.

On December 17, Coast Guard Ensign Claiborne Pell boarded the cutter *Campbell*, CG-32, an illustrious ship (fifth to bear the *Campbell* name) that would earn the title "Queen of the Seas" for its forty-six years' service in the Second World War, the Korean War, and Vietnam. The *Campbell* belonged to a naval and air task force responsible for protecting North Atlantic convoys. During the next four and a half months, Pell held a variety of positions, including deck officer, assistant censor, and assistant communications officer, which utilized his writing skills — his ticket, he hoped, for advancement into the officer corps.

▫ ▫ ▫ Pell served on convoy duty until May 1, 1942, when he was transferred to the Coast Guard's Washington headquarters as an assistant in the Office of Public Affairs, with responsibility for writing speeches and articles. He was rewarded with promotion to lieutenant, junior grade, on October 1.

One day in January 1943, Pell read a plea from the District of Columbia's Freedmen's Hospital published in *The Washington Post*. The Rev. William H. Jackson, a fifty-seven-year-old patient at the hospital, was about to undergo amputation of his right leg, which had turned gangrenous, a complication of his diabetes. "The pastor has had four transfusions to date, averaging about one a week for the past four weeks ever since he got worse," an attending physician said. "We had to remove a toe and a foot bone in an attempt to stop the infection. But it hasn't stopped, so we have to amputate."

His only chance to survive the surgery, the pastor's doctors said, was with transfusions. Pell and eight others gave blood. "He sure looks like a sick man," Pell told a reporter covering the event. "I guess this is the least we can do."

What made the story newsworthy was the minister's race: He was black, and whites customarily did not give their blood to a person of color. Even Pell's mother disapproved, in a letter she sent after he had donated.

"Thank you for your nice letter," Matilda wrote. "I must tell you, though, I really do not approve of you giving your blood so soon again. In the first place, there are plenty of civilians who would do it and should, rather than men in the service, who should do everything to keep fit and have all their strength. In the second place, as it was a Negro hospital with Negro doctors and Negro patient, I should think they could call on a Negro blood donor. I do think it was not your job. If it had been another member of the armed forces to which you gave, that is another thing and you should keep your blood for such an emergency. In a big city full of civilians and women, there are plenty of people who would have given to this man, without taking servicemen. You must not let a kind heart overrule good judgment."

Pell took advantage of the publicity to also relate, in newspaper interviews, his experiences on North Atlantic convoy duty the year before. He told the *Washington Star* that his ship had never encountered German submarines, but that he had tasted warfare — when his fleet dropped depth charges on a school of fish that had been mistaken for a sub. The weather, Pell said, was violent.

"The wind blew 100 miles an hour," he said. "No one will believe that, but it's true. Our convoy was completely broken up and the wind pushed us 100 miles backwards within a day and stove in two of our lifeboats." The story closed with the reporter's description of Pell's life during his first extended Washington stay. "Today as an officer temporarily behind a desk instead of a bridge weather cloth, Lt. Pell finds he misses a bit the extreme cold, the ever-lurking possibility of action and the vigorous exercise of his convoy days. He keeps in training as best he may by running a two-mile dog trot around the track at Western High School — in shorts."

Such dedication impressed Pell's superiors, and on April 1, 1943, they sent him to Columbia University's Naval School of Military Government and Administration, a six-month program offered, under government contract, to officers under consideration for administrative jobs in regions the Allies would liberate from Axis forces. One of only ten Coast Guardsmen in a class that included forty Navy officers, Pell studied public relations, politics, billeting, and fisheries management. In May, while still at Columbia, Pell was promoted to full lieutenant — and asked by the Chief Personnel Officer for Coast Guard Commandant Admiral Russell R. Waeschke to write an evaluation of the program. "I ask that you keep the fact that I have written you this letter and the contents of your reply strictly confidential, and that you do not talk this over with other members of the class," the personnel officer wrote. Pell obliged, giving the program high marks. An overseas administrative position appealed to him, and in August, after the Allies had advanced through Africa into Italy, he wrote to a superior requesting assignment to the European-African Theater. In addition to his Coast Guard service, Pell listed his fluent French and the Italian he had begun to study, the years he had spent living and traveling in Europe, and "newspaper writing on European conditions."

But the young lieutenant was not content with one letter. He called an officer who had known his late Navy commander stepfather in hopes he could expedite a transfer overseas, and followed the call with a hand-written note. "Thank you so very much for giving me your time on the telephone this morning," Pell wrote. "I would not have phoned you if I had not remembered the loyalty and affection my stepfather, Hugo Koehler, had for you and your own kindness to me in the past. I do hope I have not been a nuisance to you! With best remembrances from my mother I am respectfully, Claiborne Pell."

▫ ▫ ▫ On September 24, 1943, the Vice Chief of Naval Operations sent a confidential memo to Commandant Waeschke assigning Pell and two other Coast Guardsmen to the Fisheries Section of the Agricultural Division for the military government of Italian territory. They were to report to New York on October 6 for a flight to Morocco, with subsequent travel to Algiers and on to Sicily, where Pell would be based.

Before leaving, Pell visited his father and Olive. In late June, Roosevelt had named Herbert to the London-based War Crimes Commission, which would investigate allegations of Axis criminality, but final authorization had not been granted and he and his wife had been biding their time at Hopewell Junction. He would sail in November on the *Queen Mary*, but his son's earlier departure left him with a mix of emotions.

"I am, of course, very sorry to indeed to think that I shall not see you again for a pretty long time," Herbert wrote on the day his son left New York on an airplane bound for Africa, "but this is a thing for which I have been prepared and although your sudden departure does not lessen my grief it was not an unexpected shock. I certainly think that you are to be congratulated on your appointment, which was obviously the result of your very hard work and the reputation you have made in the Coast Guard. I was naturally quite impressed with Commander Labrot having made such a vigorous demand for your services. I need not say that we are all very proud of your record, which I am sure you will keep up." The commander was William H. Labrot, Pell's senior officer, a delegate to the 1940 Democratic Convention and a well-known deepwater yachtsman before the war. More praise for his son's success — and a candid admission of what he perceived as his own failure — came in January 1944, after Pell had made it to Sicily and Herbert had arrived in London. "I must say you are to be congratulated on the position you have obtained," Herbert wrote. "You have gotten it entirely off your own bat without any assistance whatsoever from me. I tried to do what I could but was unable to accomplish anything. You have a right to be proud of yourself and I am proud of you."

Based in Palermo, Sicily, with time also in Naples, Pell worked with a team charged with reviving the Italian fishing industry, a job that required writing and implementing regulations that balanced security concerns with the need for boats to go to sea. When Labrot was recalled to the U.S. and another officer transferred to the Italian mainland, Pell was left in charge of Sicily. "Many and varied were my headaches," he later wrote in a thirteen-page essay the Commandant's office asked him to write for a book about Coast Guard war experiences (the book was apparently never published). "Often the phone would ring and an angry voice from the local military or naval command would say, 'Pell, one of your fishing boats is fishing with hand grenades and blowing Hell out of our sonic buoys take care of it.' Or, 'Pell, one of your fishing boats was depth charged by an Army airplane. It was mistaken for a sub because it was in a forbidden area. See that this doesn't happen again.' And the only possible reply in every case was a quick, 'Yes, sir.' "

But he was often on the sea, and his description of some of his excursions had a lyrical touch, reminiscent of his childhood writings.

"I remember several times accompanying the Italian fishing fleet at night," he wrote. "It was a picturesque sight. Some score or so of the boats would leave Palermo Harbor before dusk and head towards the fishing grounds. There they would fish by virtually the same method that had been used since the times of the Phoenicians. They would wait for nightfall when a dinghy with a brilliant light would put out from the larger fishing boat. Then there would be a period of waiting which the Sicilians put to enjoyable use eating their oranges and bread and cheese, drinking their heady Marsala wine, and singing. And soon there would come an eerie cry from one of the men in the small boat. He had seen the sudden phosphorescent sparkles around the light that indicated a school of sardines — or better yet, of mackerel. There would be sudden energy and excitement aboard the mother fishing boat, the engines would be started, and it would make a full circle around the little boat with its bright light, at the same time dropping its purse net."

In Palermo, Pell lived in a stone house he furnished with scavenged chairs and a table. The house had no hot water, and Pell slept on a cot in a sleeping bag his mother had sent. But despite his modest circumstances, the lieutenant managed to find pleasure. He drove a government-supplied Harley Davidson motorcycle — and also a Fiat Balilla Roadster, a sporty two-seat car. He socialized. "Life continues to treat me very well indeed," he wrote to Matilda shortly before Christmas 1943. "The other day, I went to a local party which was much fun — and just what I imagine life must have been like here before the war. Here, as everywhere in Europe, there is the usual contrast between those who have and those who have not. And those who have really do have. They certainly enjoyed a grand style of living at one point. One of my fellow officers is billeted in an apartment where the original owners had their own private theater. Also, there is plenty of good food that the Army provides which, in addition, I eke out by an occasional spot of Navy chow which is even better, or a Navy shower. That is one thing we must admit: while the rationing may be severe at home, the U.S. armed forces eat better than any other." Pell gained weight, reaching 185 pounds.

"As a consequence of too much food and too little exercise," he wrote, "am as fat as a pig."

▫ ▫ ▫ Back in America, Pell's mother was struggling.

Even before the death of her husband, Matilda had experienced financial difficulties. While the commander had retired from the Navy and he and Matilda had been able to buy Eastover, their financial circumstances had deteriorated as the Great Depression wore on. Matilda's continuing poor health had been costly, and there were doctor's bills for her second son, Pell's half-brother Hugh, who himself was frequently sick. But the Koehlers had not abandoned the Newport scene, with its expensive club memberships and parties. They borrowed to support a lifestyle they could no longer afford and eventually it caught up.

By the fall of 1940, less than a year before Koehler's death, the situation was so severe that when the commander earned $50 for a lecture at a meeting of The Mayflower Society, it was sufficiently noteworthy that Matilda mentioned it in a letter to her son. The Koehlers had been renting out their apartment at 510 Park Avenue in New York for the additional income — but the rental market was soft, and for the 1940–41 winter season they had been forced to settle for "just half of what we got last year," Matilda wrote to Pell. As he had prepared to travel to Lisbon, the son had left his car with his mother and stepfather; when the muffler fell off, the commander replaced it, but could only afford a second-hand part. A lender was threatening to repossess the Koehlers' own automobile.

Pell's mother's difficulties, which stood in increasingly stark contrast to his father's comfort — and Pell's own — elicited empathy from the twenty-one-year-old, who had never lacked for anything, thanks to Herbert. He sent his mother $200 to save the Koehlers' car, which brought gratitude from Matilda. "Thank you again for helping us out about the car," she wrote. "We certainly would have been in a bad way if it had been sold at auction."

When he died in 1941, the commander left his wife and Hugh the Eastover house, but its worth had declined in a continuing bad real-estate sales market. As her ex-husband Herbert had predicted, Matilda was forced to sell the place — for $35,000, in early 1942, while her son was at sea on the North Atlantic. She moved Pell's belongings into storage, and sold things she did not need.

"I got nearly a thousand dollars besides," she wrote to Claiborne, "for the farm implements, and the coal and the wood on the place." Her circumstances were pathetic. Matilda and Hugh moved to an apartment at LaForge Cottages on the ironically named Pelham Street, a block away from the beginning of Bellevue Avenue, a busy commercial and residential district. Property values had suffered during the Depression, but the war had increased demand for rentals in Newport, home to a large Navy base on the far side of the city from Bellevue's mansions and the shorefront estates along Ocean Avenue.

The owner of LaForge took pity on Matilda.

"I have gotten our rates reduced here," Matilda wrote. "We pay $70 a week for the two of us including meals instead of $90. It really makes a lot of difference and I think it is doing well when you think how much Newport is overcrowded. There is such demand for small houses and apartments, I heard Navy people talking in the dining room and saying there was practically nothing to choose from any more and one just had to take anything they could get." In her letter, Matilda thanked Pell for quietly buying her an insurance policy. "I certainly pray I will never have [need for] it, but do appreciate your thoughtfulness and generosity more than I can say." His consideration went back years, to those times when he had been with his father or away at school on his mother's birthday, Mother's Day, Valentine's Day, and other occasions, and he had mailed her cards and gifts. He was in Sicily on his twenty-fifth birthday, November 22, 1943, when he sent Matilda a handbag.

"I am thinking of you very especially today and wishing I were with you to celebrate your birthday," she wrote back. "I am wondering how you are spending it and hope all is well with you. I had such a surprise this morning. The bag you sent arrived. It is a beauty and I shall love using it. I couldn't be more pleased. Think of me getting a present from you on *your* birthday! It was awfully sweet of you."

But status remained important to Matilda, despite her economic misfortunes. She maintained her membership with the Social Register and continued to pay her Bailey's Beach dues, although she began bringing lunch for her and Hugh, as she felt she could no longer afford the food from the club's cafeteria. She was volunteering at a Red Cross canteen and living for the off-season in an apartment at 1185 Park Avenue when she received Claiborne's gift—and she was still in New York in the spring of 1944, when Claiborne, on May 4, sent something more substantial. As a Coast Guard lieutenant, he was earning only $200 a month in base pay, but his personal fortune was significant.

"Dear Mom," he wrote. "Enclosed is a check for $1,000 which I can well spare just now—income and salary coming in and virtually no expenditures. So don't be difficult, but please, please [cash] it. Spend it now, or part of it now or do exactly what you will with it."

Matilda did indeed cash it.

"Dearest Claiborne," she wrote back. "Your letter with the perfectly enormous check has come. I think it is wonderful of you to want to give it to me, and terribly generous and I am so touched I don't know how to express it to you. It is a great deal of money and I know there are many things you could do with it yourself, and it means giving them up. I realize that very well. It is a big part of your income or pay. I know you have heavy taxes, too. A gift like that is a real sacrifice — I want you to know that I appreciate it more than I can even tell you. I will try to spend it wisely, it will be a great lift to Hugh and me in the months to come and means a tremendous lot. I just don't know how to thank you enough, but I do, with all my heart."

◦ ◦ ◦ No stranger to sickness, Pell had been ill with a fever for more than two months when he sent his check to Matilda. The Army doctors who treated him initially believed he had a cold or the flu, but they were increasingly puzzled as his symptoms persisted. He was hospitalized, released, and by May 4, he had been rehospitalized for several days. "My fever is going down now so that it is almost normal now and I am getting better," he wrote to his father. "But the doctors can't figure out what is wrong and have given me every kind of test including two chest x-rays — but none of them say anything. My own bet is the grippe."

He did not have the grippe: doctors diagnosed brucellosis, undulant fever, a highly contagious bacterial disease that can be transmitted from infected cows to people through unpasteurized milk. Characterized by recurring fevers, sweating, and joint and muscle pain, the disease can persist for months and in some cases, become a chronic lifelong condition. In June, the doctors decided Pell should be sent home to America to be treated. Pell, who suspected he had contracted the disease from eating Sicilian cheese, objected — but he was overruled. Leaving his belongings in Sicily with the hope that he would return, he was evacuated to the Army hospital ship *Acadia*, which crossed the Atlantic in early July. The condition of many of Pell's fellow patients sobered him, giving him reason to be thankful for surviving the war intact.

"As I look around on all the poor guys around me who are my fellow passengers," he wrote to his father from the ship, "I realize how lucky I am to be returning with all my arms, legs and insides. I wish the people who make wars could see this ship unload its cargo." His days on the *Acadia* left an impression of the human toll of war that would remain into his Senate years, when he would have opportunity to advance the politics of peace.

Doctors at the Navy hospital in Charleston, South Carolina, where Pell and his fellow passengers landed, treated the Coast Guard lieutenant and discharged him on three weeks convalescent leave, which he decided to take with his mother and half-brother at their summer place, the LaForge Cottages in Newport. While there, Pell reported mornings to the Newport Navy Hospital for treatment — but the rest of his time was free and he spent it playing tennis, lunching and swimming on Bailey's Beach, and attending parties. Newport Society continued with its amusements, but the war had dampened its spirits.

"Newport is very nice and informal this summer," Claiborne wrote to his father on July 24. "No great formal entertaining and a lot more healthy life. I like it very much." The war, which had drawn so many young men away, had upset the gender balance, which Pell found to his advantage. "The secret to being a social success here is to wear a pair of trousers," he told his father. "I.e., every guy my own age seems to be overseas."

One Friday night, Pell accepted an invitation to a party hosted by Mara di Zoppola, daughter of the Countess Mario di Zoppola, the former Edith Mortimer of that prominent New York family (her mother was a sister of Franklin Roosevelt's mother), and Count di Zoppola, who had achieved a degree of fame as an Italian aviator in the First World War. Mara had debuted in December 1942 at the St. Regis, site of Pell's parents' 1915 wedding reception, and was now a student at Bennington College. Mara invited a classmate and friend, Nuala O'Donnell, who had recently turned twenty, to her Newport party.

Nuala and Pell hit it off, and when they found themselves the next day at Bailey's Beach, Pell asked her out. They began dating, with trips to the movies and walks by the ocean near St. George's, Pell's alma mater.

"Have been seeing a bit of a very attractive girl named Nuala O'Donnell," Pell wrote to his father on August 14. "Though, to take the words out of your mouth, I'm afraid you may not approve of her parents — Ollie O'Donnell and a Miss Hartford. Nothing serious, though, so don't worry, Dad."

AN UNCOMMON WOMAN

Granddaughter of A&P founder George Huntington Hartford, Marie Josephine Hartford was born into one of America's great fortunes. Her mother, the former Constance Grenelle Wilcox (and later, the Princess Guido Pignatelli), was herself from wealth — and a noted author in the early 1920s. Josephine attended schools in New York and in Paris, where she studied piano under the French master Isidor Philipp. She developed lifelong interests in horse-racing and yachting. She played tournament tennis. She piloted airplanes. Before she died, she would own properties in Manhattan, England, the Bahamas, Vermont, Newport, Palm Beach, Florida, and Oyster Bay, Long Island — and she would count among her friends the author Ian Fleming, who wrote some of his James Bond series at her Vermont estate. She was an attractive but not strikingly beautiful woman, her daughter would recall after her death, in 1992 at age eighty-eight — but men fell for her. "Full of charm," Nuala Pell said. "Very sexy, according to most men." Josephine would be married four times. The first three would end in divorce, the fourth when her last husband died.

Josephine was nineteen when she married Charles Oliver O'Donnell, five years her senior, in August 1923. The first of their two children, Nuala, was born in Manhattan on the following June 30 and went home to the O'Donnells' estate in Oyster Bay. Nuala passed her childhood much as her mother had, in comfort in the elite world of private schools. Commuting by train from Long Island, she attended The Brearley School on New York's Upper East Side and then, as a young teenager, boarded at the Ethel Walker School in Simsbury, Connecticut. Josephine had planned to send her to Europe to finish her education, as she herself had done, but the advent of war ended those plans. Nuala returned for a year at Brearley and, in 1942, enrolled at Bennington College, where she majored in music and developed an interest in political philosophy.

She was increasingly (if nonconfrontationally) at odds with her mother, of whose lifestyle she disapproved.

Nuala's parents' marriage had lasted less than eight years, ending on July 15, 1931, when a Reno, Nevada, court granted Josephine a divorce (O'Donnell found a new wife, and saw little of Nuala and his son, Columbus, before his death of heart disease in January 1942). Weeks after divorcing O'Donnell, Josephine traveled to Paris to marry an older man, Vladimir Makaroff, a former Czarist Navy officer who fled Russia after the 1917 Bolshevik Revolution. That marriage ended in divorce less than five years later, after Josephine had decided to try a younger man: Barclay K. Douglas, a stockbroker from a Newport family whose own marriage had ended in Reno in 1936. Josephine and Douglas wed on March 31, 1937, in Florida. "The bride is the daughter of Mrs. Edward V. Hartford and the late Mr. Hartford, vice president of the Great Atlantic and Pacific Tea Company," *The New York Times* reported. "She is reputed to have an annual income of $500,000." In 2011 dollars, that was $7.8 million.

And Josephine was spending it all on her yachts, her horses, and her houses, which her young daughter found objectionable.

Besides acquiring material possessions, what has she accomplished? Nuala wondered. *What has she contributed?* "I always faintly disapproved of my mother's life," Nuala would later say, "because it was a life of sheer enjoyment and spending. I thought her values were a little off."

But Nuala also belonged to that narcissistic society in which her mother moved, and until an introduction to a young Coast Guard officer at a Newport cocktail party, she followed the mores of any young women of that class. Her debut (and that of her friend Mara di Zoppola) during Tennis Week on August 15, 1942, at the home of Harold W. Brooks and his wife, had been a leading story in the society pages that summer. In announcing the impending debut of Nuala, Mara, and a third friend, *The New York Times* on July 25 wrote of the building excitement along Bellevue Avenue: "All three of the young women were among those modeling hats at Mrs. Brooks's hat booth at the Red Cross garden party and fair this afternoon at Beechwood, the former Astor estate, now the home of Count and Countess Paul de Kotzebue. The fair was officially opened by Governor J. Howard McGrath."

Claiborne Pell also travelled in that blueblood world, but his intellectual Democratic father had steered him toward greater ambition than hosting Tennis Week parties and posing for the photographers on his way into Bailey's Beach. When they met in August 1944, Nuala was attracted to Pell's tall, handsome looks — but it was his political views and evolving egalitarian philosophy that set him apart from other young men of his set. He was an idealist, as was she. They both believed the world, now at war, could be a peaceful, better, place.

Predictably, Josephine disapproved of her daughter's new romantic interest, telling Nuala: *He'll never amount to anything.* Nor did Pell's parents count for much, in Nuala's mother's opinion. Pell's father had made something of a name for himself as a one-term Congressman and diplomat — but he was a Democrat and he had left Newport for good, making no secret of his boredom with its high-society ways. Pell's mother, widowed from the mysterious Koehler, who had never been accepted by the Newport aristocracy, was living at LaForge Cottages and bringing her lunch to Bailey's. Josephine that summer was living in The Waves, the spectacular oceanfront estate near Bailey's that had been designed by Jefferson Memorial architect John Russell Pope. Surely Nuala could do better than a man with parents like these: the one openly scornful of her set, the other down on her luck.

By late September, when Pell had recovered from his undulant fever and reported to a new assignment at Coast Guard headquarters in Washington, Josephine's fears were fully realized: not only was her daughter in love with Pell, she was talking of marrying him. Pell broke the news to his father in a letter he wrote on September 26:

"Now comes a slight cough of introduction. Ha-rumph!! I am really very much in love and expect to marry Nuala O'Donnell. I have been very sure myself but didn't say anything before since I didn't want to get you excited in case it didn't work out. I know that you would and will like her. Objectively, she is not tremendously good looking (though I think so), having reddish hair, brown eyes and freckles. She is 5′ 7″ tall and [has] a nice figure. In fact, you would be very pleased since she has that thickness through the chest that you admire as a sign of long life!" Pell noted that she was a junior at Bennington College studying political philosophy and would be happy after the war with pursuing a graduate degree and teaching. An academic life, he said, also appealed to him. "She thinks the same way I do," Pell wrote. "And the funny thing is that we have exactly the same tastes in likes, dislikes and, most important, friends."

Matilda approved: of all the women her son had dated (including Kathleen Kennedy, sister of John, the future president), Nuala O'Donnell topped the list. Pell wrote his father: "Mom (now don't give her Hell) really likes her and approves of her more than any other girl I have brought home, although she started out with a perfectly natural and very definite prejudice to her because of her family . . . so please trust my judgment as you have before. And consider me very lucky if we do eventually get married."

Claiborne and Nuala had not set a date or formally announced their engagement. Two issues remained: the faith in which they would raise their children, Pell's Episcopalianism or Nuala's Catholicism (rare in Newport Society, it was a legacy of her father), and Josephine's continuing disapproval.

"Her family considers me a too-unstable youth for their daughter," Pell explained in his letter to his father. "But that is fairly mutual since while I personally like and find attractive her mother and stepfather (Mr. and Mrs. Barclay Douglas), I certainly do not admire them. And Nuala fully realizes in marrying me that she would be severing her ties with their way of life. But then she has never wanted to lead it and her family have previously criticized her as being too serious-minded—which suits me fine! I have told her my idea of a life starting out academically and then, maybe, branching out into politics or writing, and it suits her fine. So, please, I hope that you and Olive wish me luck that it does work out. I know I shall be a very happy man if it does."

When Pell's letter reached his father, Herbert immediately sent a telegram: SINCEREST CONGRATULATIONS. LETTER FOLLOWS.

"As you know," he elaborated in the letter, "I have not been presented to Miss O'Donnell, but I look forward to the honor as soon as I can get back to America. I shall of course increase my efforts to return. Your descriptions sounds most charming, and your plans are very sensible. It would be a very great pleasure to you to have an intelligent girl who sympathizes and agrees with the main line of your desires. You have always been more dependent than I on appreciation and understanding, and naturally will value it more highly . . . I realize it takes a great deal of courage and determination for a girl brought up as she has been to take to an intelligent way of life; and to have done so shows a good deal of understanding, which after all is the most important thing in the world. As you justly say, I have always found your judgment sound . . . You can be quite certain that in this, as in anything else, I shall back your decision and your opinion."

Herbert suggested that Nuala marry in an Episcopal ceremony and raise his grandchildren in the Episcopal faith. "Women are more likely to get more 'churchy,' if not more religious, as they get older, and you don't want priests about the house," he wrote.

Like his father, Pell wanted to remain Episcopalian and Nuala did agree to marry and raise their children in that faith. Josephine's opposition softened when her friend James V. Forrestal, recently named Secretary of the Navy, spoke highly of Pell. With his seal of approval, she dropped her objection to her daughter marrying Pell. Eventually, she would accept him.

"Years later, when he was in the Senate," Nuala would recall, "she would constantly say, 'My son-in-law, the Senator.'"

□ □ □ Pell had been assigned as a lecturer in fisheries management at Princeton's School of Military Government when the November 16 *New York Times* published a photograph of Nuala and an announcement that she would marry Pell that December. Other papers devoted space to the impending ceremony in their society pages.

Most of '400' to See Nuala O'Donnell Wed, was the headline in the *New York News*, which reported: "Half of Newport, most of Tuxedo Park, a large delegation from Aiken, and many of the fashionable Long Island set are expected to make tracks Manhattanward a week from next Saturday. It's the day that the pretty A&P heiress Nuala O'Donnell has set for her marriage to the blue-blooded Lieut. Claiborne Pell of the Coast Guard." A *Journal-American* society writer predicted that December 16 would be "THE social star-studded wedding of the season. Nuala, who has just come down from Bennington, where she finished this semester's studies, is brightening Gotham's dark nights with the glow in her eyes, as she goes about the titillating business of completing plans down to the last orange blossom."

Pell had rented a two-room brick house in a neighborhood near the university where Albert Einstein lived. Unable to obtain an extended leave, he was planning a thirty-six-hour honeymoon with Nuala at Hopewell Junction. "My reason for preferring Hopewell to a hotel on her family's place in Long Island is that I want both our ties to be sunk mutually in my family as quickly as possible," he wrote to his father. "She is and knows she is leaving her family — they have a different way of life and have approved the marriage, anyway (although, on getting to know them, I have grown to respect them more and think they have done likewise). So I hope you are as pleased as I at the thought of our spending our first day at Hopewell."

No tension was apparent on the afternoon of December 16, 1944, at St. James' Episcopal Church on Madison Avenue at 71st Street in Manhattan. Herbert and Olive had just arrived from London and were pleased to discover Nuala to be the fine young woman Pell had described. Josephine's husband, Barclay Douglas, walked his stepdaughter down the aisle. Pell's half-brother, Hugh Koehler, served as his best man, and his new brother-in-law, Columbus O'Donnell, Nuala's younger sibling, was an usher. Nuala wore a cream-colored satin gown and carried a bouquet of white camellias, an image of youth that Olive would capture in a painting of the newlyweds that would hang in the Pells' Newport home for decades. President and Mrs. Roosevelt sent a bouquet of three dozen roses.

"A reception was given in the Viennese Room of the St. Regis, where the decorations included pink and white flowers," *The New York Times* reported.

Twenty-nine years before, Matilda and Herbert had celebrated their wedding at the same hotel.

UNITED NATIONS

After their brief Hopewell honeymoon, the newlyweds returned to Princeton, where Pell continued to lecture and take courses. As the winter wore on, he traveled to Harvard and to Yale to deliver guest lectures, making such a good impression at Yale that history professor A. Whitney Griswold, who would later be president of the university, wanted to keep him as an instructor in military government. But Pell was weighing many possibilities, including duty back at sea and an assignment again in the Coast Guard's main office of Public Relations in Washington — an assignment he accepted in early April 1945, as the war neared its end. Washington would be a good base from which to begin a career in the Foreign Service, which, his father's earlier cautions notwithstanding, appealed to him. Herbert did his usual networking, asking Rhode Island Senator Theodore Francis Green, a member of the Senate Foreign Relations Committee, to put in a good word with Secretary of State Edward Reilly Stettinius, Jr. "When I have a reply," Green wrote back, "I shall write you accordingly."

Stettinius's office was impressed with Pell's wartime experiences and his writing ability and on April 17, the lieutenant received orders to fly to San Francisco "for temporary duty on official business of the Department of State." He was headed as an assistant secretary to the United Nations Conference on International Organization, a two-month meeting of delegates from Allied nations that resulted in the writing and signing, on June 26, of the U.N. Charter. The two months in San Francisco provided Pell his first involvement in foreign policy making — an interest that would culminate decades later in his chairmanship of the Senate Foreign Relations Committee. Pell would come to see the United Nations as the vehicle for world peace and he would carry a dog-eared copy of the charter, which he could claim a small role in creating, during all his years in the Senate, showing it to presidents and ordinary folk alike.

Stettinius chaired the U.S. delegation to the San Francisco conference, whose secretary-general was Alger Hiss, a State Department official who had played instrumental roles in the 1944 Dumbarton Oaks Conference and the February 1945 Yalta Conference, two meetings at which some of the groundwork for the U.N. was laid. On the day the U.N. charter was signed in San Francisco, Hiss praised Pell in a letter to Coast Guard Commandant Waesche:

> I wish to commend the fine performance of duty on the part of Lieutenant Clayborne CQ Pell, U.S.C.G.R. while on duty at the United Nations Conference on International Organization. Lieutenant Pell was a member of the International Secretariat and serves as assistant secretary on one of the technical committees of the conference. Although the nature of the work must have been quite unfamiliar, Lieutenant Pell displayed great initiative in the competent performance of his duties. Long hours and novel tasks were the lot of the assistant secretaries, but at all times Lieutenant Pell's enthusiasm and resourcefulness were a source of inspiration to his associates. I hope it may be possible to make this letter a matter for Lieutenant Pell's official record. Sincerely yours, Alger Hiss, Secretary General.

In late June, Pell returned to Washington, where Nuala was in her last trimester of pregnancy with the Pells' first child: Herbert Claiborne Pell III, "Bertie." In August, with the defeat of Japan bringing the war to a close, Pell prepared to begin his civilian future — through a door that San Francisco seemed to have opened. On September 5, the Coast Guard granted Pell's request to be relieved of active duty so that he could accept a job in the State Department's International Security Affairs division, the ISA. Six days later, Bertie was born.

Back at Hopewell Junction, Herbert approved of his son's choice; by leaving the Coast Guard, he believed, his son would not be heading down a long, slow road to possible but hardly guaranteed distinction. "I am very glad indeed that you have gotten your discharge from the Coast Guard and therefore, they will not be able to seize you for the government of one of the occupied territories," he wrote. "I should think it would be a fine career for anyone who is interested in that sort of thing, especially starting in young, as there will be a great many resignations of older men. I do not think, however, it would interest you very much, especially in the comparatively long wait on the road to eminence. I hope you will succeed in the State Department and enjoy the work." But Herbert, sixty-one years old now, was skeptical that State Department culture, which he well knew, would agree with his son — a skepticism that would prove well founded as Pell advanced through the Foreign Service. Herbert had clashed with the State Department while serving on the War Crimes Commission, a clash that had resulted in the loss of his position and some derogatory rumors. "I shall be much obliged if you will listen, without contradiction, to State Department gossip about me," Herbert had written to his son in April, on the eve of Pell's departure for San Francisco. "It is probably pretty hostile, and it is better that I should know what it is than that you should get into a row. Let them say what they please. I am old and tough and have thriven on abuse. At your age, you can be hurt by malicious lies, but at my time of life unpleasant statements, whether true or false, do very little harm. It is however always well to know what they are, by whom they are circulated, and in what circumstances."

Bertie was an infant when Pell, having been promoted to lieutenant commander in the Coast Guard Reserves, began work as an assistant with the ISA in the same office as Dean Rusk, a rising State Department bureaucrat who would be Secretary of State under President John F. Kennedy. But Pell yearned for an overseas assignment. He passed the Foreign Service exams and in the early autumn of 1946, after completing studies at Columbia University required to earn his master's degree in Public Law and Government (his degree was awarded on December 18, 1946), he was assigned to the American Embassy in Tirana, Albania, one of the few European countries he had never visited.

He never made it to Tirana; the new Communist government severed relations with the United States, and the State Department assigned the twenty-seven-year-old as third secretary and vice consul at its Czechoslovakian embassy. With his wife, toddler son, and his son's nurse, Pell crossed to Europe for the drive across the continent to Prague. They were in Nuremberg the night before Hermann Goering, Hitler's Luftwaffe commander, killed himself rather than be executed for his conviction of war crimes and crimes against humanity. "This had particular meaning for me," Pell would later write in an unpublished memoir of his foreign service years, "as my father had been the United States representative to the United Nations War Crimes Commission and who, while he had been removed by the State Department because of the vigor of his views, had been responsible for changing the American position to agreeing with him that genocide was to be considered and treated as a war crime."

Pell initially enjoyed his Prague position, which involved assessing applicants for American visas — a job that gave him an understanding of the immigrant's plight that would last his lifetime. "It makes me wince to realize the power over a family's life that young people in my position had," he wrote in his memoir, "and I found it was very important not to be carried away by a sense of one's importance. Ours was the responsibility to determine whether an impending immigrant would not end up on welfare. If we thought such was the case, then he was called an LPC, or Likely Public Charge, and a visa was denied him. But the power one had over the fate of a particular family was awesome and I only hope it was not abused." He was a young man with a conscience.

In their leisure time, the Pells traveled outside Czechoslovakia, taking trips to Romania, Hungary, and Poland. By the spring of 1947, Pell was becoming restless; his father's warning that the Foreign Service might not be the life for him was proving true. He considered returning to America to attempt to revive and edit the *North American Review*, a literary magazine founded in 1815 that had ceased publication in 1940, but he got no further than reaching out to possible investors. He was thinking again of elective politics — and turning, once again, for advice to his father.

"The diplomatic corps is no place for an ambitious, intelligent and courageous man," Herbert wrote in a letter to Pell's mother. "In the first place, it is almost impossible for such a person to work up. The organization of the State Department is such that success comes mainly to the buck-passers who have avoided responsibility for themselves and been favored by those above them for not forcing decisions on others . . . Claiborne has grown up and has accepted the responsibility of a wife and family. He must decide for them to the best of his ability." Elective politics might be a decent bet, Herbert suggested, to Matilda and to their son — though it, too, was not without risk. "He has, as you know, a vague but permanent desire to go into public life, in which he is totally inexperienced, and he will have to do a good deal of learning on the practical level," Herbert said in his letter to Matilda. "I can do very little for him in this, as most of my friends are dead or retired. I have had nothing to do with the [New York Democratic Party] organization in a good many years and cannot really get back to any purpose."

Some while before leaving Washington for Czechoslovakia, Pell had been considering where best to establish a permanent residence in the event he one day ran for political office — Rhode Island or New York were the most logical places, and Herbert as early as September 1946 had decided the best bet would be Newport, where Pell had strong ties and where a state senate seat seemed feasible. As the spring of 1947 approached, with his thirtieth birthday only a year and a few months away, Pell was increasingly eager to follow in his father's footsteps. Herbert urged him to step back and reflect on his haste.

"In spite of what you say, thirty is still young," he wrote on March 19, 1947. "You spoke of me as being at that age enroute to Congress. As a matter of fact, I had no idea of Congress until about four months before election, when the dim possibility burst on me. Some time after that, I was criticized for saying American politics was a game and not a profession. Criticism or not, I was right. A man does not progress in politics by the slow accumulation of credits through patient merit, but by watching chances when they appear to him . . . It is a fascinating game of chance usually played with the odds somewhat against you."

In April 1947, Pell resigned from his embassy job, but after a spring and summer of travel — and contemplation of his next move — he returned to the State Department in September charged with opening a consulate general in Bratislava, capital of Slovakia. He entered the scene with what was becoming signature Claiborne Pell style: a tall, thin, rather distinctive-looking man whose thoughts were often somewhere else.

"My arrival in Bratislava was not too auspicious," he recounted in his unpublished memoir, "in that I absent-mindedly stepped in front of a trolley car to be thrown by its cow pusher high in the air, landing on wet cement. The crowning blow was to see from the top of my orbit not horrified faces but outrageously laughing ones." Pell opened the consulate in a suite he and his family took in the Carlton Hotel. "The living room became the office and the bedroom at times also became one," he wrote.

The Pells were at a diplomatic dinner in Prague in February 1948 when the Communists seized power in Czechoslovakia. They took a train back to Bratislava, where they found chaos. "The streets and particularly the railroad station were swarming with so-called Red Guards — men in civilian clothes with red armbands carrying guns," Pell recalled in his memoir. "Nuala and I were in evening clothes, made even more dressy by the fact that Nuala had a new fur coat on and I, too, was wearing one, complete with astrakhan collar, although I would add that it belonged to my father. While the Red Guards glowered at our bourgeois splendor, the other people and passengers all looked at us with a mixture of smiles and sadness." Nuala was six months pregnant with their second child, Christopher Thomas Hartford Pell, who would be called Toby.

When he reached the American consulate, Pell found that several members of his staff had fled or been arrested, which left them subject to beatings and torture. Distrusting the safe in the new office he was about to open (to replace his makeshift hotel headquarters), Pell moved sensitive documents to the security of his jacket's breast pocket — and kept a wary eye for suspicious-looking strangers as the tense days passed. Police began following him, with one officer stationing himself in the middle of a field near the Danube River where Pell took his daily jogs. Pell feared they were trying to identify Communist dissidents who, in seeking American protection, might be arrested or worse. "A thing that particularly disturbed me," he wrote, "was the awful feeling that being seen with me was like the touch of death." He was, in fact, the opposite. Pell provided temporary sanctuary for several people sought by the police — and he helped others out of the country.

"A man came who was in peril and needed to be hidden for a couple of days," Pell wrote. "The only place where one did not need identification cards was in the Red Light district so I gave my visitor a suit of mine, took him to the Red Light district, where he was deposited with a friendly lady. I am glad to say the next time I heard from him, he had crossed the border." Pell seemed to relish these clandestine adventures, which were reminiscent of his first international intrigue, in Gdansk in 1939, when he was between his junior and senior years at Princeton.

But these escapades came at a cost. The Communists accused Pell and other Americans with him of espionage, and while he was not arrested or formally charged, the accusation made the local newspapers and was reported to the Security Council of the United Nations. "Carrying the thing to absurdity," Pell wrote to his father on March 5, "we as American representatives are accused of espionage, fomenting an armed revolt and transporting people illegally over the frontier! However, I guess this is part of their old technique, and we are thriving quite impressively and happily. The Consulate General was opened officially, and there is now a large American flag sticking out in the main square . . . for the moment I have been sticking fairly close to Bratislava since they accuse our hunting trips and visits to [the spa town of] Piestany as being the purpose of our espionage." He was also concerned with the fate of Andrew Spiro, his Slovakian interpreter, "a wonderful decent chap" who had been arrested, charged with conspiracy, and imprisoned — and denied communication with the outside. Pell would later learn that he had been beaten for refusing to testify that Pell was a spy.

Spring arrived, Toby was born, and the Pells remained in Bratislava. They visited America late in 1948, spending some time with Herbert and Olive at Hopewell and in Manhattan in the apartment building Herbert owned there. Early 1949 found them back in Bratislava. That spring, Pell received a new assignment: vice consul in Genoa, Italy. On the night before Pell left Slovakia in a caravan bound for Vienna, his interpreter Spiro, who had been released from prison, called on Pell. He wanted to know if Pell could bring him with him. Pell said he could not — legally.

The trunk of my car will be unlocked, Pell told Spiro. In the overnight darkness, Spiro crawled in, to be safely smuggled to freedom.

"All that I can say," Pell wrote in his memoir, "is that as we crossed the Czechoslovak-Austrian border and later the Soviet checkpoint just outside Vienna, many of our hearts breathed a big sigh of relief."

By the fall of 1949, the Pells had been in Genoa for half a year. The vice consul was tiring of his job and eager to move toward his ambition of elective office. Having finally concluded that Rhode Island would be a better political base than New York, Pell was paying attention to Newport, from where he intended to vote and run. Herbert had joined the cause, with overtures to the few old Democratic Party friends he had left in the Ocean State — and by helping to arrange a formal, in-absentia introduction of Claiborne to the people of Newport on Independence Day 1949. Voters might have read Pell's previously published newspaper articles or encountered him on the street, but the Claiborne Pell trophy made a statement — and its widely publicized presentation, on the Fourth of July, carried patriotic symbolism. Pell, war veteran and dutiful Foreign Service officer, had yet to run or even work for the Democratic Party or on someone else's campaign — but he already seemed to understand the basics of electoral politics.

The trophy was awarded to the winner of the main event of the annual Independence Day sports contests held at a popular park next to Bellevue Avenue's Newport Casino, where Tennis Week matches had been played for decades. Herbert arranged the publicity that began days before the Trophy was awarded: morning spots on a Newport radio station, announcements at baseball games in beloved Cardines Field, and a public display of the trophy. Newport native Van Johnson, star of *Thirty Seconds Over Tokyo* and other movies, presented the trophy, and newspapers wrote about it after receiving a press release approved by Pell:

"Hon. Claiborne Pell, recently appointed American Vice Consul to Italy, has donated the principal award for the Independence Day sports observances at Freebody Park. Mr. Pell, who departed in May for headquarters in the city of Genoa, responded by cable within 24 hours when informed of the need by the Recreation Commission, the sponsoring organization." The response included a check for $100 to buy a suitable trophy. "It will be termed the Claiborne Pell trophy and has been designated for the principal contest of the day. Mr. Pell, who recently acquired business interests here, plans to make Newport his permanent home upon completion of his present assignment."

Pell's business "interests" were, as yet, only preliminary discussions with brokerages and financial-management firms, and management of his own money. Whatever firm he might join (or start), he badly wanted to return to America.

"I do not feel temperamentally in tune with the Foreign Service," Pell wrote to his father on October 7. "The thing I'm afraid of is that I will drift along until it is too late and then I will feel that fate has me by the tail rather than I fate . . .

Olive wrote us that you were coming abroad in February. Is that correct and if so, for how long? As you know, our plans are in complete flux. I hope piously that I shall be home, but the power of inertia or indecision may still have us here."

Inertia indeed affected Pell, as it had before and would frequently again; it seemed, paradoxically, to come naturally with his ambition. Thus he remained in Genoa a while longer. On April 10, 1950, a third child, Nuala Dallas, was born. In 1951, Pell transferred to Washington, taking a desk job as an assistant to the State Department's Eastern European Division. The Pells bought a house on Thirty-Third Street NW, which would give Claiborne and Nuala (who was willing to work alongside her husband), a close connection to the power center of the National Democratic Party. But the Pells were also strengthening their ties to Newport. When Nuala's mother sold The Waves mansion, she divided off an oceanfront acre of the estate and gave it to her daughter and son-in-law. Nuala and Claiborne bought an adjacent acre, and Pell, working without an architect, designed a single-story, suburban-style house on the two-acre parcel that stood in pedestrian contrast its opulent neighbors. It was a house the Pells could easily afford—and a place working-class voters, who were the majority even in Newport, birthplace of the Gilded Age, could accept.

In April 1952, Pell resigned from the State Department, this time for good. During the remainder of the 1950s, he would dabble in various business ventures, earning some income—and management credentials that might prove useful as a future candidate. Pell became a vice president and director of the North American Newspaper Alliance, the newspaper syndicate made famous by Ernest Hemingway, who reported on the Spanish Civil War for it. He was a director of WRJM, a Newport radio station owned by Columbus O'Donnell, Nuala's brother. He became a partner in Auchincloss, Parker & Redpath, the investment banking firm founded by lawyer and stockbroker Hugh D. Auchincloss, whose father had built Newport's Hammersmith Farm in the late 1800s, at the height of the Gilded Age. (After two divorces, Auchincloss in 1942 had married Jane Lee Bouvier, whose daughter Jackie married John F. Kennedy in 1953. The Kennedys celebrated their wedding with a reception at Hammersmith, which would serve as a summer White House.)

Pell's own investments occupied some of his attention. Along with managing small trusts he had established for his mother and half-brother, he was in control of a personal portfolio that (in 1953) included a mix of U.S. Treasury bonds, utility stocks, and shares of Dow Chemical, Caterpillar, General Motors, DuPont, and the Burroughs Adding Machine Co.—a conservative blend. But Pell was willing to take risks: vertical flight was still an unproven technology in the early 1950s, but it fascinated Pell. He owned $9,240 in stock in Hiller Aircraft, founded by pioneer Stanley Hiller, and stock in Doman Helicopters Inc. and Piasecki Helicopter Corp., companies built by other pioneers. With a cousin, he explored the possibility of greater investments in helicoptering with his broker at the Wall Street firm of Carl M. Loeb, Rhoades & Co. (a precursor to Shearson Lehman / American Express). "It looks as if John Pell and I are going ahead with the idea of a Helicopter Trust," he wrote on October 23, 1953. "We would first get ten people to each raise twenty thousand dollars to get the ball rolling. We would then hope that some large investment holding house such as Smith Barney (or perhaps yourselves?!) would then sell another two million dollars or so."

But the helicopter scheme never materialized. It went to the graveyard of fanciful notions, along with others Pell had conceived, such as wanting to buy a Caribbean island. An oil-field development and a uranium mine at Pellbridge, his father's estate, were among the esoteric 1950s schemes that remained unfulfilled. If there was indeed either oil or uranium beneath the ground there in New York state, it was never confirmed.

◻ ◻ ◻ Pell had not left government employment to become a full-time businessman. Business largely bored him, as it had his father.

At thirty-three, he was finally ready for politics — finally past inertia — and Democrats were happy to welcome an intelligent young man with connections and money who was willing to work enthusiastically and hard. And he came with a valuable family reputation. Many of his father's old friends were gone, but Herbert's service to his party and his country was remembered in Democratic circles. The Pell name continued to open doors.

The first significant one brought Pell to W. Averill Harriman, the banker, railroad magnate and friend of Franklin Roosevelt who sought the Democratic presidential nomination in 1952 after President Harry S. Truman decided not to seek reelection. Pell became the deputy director of Harriman's campaign. When Democrats at their Chicago convention nominated Illinois Governor Adlai Stevenson to run against Republican General Dwight D. Eisenhower, ending Harriman's candidacy, Pell signed on as the Rhode Island finance chairman for Stevenson. And he had other Rhode Island responsibilities. State Democratic chairman Frank Rao gave him charge of the Rhode Island Democratic $5 Fund Drive, a fundraising effort targeted to working-class voters, and assigned him leadership of the state party's "Nationalities Section," where Pell's extensive overseas experience, fluent French, and passable Italian and Portuguese could be an asset to Rhode Island's many immigrants and ethnic groups.

In Washington, Pell joined the fundraising arm of the Democratic Senatorial Campaign Committee and brought in $5,550, a respectable amount on his maiden effort — and one he would increase in later campaigns. He gave money of his own, $500 to various Senate candidates — with the majority of it, $300, to Montana Representative Mike Mansfield, who would become Senate majority leader in 1961, the year Pell became a senator. Pell and Mansfield would take a watershed trip to South Vietnam in 1962 that would make both men question the wisdom of U.S. involvement in that country — and start Pell down the path to becoming one of the Senate's leading critics of the Vietnam War.

"Because of my belief that your election is of fundamental importance to the welfare of our country," Pell wrote to Mansfield on October 3, "I have been making an effort to stress the importance of such a key campaign as yours." He did more than donate his own money. In a lengthy letter to other prospective donors, Pell analyzed key Senate races, including Montana's, where Mansfield was taking on incumbent Senator Zales Nelson Ecton. Pell's enthusiasm for Mansfield was expansive — and it foreshadowed many of the themes he would bring to his own Senate campaign eight years later. "Congressman Mansfield, who is running against Senator Zales M. Ecton, is a particularly good man with a fine sense of humor and propriety who has declined contributions from sources of whom he did not fully approve," Pell declared. "Mansfield, an outstanding member of the House, did a magnificent job as a delegate to the last U.N. General Assembly. He is a true liberal and believes in the democratic process. He does not care for personal glory . . . His opponent, Senator Ecton, is a consistent isolationist who has been wrong on almost all international interests as, for instance, when he voted to cut out all Marshall Plan aid just one month prior to the Communist invasion of South Korea."

In Rhode Island and in Washington, the Democratic establishment was taking notice. Leslie F. Biffle, secretary-treasurer of the Democratic Senatorial Campaign Committee, was generous in his praise of Pell, as were individual senators who received funds from Pell or through his efforts. Rhode Island Senator Theodore Francis Green, who was not up for re-election in 1952, also was impressed — and thanks to Herbert, his old friend, he learned of Pell's political ambitions.

"Do keep your eye on Claiborne," Herbert wrote to Green on January 5, 1953. "He hopes to follow in your footsteps. I'll be proud of him if he does."

In his reply, Green said that a staff member spoke glowingly of Pell. "With regard to Claiborne," Green wrote, "Eddie Higgins has told me that your son is a natural in politics and everyone at the State Committee headquarters in Providence likes him very much." Green noted that Pell was seeking a larger role with the national party. "If he does," the senator wrote, "you can look forward to my endorsement and assistance."

□ □ □ In Washington on May 9, 1953, Nuala gave birth to Julia Lorillard Wampage Pell, named for Claiborne's forbears: the tobacco side of his paternal grandmother's family and the Siwanoy Indian whose daughter Anna married Thomas, third Lord of Pelham manor.

Pell ancestry had fascinated Claiborne since he was a child, when it had been encouraged by his father. In the 1950s, fascination moved toward obsession. Pell became active in the Fort Ticonderoga Association, which managed the family's properties on Lake Champlain. He was acting chairman of the Pell Family Association when his father traveled in Europe, and with Herbert, he researched genealogy, sought connections to still-living Pells, and collected what they termed *Pelliana*: books, photographs, etchings, and other artifacts associated with the family, back to its roots in pre-Elizabethan England. Pells took unusual pride in John Pell, the seventeenth-century mathematician who is credited by some with inventing the division sign. (The claim is subject to scholarly dispute. Some maintain that the Swiss mathematician Johann Rahn invented it, but that historical asterisk was not included in Pell lore.)

Pell's expanding obsession was a serious one, but he could make light of it. In the spring of 1956, he decided to have fun with an old family tradition that dated to 1688, when John Pell sold some of the land he owned near what is now New York City to the founders of New Rochelle. John Pell charged British sterling—and the annual payment of "one fatt calfe on every 24th of June yearly and forever," if his descendants demanded it. The custom continued over the centuries until New Rochelle mayor George Vergara resisted. Tongue-in-cheek, Claiborne suggested that failure to honor the agreement might prompt Pells to take back their land—or at least exercise a sort of squatter's rights. "We might be able to set up trailer camps, or some such, in the parks," he joked. A compromise was reached: the mayor would make the 1956 payment in the form of veal served at a fundraising dinner. Claiborne sent press releases to several newspapers, including *The Washington Post*, which published a feature story, and *The Providence Journal*, which wrote an amusing editorial. The story was picked up by the wires and at least one London newspaper ran it. It did not directly advance Pell's political ambitions, but the coverage put him before the public as a man with a sense of humor—a quirky one, tinged with an obsessive interest in people long dead, but humor nonetheless.

"It has just come out that ever since 1688, the City of New Rochelle has been renting the 61,000 acres it occupies in Westchester County, N.Y., for 'one fatt calfe' a year, payable to the descendants of one Sir John Pell, the original owner," *The Providence Journal* editorialized on June 8, 1956, two weeks before the dinner.

There is something awe-inspiring about the faithfulness with which successive mayors of New Rochelle have produced a fatted critter each June 24 when the rent falls due. The Pells have been, on the whole, generous landlords. Not once have they threatened their tenants with eviction; forbearing have they ever been when wartime stringencies made fat calves hard to come by. True, they were a little strict with one New Rochelle burgomaster, former mayor Stanley Church, who was compelled in 1954 to dig into his own pocket to buy a rental calf, but, after all, the Pells had gone calfless since 1945 and we think it was mighty decent of them not to demand a whole herd of overdue stock.

Alas for a noble tradition, a survival of the days when there was so much land lying around that a good-natured fellow like old Sir John Pell could afford to let three-score thousands of acres go for a song, or rather the blat of a calf. The present mayor of new Rochelle, George Vergara, has induced a seventh-generation Pell to settle for an annual veal dinner. It's to be an annual civic affair and the city will collect $6 a plate for it from everybody but the Pells. They'll get their dinner free and their rent fricasseed.

Serious purpose absorbed Pell more than frivolity as he advanced within the Democratic Party. He worked again for Rhode Island chairman Rao in the 1954 state elections and raised money for U.S. Senate candidates that same year. In 1955, he was a delegate to Rhode Island's Constitutional Convention. In 1956, the national party put him in charge of its voter registration drive and named him Chief Delegation Clerk to the summer national convention, at which Nuala was an alternate delegate. Nuala's intelligence and warm charm were proving to be a political asset. Her down-to-earth demeanor complemented her husband, who sometimes had his head in clouds (as anyone who had been a passenger in his car could attest), and she was a gracious presence at the many Democratic fundraisers she and Claiborne hosted. Participants felt welcome in the couple's Washington and Newport homes.

In Rhode Island, the Pells put their efforts into the 1956 reelection campaign of Governor Dennis Roberts, with whom Pell had endeavored to build a close relationship in the hope that Roberts would favor his ambitions. Pell had sought the governor's counsel in the summer of 1955, when he was approached by the White House for consideration as a tariff commissioner, a job he was tempted to take if he could maintain his Rhode Island credentials. But no New England commissioner's post was available, and Pell had declined available appointment from the District of Columbia, which would have required him to give up his Rhode Island residence. And that, he said to Roberts, would of course foreclose — at least temporarily — any opportunity of a run for office.

"In view of your conversation with me in Washington," Pell wrote to the governor on July 7, 1955, "you may not think me very wise in replying this way. However, I hope instead of thinking only of the negative fact that I have not been a member of the Newport City Council, etc., you will bear in mind that I have certain positive attributes to offer the party — economic independence, governmental experience, business experience, Party service, ties with Rhode Island nationality groups, can handle myself reasonably well on my feet or TV, and am most fortunate in having a wife who is an equally enthusiastic and hardworking Democrat."

Roberts accepted Pell hospitality and Pell money but considered him something of an oddball whose prospects in a major election would be uncertain at best. Rao shared his dubious view. While weighing Democratic National Committee chairman Paul M. Butler's offer to head the 1956 national registration drive, Pell told both Roberts and Rao that he would decline the position if they would support a Pell candidacy for state senator or representative or some other office. Rao was uninterested; the Pell name on a ballot, he feared, would spell Democratic defeat. "As far as the local situation is concerned," he wrote to Pell on March 26, "I doubt it very much of there is going to be an opening for you on the state level. I feel that the honor given you by Paul Butler to be the National Registration Chairman is a very high one and I feel you should accept it . . . Hope you, Nuala and the family are all fine."

Roberts won re-election in November, and he sent Pell a brief letter of thanks a few days later. "I am deeply grateful to you and Nuala for the fine work you did during the campaign and for your many kindnesses to me," he wrote. "Hoping to see you both in the very near future."

He could never have imagined where he would indeed meet Pell in the more distant future: on the 1960 primary ballot that would end his political career.

▫ ▫ ▫ As the 1950s drew to a close, Pell had established a reputation within his party as a loyal operative skilled in organizing and raising money. Outside the party, he had earned a reputation for his knowledge of foreign affairs and his involvement in the international refugee movement.

Pell had joined the board and advanced to vice president of the Manhattan-based International Rescue Committee, founded in 1933 at the suggestion of Albert Einstein, who wanted to assist fellow Germans who were fleeing Hitler. The IRC later helped people to escape Mussolini's Italy and Franco's Spain, and was instrumental in Project Berlin, which in 1950 brought food and relief to

Berliners who were facing Soviet oppression. Pell had been personally involved in IRC resettlement efforts for refugees from Hungary after the 1956 Hungarian Revolution, which Soviet tanks and troops had violently crushed during the same week as elections were held in America. Thousands of Hungarians were imprisoned and an estimated 200,000 fled, creating a humanitarian crisis. As part of an IRC mission to Austria, Pell visited the Hungarian border. He returned home with an IRC report — and material for newspaper interviews, articles, and college lectures, all of which he diligently pursued. At Pell's request, Senator Hubert Humphrey, vice chairman of the 1956 Democratic Senatorial Campaign Committee, received unanimous consent in January 1957 to have two of Pell's *Providence Journal* op-ed pieces on the Hungarian situation entered into the *Congressional Record*. Pell's essays foreshadowed his foreign-policy views in the U.S. Senate — and brilliantly foretold, at the height of the Cold War, when fears of nuclear holocaust were widespread, the comparatively peaceful way that Communism would end in Europe:

> The free world's only comfort in watching the Hungarian revolution is that it is also watching the clearest exposition yet of the fundamental weakness of the Communist apparatus. Moreover, we are also watching the first major sign of the inevitable destruction of the Soviet Empire from within . . . We in the West should not think that Hungary's agony is in pain. Not at all. The weakness of the Soviet philosophy and apparatus is being nakedly exposed to the whole world. Moreover, the Soviets have been placed in a most embarrassing position. The coiled spring of resistance, once sprung, will never again be as secure as it was.

Similar attention surrounded Pell's presidential appointment in late 1958 as one of six American delegates to the first assembly of the United Nations' Intergovernmental Maritime Consultative Organization, held in London from January 6 to January 20, 1959. IMCO, as it was called, was charged with drafting regulations governing the safety of maritime traffic around the world, which it broadly defined to include not only protection of vessels and their crews but also protection of the oceans from ship pollution. Vice Admiral A. C. Richmond, Coast Guard Commandant, was a member of the delegation, which was chaired by Millard G. Gamble, a former executive with Standard Oil. Pell's performance brought yet more newspaper stories and a letter of thanks from Gamble. "You accomplished wonders as our representative on the Administrative and Financial Committees," he wrote to Pell, back in Washington, on February 16, 1959. "You were a tower of strength in the delegation at all times."

Pell was not, however, content; indecision seemed once again to have paralyzed him. Pell passed much of 1959 with mostly behind-the-scenes IRC work as he mounted a new effort for another government job. Senator Green brought him to the attention of Senate Majority Leader Lyndon B. Johnson. "I am very anxious to have Claiborne Pell, a native of Rhode Island whose good father once served as U.S. ambassador to Portugal and at one time was chairman of the Democratic State Committee of New York, considered for some federal appointment," Green wrote to Johnson. "Enclosed is a biographical sketch of Mr. Pell, whom I unhesitatingly recommend for a federal appointment."

Johnson was not moved by Green, who at ninety-two years of age was no longer much of a force in the Senate, whether he ran for reelection in 1960 or not. Nor was he impressed by Herbert, long out of politics and now seventy-five years old. The days of Hebert's influence had passed.

"Dear Theodore," Johnson wrote back to Green. "I am not at all familiar with the situation concerning Mr. Pell and, as you know, do not make recommendations to the president on appointments. Nevertheless, I will certainly keep your views in mind."

This was on December 5, 1959. Unknown to Green, Pell had met earlier that fall with John Lewis to discuss a run for national office in 1960 — for U.S. representative or perhaps even for Green's Senate seat, if the venerable statesman decided to retire.

His time, Pell had concluded, had come. He would finally heed his father's words during a discussion in the early spring of 1954, when the Pells had visited Herbert at Pellbridge. "I have been thinking a good deal of what you said when you were here," Herbert wrote after his son and family had returned to Washington. "I seem to have been quite unsuccessful in explaining to you that in public life, it is impossible to proceed in a straight line looking for a definite reward, as a graduate of Annapolis may look forward with great fortune and good capacity to becoming an admiral, rather than a general, an ambassador or a president of a university. A politician must sit on the bank and grab whatever drifts by. Plans are not of much value and unless you like scattering it, the cost of ground bait is very high."

In 1960, Claiborne Pell would grab the opportunity that was drifting by. If the cost was taking on his own party establishment, so be it.

FOUR □ VISION

THE DAWN OF CAMELOT

At 12:23 p.m. on January 3, 1961, outgoing Vice President Richard M. Nixon administered the oath of office to Rhode Island's new senator. A minute later, Claiborne deBorda Pell signed the Senate register and went to his seat in the second row of the Democratic section, ahead of John Pastore, the state's senior senator. Pell's wife, children and parents watched from the gallery. Five days later, Pell and his family appeared on a CBS news program profiling new members of Congress. The correspondent called him the "beardless Lincoln," an allusion to Pell's height and thin build. Pell told CBS that hard work, not money, had brought him to Washington.

"The people may be assured," Pell said, "that I shall do the best possible job for my state."

Rhode Islanders and CBS viewers may have taken notice of Pell, but the attention of the world was focused on Soviet-backed Cuba, which outgoing President Eisenhower perceived as a growing threat. Eisenhower had secretly authorized the CIA to train Cuban exiles to overthrow Premier Fidel Castro, a mission that would end in the fiasco of the Bay of Pigs invasion that spring. On the day Pell was sworn in, Eisenhower cut diplomatic ties to the island nation, while continuing with the transfer of power to John F. Kennedy, who had defeated Nixon in November. The Washington establishment was preparing for the upcoming inauguration of the charismatic Kennedy.

The Pells had known Jackie and Jack for years and sometimes saw them in Newport, where Jackie's mother and stepfather still owned Hammersmith Farm and where the president-elect like to sail and visit Bailey's Beach. Claiborne first met the Kennedys before the war, when patriarch Joseph served as Roosevelt's ambassador to England and Pell dated Joseph's daughter Kathleen, Jack's sister, while he was a student at Princeton. "A wonderful girl, gay, intelligent, bright, good-looking and thoroughly nice," as Pell described her in a 1967 oral history for the John F. Kennedy Library, Kathleen died in a plane crash after the war — second of the Kennedy children to die tragically. After the war, Pell encountered Jack Kennedy at the 1945 United Nations San Francisco conference, and occasionally in Washington and Newport at social events, as well as in 1954, when Kennedy spoke in Rhode Island at a political appearance.

Like others, Kennedy had doubted that this Newport socialite, as some of the papers had termed him, could win election to the Senate on his first run for office. "I think he was very, very startled about my election," Pell recalled in his oral history, "because of all his friends, I think I was probably as unlikely a political candidate as could have been found." The election of both men would bring them closer together, politically and personally, and begin to draw Pell into a much longer and closer relationship with Jack's youngest brother, Teddy, who would serve thirty-four years in the Senate with his Newport friend.

Kennedy was inaugurated on a frigid and blustery Friday, January 20. His address captured the fears of a nation and a world that had ended one conflict not so long before and was now under the shadow of another, the Cold War — yet a world whose inhabitants, Communist or free, also had reason to hold hopes for the future, the new president believed.

"Let both sides explore what problems unite us instead of belaboring those problems which divide us," Kennedy told the crowd at the east portico of the Capital.

> Let both sides, for the first time, formulate serious and precise proposals for the inspection and control of arms — and bring the absolute power to destroy other nations under the absolute control of all nations. Let both sides seek to invoke the wonders of science instead of its terrors. Together let us explore the stars, conquer the deserts, eradicate disease, tap the ocean depths, and encourage the arts and commerce . . .
>
> In your hands, my fellow citizens, more than in mine, will rest the final success or failure of our course. Since this country was founded, each generation of Americans has been summoned to give testimony to its national loyalty. The graves of young Americans who answered the call to service surround the globe. Now the trumpet summons us again — not as a call to bear arms, though arms we need; not as a call to battle, though embattled we are — but a call to bear the burden of a long twilight struggle, year in and year out, "rejoicing in hope, patient in tribulation" — a struggle against the common enemies of man: tyranny, poverty, disease, and war itself.

These words summarized the political philosophy of the new senator from Rhode Island, who shared Kennedy's hopes for a better future.

After a weekend of celebration, Washington returned to the business of government. In the low-key style that would characterize his Senate tenure, Pell got to work. He organized his Washington and Providence staffs and took his seats on the two committees assigned to him by Majority Leader Mike Mansfield: Rules and Administration, and Labor and Public Welfare, where he was positioned to help realize his campaign promise to better the lot of working people. Mansfield also rewarded him with a seat on the Democratic Senatorial Campaign Committee, which had benefited during the 1950s from Pell's own contributions and the tens of thousands of dollars he had raised. And Pell replaced President Kennedy on the Joint Economic Committee.

Winter turned to spring, and Pell focused his attention on matters of interest to his constituents. He started a newsletter, invited Rhode Islanders to visit him in Washington, and opened a touring "Office on Wheels" to bring him around the state on his frequent trips home. Saying it "never fired a shot in anger," he advocated turning Newport's Fort Adams, declared surplus property by the Navy, into a public recreational center.

But the economy, central theme of Pell's campaign, overshadowed all. Birthplace of the American Industrial Revolution, Rhode Island by 1961 was seeing the beginning of a shift that would eventually move most factory jobs to cheaper labor markets in the south and overseas, leaving the many workers who did not have college degrees, a growing asset in the emerging economy, with fewer options. The first bill Pell put his name to as a sponsor was the Kennedy-backed legislation extending unemployment compensation; it passed the Senate by an overwhelming majority and the President signed the final version into law in late March. Pell also joined the President in supporting legislation to raise the minimum wage to $1.25 an hour, a measure that passed Congress in May after weeks of debate. He supported Kennedy's $394 million program of aid (including worker retraining) to economically depressed areas, Rhode Island among them. He asked for a study of Rhode Island's fisheries, which employed many but were under pressure from cheap foreign imports. He won $50,000 in federal funds to study ways to turn unmarketable fish into protein-rich fish flour, which could be processed into food. He spoke of the potential expansion of tourism in the Ocean State, whose coast and cultural centers already drew visitors.

"Rhode Island is justifiably proud of its tourist facilities," Pell said in one of his first speeches from the Senate floor. "Tourism is one of our major industries and we would welcome more visitors from other countries. In addition, we are justifiably lucky in our state in that many of our people whose families have come from Europe have preserved the many original language skills and cultural habits, which would tend to make our visitors from abroad particularly welcome."

Already, Pell was planning to make a difference in areas that would improve more lives than his constituents': education and foreign policy.

In the wake of Kennedy's February 20 proposal for a $5.2-billion program of aid to American education for students from kindergarten through college, Pell joined twelve other cosponsors in introducing the Senate bill that incorporated a major provision of the program: federally funded college scholarships based on financial need, up to $1,000 per student. A precursor to what would eventually be known as the Pell Grants, the scholarship portion of Kennedy's $5.2-billion package was eventually defeated. But in announcing his overall program a month after his inauguration, the president again outlined an educational philosophy that Pell shared.

"Our progress as a nation can be no swifter than our progress in education," Kennedy said.

> Our requirements for world leadership, our hopes for economic growth, and the demands of citizenship itself in an era such as this all require the maximum development of every young American's capacity . . . This nation a century or so ago established as a basic objective the provision of a good elementary and secondary education to every child, regardless of means. In 1961, patterns of occupation, citizenship and world affairs have so changed that we must set a higher goal. We must assure ourselves that every talented young person who has the ability to pursue a program of higher education will be able to do so if he chooses, regardless of his financial means.

Like Pell, Kennedy was independently wealthy and an Ivy League graduate. Their sense of noblesse oblige and the shared beliefs of other liberal Democrats from diverse backgrounds would sustain the 1960s social revolution that Kennedy followers termed the New Frontier, which evolved into the Great Society under Lyndon Johnson, Kennedy's successor.

Pell's foreign-policy views also paralleled Kennedy's, though they were based in a childhood of travel and later foreign-service experience that differed somewhat from the president's own background—experience Pell had that Kennedy would tap later in his presidency. A hint of the role Pell would later play in the nation's foreign policy came in his second month as a senator, when he was appointed one of twenty-five Congressmen to attend the first annual Mexico-United States Interparliamentary Conference, held in Guadalajara. On his return with Nuala to Washington, Pell and other members of the delegation went to the White House to present Kennedy a silver tray from the governor of the state of Jalisco, where Guadalajara is located. Majority Leader Mansfield, who had led the delegation, proclaimed the visit "an unqualified success." Pell spoke to a reporter of his role on a committee that was examining American investments in Mexico. It was not the most thrilling assignment, but it suited Pell, the only freshman senator in the delegation.

The Mexican visit had little immediate impact on American foreign policy. A similar, though smaller and unpublicized, foreign visit led by Mansfield and including Pell would also have no immediate effect. But that 1962 delegation to Vietnam would sound a warning that would eventually be proved true, in wasted blood and treasure.

A DEATH IN MUNICH

Herbert Pell appeared with his son on CBS News after Claiborne was sworn into office, and later that January he and Olive departed Washington.

Nearing 80 now, Herbert found enjoyment in travel and the company of his grandchildren, whom he took on summer trips to Europe and for whom he established trust funds. Herbert had special fondness for his namesake, Bertie, Pell's firstborn, who was now fifteen. As winter ended, Herbert made plans for Bertie to join him in England that summer. They would tour the country, and then cross to the continent, for a trip from Paris across France to Italy, and then north through Switzerland to Germany.

As he had moved into old age, Herbert had wearied of the life he'd led through many of his adult years. His Newport estate was long gone, and after the United Nations had declined his offer in the 1940s to make its permanent home on his Hopewell Junction property, he began to think of ridding himself of it; the demands of maintaining the place and the vicissitudes of hired help were robbing it of its appeal. "I fear we are embarking on a sea of servant trouble," he wrote to his son in 1950. "Last summer was perfectly delightful, then when they all walked out on Labor Day, we got an English couple who were very nice but not very good on the job." Herbert was at the breaking point three years later. "I regret to say there has been a good deal of excitement here," he wrote in the spring of 1953. "Last night, Signa came to me and announced that she was immediately going to leave. I told her that I thought it was an outrage to go without notice and practically in the middle of the night, but she apparently had words with Edith the waitress and the result was that she got up this morning early and departed. I telephoned into New York to get another cook and was horrified to be told that cooks now cost about two hundred dollars, which seems to me outrageously high, but alas, everything is going up." In the end, Herbert decided to donate Pellbridge to a Catholic order of nuns. When they weren't traveling or visiting his son and family, Herbert and Olive lived now exclusively at private clubs in New York and Paris and a suite at the Ritz Hotel in London. The couple kept wardrobes at each.

Herbert needed clothes, of course, but he had lost interest in most of his other possessions. So he began to give them away. He donated some of his extensive book collection to the Library of Congress. He gave his vast personal archive to the Franklin D. Roosevelt Presidential Library and Museum, where they would be stored alongside the archives of his old friend. Claiborne and Nuala received some of Herbert's books and manuscripts, much of his art, and the most important pieces of Pelliana, which Claiborne used to decorate his Washington and Newport homes and his Senate office and his beloved Capitol hideaway. He gave his son clothes he no longer needed.

Ridding himself of possessions seemed to liberate Herbert. He had his wife, his son and daughter-in-law, and his four grandchildren, and that, he declared, was enough.

"Birthdays are fine things for children," he had written to Claiborne on the eve of his seventieth birthday, explaining why he did not want his son to host a party. "They mean a full year more away from the weak beginning, a marked addition to vigor, courage and freedom. Even in your twenties, each marks some progress, but after you are thirty, you begin to think in decades rather than years. Forty marks the top. Before the fifties are out, there is the beginning of a descent, and after that, it is down all the way.

"There is nobody who has had more fun in life than I or more favored by fortune, and particularly for this you are greatly responsible, more blessed in his family. You will never in your life come across a man who has been freer than I and probably will see no one who on the whole has been happier."

▫ ▫ ▫ In June 1961, Bertie Pell completed his sophomore year at St. George's, his father's alma mater, and crossed alone to England to spend the summer with his grandfather. With Herbert's chauffeur and valet, they toured England for several days, then made their way to France, and on through Italy and Switzerland into Germany. They stopped at Neuschwanstein, the castle built by the nineteenth-century Bavarian king Ludwig II. Herbert struggled for breath climbing to the top. A smoker most of his adult life, he had suffered a heart attack in the early 1950s, when his weight had exceeded 250 pounds. But he had regained his health after the incident. A medical examination in February 1960 had disclosed only mildly elevated cholesterol and "slight cardiac enlargement," according to his doctor's reading of his x-ray. For a man of almost eighty, it was a respectable finding.

Resting periodically, Herbert and Bertie made it to the top of the castle and back down. They started toward Munich, stopping for lunch along the way. Herbert rested when they reached their hotel, and in the late afternoon, he and his grandson went to Herbert's favorite Munich beer garden. "He really enjoyed himself," Bertie would later recall. "We were sitting there and we had our arms linked with people and we were drinking steins of beer. I never saw him do it, but I heard that he had been prodigious in the amount of beer he could consume. But it wasn't anything exceptional that afternoon." The Pells went from the beer garden to dinner at a nearby restaurant. Walking back to their hotel, the grandfather and grandson started across an intersection.

"Hold it," Herbert said. He reached to Bertie for support and fell to the street.

A heart attack took him. It was July 17, 1961.

The news reached Claiborne in Washington early the next day and he flew to Munich to arrange for his father's cremation, in accordance with Herbert's wishes. There would be no last goodbye, no parting letter, no grave to visit, only ashes that were scattered into the ocean.

In August, Herbert was remembered in a memorial service at Newport's Trinity Church. In his eulogy, Trinity rector Canon Lockett Ford Ballard read from Ecclesiastes, Chapter 38, which speaks of death and wisdom. "The wisdom of a learned man cometh by opportunity of leisure," Ballard read. This, he said, characterized Herbert, who had used the time and freedom his money had allowed him for public service.

"Along such a noble path trod Herbert Claiborne Pell," Ballard said. "May his son so live that countless more shall follow."

▫ ▫ ▫ Time would transform Pell's grief, turning it into a lingering sadness that his father had not lived to see his greatest achievements. Pell would wear his father's clothes, and his Senate office and hideaway would become, in part, memorials to Herbert. Toward the end of his Senate career, as his own mortality drove him to explore the possibility of life after death, he would use mediums in an attempt to reach his father.

Pell was not given to the outward expression of grief. In his private moments, he turned for support to Nuala during the remainder of that summer of 1961, and also to his mother, who herself had experienced similar loss more than once. The death of Hugo Koehler had left Matilda a widow without steady income and a child to support — but for a while, her prospects had brightened, with a man she met at her son's wedding. She fell in love with John A. Hartford, president of A&P, son of the chain's founder (and Nuala's uncle). But before they could marry, Nuala would recall, a heart attack killed Hartford in an elevator in New York's Chrysler Building, where he was attending a Chrysler board meeting. Matilda was alone, once again; and now her ex-husband, who had remained a friend after their divorce, was gone, too.

"Claiborne, dear," Matilda wrote a week after Herbert's memorial service, "your sweet letter of August 10th came this morning. I do know and understand how sad you are feeling and what deep grief this is for you. My heart aches for you. You and daddy were unusually close. You were always a great joy to him and his greatest interest. I did share in your sadness, for I feel really terribly about it myself and seem to be thinking of him all the time. I shall always be grateful that his last year was such a happy one for him. We must try to dwell on that, and that he was spared the suffering of illness. But for those left behind, the shock is very great.

"It is dear of you to say you all need me and I love you very dearly. It makes me happy to have you feel that way and you may be sure I want to be around myself for as long as possible. You all make my life very much worth living. Dear Claiborne, try not to be unhappy. Daddy wouldn't want you to. He wouldn't want sad thoughts of him to take from your strength, all of which is needed for your important work. He really was fulfilled and I know, felt his life very complete and you had such a large part in making him feel that way.

"And now, you have the privilege of being as fine a father to a wonderful family of your own. Already, I see such splendid traits of character in them. So keep your health and strength, dear, and know that you have all my love and sympathy. Your Mom"

ONTO THE STAGE

During the summer of 1961, the Berlin Crisis had emerged as the second major foreign-policy test of the Kennedy Administration. In a move that would have abrogated the Potsdam Agreement that followed the surrender of Nazi Germany in World War II, Soviet Premier Nikita Khrushchev was threatening to end American and NATO access to West Berlin, through which many East Germans had fled Soviet occupation of their land. The East German regime was stockpiling materials for a wall to divide Berlin. Kennedy was ordering troops to gird for possible battle and preparing to seek new Civil Defense funds to build and stock more fallout shelters. The Cold War now had two potentially hot spots: one in Cuba, and another, conceivably more dangerous, in Europe.

Pell's father's death opened an opportunity that Pell seized. On his trip to Germany to oversee Herbert's cremation, he spent a day in West Berlin visiting a refugee center, and when he returned to New York's Idlewild Airport (renamed for Kennedy after he was assassinated), a reporter greeted him with questions.

"The Berliners are plodding along with courage, but there's no doubt the situation is very grave," Pell told the Associated Press. In Washington, he privately briefed the president, who went on TV and radio at 10 p.m. on July 25 from the White House to speak to the American people. The next day, Kennedy said, he would seek from Congress $3.2 billion in new military spending. He would request nearly a quarter of a million more active-duty sailors, soldiers, and flyers, and the activation of additional men and women from the reserves. He wanted to increase the draft call and keep in service ships and planes that had been earmarked for retirement.

"We cannot and will not permit the Communists to drive us out of Berlin, either gradually or by force," Kennedy said,

> for the fulfillment of our pledge to that city is essential to the morale and security of Western Germany, to the unity of Western Europe, and to the faith of the entire Free World. Soviet strategy has long been aimed, not merely at Berlin, but at dividing and neutralizing all of Europe, forcing us back on our own shores. We must meet our oft-stated pledge to the free peoples of West Berlin—and maintain our rights and their safety, even in the face of force—in order to maintain the confidence of other free peoples in our word and our resolve. The strength of the alliance on which our security depends is dependent in turn on our willingness to meet our commitments to them.
>
> So long as the Communists insist that they are preparing to end by themselves unilaterally our rights in West Berlin and our commitments to its people, we must be prepared to defend those rights and those commitments. We will at all times be ready to talk, if talk will help. But we must also be ready to resist with force, if force is used upon us. Either alone would fail. Together, they can serve the cause of freedom and peace.

On August 13, construction of the Berlin Wall began, further raising global tensions. In America, citizens who had already been urged to build basement bomb shelters were advised to replenish their supplies of food, water, and medicine. School children received fresh practice in the protective routine known as "duck and cover": on seeing the flash of a nuclear bomb exploding, which could come without warning at any time, from anywhere, youngsters were instructed to dive under the nearest table or desk and curl themselves into a fetal position to await the shock wave, which would bring with it intense heat and flying debris. A new generation was learning the horrors of a new age.

The fear and hysteria accompanying the Berlin Crisis disturbed Pell. In a speech from the Senate floor on August 22, he urged negotiations with the Soviets—either in the Security Council of the United Nations, or a specially called peace conference—with the aim of American recognition of East Germany and a commitment by both the Soviets and Americans to never furnish nuclear weapons to either half of divided Germany. Diplomacy, Pell maintained, should be given a chance before war was contemplated.

"This course of action," he said, "would mean we would be acting, not react-ing. And it would result in a Soviet defeat on either the diplomatic—if Khrush-chev refused to play—or strategic front. It would also mean that, by taking the initiative, we would be taking the propaganda lead from Khrushchev."

Pell's speech drew national media attention. He was invited onto NBC's *Today* show to discuss his proposal, and several newspapers, including *The New York Times*, published letters, op-ed pieces, and reprints of the speech. Some who viewed Pell's proposal as soft, if not treasonous, criticized him—while leading Senatorial colleagues gave praise, among them one with the power to realize Pell's ambition to some day sit on the Foreign Relations Committee.

"In my opinion," Majority Leader Mansfield told *The Providence Journal*, "there is no one in the Senate—or for that matter, in the entire Congress—who is better versed in the field of foreign policy, based on expertise and knowledge, than is the distinguished junior senator from Rhode Island."

▫ ▫ ▫ As his first year in the Senate drew to a close, Pell won special appoint-ment from the Foreign Relations Committee as an alternate delegate to a NATO conference in Paris. He flew to Africa as part of a Kennedy-appointed delegation, led by Franklin Roosevelt, Jr., to celebrate the independence of Tanganyika (now part of Tanzania) from Great Britain. Traveling as a private citizen, he toured Poland and Czechoslovakia, which he had left in 1949 with his interpreter hidden in the trunk of his car. Speaking at a dinner in Rhode Island, he predicted that America would prevail over the Soviet Union.

"It is going to be a long, drawn-out, arduous process, but, thank God, strength is on our side," he said.

In Washington, the Pells had bought a new home in Georgetown, where politicians, bureaucrats, and society members were welcome at the dinner par-ties Nuala and Claiborne hosted. "Quality Hill" already had a storied history when the Pells moved in: completed in about 1798, the Federal-style house was named by Charles Worthington, a Revolutionary War physician who owned it in the early 1800s and used it as a convalescent home for soldiers wounded in the War of 1812. Destined to be placed on the National Register of Historical Places, Quality Hill was located in the heart of a power district in contemporary Washington.

"John and Jacqueline Kennedy were old friends from Newport days, so it was natural for the Pells to be in the nucleus of the New Frontier crowd which not only took over the White House but also encamped in the fashionable Georgetown district of the city," wrote *The Providence Journal*'s Washington bureau chief. "The Pell home at 34th and Prospect Streets, done in the same

Colonial style that dominates the wholly restored area, is one of the largest and most impressively decorated." The Pell residence had eight bedrooms, fourteen-foot ceilings, and original wide-plank pine floors. The library held an impressive sampling of Pelliana.

In turn, the Pells were welcome at many of the capitol city's other elite addresses. "The Pells have all the requisites to attract attention in this city — political position, taste and intellect, charm, good looks and poise, unostentatious wealth and family blood line," wrote *The Journal*:

> Most of their social life centers around the small dinner parties where some of Washington's most valuable political business is transacted. These are not exactly, as some might picture them, gatherings of the mighty where political conspiracies are hatched, candidates picked and horse trading conducted over brandy and cigars. But there is a lot of soft sell. The relaxed informal atmosphere of a dinner party is often a good place to plant ideas, form opinions and put over arguments more convincingly to a fellow congressman, administration official or newsman. Great demands are made on the listening and thinking time of these men during the working day and they often find they can think more freely and digest ideas better in a congenial atmosphere.

Pell's father had found a similar atmosphere in the men's clubs he favored, and where he lived the last years of his life.

In the inevitable end-of-first-year analyses, Pell received good grades.

The Americans for Democratic Action gave Pell (and senior senator John O. Pastore) a 100-percent rating, based on his votes on ten key liberal issues, including the minimum wage, aid to education and housing, and a four-year extension of the Civil Rights Commission, all of which Pell supported. Although its editorial board had taken issue with his Berlin stance, his hometown newspaper generally praised him. "Mr. Pell," *The Journal* wrote, "while not attempting to initiate any major legislation has made a point of aligning himself, as a co-sponsor, of most of the major liberal legislation of the season, including job retraining, education aid and foreign aid. In everything he has appeared cautious and prudent, never speaking out of turn and always deferring to his senior colleague, Mr. Pastore." Civility and bipartisanship were becoming Pell's signature legislative style.

In a story pointedly illustrated with a photograph of Pell with President Kennedy, the *Journal's* Sunday magazine was effusive in its praise. "Claiborne deBorda Pell may rank 99th out of 100 in the present official hierarchy of the U.S. Senate, but he already stands several notches higher on the senatorial ladder in the unofficial estimation of his colleagues simply because he seems to be a 'natural' for the job," the magazine wrote on December 3.

They feel that Senator Pell has gotten off to a good start because his background and experience have equipped him with the smooth touch that is so necessary to an effective entry into the upper house of Congress, where status is determined primarily by seniority. They feel that the Rhode Islander had done a masterful job of blending into the rich background of crystal chandeliers, deep leather chairs and gold ornamentation which is the atmosphere of the U.S. Senate. They also feel that Senator Pell has made few, if any, mistakes and he has succeeded in a way that can make a difference later on when the mechanical requirements of seniority are met.

The magazine noted Pell's open desire to serve on more than the Rules and Labor Committees, the two to which he had been assigned. "His admitted ambition is to become a member of the powerful Foreign Relations Committee, and his performance during the recent session would seem to indicate that he would be the likeliest candidate from the current crop of freshman as soon as the seniority escalator elevates members of that vintage to eligibility for such an assignment — perhaps as early as January 1963."

◻ ◻ ◻ Pell began 1962 concerned with the quality of rail service, particularly in the Northeast, which had declined in the postwar years as a surging automotive industry and development of the interstate highway system had put more and more Americans behind the wheel. Pell drove around Washington and Rhode Island — often carelessly — but for intercity travel, he preferred the train. He often made the trip between Washington and Rhode Island by rail, a day-long or overnight trip that he believed could be speeded up and made more reliable. His trips on the Pennsylvania Railroad, which offered service on the Washington-to-Boston line, including the historic *Congressional* and *Senator* trains — and on the New Haven Railroad, which offered similar service — gave him firsthand knowledge of rolling stock and tracks that were falling into disrepair, of late departures and arrivals, and a sense that passenger rail service, regrettably, was destined to become a thing of the past.

He had read a landmark book published in 1961: French geographer Jean Gottmann's *Megalopolis: The Urbanized Northeastern Seaboard of the United States*, which postulated that while Boston, New York, Baltimore, and Washington were separate metropolises, they were formed by their suburban areas and nearby smaller cities into a sort of super-city whose transportation, telecommunications, and other needs should be designed and constructed as a whole.

Concluding that rail service was paramount among the many issues facing this new metropolitan area, Pell would begin work on his own book, *Megalopolis Unbound*, published in 1966.

On May 20, 1962, Pell helped set in motion a process that would eventually lead to the creation of Amtrak, with its high-speed trains. His seven-page statement released that day proposed the creation of an eight-state public authority that would use $500 million in bonds to acquire tracks and rights-of-way, and modernize and operate passenger rail service in the Northeast Corridor, "this backbone of the Northeastern Seaboard megalopolis," as he called it. Pell's railroad of the future would have lightweight, air-conditioned cars, operated by a single attendant, that would move at frequent intervals at great speed along the Boston-to-Washington route.

"With the new technological advances," Pell said, "including the possibility that these modern cars might be monorails, ride on pneumatic tires or a cushion of air, or even be rocket-propelled, it would be a smooth ride and a pleasant trip." Pell submitted a Senate bill to achieve his program, and a companion bill was introduced into the House by Rep. Robert N. Giaimo, Democrat of Connecticut.

Pell's proposal prompted a national debate that played out on Capitol Hill and in the media — and was noticed by Kennedy, who in an April 5 address to Congress on America's overall transportation problems urged that revived railroads be an integral part of any solution. "An efficient and dynamic transportation system is vital to our domestic economic growth, productivity and progress," the President said. "It is equally vital to our ability to compete abroad. It influences both the cost and the flexibility of our defense preparedness, and both the business and recreational opportunities of our citizens."

In their private conversations, the President and the Senator discussed Pell's proposals. Kennedy had established a summer White House at Newport's Hammersmith Farm and during a September stay there, the Pells and Kennedys watched an America's Cup race together from the destroyer *Joseph P. Kennedy, Jr.*, named for the president's brother, a bomber pilot killed in action during Word War II. Back in Washington, Pell sent the president a formal letter urging him to take action on passenger rail service. "My job was to prick and poke them along, so that the project wouldn't die down," Pell recalled in his 1967 oral history interview for the John F. Kennedy Library.

The prodding worked: On October 9, 1962, the president, calling Pell's proposal "imaginative and constructive," wrote to Pell with word he was appointing a White House task force. That task force would bear fruit in September 1965, when President Lyndon Johnson signed into law the High Speed Ground Transportation Act.

◻ ◻ ◻ Like his advocacy of high-speed rail, the importance of another contribution Pell made in his second year would not be fully recognized until later. It was the six-week overseas trip he took in November and December with Mansfield and Republican Caleb Boggs of Delaware. Joining them was Massachusetts Democrat Benjamin A. Smith II, who had been appointed to fill President Kennedy's seat and had just passed it on to Teddy Kennedy, who had won a November 6 special election. Traveling on a presidential plane and at the request of the president, the fact-finding mission took Pell and his colleagues — and Nuala, who accompanied her husband on most of his overseas trips as Senator — to Germany, Greece, Egypt, India, Laos, and Vietnam.

Although Pell had never visited Vietnam, he had an intimate connection to the country: one of his good friends, Lt. Col. A. Peter Dewey, son of an Illinois Congressman, was in the country as a member of the Office of Strategic Services (predecessor of the Central Intelligence Agency) in September 1945 when he was shot and killed. Dewey, who had been an adviser to Ho Chi Minh's Viet Minh liberation movement, was mistaken for a French soldier. "I guess I first became conscious of Vietnam," Pell recalled in a 1979 interview, "when one of my best friends, a man who was an usher at my wedding and I was an usher at his wedding, was one of the first casualties of the Vietnam War . . . He shouted just prior to being killed to the people who were there, 'Je suis Americain,' but they still thought he was French." Although not officially recognized as such, Dewey was in fact the first American killed in what would be known as the Vietnam War. At the request of Dewey's father, Pell attempted to find the soldier's body, but was unsuccessful.

The report Mansfield gave to Kennedy on his return from Vietnam in late 1962 was not immediately made public — but Mansfield's brief exchange in Saigon with future Pulitzer Prize–winning reporter David Halberstam, then a *New York Times* writer, hinted of trouble in America's growing involvement in South Vietnam's conflict with North Vietnam president Ho Chi Minh's insurgent forces. In his story datelined Saigon, December 2, Halberstam wrote:

Senator Mike Mansfield, the majority leader in the Senate, left here today after giving the most reserved statement about the situation in Vietnam delivered by a departing American official in a long time. Informed sources said the Montana Democrat, who visited here as President Kennedy's personal representative, had rejected a statement prepared for him by the United States Embassy and had delivered a personal statement. According to these sources, Senator Mansfield was given the embassy statement — saying he was "encouraged" by the progress in the war against Communist guerrillas — at

the airport. The sources said he put it aside and jotted down his own statement . . . Senator Mansfield thus became the first American official in a year
who did not go out of his way to assert that considerable progress was being
made against the guerrillas, or Vietcong.

Mansfield completed a confidential report to Kennedy on December 18, but
outsiders did not immediately have access to its conclusions.

Christmas and New Year's passed, and legislators returned to Washington
for the start of the Eighty-Eighth Congress, Pell's third year as senator. High-
speed rail was again on Pell's agenda for 1963, along with immigration reform,
tax reform, expansion of the Peace Corps, conversion of American measure to
the metric system, and a proposed ban on nuclear-arms testing. Pell wanted to
establish a national arts council, an idea born in conversations with the First
Lady, whose husband also liked the idea. He sought to revive interest in college
scholarships for financially needy students. A divided Congress in October 1961
had failed to pass that part of Kennedy's education initiative.

Pell had hoped to be named to the Foreign Relations Committee, but the one
open Democratic seat went to George A. Smathers of Florida, who had been a
senator since 1951; Pell had floated a plan to enlarge committee membership to
accommodate him, but Mansfield had not embraced it. The majority leader instead gave Pell his first subcommittee chairmanship: of the Smithsonian Institution subcommittee. Pell wanted bigger things, but with his reverence for history,
the subcommittee chairmanship appeased him. His Newport and Washington
homes and offices constituted something of a family museum — and his family had owned and still controlled an actual one, Fort Ticonderoga, which was
open to the public.

The third-year senator had not gained the seat he wanted, but he achieved
another measure of foreign-affairs prominence in joining Mansfield on February 24, when the fact-finding panel publicly presented their twenty-one-page
report on Vietnam to the Foreign Relations Committee. The widely covered
report warned of an escalating conflict in danger of becoming "an American
war" that would senselessly drain the nation of lives and resources. Already,
Mansfield said, increased U.S. support of the Saigon regime had cost more than
fifty American lives since 1961, and these were people sent in the supposedly
noncombat roles of logistical support and tactical advice. The report went on to
describe potential developments:

This intensification inevitably has carried us to the start of the road which
leads to the point at which the conflict could become of greater concern and

greater responsibility to the United States than it is to the government and people of South Vietnam. In present circumstances, pursuit of that course could involve an expenditure of American lives and resources which would bear little relationship to the interest of the United States or, indeed, to the interests of the people of Vietnam.

If we are to avoid that course, it must be clear to ourselves as well as to the Vietnamese people where the primary responsibility lies in this situation. It must rest with the Vietnamese government and people. What further effort may be needed for the survival of the republic in present circumstances must come from that source. If it is not forthcoming, the United States can reduce its commitment or abandon it entirely, but there is no interest of the United States in Vietnam which would justify, in present circumstances, the conversion of the war into an American war to be fought primarily with American lives.

The report was rejected by Cold War hardliners, who had watched the crises in Cuba and Berlin and the ever-expanding nuclear capability of the Soviet Union; Communism, they claimed, would take over the world unless America defended freedom as it had in Korea and during World War II. Along with Mansfield, Pell would be criticized by some as unpatriotic for his reluctance to commit extensive American forces to Vietnam — and the rhetoric would turn ugly as the decade wore on and Pell emerged as an outspoken critic of the Vietnam conflict.

But Pell also found support in his early days of questioning American policy.

"We note in this morning's *Providence Journal* about something being done in Vietnam," read an unsigned typewritten letter dated February 25, 1963, that Pell received:

We have a 19-year-old son over there, for what? These people do not want to fight — they want the Americans to do the job for them. True, we should help them, with food and clothes, we agree. But lives — that is another story . . .

We are proud to be Americans and we will go along with helping the needy, but risking lives, I cannot see it. If my son knew I wrote anything like this, he would disown me. Believe me. As there could not be a more patriotic boy than he is. Came out of high school and went to the service — to get his "hitch," as he called it, over with. Then he will go to College, with the help of God, when he comes home. He has been in a little over 2 years. Only a boy, really. Never once complained.

I am leaving this letter unsigned as my son would not want me to write this, but I have prayed so hard for my son as well as all the boys over there, and believe me it is hard to think they are there for no really good reason.

This was the sort of sentiment that would help sustain Pell in the coming years as Vietnam threatened to tear his nation apart, and he was personally vilified as a "dove."

□ □ □ Pell turned forty-five on Friday, November 22, 1963, the day Kennedy was shot by Lee Harvey Oswald. In Washington, he watched TV with other Americans as the reports from Dallas grew increasingly dark until, at 12:33 p.m. East Coast time, the White House announced that the President was dead. Kennedy's body was transported from Parkland Memorial Hospital to Air Force One, where Johnson took the oath of office moments before the plane left Love Field for the flight back to Andrews Air Force Base.

"President Kennedy's death is s tragedy, not just to our country, his family and his friends, but to the whole world," Pell told a *Providence Journal* reporter in his office on the twenty-second. "I pray that our country continues on the course he set — one of domestic growth and fairness and of external peace. My wife and I extend our utter sympathy to his wife and family. I mourn the loss of a friend." Before leaving for Dallas, Kennedy had sent Pell early birthday greetings, one of the President's last pieces of correspondence.

Kennedy was brought to the White House early on Saturday, and after his widow declared that his casket be closed, he lay in repose in the East Room, where nearly a century before the slain Abraham Lincoln had lain. The Pells were among those who paid private respects.

In the years to come, Pell would draw closer to another Kennedy than he had been to Jack: Teddy and Pell would become Washington neighbors and close friends, and allies on scores of pieces of legislation. But Pell would always carry the memory of Jack and would never again celebrate his birthday on November 22. Of the thousands of mementoes he would accumulate over his long life, he would keep a special place for those involving the dead President. There, in the handful of photo albums and scrapbooks he kept within arm's reach in his Senate office — there among letters from his parents and his prized Pelliana — were photographs and letters from Jack and Jackie, including one sent August 19, 1963, thanking Claiborne and Nuala for their sympathy on the death that summer of the Kennedys' two-day-old baby, Patrick Bouvier. There among Pell's prized possessions was a first-day-of-issue John Fitzgerald Kennedy stamp.

"He could enunciate the thoughts going around in my mind with greater purity and clarity than I could," Pell told a reporter shortly after Kennedy's assassination. Discussing Kennedy, Pell could be effusive.

"I don't think I've ever, except for the death of my own father, ever been as grieved," he said in his oral-history interview,

I just remember the terribly personal and profound grief at his death as something I'll never, never forget. It may have been because it was a personal relationship and a personal admiration and also because it was a general viewpoint . . . All of us who had been through World War II for four, five years, close to that, we really had something in common, and President Kennedy was the only man in high office in government who represented this viewpoint . . .

I can honestly say that since his death, I've said in my prayers every night, "May the ideas of John F. Kennedy for our country, our earth and our universe come to be." And I believe it.

ARTS AND HUMANITIES

The month before Kennedy was shot, Pell had chaired a weeklong hearing on legislation he had co-sponsored to establish a National Arts Foundation, which would provide federal assistance to a broad range of artists and scholars. The initiative had the enthusiastic support of co-sponsors Hubert Humphrey, Majority Whip; Senator Joseph Clark, Democrat of Pennsylvania; and New York Senator Jacob Javits, a moderate Republican who had become one of Pell's closest Senate friends. Pell held the hearing after Mansfield had appointed him to chair the Special Subcommittee on Arts and Humanities of the Senate Committee on Labor and Public Welfare.

Pell's appreciation for the arts dated to his childhood, with his father's collections and his stepmother Olive Pell's successful career as an artist. Financially secure, Olive could afford her passion — but other artists, Pell knew, were not so lucky. Given their contribution to the culture, he believed they deserved government support, much as talented young students unable to afford college deserved federal scholarships.

Pell had begun to develop his idea of federal assistance to the arts — and to the humanities, which others in Congress were pushing — during his first days in Washington, when he discussed the issue with Jackie Kennedy. The First Lady had turned the White House into a showcase for the arts, with dinners featuring musicians, artists and scholars, and ballet performances, music recitals, and Shakespeare readings. She envisioned a cabinet-level Department of the Arts, but given the political realities, was receptive to something short of that. Pell proposed that the White House name an official Arts Advisor with influence in the executive and legislative branches of government and a close connection to the private sector.

"The White House Advisor should maintain as close touch as possible with spokesmen for the various fields of art," Pell wrote to Jackie on Oct. 24, 1962, after a recent discussion. "In this connection, he should pay special attention to keeping a nice balance between the leaders of the visual [and] the performing arts. He should also bear in mind the political facts of life, in that the leaders of the folk arts — Indian crafts and the like — should be recognized to help insure federal acceptance of any overall legislation in this field."

Pell's vision was all-inclusive, but it was not new to him. In his 1955 State of the Union address, President Eisenhower had proposed creation of an advisory arts commission within the Department of Health, Education and Welfare. "In the advancement of the various activities which would make our civilization endure and flourish," Eisenhower said, "the federal government should do more to give official recognition to the importance of the arts and other cultural activities."

A bill to establish the commission passed the Senate in 1956, but the measure died in the House. Similar bills were introduced into the next session of Congress, including one sponsored by Humphrey and Javits, but after a public hearing, they did not advance. President Kennedy repeated Eisenhower's call on February 6, 1962, in his Special Message to Congress on Education:

Our Nation has a rich and diverse cultural heritage. We are justly proud of the vitality, the creativity and the variety of the contemporary contributions our citizens can offer to the world of the arts. If we are to be among the leaders of the world in every sense of the word, this sector of our national life cannot be neglected or treated with indifference. Yet, almost alone among the governments of the world, our government has displayed little interest in fostering cultural development. Just as the Federal Government has not, should not, and will not undertake to control the subject matter taught in local schools, so its efforts should be confined to broad encouragement of the arts.

Once more, bills were drafted and hearings held, but with the nation's attention focused on the economy and the Cold War — and some members of Congress believing that taxpayer dollars were better spent on weapons than on paintings or plays — the notion did not advance.

As chairman of the special subcommittee, Pell was determined to finally realize what had become a shared vision in the White House and the Democratic-controlled Senate and House. Pell opened his October 1963 arts and humanities hearings with a call to action that put American arts in a global perspective: "I believe that this cause and its implementation has a worldwide application, for as our cultural life is enhanced and strengthened, so does it project itself into the world beyond our shores. Let us apply renewed energies to the very concept we seek to advance: a true renaissance, the reawakening, the quickening, and above all, the unstinted growth of our cultural vitality."

Humphrey elevated the argument to an almost spiritual level he hoped would resonate with taxpayers who were stocking canned goods in their basement shelters and fearing the end of the world.

"The arts have a significant place in our lives, and I can think of no better time to place some primary emphasis on it than in this day and age when most people live in constant fear of the weapons of destruction which cloud man's mind and his spirit and really pose an atmosphere of hopelessness for millions and millions of people," Humphrey said. "The arts seldom make the headlines. We are always talking about a bigger bomb . . . I wonder if we would be willing to put as much money in the arts and the preservation of what has made mankind and civilization."

During the five days of Pell's hearing, people traveled from across the country to testify to their support. Performing and visual artists joined business and labor leaders, state and federal officials, educators and senior citizens, among others. Kennedy's Commissioner of Education Francis E. Keppel, whose vision for college accessibility would influence Pell in the legislation that became the Pell Grants, blessed the concept.

"The true state of the arts in America," Keppel said, "is found in the fact that public interest and participation in the arts are not matched by adequate financial support."

A month after Kennedy was buried at Arlington National Cemetery, the Senate passed SR 2379. Combining provisions of separate bills that had been co-sponsored by Pell, Humphrey, Javits, and others, the measure called for creation of a National Arts Foundation and a National Council on the Arts, an advisory body. But once more, the initiative languished. Finally, in August of 1964, the House passed similar legislation, which the Senate approved the next day on a voice vote. On September 3, 1964, Johnson signed Public Law 88–579, the National Arts and Cultural Development Act, creating the National Arts Council. An endowment to distribute funds was yet to be established, however.

The endowment was not forgotten—but its creation had become more complicated.

▫ ▫ ▫ Pell's efforts coincided with a movement to win similar support for the humanities. The effort began with the American Council of Learned Societies, the Council of Graduate Schools in America, and the United Chapters of Phi Beta Kappa, which joined to create the National Commission on the Humanities, chaired by Brown University President Barnaby C. Keeney.

In announcing creation of the commission, which would be headquartered in New York, on June 1, 1963, the effort's leaders explained its purpose. The commission would seek ways in which private and government entities could encourage creativity and improve the study and teaching of history, philosophy, the law, political science, psychology and related humanities disciplines — the sisters to the arts in American culture. Yale President Kingman Brewster had joined the commission, as had Notre Dame President Rev. Theodore M. Hesburgh, and Glenn T. Seaborg, chairman of the Atomic Energy Commission.

"Those who are concerned for the future of the humanities in America should cease to speak in platitudes and should undertake to demonstrate the national relevance and importance of humanistic teaching and scholarship," said Frederick Burkhardt, president of the American Council of Learned Societies. "Rather than simply bewailing the 'imbalance' between the sciences and the humanities, we must specify as precisely as possible the present and future needs of the humanities." '

Nearly a year passed. In the spring of 1964, the humanities commission issued a report calling for the president and Congress to establish a National Humanities Foundation; that August, Pennsylvania Democrat William S. Moorhead introduced legislation into the House to create it.

In the White House, the President was watching both the arts and the humanities initiatives, which seemed to complement each other. Invited by Brown President Keeney to speak at the university's 200th convocation, Johnson, in Providence on September 24, 1964, endorsed support for arts and the humanities — and with Keeney by his side, praised the humanities commission's work. Pell attended, and while he was beginning to question LBJ's Vietnam policies, the President singled him out for praise at the start of his address. "Your brilliant young Senator Claiborne Pell is taking his place as a leader and a statesman," the President said. He was, in the President's view, a worthy successor to Green, with whom Johnson had served in the Senate for two terms.

"In the sciences, in the arts, in our understanding of human behavior, all of our tools must be sharpened," Johnson said. "And there just simply must be no neglect of humanities. The values of our free and compassionate society are as vital to our national success as the skills of our technical and scientific age. And I look with the greatest of favor upon the proposal by your own able President Keeney's Commission for a National Foundation for the Humanities."

▫ ▫ ▫ By the time of his 1965 State of the Union Address, Johnson had decided that a single bill creating endowments for arts and humanities made sense, and on March 10, he transmitted versions to the House and to the Senate, where

Pell was chief sponsor. Modeled after the National Science Foundation, which Congress had created in 1950, Johnson's proposed National Foundation on the Arts and the Humanities — origin of today's separate National Endowment for the Arts and the National Endowment for the Humanities — would provide $10 million in federal assistance (plus matching federal funds for private contributions) to individuals and groups in both fields of endeavor.

The public reaction was favorable.

"For the first time since the New Deal, the federal government would provide direct aid to creative artists," *The New York Times* reported on March 11:

> President Johnson's proposals are aimed directly at the creative world. They would be the first, for example, to provide federal matching grants to nonprofit groups and individual artists and scholars. The definitions in the bill for "arts" and "humanities" are sweeping. Arts includes not only such traditional fields as drama and creative writing but also photography, costume and fashion design, motion pictures, television and radio. The humanities, the measure says, includes but is not limited to "language, literature, history and philosophy; archeology; criticism and theory of the arts . . . and those aspects of the social sciences which have humanistic content and employ humanistic methods."

Meanwhile, Johnson had named the first members of the National Arts Council, created by the 1964 National Arts and Cultural Development Act: composer Leonard Bernstein, along with authors John Steinbeck and Harper Lee, jazz musician Duke Ellington, violinist Isaac Stern, choreographer Agnes de Mille, and actors Helen Hayes, Rosalind Russell, Charlton Heston, Gregory Peck, and Sidney Poitier.

"I believe that a world of creation and thought is at the very core of civilization and that our civilization will largely survive in the works of our creations," Johnson said in swearing them in at a White House ceremony on April 9. "That quality, as I have said many times before, confirms the faith that our common hope may be much more enduring than our conflicting hostilities. And I want that each hour of the things that we do will be enduring. Right now, the men of affairs are struggling to catch up with the insights of great art. The stakes may very well be the survival of our entire society."

At 9:50 a.m. on September 29, Johnson took the podium in the White House Rose Garden. He was surrounded by a crowd of private citizens and politicians, including now–Vice President Humphrey, Mansfield, and Pell, who stood directly behind him. Johnson had brought everyone together to witness the signing of PL 89–209, the National Foundation on the Arts and the Humanities Act of 1965, which realized an old ambition that his slain predecessor had not lived to see. Johnson's remarks were eloquent:

> In the long history of man, countless empires and nations have come and gone. Those which created no lasting works of art are reduced today to short footnotes in history's catalog.
>
> Art is a nation's most precious heritage. For it is in our works of art that we reveal to ourselves, and to others, the inner vision which guides us as a Nation. And where there is no vision, the people perish. We in America have not always been kind to the artists and the scholars who are the creators and the keepers of our vision. Somehow, the scientists always seem to get the penthouse, while the arts and the humanities get the basement.
>
> Last year, for the first time in our history, we passed legislation to start changing that situation. We created the National Council on the Arts. The talented and the distinguished members of that Council have worked very hard. They have worked creatively. They have dreamed dreams and they have developed ideas. This new bill, creating the National Foundation for the Arts and the Humanities, gives us the power to turn some of those dreams and ideas into reality.

Johnson thanked the key legislators, including Pell, who had brought them to this moment. He enumerated some of the programs the new endowments would help support or create: national opera and ballet companies, symphony orchestras, a national theater, an American Film Institute, new works of music by American composers, and grants for artists-in-residence in schools.

"Those are only a small part of the programs that we are ready to begin," Johnson said.

> They will have an unprecedented effect on the arts and the humanities of our great Nation. But these actions, and others soon to follow, cannot alone achieve our goals. To produce true and lasting results, our States and our municipalities, our schools and our great private foundations, must join forces with us. It is in the neighborhoods of each community that a nation's art is born. In countless American towns there live thousands of obscure and unknown talents.
>
> What this bill really does is to bring active support to this great national asset, to make fresher the winds of art in this great land of ours. The arts and the humanities belong to the people, for it is, after all, the people who create them.

By the time he realized success with the national endowments, Pell was no longer the new man in town. His foreign-affairs expertise especially had impressed Washington, and his reputation was spreading beyond the capital city and Rhode Island. Pell began to think on a grander scale.

He began to imagine he could be vice president.

As the August 1964 Democratic National Convention in Atlantic City approached, Pell floated his name as a possible running mate for Johnson. Former *Providence Journal* reporter Ray Nelson, the 1960 campaign press secretary who had gone to Washington with Pell to become his administrative assistant, distributed a press release proclaiming Pell's appeal. Pell's 1960 primary win and landslide general-election victory were attributable, Nelson wrote, "in part to his singularly successful ability on television, his sincerity, and his direct personal style in campaigning. He is the first former Foreign Service officer to become a senator. Senator Pell has particularly concerned himself with the problems of intercity transportation, youth and Germany. In each of these areas, he has delved deeply, coming up with solutions and ideas that have received national attention." The release noted Pell's father's history in politics and international diplomacy, and the fact that he was a family man with a wife and four children.

Journalists picked up on Pell's ambition. In an early July column evaluating possible vice-presidential candidates, Columnist and broadcaster Walter Winchell wrote: " 'Who is the darkest horse of them all?' A newspaper executive pal (he co-spooked FDR speeches) informed: 'It could very well be U.S. Senator Claiborne Pell of Rhode Island. He polled the heaviest vote in the East — outside of JFK — in '60. Not many people know Senator Pell in other states, but Mr. Johnson seeks a vote-getter. Besides, he's an Easterner.'" Papers in Boston, Baltimore and New York, among other cities, ran with the story. After Pell appeared at a Democratic fundraising dinner in Topeka, Kansas, *The Junction City Daily Union* editorialized about the favorable impression he had made.

"In fact," the paper wrote, "the impression was so strong, we had several Democrats who are delegates to the National Convention remark that they intend to stir up interest in Sen. Pell as a possible candidate for the vice-presidential nomination." Pell reprinted copies of the editorial and Nelson distributed them. The national party commissioned an internal poll to test the appeal of Pell and others, and NBC News broadcast the results on the opening day of the convention, August 24, after obtaining a copy. It showed Johnson and Pell was almost as strong a ticket as the president with Humphrey. But Humphrey, the president's man, won the vice-presidential nomination that week.

Pell would resurrect his vice-presidential desires in 1968, but he left Atlantic City with much else to preoccupy him — and a more realistic ambition about to be realized.

In early January 1965, Mansfield appointed him to the Foreign Relations Committee.

▫ ▫ ▫ Pell was starting his fifth year in the Senate — and for the first time in his political career, a reelection campaign loomed. No Rhode Island Democrat was eager to face the popular Pell in a primary — but Republican Governor John Chafee was interested. The state's most prominent Republican, Chafee was a decorated Marine Corps veteran of World War II who had fought in the battles of Guadalcanal and Okinawa. His moderate political views had helped him to win the governorship in 1962 and reelection two years later. Like Pell, Chafee came from wealth, which would allow him to spend freely in a campaign.

As he tested the possibility of a senatorial run, Chafee in 1965 publicly criticized Pell, who had tailored his schedule to be in Rhode Island more often — a fact that John Lewis, his 1960 campaign manager and now head of his Rhode Island office, acknowledged in a *Providence Journal* article.

"We welcome him back after a four-year absence," Chafee said in a gubernatorial press conference that spring. "His presence is noticeable quite possibly due to his long absence. Too bad that it takes an election to get him back." Chafee told a reporter at the conference that he had not decided his plans for 1966, but should *he* ever be elected to Congress, *he* would be in his home state often "because I like it here."

Chafee continued his criticism in the fall, when in another press conference he called Pell "Rip van Winkle" who had enjoyed a "five-year-sleep" in Washington. Pell responded with a list of 122 trips to Rhode Island that he said he had made since his term began. Saying he had visited every city and town at least once a year since January 1961, Pell declined Chafee's offer to accompany him on a tour of the state

By the start of 1966, more substantial issues had emerged in a potential Pell-Chafee race, notably their difference on the Vietnam War, which under Johnson had expanded into full American involvement involving nearly 200,000 troops. Pell was increasingly strident in his opposition, while Chafee supported U.S. policy.

In March, Chafee decided to seek reelection to the State House — but he had not abandoned his senatorial ambitions. He would run in 1972, in a fierce race that would not only test Pell but reflect the raw emotions of a country divided by war.

With the popular Chafee out of contention, Republican Ruth M. Briggs, fifty-five, a decorated lieutenant general in the Women's Army Corps who had served in the military until her retirement in 1964, threw her hat in the ring. Briggs had never held elective office, unless her presidency of the state chapter of the Daughters of the American Revolution was counted. She was the first woman to run for Senate from Rhode Island. Poorly financed, she polled poorly against the incumbent.

Pell mounted a modest campaign that stood in contrast to the investment he had made six years before. Lewis had planned to spend more than $300,000 in a Chafee race, but with the weaker Briggs as the opponent, he decided to spend some $100,000 less. Media ads would emphasize Pell's local initiatives; his national stature, particularly on foreign affairs; and his "Kennedy-like" appeal, which Ted Kennedy would reinforce in person on a swing through the state. Voters would be reminded of the excitement of Pell's 1960 victories, when a newcomer defied odds to slay giants.

"Was virtually unknown and swept state like wildfire in becoming first unendorsed candidate to win statewide primary and in general election to become best vote-getter in Rhode Island's history," a Pell briefing manual declared. The manual sought also to emphasize Pell's physical appearance, fitness, affinity with young people, and family image. "Is considered handsome and would have much appeal to women's vote. Wife is very attractive, personable and friendly, and is willing campaigner. Identified with physical fitness by keeping in shape through sports of tennis and running . . . Has a young family of four . . . has growing national identification with youth through his work and speeches in the Senate on the problems and challenges of youth."

Briggs met Pell in an October televised debate and they clashed on government spending and Vietnam. Pell opposed an ultimatum for the North to leave the South, deeming such a measure dangerously provocative. He favored diplomacy.

"Did you really mean that or were you just talking?" Briggs responded. "One-sided restraint is tantamount to murder, cold-blooded murder."

She renewed her demand for Ho Chi Minh's forces "to either pull out or we will fight this war the way it should be fought."

Pell patiently disagreed. "The best course we can have in Vietnam," he said, "is to cool it rather than heat it."

It was a rare moment of drama in a campaign that seemed to put Rhode Islanders to sleep — a campaign that found "Senator Pell steam-rollering an under-financed and over-matched opponent," as the *Journal* described it shortly before the vote.

On the eve of Election Day, Briggs predicted an upset win.

"I think it's going to be one of the biggest surprises the state has ever seen," she said. "The polls be darned. The people that are going to make a difference to us aren't the people being reached by the polls."

She was wrong.

When the votes from November 8 were counted, Pell had won 214,885 votes to Briggs's 101,611, more than two-thirds of the vote, roughly the same margin by which he had defeated Raoul Archambault Jr. in 1960. Briggs had not even carried her hometown of Bristol.

Like Archambault and ex-governor Roberts, Pell had buried her politically.

Five □ History Making

AGAINST WAR

On March 10, 1967, Pell received a letter from a woman in Manhattan, Kansas. Helen Melaragno wrote of the disgrace she felt in America's still-escalating role in the Vietnam War. By that point, Johnson had committed nearly 400,000 troops to the conflict and additional tens of thousands were on the way. More than 8,000 Americans had died. North Vietnam was under attack from U.S. B-52 bombers, which were killing untold numbers of civilians. On the present course, no end seemed in sight.

"My Dear Senator Pell," Melaragno wrote,

> I am writing to you as a former resident of Rhode Island who is very concerned about our country's involvement in Vietnam. Frankly, I am ashamed of what we are doing there. I feel, as people in Hitler's Germany must have felt, that I must speak out against inhumanity, and this to me is inhumanity.
>
> In view of the fact that pressure in this country seems to be building up recently, I am hopeful that we can soon, as [United Nations president] U Thant suggests, terminate the bombings as prelude to peace talks. I do hope you will do all you can. Perhaps soon we can again be proud of our country.
>
> Very truly yours, Helen Melaragno.

The letter was but one in a growing volume of correspondence that Pell had been receiving. Some writers supported the war—but others, like Melaragno, were in agreement with an increasing number of opponents who were moved to action. Petitions were being circulated and protestors had taken to the streets. University students had staged sit-ins and strikes. Heavyweight champion Muhammad Ali had declared himself a conscientious objector. Two days after Pell received Melaragno's letter, *The New York Times* published a three-page ad signed by thousands of professors and teachers against the war. Pell's position was closer to theirs than to the declining majority that continued to support the president. Pell was in agreement with Martin Luther King, Jr., who in a sermon on April 4 at New York's Riverside Church urged fellow clergy to speak against the war:

> I come to this magnificent house of worship tonight because my conscience leaves me no other choice. I join you in this meeting because I am in deepest

agreement with the aims and work of the organization which has brought us together: Clergy and Laymen Concerned about Vietnam. The recent statements of your executive committee are the sentiments of my own heart, and I found myself in full accord when I read its opening lines: "A time comes when silence is betrayal." And that time has come for us in relation to Vietnam.

Pell wrote back to Melaragno a week after her letter arrived.
"As you may know," he said,

I have opposed escalation in general and believe we should do everything we can to cool down the military conflict in South Vietnam, as well as terminate our bombing of the North.

As early as November 8, 1965, in a speech in Providence, I declared that "we should not escalate but rather should deescalate our bombing of North Vietnam." I also said at that time that "while our bombing may seem to be successful in its immediate tactical objectives, I believe it is counterproductive in its political effects, in that it tends to strengthen Communist unity and morale."

I urged in that speech that we seek a neutralization of Vietnam, Cambodia and Laos, through the Geneva Convention; that we encourage the greatest possible participation by the United Nations; and that we be prepared to "talk and negotiate with whomever was at the conference table." I continue to support all of these positions and will pursue them vigorously in my work on the Senate Foreign Relations Committee in the coming weeks.

Pell invariably responded to those who wrote him, on whatever issue — but as spring came to Washington that year, he did more than answer letters protesting the Vietnam War. His opposition had intensified since his November 8, 1965, Providence speech, and he wanted a larger platform to express his views. It would have power that personal correspondence lacked, particularly if it received widespread media coverage, as it would. He began to work on a major foreign-policy speech, the first on Vietnam that he would deliver in the Senate.
On May 23, 1967, Pell took the Senate floor. Reporters, including *The New York Times*' Hedrick Smith, a future Pulitzer Prize–winner, had been alerted.
"I wish to express my concern about what seems to be a growing sense of impatience and frustration regarding the Vietnam War," Pell began.

So often we hear people say: "Let us escalate the war, get it over with and bring our young men home." This view is reflected in the latest Gallup Poll. Our administration reflects this view, too, without recognizing that achieving a military victory through constant escalation will lead, at best and only after many more deaths, to a permanent commitment of thousands of our young men and billions of dollars for many years to come. More important, such a so-called victory will contain the seeds of far greater future bitterness and disaster.

Without specifically mentioning America's nuclear arsenal, Pell said the U.S. could "erase the entire nation of North Vietnam, which is about the size of the state of Nevada," in no time, if it chose to. China would then move in to fill a vacuum of power, Pell said, which would be contrary to America's national interests. Complete and unilateral U.S. withdrawal, he said, would have the same effect:

> To my mind, American national interest, Vietnam's national interest and the world's self-interest are all the same when it comes to the common aim of achieving a sane resolution to the conflict in Vietnam. To cool it down, to slow down, would appear to me to be the correct, common-sense, immediate course to follow. The best permanent solution to Vietnam, in my belief, is to strive for and accept a settlement that reasonably represents the actual political forces in being there: the relatively small Ky right wing and Communist left wing, and the large middle ground of neutralists of all complexions. From the standpoint of the unfortunate Vietnamese, such an outcome would obviously be preferable, too; and it is one that would permit us to bring back our young men and substantially reduce our expenses. In pursuing these objectives, we should work within the framework of the United Nations to the maximum extent possible.

Listening, one could imagine Pell's diplomat father speaking.

◻ ◻ ◻ Although he had joined Mansfield in his written warning to Kennedy after their late-1962 visit to Vietnam that American involvement there was potentially problematic, Pell initially had supported White House policy. He initially believed, as did Mansfield and most other Congressmen of the time before so many troops were on the ground and losses had mounted, that the United States had strategic interests in Southeast Asia. Success for Ho Chi Minh would not be success for America and its Cold War allies.

In a 1964 letter to a constituent, Pell summarized the three options he saw facing America then. Pulling out of Vietnam, he wrote, "would be very harmful indeed to our national interest" since it would "break faith" with an ally, South Vietnam; set a poor precedent undermining America's position as a world leader; and create a risky vacuum, "which the Communists would inevitably fill." One more domino would fall. A second option would be to expand the conflict into the north — perhaps with the use of nuclear weapons — but this, Pell wrote, would be "a bad error in judgment" that could lead to a greater war with China and, possibly, "World War III." He preferred a third course, one that, predictably, stressed diplomacy:

> To continue and intensify our present campaign, all the time probing and searching for a firm settlement. I realize that this third alternative is a frustrating one and that it does not offer a quick solution. But this last alternative is a bearable course and, to my mind, it is preferable to either of the first two. In fact, I believe that this latter course is the only sensible one open to us at the present time, and I shall be doing what I can to see that it is used with imagination and caution.

On August 2, 1964, the U.S. destroyer *Maddox*, on an intelligence-gathering mission in the Gulf of Tonkin, opened fire on three North Vietnamese torpedo boats. One North Vietnamese vessel was sunk. Two days later, a second engagement was reported by Johnson in an address to the American people from the White House.

"The initial attack on the destroyer *Maddox*, on August 2, was repeated today by a number of hostile vessels attacking two U.S. destroyers with torpedoes," Johnson said. (In truth, the second "attack" probably did not happen. A North Vietnamese boat may have fired a single torpedo that missed its target, but the evidence was inconclusive; no visual sightings were made, and a thunderstorm in the area may have distorted radar and sonar readings. War critics would believe Johnson used the two incidents, whatever they really were, as an excuse to escalate the war.) Johnson said in his address,

> It is a solemn responsibility to have to order even limited military action by forces whose overall strength is as vast and as awesome as those of the United States of America, but it is my considered conviction, shared throughout your Government, that firmness in the right is indispensable today for peace; that firmness will always be measured. Its mission is peace . . .
>
> I have today met with the leaders of both parties in the Congress of the United States and I have informed them that I shall immediately request the Congress to pass a resolution making it clear that our Government is united in its determination to take all necessary measures in support of freedom and in defense of peace in southeast Asia. I have been given encouraging assurance by these leaders of both parties that such a resolution will be promptly

introduced, freely and expeditiously debated, and passed with overwhelming support.

The next day, American pilots from two aircraft carriers bombed North Vietnamese torpedo-boat bases and an oil storage depot. Two U.S. aircraft were lost. One pilot was killed and a second, Everett Alvarez, Jr., survived to become the first prisoner of war. By any definition, the Vietnam War had begun.

On August 7, Congress passed Public Law 88–408, the Gulf of Tonkin Resolution, which gave Johnson authority to use military force in Vietnam — without a formal declaration of war. The House supported the resolution on a 416–0 vote. Pell and 87 other senators approved, with only two senators voting against it.

"I trust the people and press of the world will be aware that as the world's strongest nation and defender of freedom," Pell said in a statement, "we will not stand for unprovoked attack or aggression, but at the same time be aware that we do not seek material or territorial gain. We only desire freedom, for ourselves and for the people of other nations."

In later years, Pell maintained that if he had known the true circumstances of the Tonkin incidents, he might have joined Senators Ernest Gruening, Democrat of Alaska, and Oregon Democrat Wayne Morse, a member of the Foreign Relations Committee, in voting against the resolution. Morse and Gruening were among the first prominent — and most persistent — Americans to oppose the war. Both were on record against the conflict by March 1964, when Morse loudly criticized Johnson's Vietnam policies. "We should never have gone in. We should never have stayed in. We should get out,'" Morse was quoted as saying by *The New York Times* in its March 21, 1964, edition.

Pell spoke of being misled on Tonkin most emphatically in a 1979 interview conducted by the Library of Congress's Congressional Research Service, which was preparing a study on the federal government's role in the war for the Foreign Relations Committee. "In retrospect," Pell said,

I don't think we were adequately informed . . . I regret I did not have the gumption to vote against the Gulf of Tonkin resolution, but at the time I just knew that an action hostile to us had been taken without, I thought, provocation. Later on, I realized it was an incorrect assumption on my part that was based on the information available at the time. And I felt it was necessary to back up the president in his regard that we would not stand idly by and see our ships attacked.

The president was committed. On March 8, 1964, a contingent of 3,500 combat Marines landed at China Beach, near Da Nang Air Force Base, joining more than 20,000 American military advisers who were already in Vietnam. The ground war was underway, in force.

Pell continued to generally support Johnson's pursuit of the war as 1965 unfolded. He was motivated, in part, by practical political considerations: he backed Johnson on most major issues, including the president's Great Society initiatives on education, civil rights, poverty, and the creation of Medicare, through the Social Security Act of 1965. Johnson had signed into law Pell's National Endowments for the Arts and Humanities legislation. And the president agreed with Pell's ideas for high-speed rail transportation, particularly along the Northeast Corridor. Saying the nation had "imminent need" of improved intercity transportation, Johnson introduced legislation for research and development of a new system on March 4, 1965.

"I admired President Johnson," Pell said in his 1979 interview. "I think he got through more legislation of a domestic nature than any man in a long time. He was just nailed to the cross on this Vietnam War."

Johnson introduced his 1965 rail legislation as the bankrupt New Haven Railroad and the financially ailing Pennsylvania Railroad struggled to maintain track and rolling stock. Pell, who preferred the train to airplanes on his trips between Rhode Island and Washington, often experienced the sorry state of passenger rail service — most poignantly in the spring of 1965, when he and Nuala were leaving the capital on their way to a meeting of the Democratic State Committee in Providence's Biltmore Hotel. The Pells were on a Pennsylvania Railroad train when a piece of brake on the car ahead of them broke off and shattered the window where they were sitting. Nuala suffered cuts to her legs — and Pell required a hospital visit to remove glass splinters from his eyes. *The Providence Journal* reported the story:

> Senator Pell was discharged from the hospital this morning with a patch over his left eye. He said the patch may be removed tomorrow. Both eyes feel "a little badly" but "will come along," he reported this morning. He is unable to read, but can see well enough for walking, he said. The senator, who has given much of his attention to studying proposals to improve rail service between Washington and Boston, added a wry comment. "This has elements of sardonic humor, that the fellow who is very interested in the railroad gets beaned on it," he remarked.

Nuala took a commercial flight home. Pell returned to Rhode Island on a National Guard plane with Governor John Chafee, who was in Washington on state business.

"I was very appreciative of the governor's offer to give me a ride back," Pell told *The Journal.* "We had a pleasant discussion. We talked about a number of things affecting the state but didn't come to any conclusions."

It was a friendly encounter, despite Chafee's well-known interest in running for Pell's seat.

▫ ▫ ▫ Championed by Pell, the High-Speed Ground Transportation Act of 1965 passed Congress and Johnson signed it into law on September 30. But Pell and LBJ were parting company on another issue: Speaking on November 8, 1965, at St. Francis School in Providence, Pell signaled a break with the president on Vietnam. The autumn brought new protests and troop levels continued to increase. Pell's 1962 fears had materialized: by November 8, more than 2,000 American lives had been lost in Vietnam, nearly 1,800 in 1965 alone.

In his speech at St. Francis School, Pell said he continued to support Johnson's overall policy—but he broke with the president on the bombing of the North.

"It is counter-productive in its political effects, in that it tends to strengthen Communist unity and morale," Pell said. He called for a "systematic, step-by-step plan not only for concluding the military engagement but securing the peace which should follow." He urged negotiations with the Viet Cong and he said he could accept a coalition government with Communists in Vietnam— diplomatic solutions that Johnson opposed.

In January 1966, the Foreign Relations Committee began televised hearings on the war. Led by Arkansas Senator J. William Fulbright, the sessions featured testimony from Secretary of State Dean Rusk and General Maxwell Taylor, former ambassador to South Vietnam and an adviser to the president. Some of the testimony at the hearings, the first full Congressional examination of the war, profoundly disturbed Pell.

"We were shocked by the way they were talking about body counts," he recalled in his 1979 interview. "It reminded me of a Scottish laird laying out the grouse at the end of a day's shoot. We started losing our own humanity and sensitivity as a result of what was going on there. We knew that fingers and ears were being taken as trophies. I have Indian forbears. I'm not proud of the fact that they scalped people, but we were doing almost the same thing in Vietnam."

Pell's presence on TV brought growing visibility, reflected in letters he received—pro and con. Pell had still not completely broken with the president, and as 1966 wore on, he entered his first re-election campaign, against the retired Army general Ruth Briggs. With the nation and his state divided, Pell kept to his public position of general support for the war while supporting efforts for a negotiated peace—and an end to the bombings. He wanted, as he said in his debate with Briggs, "to cool it rather than heat it."

As 1967 unfolded, the tone of the Vietnam debate was changing: the rhetoric had continued to heat and people had taken to the streets and campus greens to protest. On March 17, protestors marched on the Pentagon; a week later, King led a march in Chicago. On April 15, King, joined by Dr. Benjamin Spock and Harry Belafonte, led the largest antiwar demonstration in New York since the war began: a crowd estimated by police at more than 100,000 people (and said by others to be three or four times that) marched from Central Park to the United Nations.

"Hell no, we won't go!" some marchers chanted. Cried others: "Hey, hey, LBJ, how many kids did you kill today?"

In Washington, the war was prompting public criticism from several leading senators, including Mansfield, Idaho's Frank Church, and Robert F. Kennedy, whose much-publicized late-winter Senate address brought public praise from Pell.

The time had come for Pell to proclaim himself unequivocally against the war.

◻ ◻ ◻ In his May 23, 1967, Senate speech, Pell proposed an end to the bombing of the North and a commitment not to increase U.S. forces as a first step toward negotiations resulting in a lasting peace. He proposed "verified free elections" in South Vietnam and an "agreement in principle" to withdraw all American troops after the election, simultaneous with North Vietnam's agreement to withdraw its forces from the south. Pell wanted "immediate release of all political prisoners, amnesty for any political actions in past, and right of asylum for any South Vietnamese wishing it." Finally, he sought "general military neutralization of the whole area."

Fellow senators praised Pell and his speech made major national news, with reports in *The New York Times* and many other newspapers. Pell reprinted it under the Congressional Record banner and sent copies to leading politicians, including Johnson, Vice President Humphrey and U.N. President U Thant — and to anyone who wrote in response to his speech. Many did, and not all agreed with Pell's opposition.

The father of a soldier in Vietnam with a second son who was scheduled to go said he did not like the danger the two boys faced — but that their lives were worth the risk, given the larger peril he saw if North Vietnam succeeded. A Washington resident Raymond P. Flynn sent this letter:

Although you apparently wish it were not so, it is an inescapable fact that the United States is the only great non-Communist power in the world today. This means that while it has the means to prevent it the United States cannot permit the communists to extend their power over other non-communist nations or people. The communists are using every means at their disposal to impose their social and political system on the free people of the world. Their direct confrontation in Korea failed, so they are now using more subtle techniques, such as the fiction that their campaign to take over South Vietnam is an internal revolution. It is worth any price we have to pay to prevent their succeeding.

Pell was gentle but firm in his response:

It seems to me that our differences result from a very basic divergence in judgment regarding the historic evolution of Communism. I can only assure you that my own judgment is based on my experience as a former Foreign Service officer who served behind the Iron Curtain and on my work on the Senate Committee on Foreign Relations. I assure you, also, that I value the challenge of your opposing viewpoint, and hope that we can at least agree to disagree in an honorable way.

Other supporters of the war were not as measured as Flynn in their rebukes of Pell. "We who were doves suffered at the time, in both respect in our communities and politically, and in personal anguish," he said in his 1979 interview. "I was booed and censured by different veterans organizations in [my] state."

Polls confirmed what the 1967 headlines suggested: that Americans were increasingly opposed to the war. Encouraged, Pell believed he could do more than give speeches and write letters. What resulted was an adventure whose spirit was reminiscent of his daring 1939 visit to Gdansk.

On the day after his May 23 Senate speech, Pell flew to Europe to attend the *Pacem in Terris* International Convocation, a gathering in Geneva of peace activists from around the world. Scientist Linus Pauling, winner of the 1954 Nobel Prize in chemistry and the 1962 Nobel Peace Prize, was among those who spoke. Pell's attendance would lend support to the antiwar movement—but he also had clandestine intent.

He was hoping to secretly meet with Mai Van Bo, Hanoi's representative in Paris.

On the morning of May 25, Pell, en route to Geneva, called on John Gunther Dean, a friend who was assigned to the American embassy in Paris. He wanted Dean's help in arranging a meeting with Bo. Two years before, Pell had expressed a desire to sit with Bo, but Johnson's assistant secretary of state for East Asian and Pacific Affairs, William Bundy, had persuaded him not to. This time, Pell was determined.

"Senator is interested in obtaining some reaction from North Vietnamese to his Vietnam speech," Ambassador Charles E. Bohlen wrote in a confidential memo to his State Department superiors on the day Pell met with Dean, who tried to dissuade Pell from contacting Bo. "It appeared to him," Bohlen wrote, "that Mai Van Bo might interpret and publicize senator's initiative as evidence of increasing lack of support for administration's policy and that therefore senator's initiative might harden DRV position and make North Vietnamese persist in their present inflexible policy rather than move Hanoi closer to accepting compromise solution . . . we do not know whether senator will persist in effort to see DRV reps in Paris, but we have made it clear to him that embassy cannot be helpful to him in this field."

Pell did persist. He sent a message to Bo through an old Foreign Service friend, and continued on to Geneva.

On his return to Paris after the *Pacem in Terris* convocation, Pell found no word from Bo. There had been a miscommunication: Bo had accepted Pell's invitation, but his response had not reached Pell. Pell flew back to America.

On June 17, he received a letter from his Foreign Service friend: Bo, the friend wrote, not only was willing to meet with him, he was "desirous" of secretly getting together. Two days later, Pell flew to Paris and talked for an hour and a half with the North Vietnamese delegate, who had postponed a trip home to Hanoi to see Pell. Both Pell and Bo spoke in French. The Senator "thus became the highest level government official in direct communication with an official of the Vietnamese government," Johnson's Senate liaison Mike N. Manatos wrote to Johnson on June 20. Back in Washington, Pell had asked Manatos to arrange a personal briefing of the President.

The briefing was scheduled for July 13, when the President and Senator met in the White House for an off-the-record session. Although Pell had emerged as one of Johnson's more vocal (if polite) critics, the President had not publicly taken Pell to task for his stand. "He was always very fair and very friendly with me," Pell recalled in his 1979 interview. "He knew I disagreed, but he knew that I disagreed within the rules of the game, that I was a good Democrat, and that generally I was supportive of him except for this one area. So I must say that President Johnson only rarely made me feel that he did not approve of me. In general, I would say that he was absolutely correct in his behavior toward me and quite kind."

In their off-the-record conversation, Pell informed the president of Bo's statement that if the bombing of the North were stopped "without condition," Hanoi would be willing to enter into negotiations to end the war. Pell had attempted to get Bo to respond to the specific points of his May 23 speech, but Bo,

Pell told Johnson, said these were issues to be discussed at the conference table. Pell had then advised Bo that if he wished to open a dialogue with the United States, he should begin by talking with Dean — an option that Bo categorically rejected, as long as the bombing continued.

Manatos wrote in his memo to Johnson,

> Bo's motive in seeking the conversation seems obscure. However, it is noteworthy that since mid-May, he has been much more available to unofficial Americans than in the preceding months. He may well have wished to see whether Pell had anything new to offer. But the most likely explanation would be that he wished to convey to a respected "semi-dove" the most forthcoming possible picture of North Vietnamese willingness to talk seriously if we stopped the bombing . . . the fact that Bo had ample time to get instructions from Hanoi before he made the date with Pell clearly indicates that he was speaking with authority.

The president listened without emotion to Pell on that July day and did not accuse the senator of violating the Logan Act, which forbids unauthorized citizens from negotiating with other governments, as Pell feared he might.

"He could not have been more courteous and listened to me most attentively," Pell recalled in his 1979 interview. But Pell's contact with Bo and his off-the-record session did not influence Johnson or the course of the war: the bombing continued, and by the end of 1967, the president had sent nearly a half million troops to Vietnam.

Pell's only regret about meeting Bo, he later recalled, arose from his infamous frugality.

"The thing that burned me up about the trip," Pell declared, "was that since it was not an official trip and I took it secretly and privately, the IRS did not permit me to deduct it — although I was trying to achieve peace for our country."

For all his wealth, Pell remained tight with a dollar.

▫ ▫ ▫ The prospect of peace preoccupied Pell in 1967 and through the remainder of the decade — and not only peace for Vietnam, but the planet.

With its successful detonation of a nuclear weapon, China had joined the Soviet Union (and France and England) in having the bomb, exacerbating Cold War fears. Pell was particularly concerned with the possibility that nations would base nuclear weapons on or in the ocean bed, where they would be difficult for anyone to find — an option with appeal to certain military minds, who sought better protection than silos and B-52 bombers. Inspired in part by the minor role he had played in helping build Congressional support for the Outer Space

Treaty, which the United Nations opened for signature on January 27, 1967 — a treaty that banned weapons in space and was the basis for international space law — Pell wanted a similar pact for the sea. It was a passion that brought him early in his long tenure on the Foreign Relations Committee to chairmanship of its Subcommittee on Arms Control, Oceans, International Operations and Environment.

"I'm not sure whether my life has just naturally revolved around the sea or whether, because I love the sea, I have made my life revolve around it," Pell wrote in the preface to his book *Challenge of the Seven Seas: The fascinating story of man's discovery of new worlds under the sea*, published in 1966, the same year as *Megalopolis Unbound*. *Challenge of the Seven Seas*, written with a collaborator, was a 306-page, wide-ranging look at the world's oceans and their uses, and a prescription for preservation and sustainable development in an age of increasing global pressures. Even before publication of *Seven Seas*, Pell was establishing a reputation as an early environmentalist, a word that would not enter the vernacular until later. His preface continued,

> Whatever the reason, the sea is part of me. As a boy, I sailed on Narragansett Bay and played on the shore. As a man, I enlisted in the U.S. Coast Guard, taking part in patrols and escort duty in the North Atlantic during World War II. On cessation of hostilities, I found myself assigned to reestablishing the Sicilian fishing industries. I take a sailing vacation whenever possible and my home in Newport keeps me close to the sea at other times. The house is built on the Atlantic Ocean, so close that the last hurricane piled the seas on the lawn, where they lapped at the foundation. Now in the Senate, I press for development of the oceans and for Sea Grant College legislation. In hearings, in discussions on the Senate floor, I became convinced that ocean development needs more resources. This book is the result.

As he noted in his preface, Pell had submitted legislation the year before to create university-based centers of excellence in the study, responsible use, and long-term development of America's coastal and ocean resources; the legislation became the National Sea Grant College and Program Act of 1966, which Johnson signed into law that year. Five years later, the University of Rhode Island would be designated one of the first four Sea-Grant colleges, and its Graduate School of Oceanography would become one of the world's foremost, a magnet for researchers and research dollars.

But one nation alone could not be steward of the world's oceans, and the threat from nuclear weapons overshadowed any other. Pell wanted the broader protection that only an international treaty could provide.

In an address on September 5, 1967, to officers at the Newport Naval Base that was covered by the Associated Press, Pell spelled out his concerns.

We are moving toward dangerous legal confrontations with foreign nations over the ownership and jurisdiction of the extraterrestrial sea bed and the super adjacent waters. We stand on the threshold of a vast technological breakthrough which may suddenly advance this nation's—and others'— ability to carry out every type of ocean logic activity, at any depth, and in any area of the ocean. To date, there is no adequate regime to provide for order when this breakthrough comes.

The AP story ended with Pell's belief "that recent agreements with the Soviet Union for peaceful use of Antarctica and outer space led him to hope that a similar declaration might be made on inner space."

Pell elaborated during a later speech at graduation exercises for the Coast Guard's Officer Candidate School.

In this vast area of ocean space, both the sea beds and the water above, there is virtually no law present. Anarchy really exists. If the explorers of one country find a rich deposit of mineral resources on a sea mount, there is nothing to prevent men of another nation coming along, killing its original discoverers, and hijacking the produce. Or, from the viewpoint of disarmament, this 70 percent of the earth covered by ocean is presently virginal when it comes to the installation of nuclear weapons.

Pell introduced Senate Resolution 186, his first draft of what eventually would be known as the Seabed Treaty, on November 17, 1967. The Foreign Relations Committee held hearings, but progress in Congress stalled when the Johnson Administration resisted. The idea, however, had taken root in the United Nations, to which Pell had been named an adviser—and where Pell had a strong ally and friend, Arvid Pardo, Malta's U.N. delegate and Maltese ambassador to America (and driving force behind the later Law of the Sea treaty, a companion pact to the Seabed Treaty).

That December, the U.N. General Assembly named a committee to explore ways to ensure "that the exploration and use of the seabed and the ocean floor should be conducted in accordance with the principles and purposes of the Charter of the United Nations, in the interests of maintaining international peace and security and for the benefit of all mankind." Seabed concerns were brought to the table in 1968 during continuing negotiations at the Geneva-based disarmament talks among 18 nations—and received a boost in March 1969, when President Richard Nixon responded favorably to a Soviet recommendation to embrace a treaty prohibiting all military installations on the ocean floor (submarine-based ballistic missiles were not included). In a letter to Gerard C. Smith, head of the U.S. Arms Control and Disarmament Agency, Nixon wrote of his support for a ban that would "assure that the seabed, man's last frontier, remains free from the nuclear arms race."

On December 7, 1970, the U.N. General Assembly voted 104 to 2 to adopt the Seabed Treaty. Two months later — on February 11, 1971, in simultaneous ceremonies in Washington, London, and Moscow — American, British, and Soviet statesmen joined representatives of dozens of other nations in signing the treaty. At the State Department, President Nixon sat with Secretary of State William P. Rogers to ink the pact, which still required Senate consent to be formally ratified. Nixon and Soviet Premier Aleksei N. Kosygin spoke of their hope that the agreement to prohibit nuclear arms on the ocean floor would encourage negotiators to continue on the path to ending the arms race everywhere on earth, thus making this thaw in the Cold War permanent.

"Speaking for the United States," said Nixon, "I pledge that as we sign this treaty in an era of negotiation, we consider it only one step toward a greater goal: the control of nuclear weapons on earth and the reduction of the danger that hangs over all nations as long as these weapons are not controlled."

New York Times coverage of the signings credited Pell with doggedly moving his country to this historic moment. The article stated,

> The seabed treaty represents the fruits of more than three years of negotiation, principally between the United States and the Soviet Union. The Americans had no formal negotiation position on the problem of exploiting the ocean floor for peaceful purposes but were spurred into adopting one through the prodding of Senator Claiborne Pell of Rhode Island . . . Senator Pell's interest in peaceful exploitation of the seas under international verification began as a young Coast Guard officer in World War II. Mr. Pell and Arvid Pardo, Malta's delegate at the United Nations, are widely credited with having spurred United Nations interest in peaceful uses of the underseas areas of the world.

A year later, the Foreign Relations Committee reported the treaty out of committee with a recommendation that the full Senate give its consent. Speaking from the Senate floor on February 15, 1972, Pell said:

> It is true that the United States and the Soviet Union have not deployed any weapons systems which the treaty would prohibit and no such weapons have yet been actively produced. But such weapons were on the drawing boards.

While an actual arms race in this environment has not yet started, this does not mean that one could never start. Indeed, the developments of technology have already brought into focus some possible applications of nuclear weaponry on the seabed. Consideration has apparently been given to the feasibility of placing remote-controlled missiles off the coast of target states, and even to the possibility of underwater ABM systems.

Furthermore, a futuristic seagoing tank — appropriately called a "creepy crawler" — has received widespread attention. While these weapons systems are now prohibited under the treaty, there is no guarantee that man's ingenuity could not contrive new, equally clever means of wreaking destruction from the ocean floor. Indeed, our experience with military technology and the arms race suggests the contrary — if they are not banned, some such contraptions will ultimately be invented and sold. This treaty will substantially eliminate the incentive to pursue research programs in this direction.

Funds for such programs, Pell believed, were better spent on people.

Three months after Pell spoke, on May 18, 1972, the Seabed Treaty entered into force when the U.S., Britain, the Soviet Union, and several other nations deposited instruments of ratification. Pell often called Pell Grants his most important achievement — but less remembered was his assertion that the Seabed Treaty was equally momentous.

"It removed 70 percent of earth's surface from the implantation of nuclear weapons," he said in a 1996 television interview. "It is an abstruse subject, but it means that more than two-thirds of the earth's surfaces would not have nuclear weapons implanted on them."

MAI VAN BO

Democratic presidential candidate Eugene McCarthy, a strident Vietnam peace proponent, stunned the political world on March 12, 1968, when he won 42 percent of the vote in the New Hampshire primary — just seven points behind Johnson, whose prosecution of the war had overshadowed his many Great Society domestic initiatives and bitterly divided the Democratic Party. The president knew he would have a difficult time, at best, at the August Democratic National Convention — and when the popular Robert F. Kennedy, another antiwar senator and heir-apparent to the Camelot legacy of his brother, announced his candidacy on March 16, Johnson's odds of renomination grew longer still. Two weeks later, a Gallup Poll showed the president's popularity at an all-time low: only 36 percent of Americans approved of his overall performance, a drop of five points in just four weeks.

On March 31, Johnson addressed the nation on Vietnam. As a sign of his willingness to negotiate, he said he was stopping air strikes over most of Vietnam.

"Our purpose in this action is to bring about a reduction in the level of violence that now exists," the president said. "It is to save the lives of brave men — and to save the lives of innocent women and children. It is to permit the contending forces to move closer to a political settlement. And tonight, I call upon the United Kingdom and I call upon the Soviet Union — as cochairmen of the Geneva Conferences, and as permanent members of the United Nations Security Council — to do all they can to move from the unilateral act of de-escalation that I have just announced toward genuine peace in Southeast Asia."

Johnson continued for several minutes on Vietnam, and then he began to speak of his country.

There is division in the American house now. There is divisiveness among us all tonight. And holding the trust that is mine, as President of all the people, I cannot disregard the peril to the progress of the American people and the hope and the prospect of peace for all peoples. So, I would ask all Americans, whatever their personal interests or concern, to guard against divisiveness and all its ugly consequences.

Fifty-two months and ten days ago, in a moment of tragedy and trauma, the duties of this office fell upon me. I asked then for your help and God's, that we might continue America on its course, binding up our wounds, healing our history, moving forward in new unity, to clear the American agenda and to keep the American commitment for all of our people. United we have kept that commitment. United we have enlarged that commitment. Through all time to come, I think America will be a stronger nation, a more just society, and a land of greater opportunity and fulfillment because of what we have all done together in these years of unparalleled achievement.

Our reward will come in the life of freedom, peace, and hope that our children will enjoy through ages ahead. What we won when all of our people united just must not now be lost in suspicion, distrust, selfishness, and politics among any of our people. Believing this as I do, I have concluded that I should not permit the Presidency to become involved in the partisan divisions that are developing in this political year. With America's sons in the fields far away, with America's future under challenge right here at home, with our hopes and the world's hopes for peace in the balance every day, I do not believe that I should devote an hour or a day of my time to any personal partisan causes or to any duties other than the awesome duties of this office — the Presidency of your country.

Accordingly, I shall not seek, and I will not accept, the nomination of my party for another term as your President.

Johnson's surprise decision stunned the nation and left Democrats to choose between two politically similar candidates, McCarthy and Kennedy.

Pell threw his support behind Kennedy almost immediately. But the possibility of a second act of Camelot ended when Kennedy was assassinated on June 4, after winning the California primary.

"We couldn't believe it," Nuala Pell would say many years later. "We wondered what had happened to America."

The death of a second Kennedy brother by assassin's bullet was the latest tragedy in a year of unrelenting violence. Martin Luther King, Jr., had been shot and killed two months before, and his assassination had touched off rioting in dozens of cities. In Vietnam, the Tet Offensive and the fighting that ensued continued to raise the American death toll. The year 1967 had ended with 11,153 deaths, the most to that point in the war — and 1968 was on track to be the deadliest year, with 16,592 American lives lost by December 31, when the total for the war since its beginning surpassed 36,000 American lives. Popular support for the war continued to tumble.

As the riot-torn 1968 Democratic National Convention approached, Pell continued with his public criticism of the war. He worked for a peace platform — and campaigned, quietly and without encouragement from the national party or Humphrey, for consideration as the Democratic candidate for vice president.

The literature that he circulated to Democrats and the press echoed his unsuccessful 1964 vice presidential nomination bid.

"Has television charisma," read one of the ten points of appeal in a background paper distributed to the press on August 10, two weeks before the Chicago convention. "Youth," read another. "Family. Wife, Nuala, is attractive, friendly and willing campaigner. Four children between 15 and 22," read a third point. "Pell has been identified with Kennedy wing of Democratic Party and as such would bring much of the Kennedy luster to the national ticket." The backgrounder mentioned Pell's father, noting that Herbert was not only a congressman but a friend of FDR, and his great-great granduncle George M. Dallas, Democratic vice president "whose father was co-founder of Democratic Party."

Four years after his first effort to be nominated for vice president, Pell had more substantial accomplishments to offer. In the literature he distributed, Pell listed the National Foundation on the Arts and Humanities Act of 1965, his passenger-rail initiatives, and the National Sea Grant College and Program Act of 1966. "Pioneer in oceanology, arts and humanities, high speed ground transportation," the paper read. He emphasized his foreign-policy experience and his view on the most pressing foreign-policy issue of the era: "Dove approach," the paper read. "Has long been outspoken advocate of de-escalating war in Vietnam and seeking a negotiated peace."

A story in *The Providence Journal* on the eve of the Chicago convention described Pell's possible appeal to Humphrey: "His connections to the Kennedy family, his association with big city programs and his position as a wealthy member of the Eastern Establishment."

But the Humphrey camp had sent no signal that they wanted Pell, and the *Journal* story noted his liabilities. "Senator Pell is not well-known nationally and is from a state which has four electoral votes. Thus he figures only peripherally in the speculation. Ahead of him on the list are such senators as Fred Harris of Oklahoma and Edmund S. Muskie of Maine."

In typically reserved fashion, Pell professed only to being "a little bit active" in seeking the nomination. "One cannot run for the vice president," he said; one had to be asked, or so Pell maintained. Humphrey, who favored Muskie, the eventual vice-presidential nominee, gave no sign of interest.

As delegates headed off to Chicago, Pell's last, tentative run for higher office collapsed.

"Asked about the Pell candidacy, a source prominent in the Humphrey camp said that whenever Mr. Humphrey thinks about an Eastern liberal, Sen. Edmund Muskie of Maine is the man," *The Providence Journal* wrote. "Senator Pell's only public backing so far has come from Rhode Island business executive and loyal Democrat G. William Miller, president of Textron, and even that may have slightly embarrassed Mr. Pell, who is not committed to a presidential choice since Mr. Miller also announced that he supports Mr. Humphrey for president."

The *Journal* story noted that Pell's ambition had been covered by *The New York Times* and the *Los Angeles Times* and traced its beginnings to a syndicated column in the August 2 *Washington Star* by "Clayton Fritchey, an old friend of Mr. Pell." The story ended with a blunt, if correct, assessment of Pell's legislative style, which was informed but gentlemanly, sometimes to his detriment.

"After eight years in the Senate," *The Star* wrote, "the junior senator from Rhode Island has established himself as an expert on foreign relations and on selected domestic problems. But so far, he has not been seen by his colleagues as one of the up-and-coming younger liberals like Fred Harris or Ted Kennedy or Ed Muskie, who do the hard chores, handle themselves capably on the floor and in horse-trading on bills, and have enough of a grasp of the uses of the Senate to be talked of in the cloakroom and the press gallery as future leaders of that body."

Pell returned from Chicago without the nomination — but with a continued commitment to opposing the war while supporting peace negotiations, which had formally started in Paris in May when Xuan Thuy, leader of the North Vietnamese delegation, sat down with U.S. Ambassador-at-Large Averell Harriman, whose short-lived presidential aspirations had drawn Pell into his first national campaign many years before.

November 1968 brought victory for Nixon and running mate Spiro Agnew, and when they assumed office in January 1969, they took leadership of a nation torn by protests and counter-protests. Pell's own opposition to the war intensified in 1969, notably in a June 17 Senate speech and the October 14 introduction of a resolution calling for all combat troops to leave Vietnam by December 31, 1970 (and for the termination of the Gulf of Tonkin Resolution by that date). Pell's cosponsor was New York Republican Jacob Javits, a fellow member of the Foreign Relations Committee and Pell's ally on many earlier initiatives, including the National Endowments. The Pell-Javits resolution, one of several introduced that fall, failed to pass the Sentae.

Part of an international series of events during that period, the Moratorium to End the War in Vietnam brought millions of people onto American streets, including a march on Washington on November 15, 1969, that drew hundreds of thousands and ended with police tear-gassing demonstrators.

▫ ▫ ▫ According to a January 28, 1970, Gallup Poll, 65 percent of Americans approved of Nixon's policy of Vietnamization, under which South Vietnam would take increasing responsibility for the war as Nixon drew down American forces. But the president's announcement on April 30 that U.S. forces had invaded Cambodia brought global outrage and protests unlike any before, in America and abroad. Pell did not march, but he called the invasion a "tragic mistake." He urged the United Nations to step in.

On May 4, National Guardsmen fired at a crowd of students protesting the war at Ohio's Kent State University. They killed four, including twenty-year-old Jeffrey Miller, who was photographed lying dead on the ground with fourteen-year-old Mary Ann Vecchio kneeling by his side in profound anguish. The photograph would bring the Pulitzer Prize for journalist John Filo — and would be published around the world, becoming one of the iconic photographs of the war, along with Associated Press photographer Nick Ut's shot of a Vietnamese girl burned by a napalm attack. Bodies of Americans had been coming home in flag-draped coffins and now innocent American blood had been shed in America.

The day after Kent State, Pell took the Senate floor.

"It is a wrong war," he said. "Some of us have opposed it for years. Usually we are calm and quiet but my voice rises in anger and anguish because I feel this war is based on wrong moral premises. It is the war in Vietnam that is alienating the younger generation—in fact, our whole way of life. It has resulted in increasing inflation, interest rates, unemployment, violent crime, disturbances on campuses, and most important, the death of 40,000 American youths as well as countless Vietnamese." These were unflinching words.

Two weeks later, Pell spoke to students at Providence College in Rhode Island. He urged opponents of the war to reject violence and work within the political system to end the conflict. Some of the students criticized him stingingly, with one saying that Pell had put forth only "symbolic" actions and that he had chosen "political expediency over moral expediency." Pell acknowledged his own belief that the democratic process was the best course—but said he understood the students' frustration.

A week later, Pell and Javits introduced another Senate resolution calling for all American combat troops to leave Vietnam by the end of the year, and for funding of most military operations in the country to also end by that time. Similar to their autumn 1969 resolution, this latest try also failed. But the "dove" faction within the Senate now numbered about three dozen, and their ranks were growing. They joined other Senate colleagues on June 24 in voting to approve a nonbinding resolution repealing the Gulf of Tonkin Resolution, which gave the President authority to conduct the war.

Pell continued his high-profile opposition to the newly broadened conflict on June 29, when he made a major presentation to the Senate during debate over an End The War resolution offered by Oregon Republican Mark Hatfield and South Dakota Democrat George McGovern, an early opponent of the war who had run unsuccessfully for his party's presidential nomination in 1968 and would be the nominee in 1972.

"I believe there is only one way to get out of Southeast Asia," Pell said,

and that is to accept the fact that the damage caused by our continued military presence there to our true national interests and to our economy and social structure far outweighs the questionable advantages that result to our national interest by maintaining the corrupt, inept Thieu-Ky government in South Vietnam or even of maintaining the division of Vietnam into two countries. When we have accepted that fact, we should firmly carry out the resulting decisions as best we can, recognizing the fact, as France did in 1954, that the decisions may well result in a unified Vietnam under Hanoi. If the President and Executive Branch will not make this decision, then I believe we in Congress should make it and require the Executive Branch to implement it. It would be more orderly if the President made it himself, but if he does not, then we in Congress who feel as I do have no alternative but to support the McGovern-Hatfield "End the War" resolution or a similar one.

The Hatfield-McGovern resolution failed, but Pell's prominence during testimony earned him editorial praise in several newspapers and an invitation to appear on NBC's top-rated morning *Today* show, which opened the floodgates to letters and calls from people across the nation to his office. The White House and Pentagon were also following Congressional debate carefully—but one who was following Pell had unusual self-interest.

After the surprising loss of his 1968 gubernatorial reelection bid, John Chafee had been named Secretary of the Navy by Nixon. The job had not dimmed his desire to one day be Senator. A past chairman of the Republican Governor's Association, Chafee would likely have the blessing of his national party when the time was right. And that time, the party reasoned, would be 1972, when Pell, completing his second term, faced reelection.

On the day after Pell's June 29 speech, during a Washington press conference the Navy Secretary called after returning from a ten-day trip to Vietnam and other Southeast Asian nations, a *Providence Journal* reporter asked for Chafee's reaction to Pell's End The War resolution comments.

"I find it difficult to understand why anybody would take that position when we've had the experience of a unified North Korea and what that's meant to our country," Chafee said. "They've been shooting down our aircraft and seizing our ships." He referred to North Korea's January 1968 seizure of the Navy vessel *Pueblo*, whose crew was held in captivity until the end of that year.

It would not be the last time Chafee would rebuke Pell over Vietnam.

"The differences between Mr. Pell and the Secretary of the Navy on the war issue are of interest to observers here," *The Providence Journal* wrote, "since many regard it as highly likely that Mr. Chafee may seek the Rhode Island Senator's seat in the 1972 election."

And he would, in the first true challenge to a man who after two terms was becoming a Rhode Island institution.

▫ ▫ ▫ The autumn of 1970 saw Nixon reducing America's involvement in Vietnam. The year would close with 334,600 American troops in Vietnam, the smallest force since 1965. American deaths for the year would total 6,081, also the lowest since 1965.

But the war was not over, and Pell was not done. The fate of American prisoners still held in North Vietnam and soldiers listed as missing in action now concerned him. He had addressed the Senate on the POW issue in August—and now, as he had three years before, he set off on another solo mission, this time to meet Xuan Thuy.

They talked privately for ninety minutes on September 23 at the North Vietnamese compound in Paris, where the Peace Talks, begun in 1968, continued.

Pell told Thuy that, as Senator, he had no direct role in negotiations and was only interested in the welfare of Americans held prisoner. Pell gave Thuy a copy of a speech on the POW issue that he had given on August 5 in the Senate. According to the confidential report Pell later sent to the State Department, Thuy assured him that POWs were being treated properly.

"Thuy stated that prisoners were treated in a humane way," Pell wrote, "permitted to play chess, to play musical instruments, and to go to church. He said that they were permitted to communicate at will through the 'committee of liaison.'"

Pell disagreed with Thuy: what he had learned had led him to believe that American POWs were being treated inhumanely. In his State Department report, he wrote:

> I reiterated to him that those opposed to the war and those supporting the war were united in their feeling with regard to the bad treatment on the part of the North Vietnamese government toward prisoners of war and that I would have thought his government would have seen their policy of maltreating prisoners of war is strengthening those who support the war in the United States. I said that if North Vietnam released every one of their prisoners immediately, they would have removed one of the primary elements of support for our present policy vis-à-vis North Vietnam.

A visit to North Vietnam, Pell said, might disclose the truth. He offered to go himself, provided the Nixon Administration approved. Thuy, according to Pell's report, "said that he would report these suggestions to his government and re-emphasized that it was exceptional on his part to be willing to discuss prisoners of war with a visitor. When I opened the door for him, saying, 'Is there any point you would like to present on any other subject,' he did not have much to add."

The State Department encouraged Pell's initiative, and Pell followed his visit with a letter to Thuy thanking him for his time and repeating his desire to visit North Vietnam accompanied by a medical doctor, a Senate staff assistant, and Rita Hauser, the American representative to the U.N. Human Rights Commission. Pell told Thuy that he had not disclosed their visit to the press "since this seems the most responsible course."

On November 6, Pell testified on the POW issue before the United Nations. Then he flew to Paris, where he hoped to meet again with Thuy. For four days, he tried by telephone to arrange a meeting with the chief delegate; for four days, Thuy's staff said Thuy was too busy.

Finally, the North Vietnamese arranged for Pell to meet, once more, with Mai Van Bo.

They talked for an hour and a half, without progress: Bo repeated Thuy's contention that American POWs were being treated fairly, and Pell again disputed that. Pell presented Bo with a letter and list of POWs and soldiers missing in action in Southeast Asia, which he asked Bo to deliver to Hanoi.

As the meeting wound down, Bo asked Pell to keep their session out of the news. In his report to the State Department, Pell wrote: "He said that in order to preserve the private nature of our conversation (he referred to our old acquaintanceship several times in the course of our conversation), it would be better not to mention my visit to the press and left me with the inference that it could harm our relationship if it did." Pell agreed.

The meeting had started at noon.

"Finally, at 1:30 p.m.," Pell wrote, "we parted company on cordial terms, but without much sense of accomplishment."

HIGHER EDUCATION

When Pell took the Senate floor on February 22, 1972, to urge passage of what he would later deem his most important legislative accomplishment, he was no longer the novice who had arrived in Washington fresh from elections he had won on youthful promise.

He was beginning his twelfth year in Congress, and his seniority had brought him, in 1969, chairmanship of the Labor and Public Welfare Committee's Education Subcommittee. He had a bipartisan record of joining with key Senators from both sides of the aisle to advance major legislation, and while by nature he did not enjoy the conflict sometimes required in reaching legislative compromise, he accepted the reality of Washington, which could be contentious. He was a man of ideas who now had experience in translating some of them into action on the Senate floor. Managing the legislation he was addressing on that late-winter day would prove more challenging than anything he had experienced in Congress.

In its broad terms, the Higher Education Act of 1972 was a $20-billion assistance package to America's colleges and universities that had appeal to many Republicans and Democrats alike. Unlike previous bills, which provided assistance to specific school programs, this legislation would give schools the unrestricted funds their leaders said they desperately needed for general operations. A provision of the bill would correct what Pell and others saw as a flaw of the 1965 act and the 1968 reauthorizations — a flaw by which grants to students were determined by individual schools, not by the financial need of the student regardless of which college she or he attended. Through a program he was already describing as "Pell Grants" (he used quotation marks) in letters to constituents, Pell proposed that any student at any college who needed help should get it — and that a federal formula, not individual ones set by individual schools, be used in awarding the money.

But the education act had become entangled in a bitter national debate about busing as a means to desegregate racially divided schools. The House was on record in opposition to busing, and many senators concurred.

In his speech, Pell recapped the debate that had unfolded in the Senate and House so far, and he outlined the compromise on busing that he and Senate leaders proposed. He expressed his hope that busing would not bring the bill down, as many feared it would in an election year in which race would be a dominant — and intensely divisive — issue throughout much of the country.

"I would like to say that this education bill is really one of the major pieces of legislation to be considered by this Congress," Pell said. "The Carnegie Commission on Education has characterized the higher education bill as the most important piece of legislation to be put before the country since the passage of the Morrill Land Grant Act of 1862. I would hope that we would not lose sight of the deep foundation of this legislation as we discuss the question of busing, which is extraneous to the higher education bill."

Javits, Pell's Republican ally and friend, joined Pell in urging colleagues not to let the busing issue derail "a magnificent bill" and he praised Pell for his long support of education and work on this 1972 legislation. "I express my satisfaction to the chairman of the subcommittee and I pay tribute to the nobility of his effort and to the skill he has brought to the bill to the point where a bill will be passed by the Senate. I know perhaps better than anyone else of his decisive contribution to the various matters before us and the highly constructive legislation for the education of the young people of our country."

Pell, in turn, thanked Javits. "To have worked with him as a team has been very good," Pell said. "This bill has been reported with a minimum of partisanship and working together we have a bill of which we are very proud."

Pell struck a note of harmony, but the next three months would be anything but harmonious.

▫ ▫ ▫ Pell's interest as a Senator in financial aid to college students dated to the first weeks of his first term, when he joined twelve cosponsors in introducing the bill that would have established the scholarship program that Kennedy asked for in the $5.2-billion education package he proposed in February 1961.

The scholarship program was defeated, but Pell had staked out his signature cause. He believed, as he would state many times, that every American has "a right to a college education." He was determined to realize a vision that had taken root in his World War II Coast Guard days, when he, a prep school– and Ivy League–educated man of means, had lived for the first time with working people as a peer, not someone who knew them only as nannies and tutors.

Senator Jack Reed, the son of a janitor, many years later would recall how the Senator he succeeded in 1997 harbored no illusions about how privilege, and not merit alone, had allowed him a premium education.

"He got to Princeton—and I think he was very frank—because he had a name, he had the connections, and he had the resources to go to the right prep school," Reed said.

But Pell had graduated with a different perspective than many of his classmates. "As I said in his eulogy," Reed said, "here's someone who made a conscious decision in 1941 to enter the Coast Guard as an enlisted person, on a ship—with other folks, none of them from Princeton and those places. He not only wanted to be part of this great endeavor, on the ground floor if you will—but also he learned a great deal about people not just from his social circle, but people from a whole spectrum. He saw, particularly during the war, a bunch of very, very smart people who had more talent probably than some of his colleagues at Princeton but they would never have the resources [for a college degree] or the universities would never be receptive.

"And then he saw the G.I. Bill, which was a transformative event. Really, that began to just confirm what he saw intuitively or viscerally: that you have these very talented people who just got out of high school and they can fix anything on this boat, they can draw plans, they can do all these things—but if they don't get a college degree, they're going to be in these entry-level or nonsupervisory jobs. That, together with the success of the G.I. Bill, gave him a legislative model and the instincts to do it."

Vice President Joe Biden, who became a close friend of Pell during their twenty-four years together in the Senate, attributed Pell's passion for education to something instinctive in the man.

"My mom had this expression," Biden said, "She said if someone has the ability to sort of instinctively know something or know what's troubling or concerning or motivating someone else—she always said, 'you know, Joey, so-and-so has that sixth sense.' Our five senses, plus one, the one you can't define. And

Claiborne sort of had that sixth sense. Claiborne never was confused about the fact that there wasn't a single black woman living in the ghetto who didn't dream about her son going to college. How he got it I don't know, but he got it. He knew it. Yet if he had to talk to and relate to that woman, it was not the ability to hug her and to empathize with her and to communicate that he understood her plight or her aspirations, but he knew. And he acted on that certitude.

"It sounds corny, like 'oh, Claiborne really *did* think all men are created equal. Some went to Groton, but all men were created equal.' But there was this notion that everyone's entitled to have a shot. That was the thing about him — and maybe I shouldn't have said it at the eulogy — but that was the thing about him that separated him from other very wealthy old-money, patrician, noblesse-oblige school of leaders that I've met in my career."

◻ ◻ ◻ Although lacking the seniority in the early 1960s to advance major legislation, Pell had lent his support to a number of education initiatives, including expansion of vocational training. His passion for the subject was rewarded in 1963 with his appointment to the Education Subcommittee. The next year, Pell followed the progress of the task force that Johnson named to study the role the federal government should play in expanding financial assistance to college students, among other education issues.

Chaired by John W. Gardner, who would become Johnson's Secretary of Health, Education and Welfare, and assisted by senior domestic policy aid Joseph Califano, Jr., who would hold the same post under President Jimmy Carter, the task force gave Johnson the foundation he would need in realizing his own ambition of opening college to everyone. It was an ambition he touched on during his September 28, 1964, address at Brown University, which Pell attended — the address in which he put his support behind a national endowment for the arts and humanities.

"At the desk where I sit in Washington," Johnson said, "I have learned one great truth: The answer for all of our national problems, the answer for all the problems of the world, comes down, when you really analyze it, to one single word: education . . . Universal, free, public education is the very foundation upon which our entire society rests today. So our goal must be to open the doors to education beyond the high school to all young Americans, regardless of station or the station of their families."

The task force concluded that a substantial number of high school students who wanted to continue on to college were restrained by financial considerations. That conclusion was reinforced by a study that showed that one of six high school students who took the National Merit Scholarship test did not go to college; of the one-sixth who did not, a majority of those whose families could contribute only $300 or less to their child's education said they would have attended college if they'd been able to afford it. To Johnson, that was an unacceptable end to a young person's ambition — and a waste of human capital that the nation in an increasingly sophisticated age needed.

The president incorporated the task force's recommendations in legislation he submitted in 1965 to Congress, with Senator Morse and representative Edith Green of Oregon as the primary sponsors. The Higher Education Act of 1965, Public Law 89–329, reflected the belief of Johnson and others who shared his Great Society vision that a college education should be an American birthright for anyone wanting one, just as a high school diploma had been accepted as a birthright decades before. Not everyone agreed: some citizens and their elected officials feared that increased federal aid to education would mean forced in-tegration (through busing, for example), money for private (mainly Catholic) schools, and intrusive (i.e., Communist) government control of people's lives — the "Three Rs" of race, religion and Reds, as some called it. The landmark Civil Rights Act of 1964 had outlawed racial segregation of schools, among other discriminatory practices, but prejudice persisted, and not just in the South, as the 1972 Congressional debate over busing would illustrate.

On October 20, 1965, Pell had joined other senators in the voice vote that sent the House version of the Higher Education Act of 1965 on to Johnson for his signature. The $2.3-billion act, which would require reauthorization after three years, provided greater federal support for college- and university-based community-service programs and libraries, establishment of a Teachers Corps, and funds for construction of educational facilities. Title IV of the act provided financial assistance — grants and federally insured loans — to needy college students from all walks of life. A student no longer had to be a veteran (eligible for the G.I. Bill) or be pursuing a specific course of study (such as math and science, where help was available from the National Defense Education Act) to qualify for higher-education aid.

Johnson was recovering from gall bladder surgery and did not sign the bill until November 8, 1965, when he went to Southwest Texas State College (now Texas State University), his alma mater, for the ceremony. In his remarks, he praised Congress for its passage not only of the higher-education bill but of his other Great Society measures, among them the establishment of Medicare, the creation of the national endowments, the Voting Rights Act of 1965 and the Ele-mentary and Secondary Education Act of 1965, all signed into law by Johnson during the 1965 calendar year.

"Too many people, for too many years, argued that education and health and human welfare were not the Government's concern," Johnson said. "And while they spoke, our schools fell behind, our sick people went unattended, and our poor fell deeper into despair. But now, at last, in this year of our Lord, 1965, we have quit talking and started acting. The roots of change and reform are spreading, not just throughout Washington, but throughout every community in every State of this great Nation."

With the stroke of a pen, the president said, a new era in education was opening. He went on,

> In a very few moments, I will put my signature on the Higher Education Act of 1965. The President's signature upon this legislation passed by this Congress will swing open a new door for the young people of America. For them, and for this entire land of ours, it is the most important door that will ever open — the door to education. And this legislation is the key which unlocks it.
>
> To thousands of young men and women, this act means the path of knowledge is open to all that have the determination to walk it. It means a way to deeper personal fulfillment, greater personal productivity, and increased personal reward. This bill, which I will make law, is an incentive to stay in school. It means that a high school senior anywhere in this great land of ours can apply to any college or any university in any of the 50 States and not be turned away because his family is poor.

The new program of Educational Opportunity Grants indeed opened a college education to more financially needy students — but it contained a provision that Pell disliked, which limited a student's choices. Under the EOG formula, federal funds were appropriated to the states based on the ratio of a state's full-time college students to the total number of such students in the country; the states then allocated the money to each college or university, which in turn allocated them to individual students.

The final decision on which student received what size grant was thus left to each school — meaning that two students of equal need could receive different levels of assistance. In some cases, the student receiving less aid might be forced to forgo college.

Pell was determined to change the inherent inequities of the formula, but in 1965, he did not yet have the stature to lead the charge.

▫ ▫ ▫ Out of public view, Pell was receiving encouragement in his ambition to broaden opportunities for a college education. Among those who were influential was Ray Nelson, who had left his reporter's job to become his press secretary in 1960, when his Senate candidacy seemed Quixotic to many. Nelson was now his trusted administrative assistant.

Born in 1921, Nelson himself had never been to college. Grandson of Swedish immigrants and the son of a housewife and a third-grade dropout who became a mechanic and advocated reading as a key to success, Nelson graduated from high school and took jobs as an orderly and a factory worker before joining the Navy and serving in World War II. A newspaper career appealed to him. Out of the service, he briefly took a job in the mailroom of *The New York Times*, then became a dictationist at *The Providence Journal* in 1946. In 1947, he was promoted to reporter, a position he kept until 1960, when Pell, having been turned down by others who believed he had no chance of winning, hired him.

"I don't believe he ever considered going to college," his son, David C. Nelson, recalled. "He had both admiration and disdain for higher education, believing he was as smart as any college graduate. This may have been a class thing, because he always identified himself as a 'peasant,' and my grandfather referred to the 'upper crust' as 'a bunch of crumbs, held together by a little dough.' They almost lost their home several times during the Depression and were very traumatized during that period."

Recognizing the complexities of the new world that his children would inherit convinced Nelson of the value of a college degree, and he brought that perspective to his boss in their discussions. Like Pell, Nelson saw a model in the G.I. Bill.

Son David recalled a conversation from 1965, when education had become such a prominent part of Johnson's Great Society vision: "He was sitting on the couch in the living room and reading one of the six to eight books he got weekly from the library. He said something to the effect that I really needed to go to college. I responded that he hadn't gone to college, so why should I? He explained that not going wasn't an option anymore, that if I wanted a fulfilling and well paying job, that I had to get a college degree.

"He then stated that he had discussed with Senator Pell the idea of proposing legislation that would help families who couldn't afford to pay for tuition for their children to attend college. He was very clear that it would be a grant and not a loan. I remember asking if I would be eligible, as I didn't have the money to attend college. He said something like 'Don't be a smart-ass. I'll pay but you are damn sure going to work while you attend school.'"

In 1966, Pell joined Senate and House colleagues in unanimously passing the Veterans Readjustment Benefits Act, which broadened Roosevelt's 1944 G.I. Bill to offer education assistance and other benefits to veterans who had served since the Korean War, whether they had been to war or not.

The next year, Pell introduced a bill that would provide grants of up to $1,000 a year to students, regardless of need, who were in their first two years of post-secondary school study. Calling it the first step toward "extending the range of free and universal education" beyond high school and "the first line of defense against the mounting avalanche of educational costs for millions of families," Pell said that his 1967 Higher Education Scholarship Act would cost $3.3 billion annually, according to an estimate prepared for him by the Department of Health, Education and Welfare.

"Astronomical as it may seem," he said, "I believe that this is the sort of public commitment which is going to have to be made if we are going to make the best possible use of our national manpower and open new doors of opportunity to all citizens alike, whether they come from the ghetto or the suburbs."

The national interest would be served with a more highly educated work-force, Pell believed—and also the individual, whose mind would be enriched. Pell said that his program would result in a better-educated citizen who would make choices "be they political or commercial on a rational rather than an emotional level."

Listening, one could hear an echo of his father, who was ruled by logic.

The Higher Education Scholarship Act did not clear the Senate; with the costs of the Vietnam War bleeding resources from already-established domestic programs, one with significant additional cost had little chance of passage.

Pell voted in 1968 to reauthorize the Higher Education Act, which amended provisions of the 1965 legislation, although not by establishing the more equitable granting formula that he sought. But Pell would soon be in a position to champion change. He had been a loyal Democrat, in office for eight years, and party leaders rewarded him at the start of the 1969 session with the chairmanship of the Education Subcommittee.

In one of his first moves as chairman, Pell introduced an amendment to the 1965 act to provide college scholarships "as a matter of right" to all needy students, not just those selected by colleges receiving federal aid according to the 1965 formula. And the way to provide it, he maintained, was to create a calculation that entitled a student to a certain amount of aid minus the amount his or her parents paid on federal income taxes—a calculation he deemed a fair assessment of need, since taxes paid were an indication of a family's financial situation. The idea had come to him over the winter, while he was skiing during a vacation in the Alps. He wrote his notes on a placemat, and when he returned to Washington, directed the subcommittee staff to fashion a bill.

Staff drafted an amendment under which any student could receive $1,200 in aid, minus the amount parents paid in federal income taxes; the neediest students, under this formula, would receive the full amount, enough to cover costs at most public and private two- and four-year universities. Another provision of Pell's proposed amendment would give colleges a $1,000 grant for every scholarship student who was attending the institution, an enticement to abandon the existing formula, which rewarded certain schools over others.

"It is time for us to recognize the role that our government must take to insure that a higher education is available to all who are capable of assimilating it," Pell said from the Senate floor.

The amendment did not pass. But Pell was chairman now. No longer could he be viewed as merely another outspoken dove or the driving force behind the National Endowments, whose constituency was not nearly as broad as education. No longer could he be dismissed, as he was by some, as the quirky patrician politician who wanted America to go metric, and who preferred trains over jets. At a time when public education was in the forefront of the national dialogue, his name was now increasingly associated with it.

"Seniority early this year brought him to the position of chairman of the education subcommittee, by custom the primary spokesman in the Senate on education issues," wrote *The Providence Journal*. "He becomes the educational spokesman at a time of unprecedented upheavals in the field, making the Rhode Islander's first major subcommittee chairmanship the most difficult test of his Senate career. The issue of violence on college campuses and in the high schools is on full boil. The financial squeeze on school systems grows at every level and administrators cry for help. Administrative problems abound."

Pell, the paper declared, now had a prominent platform—but no reputation for the bargaining often required to move legislation. Good with forging alliances, he was largely unproven in battle with tough adversaries.

"It is a new role for the Rhode Islander, now in his second term in the Senate," *The Journal* wrote:

His record thus far has been marked by the sponsorship of legislation on high-speed ground transportation, oceanography, a study of the metric system and a new commission on the arts and humanities. He has done this slowly and patiently, courteously and with an almost painful diffidence, letting the merits of a bill speak for itself and often stepping aside for another senator to push the legislation through. As a result, he is regarded with a sort of vague goodwill by his colleagues. But most observers agree they have not really taken him seriously.

On education, they soon would.

In 1970, Pell successfully managed nearly two weeks of contentious debate over anti-busing provisions in an unprecedented $35-billion aid-to-education bill, winning a compromise with southern Senators who opposed integration of public schools that led to unanimous passage of the bill — and earning praise from a skeptical press.

"Sen. Claiborne Pell was predisposed to roll with the punches when he stepped onto the Senate floor two weeks ago as manager of the largest education bill in the history of Congress," *The Journal* wrote. "Last night, after eight exhausting days of debate, he was still on his feet — and the bill was passed."

Pell's performance impressed reporters: this low-key man who shunned conflict seemed to have found a knack for horse-trading. Less notice was given to what was becoming an annual ritual for Pell: introduction of legislation that would provide grants directly to needy college students, a method modeled after the G.I. Bill, whose benefits were not determined by individual colleges considering the applications of individual students.

Pell in 1970 again proposed grants of $1,200, minus what the student's parents paid in income taxes. Under the formula, a student from a family with an income of less than $3,000 (nearly $17,400 in 2011 dollars) would get the full amount. Families with incomes between $6,000 and $7,500 would qualify for a $630 grant, and families with incomes up to $12,000 would get some aid. Depending on the school, the poorest students would be able to attend college for free: in 1970, average tuition (and required fees, excluding room and board) for a public four-year university was $480, and it was $1,980 for a private four-year school, according to a study by the Congressional Budget Office.

But once more, Pell's proposal failed to clear Congress. In 1971, he resubmitted his idea with a bill that provided up to $1,400 a year in grants. He found support from fellow subcommitteemen Ted Kennedy, Walter Mondale of Minnesota, Thomas J. Eagleton of Missouri, all Democrats, and Republican Javits, among others. It finally seemed an idea whose time had come.

By now, Pell's advocacy had won him growing public support, reflected in favorable press coverage, the many encouraging letters he was receiving from educators and students, and the numerous prominent Senators who had signed on to the concept, both on and outside his subcommittee. After fifteen subcommittee hearings, Pell brought S. 659, a $20-billion higher education bill that included the Pell Grant program, to the full Senate for consideration on August 4, 1971.

During three days of debate that the press largely ignored (*The Washington Post* published a favorable editorial), Kennedy, Mondale, Javits, and others joined Pell in arguing for passage. In one of his last speeches before dying the next month of cancer, Republican Winston L. Prouty decried the seeming lack of interest by the media. "This bill is good news for millions of young Americans who need the assurance that their aspirations will not be limited by their economic circumstances," Prouty said. "This is good news for the nation."

In his closing remarks of the debate, Pell struck a familiar theme: "For the first time in the history of our nation, there will be established the right to a post-secondary education."

On August 6, the Senate voted 51 to 0 to approve S. 659, sending it to the House for consideration after the summer recess. Pell went home to Newport for a short vacation and then to Geneva for a meeting of the United Nations Committee on the Peaceful Uses of the Seabed and Ocean Floor, which was considering a U.S. concession to extend nations' territorial waters from three to twelve miles. Pell was serving as a Congressional adviser to the committee.

Before heading overseas, Pell hailed passage of what he called "landmark" legislation. "No longer will higher education be the province of some of us," he said. "It will be the birthright of all." Long a promise, it seemed soon to be realized.

Passage of S. 659 drew praise from individuals and educators, including Alan L. Baker, president of the Katharine Gibbs School. "It is with a great deal of interest that I read during my vacation about the Senate passage of the landmark Higher Education Bill," Baker wrote to Pell. "You and your associates in the Senate are to be complimented on the measure. This support for higher education represents an intelligent investment of public resources . . . I extend personal congratulations and appreciation to you for your leadership."

But when House debate began after Congress returned from its summer recess, Pell's hope met the reality of a nation still divided by race.

In the House, Southern representatives joined nearly all Republicans and several Democrats to attach a rider to the higher-education bill prohibiting the use of federal dollars for busing to desegregate public schools — a move that defied the Supreme Court, which earlier that year had unanimously upheld the constitutionality of busing to achieve integration in southern school systems.

The high court's twenty-eight-page decision, handed down on April 20, 1971, did not order elimination of all-black schools, which had persisted despite the court's landmark 1954 Brown v. Board of Education ruling that a system of separate schools for blacks and whites that denied blacks equal educational opportunities was unconstitutional. But it did prompt federal judges to order desegregation in several southern districts in 1971 — and also in some northern communities, notably Michigan, where white parents were outraged after a federal judge issued an order they believed would result in suburban white children being bused to Detroit, and black city children being bused to outlying communities. By the fall of 1971, with protest from whites in many parts of the nation reaching Washington, many observers were predicting that busing would be a major issue in the 1972 presidential election, and in many Congressional and local races as well. They would be proven right.

Well over a year before the election, Nixon went on record against busing: On August 3, 1971, he responded to a federal court order requiring that extensive busing be used to achieve racial balance in Austin, Texas, schools by instructing the Justice Department to challenge the decree. In remarks that day, he reaffirmed his position on the issue:

> I am against busing as that term is commonly used in school desegregation cases. I have consistently opposed the busing of our Nation's schoolchildren to achieve a racial balance, and I am opposed to the busing of children simply for the sake of busing. Further, while the executive branch will continue to enforce the orders of the court, including court-ordered busing, I have instructed the Attorney General and the Secretary of Health, Education, and Welfare that they are to work with individual school districts to hold busing to the minimum required by law.

The House debate reached its climax on November 4, 1971, the day after Michigan governor William G. Milliken, a Republican, announced on a statewide TV broadcast that he would appeal the federal court order affecting Detroit. With the vote on the education bill's busing rider looming, Pell's House counterpart, Rep. Edith Green, weighed in.

"As midnight approached," *The New York Times* reported, "the more than 200 representatives on the House floor were growing restless, but a hush fell over the chamber as Representative Edith Green, the foremost House expert on education, rose to speak."

Democrat Green, a former schoolteacher and lobbyist for the Oregon Education Association, that state's largest teachers' union, would be remembered for her work in passing legislation forbidding sex discrimination in federally funded schools.

But she did not believe busing was the answer to the discrimination of race.

"We cannot go back 100 years to make up for the errors of our ancestors," Green said. And, she maintained, "the evidence is very strong that busing is not the answer to our school problems." Green said that parents alone should have the right to decide where their children were educated. "I never bought a home without looking first to find out about the schools my boys would attend. Now, the federal government is reaching its long arm in and telling me I can't send them to that school. And that's going too far."

Brooklyn Democrat Shirley Chisholm, the first black woman elected to Congress, smelled racism.

"Let me bring it down front for you," she said. "Your only concern is that whites are affected. Come out from behind your masks and tell it like it really is. Where were you when black children were bused right past the white schools?"

By a vote of 332–38, the House approved the anti-busing amendment.

Pell only wanted college for all. He had not imagined his noble ambition would become entangled in the politics of race, but as 1972 began, it had.

▫ ▫ ▫ In his speech on February 22 of that year, Pell offered his colleagues compromise language on the busing issue that had been drafted in concert with Minority Leader Hugh D. Scott, Jr., Republican of Pennsylvania, and Pell's longtime Vietnam ally Mansfield, Majority Leader of the Democrat-controlled Senate.

The Scott-Mansfield amendment did not outright prohibit federal funds for busing, as opponents of desegregation wanted, but rather left acceptance or rejection of such funds a decision to be made locally. Pell read the simple language from the Senate floor: "No provision of this act shall be construed to require the assignment or transportation of students or teachers in order to overcome racial imbalance." The hope was that not only would some busing opponents sign on — but also Democrats who wanted stronger measures to force integration of the schools.

The hope was immediately dashed when liberal Democrat Abraham Ribicoff, who had succeeded George W. Bush's father in the Connecticut seat (and who would be succeeded by Christopher Dodd on his retirement in 1981) condemned the compromise and reintroduced legislation he had sponsored in 1970 to impose a strict ten-year deadline to end desegregation. Speaking after Pell and Javits, Ribicoff appealed to the conscience of those like Pell who, he believed, sadly were prepared to sacrifice long-held principle for the short-term gain of a higher education bill, worthy though it may be in many regards.

"I have been dismayed by the developments of the last year," Ribicoff said.

The arguments we rejected for years when raised by southerners are now embraced by liberals throughout the north. After years of presidential leadership on civil rights, we have an administration anxious to and willing to abdicate its constitutional responsibilities by appealing to the worst fears and stereotypes rather than trying to eliminate them. After years of forcing the issue onto the courts, the Congress of the United States seems more determined than ever to hide behind a few courageous men in judicial robes . . .

Some are talking now of compromises on the question of busing, perhaps resulting in an amendment that would appear to be against busing without really ending it. Senators will therefore be able to vote against busing without, hopefully, destroying our efforts to end segregation. This may be fine for our conscience and may allow us to appear to be all things to all people, but it hardly qualifies as effective leadership. Nor does it do anything to dissipate the fog resulting from the irresponsible dialogue surrounding the entire question of busing and school integration. At a time when our future is threatened and people are seeking leadership and guidance, fancy legislative footwork is not enough.

During debate the next day, Pell rebuffed Ribicoff while defending the Scott-Mansfield amendment. While his voting record showed long support for civil rights, Pell argued that busing alone was not the solution to integrating schools; he sought, as he always attempted, to bring two sides together. But this divide was not easily bridged.

"Busing has become really a red-letter word," Pell said.

What we sought to do was to make sure that busing would not be used in a forced situation. We would rather, if it is used, it be used at the discretion of local school boards . . . Busing is not a tool that should be used to extreme, but in moderation. It is one means of achieving a degree of the integrated society which we seek. Of course, we seek to be reasonable men. What one man might consider moderate, another would consider extreme.

Extremism prevailed during the third day of debate, with an amendment offered by Minority Whip Robert P. Griffin, Republican of Michigan, northern battleground of the busing issue. Griffin's amendment, which even he conceded might not have passed constitutional muster, would have prohibited all federal courts from ordering the busing of schoolchildren "on the basis of their race, color, religion or national origin."

On Friday, February 25, Griffin's measure came to a vote. By then, several supporters of Scott-Mansfield had left Washington for the weekend. Presidential aspirations in this election year had drawn four to the campaign trail: Democrats Humphrey, Muskie, McGovern and Henry Jackson of Washington.

With key compromise supporters absent, Griffin's prohibition passed, 43 to 40.

Mansfield and Scott (who was risking his own political standing back home in Pennsylvania by supporting compromise) were irate at the missing senators. "They are being paid $42,500 a year plus travel expenses and stationery allowance to be here," Scott said. "This is where they are needed." If they were not back the following week, when Mansfield would bring their compromise to a vote, Scott said "we are going to make them responsible."

They were indeed back the following week, when, on February 29, the Senate resumed consideration of the Higher Education Act. Pell called the Griffin amendment "a step backwards" and he introduced into the record a "most interesting and meaningful" editorial, published in *The Providence Journal*, that supported Scott-Mansfield. Pell again urged passage of the compromise measure. Again, the debate was contentious. Vice President Agnew presided, prepared in the event of a tie to cast his vote — most likely in favor of Griffin, Senate leaders believed, given Nixon's opposition to busing.

But this time, Griffin's amendment failed, 50 to 47. Ribicoff's measure to end all school segregation in ten years also failed, by a 65-to-29 margin. Those measures having been defeated, Scott-Mansfield was adopted, 63 to 34.

Busing opponents tried once more the next day for a prohibition, but the measure, sponsored by Republican Robert Dole of Kansas and nearly identical to Griffin's, failed. The Senate then passed the Higher Education Act, 88 to 6, and sent it to House-Senate conference, with Pell leading twelve Senate conferees, including Kennedy, Mondale, and Javits, all of whom were in basic agreement, unlike the divided House.

◘ ◘ ◘ The conference committee met for the first time on March 15 in room S-207 of the Capitol, a grand space with high ceiling, white marble fireplace, and crystal chandelier. There, the politicking intensified. In the House, support for anti-busing legislation was stronger than in the Senate, and House leaders were adamant that any bill contain a strong prohibition. The House had approved three anti-busing amendments: one prohibiting the use of any federal funds to bus children, another forbidding federal officials from encouraging communities from using their own funds for busing, and a third that would delay implementation of any court order to bus until all appeals had been exhausted, a process that could take many years, precisely what sponsors intended.

Pell's grant program was lost for the moment — and possibly for another year or longer when the House, in an unusual parliamentary maneuver, voted on March 8 to instruct its conferees to "insist" on a prohibition against busing in discussions with their Senate counterparts. The vote was in part intended to rein in the House conference chairman, Carl D. Perkins, Democrat of Kentucky, head of the Education and Labor Committee, a key leader in passage of the Economic Opportunity Act of 1964, which led to the creation of the Job Corps and the Head Start program for low-income children. In the debate leading up to the

House vote that conferees not accept the Senate compromise, Perkins criticized colleagues who supported it, saying that their unbending opposition to busing would "overshadow and perhaps destroy the greatest higher education bill that has ever been written." Perkins was on Pell's side.

But Democrat Joe D. Waggonner Jr. of Louisiana, a leading southerner who had opposed civil rights legislation and been a strong supporter of the Vietnam War, was looking to November—when he and many fellow representatives would be up for reelection. "You cannot vote for the motion to table [the insistence to conferees] without telling your constituents, 'I like busing and I want some more,'" Waggonner said. "This is a vote the people of the country are going to look at."

Nixon understood the implications for his own reelection chances. In a special message to Congress on March 17, he asked lawmakers to pass a moratorium on busing—and for legislation to be enacted during the moratorium to permanently curb the practice:

Conscience and the Constitution both require that no child should be denied equal educational opportunity. That Constitutional mandate was laid down by the Supreme Court in Brown v. Board of Education in 1954. The years since have been ones of dismantling the old dual school system in those areas where it existed—a process that has now been substantially completed. As we look to the future, it is clear that the efforts to provide equal educational opportunity must now focus much more specifically on education: on assuring that the opportunity is not only equal, but adequate, and that in those remaining cases in which desegregation has not yet been completed it be achieved with a greater sensitivity to educational needs.

Acting within the present framework of Constitutional and case law, the lower Federal courts have ordered a wide variety of remedies for the equal protection violations they have found. These remedies have included such plans as redrawing attendance zones, pairing, clustering and consolidation of school districts. Some of these plans have not required extensive additional transportation of pupils. But some have required that pupils be bused long distances, at great inconvenience. In some cases plans have required that children be bused away from their neighborhoods to schools that are inferior or even unsafe. The maze of differing and sometimes inconsistent orders by the various lower courts has led to contradiction and uncertainty, and often to vastly unequal treatment among regions, States and local school districts.

In the absence of statutory guidelines, many lower court decisions have gone far beyond what most people would consider reasonable, and beyond what the Supreme Court has said is necessary, in the requirements they have imposed for the reorganization of school districts and the transportation of school pupils. All too often, the result has been a classic case of the remedy for one evil creating another evil. In this case, a remedy for the historic evil of racial discrimination has often created a new evil of disrupting communities and imposing hardship on children — both black and white — who are themselves wholly innocent of the wrongs that the plan seeks to set right . . .

Until now, enforcement has been left largely to the courts — which have operated within a limited range of available remedies, and in the limited context of case law rather than of statutory law. I propose that the Congress now accept the responsibility and use the authority given to it under the 14th Amendment to clear up the confusion which contradictory court orders have created, and to establish reasonable national standards.

On its surface, Nixon's proposal seemed in the best interests of all Americans. But people on both sides of the issue saw it for what it was: a proposal to end, for good, busing as a means to achieve true equality of education.

Predictably, Nixon's proposal touched off new fury, with candidates for many offices believing they must take a stand for or against it — and key players in the Congressional impasse over the higher education bill finding themselves further hardened in their respective positions. It did not bode well for compromise.

Griffin of Michigan was encouraged by Nixon, saying the president's proposal "should be enough to make the difference in Congress." But another busing opponent, Democrat Senator Sam J. Ervin Jr. of North Carolina, did not believe Nixon had gone far enough, since his proposal would apply to future busing, not reverse busing already underway in the south. "If it is wrong," Ervin said, "it ought to be uprooted forever and thrown on the scrap heap of history."

Civil-rights activists saw the proposal as racist, with New York Mayor and Democratic presidential candidate John Lindsay calling it a "cave-in" to the segregationist beliefs of presidential candidate George Wallace, governor of Alabama, and Representative Chisholm decrying it as "final evidence of [Nixon's] desire to shut the door to racial equality in this nation."

In testimony before Pell's Education subcommittee, lobbyist Clarence Mitchell, director of the NAACP's Washington office, was more blunt.

Mitchell said Nixon's proposal and others that were similar were "blatant products of racism." Nixon, he said, had "joined forces with George Wallace."

▫ ▫ ▫ Spring came, and the higher education act remained mired in conference. Opponents of busing maintained their heat on the issue — while on the other

side, students came to Washington to lobby lawmakers, editorials were published, and letters written urging legislators to stop keeping the education act a
hostage to race.

"Thank you very much for your letter in which you so succinctly stated the
urgent need on S. 659, which is presently in conference," Pell wrote back to
Harry F. Evarts, president of Bryant College in Smithfield, Rhode Island, one
of many who expressed his views to him. "You may be assured that I am well
aware of this urgency. Unfortunately, the House took a ten-day recess which has
slowed up our work. The conference is now moving ahead diligently with a view
toward bringing out a bill at the earliest possible time."

It was a rosy assessment that belied what was actually happening. What was
happening was stalemate seemingly without end. By May 7, when *The New York
Times* published an update, conferees, after meeting seventeen times, remained
deeply divided.

"Members who have been in dozens of conferences over the years," the newspaper reported, "among them Senator Jacob K. Javits, Representative Edith
Green and Representative Albert H. Quie, said last week that this conference
was the most difficult they had ever experienced."

Said Javits: "The breadth of the issues and the really deep differences in philosophy are the greatest I have ever seen."

Busing was the major point of contention — but it was not the only issue
that divided the conferees. By the first week of May, more than 200 differences
remained, and one of the more substantial was Pell's grants program.

Representative Green strongly opposed it.

She wanted to maintain the 1965 formula, under which schools determined
which students received federal aid. She had the backing of several post-
secondary schools associations, including the powerful Association of American Universities and the American Council on Education, which feared that
under Pell's plan, federal funding to their member schools would suffer. They
feared receiving less money. And Green was their champion.

Election-year politics were now affecting Pell directly. Although he would
not formally announce his candidacy for another week, Navy Secretary Chafee
was widely known to be assembling a campaign to challenge Pell for his seat in
November. The early polls gave Chafee a commanding lead. And Chafee opposed busing.

The even-tempered Pell was beginning to lose his composure.

"Mrs. Green, a 62-year-old former schoolteacher, has alienated some of the
senators," *The Times* wrote. "Senator Claiborne Pell, the head of the Senate
Democratic conferees, who faces an uphill fight for re-election in November,

stood up and shook his finger at Mrs. Green at one session and accused her of drumming up a lobbying campaign against him in his home state, Rhode Island. Mrs. Green denies the charge, but other House members say it is a tactic she has employed in the past."

Backed by Mansfield, Javits, and other Senate leaders, Pell refused to take his grants program off the table; ordinarily inclined to compromise, he had worked too long for this to give in. It would be all or nothing.

At 2 p.m. on May 16, conferees assembled in the Old Supreme Court Chamber, a historic chamber adorned with busts of prominent justices where the nation's highest court had met for forty-one years, beginning in 1819.

"As the conferees gathered on May 16 and the voluminous accumulation of conference documents was wheeled on carts into the room by the committee staff, there was a sense of being in the eye of a raging political storm," wrote Lawrence E. Gladieux and Thomas R. Wolanin in their 1976 book, *Congress and the Colleges: The National Policies of Higher Education*. "There was also a sense of historical drama, of writing another page in the saga of American race relations."

More than fifteen hours later, at 5:13 a.m. on May 17, the conferees had reached agreement. Green had relented. In return for controls guaranteeing that other programs would not be cut to provide funds for Pell's Basic Educational Opportunity Grants, she would drop her opposition. After years of working doggedly but without fanfare, Pell had prevailed. He had been, Jack Reed would later recall, "someone who was patient, someone one who was very bright intellectually, and someone who believed — maybe in the old-fashioned way — that right-thinking and hard work and tenacity will pay off, rather than shrill rhetoric and grandstand plays."

The marathon session had exhausted participants — and left the Old Supreme Court Chamber, site now of another historic occasion, a mess.

"Gray with fatigue, but nevertheless managing broad smiles, Democrats and Republicans, House members and Senators shook hands all around congratulating each other," wrote Gladieux and Wolanin in their account. "They trailed out leaving a littered landscape: every surface in the august chamber was covered with discarded notes, memoranda, draft amendments, paper cups half-filled with stale coffee, food wrappers and overflowing ashtrays."

On May 23, the Senate opened debate on the bill that had resulted from legislators meeting twenty times since the bill was sent to conference. It included the Pell program — and a new compromise on busing, under which enforcement of lower-court busing orders would be delayed until Jan. 1, 1974, or until all appeals had been exhausted, a provision that fell short of what Nixon wanted. Congressional leaders hoped the president nonetheless would sign in light of the bill's purely educational elements, which he supported. Pell urged senators to look to the primary purpose of the bill, which was to give students and schools the support they needed to prosper.

"I would remind my colleagues," Pell said as the Senate opened debate,

> that if the bill is to be attacked, from the right and from the left, those efforts can result in the defeat of the bill. If that should happen and the conference bill is not approved, I can see that with the mood of the country and the intensity of feeling on these subjects, that there would be no higher education bill through this and perhaps next year . . . I would therefore hope that those who criticize the bill, from both the right and the left, as being too pro-busing or too anti-busing would bear with the conference managers who worked laboriously and very hard — as some of my colleagues may not be aware, until 5:30 one morning — to try to get some ground of agreement. In order to get agreement, there had to be some "give" on both sides. This is the best job we could do. In connection with the bill, the higher education portion is really the main portion, but like an iceberg, only a small bit shows through. The educational part is of the bill is the least visible — with the extraneous issue of busing, which has been added as the iceberg's tip, gaining the attention of our nation.

Pell summarized the key features of the amended S. 659: greater aid to institutions of higher learning for them to use as they saw fit, not in specific programs that had been federally targeted; an end to federal aid to any school that discriminated against women in hiring, promotion, or admissions, a provision for which Green had long fought; and the new program of grants based solely on a student's need, as judged by a national formula, not by an individual school. Pell spoke extensively of the historic nature of the latter:

> A major new program of assistance to students is now established. The Basic Educational Opportunity Grant program provides for an entitlement — not as a privilege but as a matter of right — of $1,400, from which is deducted an expected family contribution, to every student in good standing who desires to attend a post-secondary institution. This program would be limited, of course, by considerations revolving around appropriations — and the formula we worked out gives a break, in any case, to those students who have the greatest need. It also helps not only children from poor families, but also children from lower middle-income and middle-income families who have responsibilities that presently make it very difficult to send their youngsters to college.

The debate continued for two days, mostly over the busing provisions. A final move for tougher language was defeated, and on May 24, the Senate passed the bill, 63–15.

"Last Wednesday afternoon was Claiborne Pell's finest hour in the U.S. Senate," wrote *The Providence Journal*, which over the years had become more critical of Pell. "His colleagues passed by a wide margin a landmark aid to education bill, a measure that could rework the system of financing college education for lower and middle income students. If adequately funded, it will rival in impact the post World War II G.I. Bill. It is the most important basic piece of education legislation since the establishment of land grant colleges." (Signed into law by Abraham Lincoln in 1862, the land-grant Morrill Act gave states the resources to found colleges to educate the new class of industrial workers. In Pell's state, the University of Rhode Island, chartered in 1888 as a public agricultural school, was the beneficiary of this act—and also of the National Sea Grant College and Program Act of 1966, which Pell championed).

"Most of the public notice concerning the bill involved its anti-busing provisions," *The Journal* continued, "but its heart is the system of grants designed by Pell. It is the first piece of major legislation that he has conceived, written and steered to passage through the most dangerous and tricky congressional waters. Many senators, including many capable and powerful ones, never achieve anything like it."

The newspaper noted that Pell's success came in conflict with Rep. Green, "patron saint and dragon lady of education," as the reporter described her.

"Pell has never functioned well on the Senate floor, and in tough debate. He was been, in fact, one of the least impressive movers and shakers in the Senate: a good idea man but a poor mechanic. Mrs. Green, by contrast, is as tough as a fence post. She is used to having her own way . . . During hours of negotiations, Pell managed to hold both the Republican and Democratic Senate members of the conference in support of his position. He had some Republican support among the House members, and with considerable effort he managed to move three and sometimes four Democrats away from Mrs. Green. When the conference finally wound up after an all-night session, Pell had his bill and Mrs. Green had a rare defeat."

With Chafee intent on Pell's seat, *The Journal* wrote, Pell's springtime success could be a factor in the November election.

"Although the bill must still be approved by the House, and there could be trouble there," the paper wrote, "the job has been done in the Senate, and it is something new in Pell's career. He has been identified with several areas of legislation since he went to the Senate in 1961. But most of them were faintly exotic in congressional terms: the arts and humanities legislation, the high-speed trains that not many people ride on anyway, the oceanography legislation, the metric measurement bill. In each case, Pell was operating on the margins of the Senate, working on legislation that, put bluntly, not many people were interested in. Pell's supporters in Rhode Island have never been much impressed with it. Do something that affects ordinary people, they have told him. The education bill is it . . . Facing the most difficult reelection campaign yet, he certainly needs it."

▫ ▫ ▫ On June 8, 1972, the House narrowly passed the Higher Education Act and sent it to Nixon, whose signature was uncertain. Pell was in Stockholm, serving as the Senate Adviser to the United Nations Conference on the Human Environment, the first major U.N.-sponsored conference on global environmental issues — a conference that would prove to be a milestone in international consideration of environmental problems, including global warming. Pell, again, was ahead of his time.

In Washington, Nixon sat on the bill. With the deadline approaching for his action, reporters at a June 22 Oval Office news conference were eager to learn what he would do.

The higher-education bill was not the initial issue the reporters raised. The first of fourteen questions they asked was about the June 17 burglary of the Democratic National Committee headquarters in Washington's Watergate complex, which had just hit the news — and which, until now, Nixon had let press secretary Ron Ziegler handle. "This kind of activity," Nixon said, "as Mr. Ziegler has indicated, has no place whatever in our electoral process, or in our governmental process. And, as Mr. Ziegler has stated, the White House has had no involvement whatever in this particular incident. As far as the matter now is concerned, it is under investigation, as it should be, by the proper legal authorities, by the District of Columbia police, and by the FBI. I will not comment on those matters, particularly since possible criminal charges are involved."

Later in the conference, Nixon did not tip his hand about the education bill.

"I have to make the decision tomorrow," he said. "I will be very candid with you to tell you that it is one of the closest calls that I have had since being in this office. Some of the members of my staff and members of the Congress are enthusiastic for signing it, and others are just as enthusiastic for vetoing it. I have mixed emotions about it. First, as far as many of the education provisions, strictly education provisions, they are recommendations of this Administration. I think they are very much in the public interest. If they could be separated from the rest of the bill, and stand on their own, there would not be any question about signing the bill."

Nixon did sign the bill, on June 23 — reluctantly and with an attack on Congress.

In a terse statement, Nixon devoted just one sentence to what he called the "comprehensive higher education provisions" of the bill; he did not mention the Pell program, which would prove to be the most momentous achievement of the legislation. The rest of his comments castigated the House and Senate for failing to take a stronger stand against busing:

> Congress has not given us the answer we requested; it has given us rhetoric. It has not provided a solution to the problem of court-ordered busing; it has provided a clever political evasion. The moratorium it offers is temporary; the relief it provides is illusory. Confronted with one of the burning social issues of the past decade, and an unequivocal call for action from the vast majority of the American people, the 92d Congress has apparently determined that the better part of valor is to dump the matter into the lap of the 93d. Not in the course of this Administration has there been a more manifest Congressional retreat from an urgent call for responsibility.

Speaking from the Senate floor that day, Pell marked the occasion, in language that, for him, passed for excitement:

> President Nixon's signing of the higher education bill is a most memorable event in my life," he said. "One of my desires on entering the Senate was to work on education, with the goal that post-secondary education would be available to all. The provisions contained in S. 659 go a long way to accomplishing this goal. I have worked on this specific legislation for three years. To have it signed into law and know that in the future, higher education will be available to so many more people, is a most gratifying event.

CHOO-CHOOS AND SEAWEED?

When Chafee resigned as Secretary of the Navy on May 4, 1972, the news made national headlines, and not for the Navy's loss.

As *The New York Times* and other media outlets reported, Chafee had resigned in order to run for the Senate — a decision he confirmed eleven days later, when he formally announced his candidacy with the declaration that "I do so because I firmly believe that I can do a better job than is being done by the incumbent."

Moderate Republican Chafee said he would emphasize local job creation, improved health care and protection of the environment. He hoped voters would look favorably on his long service to state and federal government. He did not sharply attack Pell, but he did say his opponent had not used his Senate seniority wisely; he did not serve on any committees, Chafee said, "that have any direct bearing on Rhode Island." Put charitably, this was poetic license.

Among Washington insiders and widely throughout Rhode Island, the announcement was anticlimactic. Chafee's publicly stated desire to become Senator dated to 1965, when the then-governor hinted at challenging Pell in his first reelection bid. Appreciative of his party loyalty, Nixon appointed him Navy Secretary—but as the 1972 race approached, he and the national party saw greater value with him in Congress. While Republicans seemed unlikely to win a majority in the Senate, which they had not enjoyed since the 83rd Congress (from 1953 to 55, the first two years of Eisenhower's presidency), they hoped at least to strengthen their hand. And they viewed Pell as vulnerable. They believed they could paint him as an oddball, passionate for esoteric causes, who was out of touch with his constituents, while presenting the more charismatic Chafee as the right man—this time, on a larger stage—for Rhode Island.

As 1971 had unfolded, the polls showed Chafee in front—and one, by the respected Boston-based Becker Research Corp., gave Chafee a commanding lead, 53 to 25 percent, with 22 percent undecided. That poll, conducted in spring 1971, had generated extensive coverage. Not only did it show Pell trailing badly overall—it showed him behind in Providence, heart of the electorate; behind with both men and women; and behind with independents. With 43 percent of Democrats saying they would vote for him compared to 42 percent of Democrats who favored Chafee, Pell was barely ahead among voters of his own party. It did not look good. The 1960 and '66 air of invincibilty was gone.

Encouraged by these results and another independent poll in August 1971 that also showed him in the lead, though more narrowly, Chafee had done nothing to discourage the growing speculation that he would run; indeed, he never had during his tenure as Navy Secretary. Pell was in Geneva at the United Nations Committee on the Peaceful Uses of the Seabed and Ocean Floor and could not be reached for comment when the August 1971 poll results were released. But chief *Providence Journal* political reporter John P. Hackett reached Chafee, who told the paper, in an article headlined "Chafee Hints Race Against Pell": "I certainly appreciate and am grateful for the confidence the people of Rhode Island have shown in me. I very much enjoyed working for Rhode Islanders in the past and hope to have the opportunity to do so again some day." Regarding the 1972 election, Hackett concluded: "Mr. Chafee has not heretofore gone beyond describing his participation as 'a possibility.' Thus, his expressed anticipation of resuming a Rhode Island role in the future opens the door a bit wider to his making a senatorial bid in 1972. Mr. Chafee served as governor from 1963 to 1969. He is expected by Republican Party officials here [in Rhode Island] to go against Senator Pell next year. They believe he will return from Washington sometime next spring from the Navy Department post to which President Nixon appointed him in 1969."

Journal stories in the fall of 1971 and the early months of 1972 spoke of a Pell-Chafee match up as a virtual *fait accompli* — "A Titanic Struggle Takes Shape," as one headline described it. Rhode Islanders, who took their politics as seriously as their heart-breaking Red Sox, anticipated a battle the likes of which they hadn't seen since 1960, when Pell had pulled off an upset playing David to former governor Dennis Roberts' Goliath. This time, the narrative would be different: this would be Goliath against Goliath, two men of financial means, two veterans of World War II, two veteran politicians facing off across the great divide of the Vietnam War, now winding down but still among the dominant foreign-policy issues of the time.

Untested in his 1966 landslide reelection, Pell in the latter half of 1971 began to plan a campaign that would draw on his 1960 success for its strategy; with no credible primary opposition to consider, he focused his efforts on the general election against Chafee, who also was guaranteed his party's nomination. Reviving the organization that helped send him to Washington in 1960 would be crucial, and Pell began visiting local Democratic committees, prompting state Republican chairman Thomas E. Wright to complain: "I understand he has already given money to the Democratic town committees. In some towns, he has his coordinators set up. He is out campaigning. He is everywhere. He is sponsoring every bill in sight down in the Senate." Pell revived his practice of taking long walks through the state, which gave him direct contact with voters in their workplaces and homes.

As they had in the re-election year of 1966, reporters noticed Pell's increased presence in the state. The *Journal* wrote:

> One step has been the quiet and entirely unpublicized use of walking tours around the state. Over the last several weeks, Pell has walked from the Pawtucket City Hall to the Providence City Hall, from Broad Street in Cranston to downtown Providence, through Federal Hill, through downtown Woonsocket, and in the Little Compton area. This sort of thing should be very effective for Pell. He is not an easy stump speaker; low-key personal campaigning in neighborhoods, on the other hand, fits his style well.

As 1972 neared, Pell commissioned his own polls and reached out to organized labor, winning the early support of the AFL-CIO. He began raising money, knowing that he could tap into his and Nuala's wealth if need be. He worked with other Democratic leaders to discourage two-term Democratic governor

Frank Licht, who had upset Chafee in 1968, from seeking re-election; Licht had alienated Rhode Island voters by reversing campaign promises when he established the state's first income tax, and Pell and others feared that his name on the ticket would spell disaster for all Democrats.

And Pell began framing his issues.

By the beginning of 1972, his platform had crystallized: his long opposition to the Vietnam War, which so clearly divided doves from hawks, and which in internal documents topped every list of issues; oceans and the environment, notably his authorship of the Seabed Treaty and the Sea Grant College Act and his co-sponsorships of the Clean Air and Water Acts and their amendments; jobs creation; his proposal for a national health care bill; his support for programs to benefit the elderly; and education, notably the Pell Grant program, which he bundled with other issues in a category he called "middle class problems." In one way or another, Pell's every major plank had local impact for Rhode Islanders. Left almost as an afterthought were his metric proposals and high-speed rail. The esoteric Pell was not the image Pell and his strategists wanted to project, though they knew Chafee would seek to exploit it.

The essentials of Pell's campaign were all in place by March 1972, when *The Journal* released the results of its first "Rhode Island Poll" for the year. Based on a telephone survey of 417 voters from January 29 to February 13, the "scientifically balanced survey," as the paper described it, confirmed the uphill task Pell faced: 54 percent of respondents would vote for Chafee if the election were held on the day they answered, compared to 28 percent for Pell, an almost unbelievable margin of 26 points (17 percent were undecided). Independents favored Chafee by a wide margin, another ominous sign — as did men, women, and voters under twent-five, a group that been a key to Pell's 1960 and 1966 victories. Only among Democrats did Pell come out on top: 48 percent to Chafee's 35 percent. That more than a third of Democrats in heavily Democratic Rhode Island would vote for the Republican was a sobering message to the incumbent, who believed he had served his constituents well.

In the wake of its publication, new state Democratic chairman Lawrence P. McGarry tried the old tactic of dismissing the poll as irrelevant — and he accused the newspaper, whose owners included Chafees, of bias toward the Republican. (A similar charge would be leveled in 2010, when Chafee's son Lincoln, a Republican-turned-Independent, ran successfully for Rhode Island governor.)

"This whole poll is full of hogwash," McGarry told the Associated Press. "When the undecided run this high, the poll ought to be thrown out." The AP account continued: "McGarry said the Chafee family is a large stockholder for the *Providence Journal* Company, adding that the newspaper has a large Republican slant. He said the appearance of the poll story across the top of the front page 'is a subtle way in which the newspaper is using the power of suggestion to brainwash the people that the Republican Party is a winner in the state of Rhode Island.' The paper would not have run the story 'in such a prominent place' if the results had shown Pell to be the favorite, McGarry said."

But Pell himself was not so dismissive.

"I realize I am trailing at this point," he said. "I have had private and very scientific polls taken and I believe the gap at this point is between six and ten percentage points. Though it will be difficult, I believe I can close the gap and win in November."

If there was a silver lining, it was the goodwill that many voters felt toward Pell, as evidenced by his favorability ratings: asked their opinion of Pell's performance as senator, 64 percent of all poll respondents approved. Even a third of Republicans liked the job he had done. The problem was that voters seemed to like Chafee more — and seemed to know him better, since he had lived in their state full time during most of Pell's two terms and had returned frequently during his Navy tenure.

A *Journal* canvas of voters perhaps illustrated Pell's challenge better than poll numbers. "Pell is a good man but Chafee deserves a chance; we should have kept him as governor," a woman told the paper. Said another: "Pell is doing a very good job but Chafee will do even better." Added a man: "Pell is a real gentleman who cares about his people, but Chafee is the greatest." Others saw Chafee as "the most honest man in politics" and someone who "can be trusted."

The next *Journal* poll, conducted during the last week of April 1972 and released during the week that Chafee resigned as Navy Secretary, held slightly better news for Pell: Chafee kept a commanding lead over his rival, but his margin had shrunk from 26 points to 17 points: 49 percent of voters favored Chafee to 32 percent for Pell, with 19 percent undecided. Pell remained in trouble — but by early summer, when the campaign began in earnest, he was ready to step into the ring for the fight the state had been awaiting.

As he had in 1960 and 1966, Pell rented a suite in Providence's Biltmore Hotel for his operational base. He was raising money at a brisk pace, and he had recruited a sizeable volunteer corps. He had hired outside consultants and an outside polling firm, and approved intensive media, telephone, and direct-mail campaigns. He had shuffled his staff, placing Paul Goulding, who had experience in the 1968 presidential campaigns of Robert Kennedy and Hubert Humphrey, in charge of the overall effort — ahead of longtime aides Lewis and Nelson, who had been with him from the start. It was a difficult decision for Pell, who valued loyalty, but a decision he deemed necessary given the changes in campaigning in the twelve years since he had been truly tested. He needed fresh blood.

He had done all this along with shepherding the Higher Education Act to passage — and while watching his elderly mother's already frail health break down further.

□ □ □ In the years after his father's death, Pell had remained close to Matilda, who was sixty-six years old when a heart attack claimed Herbert in July 1961.

From his Senate office, he continued the tradition begun in childhood of sending her cards and gifts. He provided the financial support she needed to maintain a comfortable, if not extravagant, existence. Matilda lived in the apartment building at 115 East Ninety-Second Street in New York that her ex-husband had once owned. She stayed frequently with her son, daughter-in-law, and grandchildren at Pelican Ledge in Newport, where she could experience again some of the pleasures she remembered from the early days of her first marriage and the early part of her second, to Commander Koehler — times she belonged in Newport society, and was not living on its fringes as a debt-ridden widow with a fatherless young child.

Matilda had neither the expertise nor the interest in politics that Herbert possessed, and she rarely offered her son political advice. But she followed his career through the newspapers and TV, and wrote frequently to him of her pride in his accomplishments. Along with citations and photographs and letters from presidents and European royals, Pell kept favorite letters from his mother in his hideaway office. One described Matilda's reaction on one of his first national television appearances, which had been an anxiety-provoking opportunity for the young Rhode Island politician in the early 1960s, when TV was supplied by only three television networks, and TV sets had rabbit ears. Matilda watched her son from her home, after alerting her mother, Bomba.

"Dear Claiborne," she wrote, "You were really wonderful on T.V. last night. It came over very clearly, both voice and picture. You couldn't have been better. You gave the impression of complete honesty and a fine thoughtful mind, and answered all questions with great ease and clarity. In fact, there wasn't one single thing that I could critique in any way. I thought you were perfect. Audrey Clinton, who watched the show with me, thought you were 'awfully good' and that I must be very proud.

"Bomba gave strict orders that she was to be awakened, which she was ten minutes before. The nurse got her out of bed and in the big easy chair right in front of her T.V. and she listened to every word and called me right afterwards with much enthusiasm, as did the night nurse. Mrs. Ratchford, the day nurse, listened to it from her home with all her young people. They had it tuned to Channel 9 from nine o'clock as they were so afraid of missing any of it. The nurse thought it terribly good, and the girls thought you so handsome — 'a real doll.' You certainly made a hit.

"And what a terrific advantage it is in politics to look and speak well on T.V. You were absolutely natural and anyone could tell that. Dear Claiborne, you must do it as often as possible and you don't need to worry about a thing. I only felt badly that you and Nuala couldn't see it in Washington. You would have been very delighted with it. Audrey and I were so sorry when it was over. It held our interest every minute. You did not look tired or thin, or have circles under your eyes! I thought you might wonder about that . . .

"With much love and all congratulations, from Mom"

When Bomba — Mrs. Sophia de Borda Padelford — died at ninety-eight, on July 7, 1963, in her New York apartment, Claiborne and Nuala handled the funeral arrangements with Pell's half-brother, Hugh Koehler, and then invited Matilda to Pelican Ledge to pass the rest of the summer. Matilda was grateful.

"Claiborne Dear," she wrote on July 11, before leaving New York, "your very sweet and sympathetic letter has just come and it means so much to me. Thank you for all your goodness to me and your help and understanding. You did so much, and coming down with me and helping me in every possible way. I am indeed fortunate.

"Yes, I shall miss Mother greatly and she was so brave all these hard years and showed such courage and patience. She was so proud of you and I am thankful she was here to see her grandson a United States Senator as well as a very fine man. Nuala was really sweet and I was so glad she stayed with me that night. The children were perfect and I had a dear letter from Toby. I though you and Hugh arranged everything with great care and thoughtfulness. I appreciate it, beyond words.

"I know what a deep sadness you suffered two years ago, and that you still miss Daddy a great deal. There are some things that time softens but cannot erase.

"With love and gratitude, Mom"

Matilda had survived breast cancer, but by 1971 cancer had returned, this time in her bones, which left her vulnerable to fractures. After Pell had the guest room at Pelican Ledge rebuilt to accommodate her increasing disability, she spent that summer with her family there. Perhaps sensing that Matilda's failing health would leave her unable to communicate with loved ones, or perhaps fearing she would die suddenly, as his father had, Pell penned an uncharacteristically affectionate letter to his mother.

"Dearest Mom," he wrote, "Rarely do I find it easier to write than speak, but this is one time since I get so choked by emotion when I try to say these thoughts.

"I want you to know how hugely I respect you . . . your common sense, and your intelligence. You are and have been a wonderful mother—in fact, your advice and counsel have been all any parent could [want] for the past 60 years. And you have been a far better parent and given more to me than I have to my children. I could not respect or love a parent more than I do you.

"For all these reasons, I and the grandchildren need you. How I want more than I can say—and this I pray every night—that your life continues on free of pain, and healthy as God or I can will. So please get as well as you can.

"With immense and proud love from your son, Claiborne"

But Matilda experienced more pain and another hospitalization in the autumn of 1971. She instructed Claiborne on her will, and in a December letter apologized for not doing more for her son, daughter-in-law and grandchildren for Christmas.

"I wish I had some lovely Xmas presents for you," she wrote in an unsteady hand, "but there is only this letter, telling you that I thank you with all my heart for your goodness to me and all the care and trouble you have taken. I do realize what a hard time and an anxious one you have had with this worry. You were both just perfect to me and did everything you possibly could. I love you both dearly and feel deep gratitude. Your children were all so thoughtful, and Hugh is doing all he can and brings in Polly and the children to see me. I am feeling much better and so happy to be home. So don't worry.

"Merry Xmas, Happy New Year. Much love, Mom"

The New Year brought brief improvement, and in the spring of 1972, Matilda was living in an apartment on Bellevue Avenue that she had rented before. But as summer approached, she was failing again. Back in Washington from the Stockholm environmental conference on June 19, on the eve of Nixon's signing the Higher Education Act into law, Pell completed arrangements to bring his mother to Pelican Ledge.

"Dear Mom," he declared in a handwritten letter sent that day, "I just want you to know how very much I—and all of us—are looking forward to you being with us this summer. I think you know, too, how awfully sad I am at the state of your health. When one's mother, whom one loves dearly, is in pain or sick, it's just as if one's sick oneself.

"I think of you often and just (and actually) pray for improvement. I really believe—and hope—that Newport may do it. And never forget how very much I want you to get better. You are much needed and wanted, too, not just by me but by all of us.

"So please continue to be as stout hearted as you have. I admire and love you hugely.

"Love, Claiborne"

Thirty-eight days later, on July 27, Matilda died at Pelican Ledge. She was seventy-seven.

Pell was distraught.

"He was really, really upset," his son Toby would recall. "I had never seen my father cry before." Nor had Toby ever seen a dead person, but Claiborne kept the body of his mother in her room for two days before releasing her, so that her family and friends could say goodbye in a familiar place. "He didn't want to let go of her," Toby said.

Pell suspended his campaign for ten days and Chafee cancelled his events so that he could join the Pells at Matilda's funeral, which was held at Trinity Church, where Herbert had been remembered eleven years before. Matilda was buried next to Koehler at Saint Columba's Chapel cemetery. Nuala's father was already buried there, too, and she and Claiborne owned a plot of their own beneath the shade of an old copper beech tree.

◦ ◦ ◦ Pell went back to Washington, where on August 3 he voted for a measure sponsored by Massachusetts Senator Edward Brooke calling for Nixon to withdraw all troops from Vietnam within four months. And then he returned to the campaign.

A poll released on August 20 indicated that Pell had made significant inroads against Chafee: The Republican still led, with the support of 45 percent of respondents, but Pell, at 41 percent, was right behind, a statistical dead heat. Pell had improved appreciably among independents, and with 14 percent still undecided, he saw an opportunity for further gains. It would take work. The perception still persisted among some voters that Pell was disconnected: as a Providence man told *Journal* reporter Hackett, "all Pell worries about is the railroads, there's something funny about that." And while a majority of Americans now opposed the Vietnam War, not all did. "Pell would sell us out in Vietnam," a Chafee supporter told *The Journal*.

But Pell's overall message was taking hold, and he was scoring points with "his so-called Pell Grants," as reporters called them, describing the program in a radio interview on August 30 as his most important achievement during his 12 years in the Senate. Chafee, whose support had dropped to 45 percent from 49 percent in April, had failed to connect on the substantive issues that would decide the election, political observers believed.

"Every indication on the stump is that Mr. Chafee still retains the personal magnetism he held in the 1960s," wrote young *Journal* staffer M. Charles Bakst, who would soon establish himself as the dean of Rhode Island political reporters. "But there is a widely-held feeling his campaign has not caught fire, that he still needs a big and interesting issue, bigger and more interesting, for example, than which committee Mr. Pell does or does not serve on."

Election developments were followed closely in Miami, where Republicans were holding their late-August national convention, marred by the antiwar protests of *Born on the Fourth of July* author Ron Kovic and others. The party nominated Nixon and Agnew for second terms, and a giddy Colorado Senator Peter H. Dominick, chairman of his party's Senatorial Campaign Committee, declared: "This is the year we take control of the Senate." He was bolstered by polling that indicated that Nixon was headed for a sweeping victory, which would improve Republicans' chances in Senate races. With fifty-five Democrats and forty-five Republicans in the Senate, the GOP needed to gain six seats to regain control, or five to achieve a tie that could be broken by Vice President Agnew's vote. Leaders saw several seats that appeared promising — but despite Chafee's early promise, Pell's improvement in the polls had tempered early enthusiasm for Republican chances in Rhode Island. It was becoming a race.

"Rhode Island Republicans have conceded," *The New York Times* reported on August 24, "that Senator Claiborne Pell seems to be closing the gap on former Gov. John H. Chafee, who served as Secretary of the Navy early in the Nixon administration. Mr. Chafee had a broad lead in several early polls."

Labor Day passed, and with vacations over and children back in school, more voters began tuning in to the campaign. Pell and Chafee stepped up their appearances, continued planning for the two debates they had agreed on, increased their advertising, and boosted their fund-raising. Both had raised substantial sums over the summer, but Chafee, whose pockets were not quite as deep as his opponent's, did better, bringing in $300,909 to Pell's $109,688 for the June 1–August 31 period. Republicans in Rhode Island and across the country were still betting big on Chafee. At the suggestion of Dominick, who headed the GOP Senatorial Campaign Committee, the Washington-based Republican Boosters Club made the biggest investment: $35,000, which qualified as one of the club's "top category" expenditures, a spokesman told *The Providence Journal.*

By the first week of October, the investments had paid off: the latest *Journal* poll showed Chafee rewidening his lead over Pell, 43 percent to 33 percent.

"One of the nation's top U.S. Senate races is entering the home stretch in Rhode Island with the outcome still uncertain, but with important developments beginning to be felt," Hackett wrote in early October. "One of those is a definite pickup in the campaign of John H. Chafee to something resembling the style and pace he used when he ran for governor in the 1960s." Hackett noted "Chafee's ability consistently to dominate the news lately with campaign activities and statements on issues that frequently have put Pell in the position of reacting to them" and what he described as the Republican's "renewed buoyancy in campaigning, as used to be his trademark."

After three years inside the Pentagon, Chafee seemed to have hit his political stride. He was succeeding in presenting himself as a practical, take-charge leader who stood in contrast to a man with fanciful ideas about high-speed trains and Sea Grant colleges who was disparaged by some Chafee supporters as the candidate of "choo-choos and seaweed."

But Hackett cautioned against writing Pell off, despite the latest poll.

"Throughout the spring and summer," he wrote, "the Pell team has conveyed an image of knowing what it was about and doing it quietly and proficiently, especially in scheduling the senator into every nook and cranny of the state."

Hackett was right: The Pell campaign was playing to their candidate's strength in personal contact with voters, and they continued down that track in finalizing his appearances for the month of October and the days in November leading up to the election. The internal schedule had Pell appearing at events on every day from Monday, October 2, through Monday, November 6, the eve of the election. On some days, he was scheduled for as many as six appearances. Other days were themed: October 28 would be a Whistle Stop Tour of the state; "blitzes" were scheduled for Providence, Warwick, Cranston, Pawtucket and Woonsocket, the state's largest cities; and there was an "Ethnic Heritage Day," with Pell giving speeches in Italian, French and Portuguese, and in English at a Jewish community center. Joining him would be VIPs, including Joan and Ted Kennedy, on separate visits, and Senator Ribicoff, who would appeal to Jewish voters. McGovern, trailing in the polls, was not invited.

As she had so effectively in 1960, Nuala reached out to women's groups. In her speeches, she noted Pell's jobs and economic initiatives, his support for increasing the minimum wage, the research funds that came into the state as a result of the Sea Grant College act, and his education initiatives. She stressed the value of Pell's seniority.

"A senator's effectiveness as a legislator, who can best help his state, is increased as he gains experience," she said during one speech. "It is increased as he gains seniority. Each new senator begins at the bottom of the ladder, so to speak, in terms of the positions he holds on committees and subcommittees . . . My husband holds four subcommittee chairmanships, including one of the most influential, the Subcommittee on Education. He is responsible for all education legislation in the Senate. During his first years as a Senator — in keeping

By the age of eight, the young Claiborne Pell was already a world traveler.
Special Collections, University of Rhode Island Library

Fourteen-year-old Claiborne and his young half-brother, Hugh Koehler, in
London in the summer of 1933. Special Collections, University of Rhode Island Library

At Princeton, Pell was active in student political groups and participated in sports, including rugby. He is back row, fifth from the left. The Pell family

The young senator views a painting of him as a boy with his father, Herbert C. Pell Jr., diplomat and one-term Congressman.
Dennis P. Riley

Musicians serenading Pell were an important feature of the Senate candidate's primary and general elections in 1960. *The Providence Journal*

below:
The Pell "bandwagon," a 1940 truck that a Coast Guard buddy donated to Pell for the 1960 elections. He won both, and never did lose an election. *The Providence Journal*

In christening the bandwagon, Pell's wife, Nuala, broke a bottle of champagne. Pell picked up the pieces. *The Providence Journal*

Nuala and the Pells' four young children appeared frequently during the 1960 campaigns, both in person and in newspaper advertisements.

The Providence Journal

Pell, who had never run for office before 1960, understood the importance of media, and was regularly on the radio and TV.

The Providence Journal

Despite his wealth and aristocratic upbringing, Pell presented himself as a man of the people. Blue-collar Rhode Islanders embraced him.

The Providence Journal

One of the earliest photos of Pell, new senator from Rhode Island.

Dennis P. Riley

President Kennedy backed fellow Democrat Pell, despite considering him one of the least likely candidates to win a major election. *The Providence Journal*

Kennedy, who kept a summer White House in Newport, often invited the Pells aboard his yacht. Special Collections, University of Rhode Island Library

JFK's youngest brother Ted became one of Pell's best Senate friends. One of Ted's last speeches before he died was his eulogy of Pell in January 2009. Dennis P. Riley

Pell disagreed with President Johnson on Vietnam but was a supporter of his domestic programs. Dennis P. Riley

Opponents ridiculed Pell's interest in high-speed passenger rail, but supporters saw him as a visionary.
Dennis P. Riley

Pell was no gifted speaker, though he was comfortable with a crowd.
Dennis P. Riley

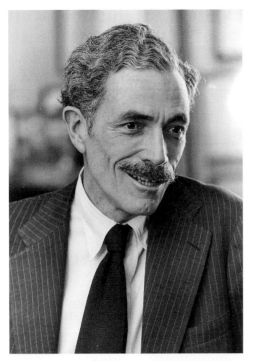

After his tough 1972 victory over the popular John Chafee, Pell grew a mustache.
The Providence Journal

Pell himself could make light of his sometimes quirky ways. Dennis P. Riley

A Coast Guardsman during World War II, Pell remained an officer in the reserves until mandatory retirement at 60. The Pell family

One of the keys to Pell never losing a re-election bid was his connection to his constituents. Dennis P. Riley

Pell with Presidents Gerald Ford, Jimmy Carter and Richard Nixon, in an undated photo likely taken during Carter's term in office. Special Collections, University of Rhode Island Library

With former Chrysler CEO Lee Iacocca and Ted Kennedy in the late 1970s. Dennis P. Riley

The Pells were fixtures on the Washington social scene for nearly
four decades. Dennis P. Riley

Pell presiding over the Senate Foreign Relations Committee in January 1988 during a debate on the INF missile treaty. U.S. Senate

During his years as member and chairman of the Foreign Relations Committee, Pell met with many world leaders, including Nelson Mandela.
Dennis P. Riley

Pell did much of his behind-the-scenes work in his beloved Capitol hideaway office. Dennis P. Riley

Nuala with her husband near the end of Pell's life. Behind them is their wedding painting, by Pell's stepmother Olive Bigelow Pell, noted artist.
The Providence Journal / Connie Grosch

Flanked by her family, Nuala holds the flag that draped Pell's coffin at his burial ceremony. *The Providence Journal* / Bob Breidenbach

with Senate procedures—he held no such positions of authority. They have come over a period of time, and they benefit Rhode Island." Twelve years after running as an outsider, Pell now sought advantage from his insider status.

"My husband's reelection could well determine how the next Senate is organized," Nuala said. "If the opposite party gains control, they would hold the chairmanships and the positions of greatest Senate authority. That is one chief reason why a national focus has been placed on our Senatorial campaign in Rhode Island, why such emphasis has been placed on this campaign by the administration in Washington."

▫ ▫ ▫ In his opening statement of his first debate with Chafee, on October 16 at Bryant College, which had awarded him the first of his many honorary degrees in 1962, Pell also struck the themes of seniority and Senate control. As cameras for the national networks rolled, he spoke of his participation in legislating, "more than 3,100 Pell votes on record in the Senate over a twelve-year period," which, he said, would confirm his "record of independent judgment." He listed initiatives and bills that had directly benefitted Rhode Islanders, noting especially the long battle during the spring to win passage of the Higher Education Act and its provision "providing, for the first time, an assurance to every young person in this country that he will get the money, if he needs it, for career training or a college education after high school. This legislation, and it is a Pell Bill, is regarded as the most important step in higher education in this century."

He spoke, without using the word, of his conscience.

"You will find in the Pell record no long periods of silence on major issues facing our state and our nation," he said. "I have never hidden my views behind claims of governmental secrecy. I have never declined comment for fear of offending a president." It was a gentle slap at the former Navy secretary.

Pell spoke, eloquently and forcefully, of the Vietnam War.

By then, the war was winding down. In 1972 alone, Nixon had ordered four troop withdrawals that would bring U.S. forces in Vietnam to less than 25,000 by year's end. The Paris Peace Talks had resumed (and would lead to a cease fire in January 1973). Pell could legitimately claim a long and prominent role in the opposition that had been a factor in ending the war: he had spoken against the war early, and he had continued to be vocal even as Nixon moved to end U.S. involvement. In the middle of his campaign against Chafee, he had taken the time, in July, to sponsor hearings as chairman of the Foreign Relations Committee's subcommittee on oceans and the environment into the Pentagon's covert practice of seeding clouds to create disruptive rain over Vietnam—"weather warfare," as it was called.

The end of the war was indeed in sight—after more than 56,000 lives lost, hundreds of thousands injured, and billions of dollars spent. Even many Americans who had supported the war now wondered if it had been worth the cost. When all was said and done, Pell had been on the right side.

As Navy Secretary, Chafee had not only backed the war, he had helped to wage it.

"The War in Vietnam, I believe, is a pretty good key to a man's thinking," Pell said during the Bryant College debate. "A man's position on the war is a good indication of what his priorities are. A man's position on the war, I believe, gives us a clue about his deepest convictions. And this is true because the war in Vietnam is not really a political issue or a tactical issue. The war is a moral issue, the kind of issue that makes a man consult his conscience."

Chafee in his opening remarks emphasized jobs, welfare, ethics and the environment, the "important issues of the campaign," he called them; he did not dwell on Vietnam during the debate, wisely, although he did say America should not leave until all soldiers had been accounted for. "We have done our part over these eight to twelve years," he said. But "We don't get out of Vietnam until we get the prisoners of war and missing in action accounted for. We don't leave before that."

The debate received front-page coverage, with reporters noting what one described as its "tension-packed" atmosphere. Chafee announced that he and his wife would publicly disclose their financial assets and challenged Pell to do the same. Pell agreed. The disclosures a few days later confirmed what most observers had surmised:

The Pells were wealthier by far. Claiborne and Nuala listed assets of $3,157,818 (almost $17 million in 2011 dollars), with the Chafees disclosing assets of $267,068 ($1.4 million in 2011 dollars). To the average Rhode Islander, either sum was all but unimaginable. Unlike in 1960 and 1966, wealth was not an issue that could be used against Pell.

Ten days later, the candidates debated once more—and this time, Pell was uncharacteristically aggressive, putting Chafee on the defensive for his many trips back to Rhode Island while Navy Secretary aboard government aircraft and at government expense—what Pell called a "magic carpet" designed to keep his opponent visible to voters. In turn, Chafee criticized Pell for improperly—though not illegally—using staff members for his campaign, a charge Pell refuted.

As the campaign entered its final phase, some of the biggest names from both national parties came to Rhode Island on behalf of their local candidates. Ed Muskie came and Ted Kennedy campaigned with Pell twice, including a day on which he said ordinary citizens should be alarmed by the burgeoning Watergate scandal, which the FBI had now concluded was part of, in the words of *Washington Post* reporters, "a massive campaign of political spying and sabotage conducted on behalf of President Nixon's re-election and directed by officials of the White House and the Committee for the Re-election of the President." Watergate, which would eventually bring down Nixon, was no longer viewed as a simple burglary.

At a press conference for one of his Rhode Island appearances, Kennedy said: "When you have an administration that is prepared to bug the political headquarters [of its opponents], what will they do to the homes of people in the next administration? Or to a university or a labor hall? I think they're prepared to take these kinds of steps for the reelection of this president. I think everyone who lives in a home or works in a business or attends a university or visits a labor hall would feel that this administration wouldn't think twice about doing the same thing [if] they're reelected. I think that, on the face of it, is enough to indict this administration."

Popular New York Governor Nelson Rockefeller visited Rhode Island on Chafee's behalf, making stops in Pell's home town of Newport and conducting a press conference in the Biltmore Hotel, where Pell had his suite.

But the biggest appearance was by Nixon, who addressed Chafee supporters at the state airport on November 3, four days before the election.

"I speak about a man that I know, and that you have known for many years," Nixon said. "I remember when he was the Governor of this State and rated by all of the objective journalists as one of the top Governors in the Nation. I remember him, too, as the Secretary of the Navy in our Administration for three years. John Chafee, without question, is a man who was born to be in public service. He is a man that the Nation needs in public service. Let me just put it quite directly to you: Rhode Island needs him in the Senate, America needs him in the Senate, I need him in the Senate, and you are going to put him in the Senate. John Chafee.

"I would like to say a word for another candidate, for myself. I would like to say in that respect that I have had the great honor of being a candidate for the highest office in this land on three occasions, in 1960, in 1968, and again this year, in 1972. I lost the first time in a narrow election. I won the second time, and now comes the third. As I stand here in Rhode Island, it just occurred to me that while in those elections to which I referred, in '60 and '68, I have at one time or the other carried most of the States, Rhode Island is a state that I have never carried. Let me say, the third time will be the charm. This is the year when we take Rhode Island."

Nixon's words would prove prophetic—for his presidential candidacy. The final poll of the season, released a week before Election Day, was also prophetic.

It showed Pell beating Chafee—narrowly.

Only the margin proved wrong.

▫ ▫ ▫ With 52 percent of the vote, Nixon carried Rhode Island, the first time since 1956 that a Republican presidential candidate had. But Chafee did not benefit, nor did his party in the Senate: Pell won, and Democrats kept their majority in Washington.

The final tally for Pell surprised many, just as his election had in 1960, though not as completely: he took 54 percent of the votes to Chafee's 45, a convincing margin that no one had predicted. Pell trounced Chafee nearly two-to-one in Providence, and he took the state's seven other cities—including Warwick, Chafee's home (by 33 votes). He won the large towns of Johnston, North Providence, West Warwick and Westerly. It now seemed that Pell would now achieve the status of Theodore Francis Green, the man he succeeded: Senator for life, or as long as he wanted the job.

"Six more years! Six more years!" supporters chanted, in mockery of Nixon, when Pell walked into the victory party at the Biltmore.

"Victory is not enough," Pell answered. "What does it mean? First, it recognizes that this Senate seat belongs to you: to we, the people of Rhode Island, and not to the President of the United States."

The Republican-leaning editorial board of *The Providence Journal* again praised the Democratic victor.

"Senator Claiborne Pell has survived his toughest election fight in convincing fashion, demonstrating once again the value of incumbency, the muscle of the Democratic Party in Rhode Island, and the asset of a solid legislative record," the paper wrote.

By defeating John H. Chafee to gain a third term in the U.S. Senate, Mr. Pell showed himself able to trade impressively on his previous work, especially his activity on behalf of education and aid to the elderly.

Mr. Pell won with the help of a massive outlay of money, a vigorous volunteer force, and heavy party backing in Providence. His wife, Nuala, was a tireless campaigner for her husband. But more telling than these techniques, perhaps, was the evident impression in the minds of many voters that Mr. Pell had not made any serious blunders during his twelve years in the Senate. Quiet and self-effacing, he has been a conscientious and creative legislator who has represented the best interests of the state . . . Senator Pell, having triumphed in the big one, now returns to what is certain to be a challenging congressional session.

During the campaign, Pell had taken a bet from his children that if he won, he would grow a moustache. Back in Washington, he let it grow. The new look it gave him, a look that hinted of mystery, would prove symbolic of the next period of his life, in which paranormal phenomena and the afterlife captivated him.

Six □ Heart and Soul

MR. MAGOO

The year 1973 began on notes of triumph and promise for Pell.

When he returned to Washington after the holiday break, he could look forward to six more years in the Senate; his Pell Grant program was firmly in hand; and the war he'd so long opposed was about to enter its final stage with the signing, in Paris, of a cease-fire agreement. Pell's legislative agenda for the start of his third term included a mix of initiatives, some old and some new, that he believed would improve America internally and in its relations with the rest of the world: conversion to the metric system, an end to weather warfare, extension of healthcare to all workers, year-round daylight savings, changing federal elections to the first Saturday in November as a means of encouraging voting, and campaign finance reform, among other measures. It was, characteristically, a mix of down-to-earth and pie-in-the-sky.

And Pell's third book, on the subject that, after education, was closest to his heart, was in bookstores.

A slim but readable volume at 174 pages, *Power and Policy: America's Role in World Affairs*, released during his 1972 reelection campaign, was an exploration of America's role in a world that had changed dramatically since Pell, now fifty-four, had come of age in the period between the world wars.

Beginning with a discussion of America's place in world history — major chapters of which, the Second World War and the Cold War, he had directly experienced, as a Coast Guard officer and a member of the Foreign Service — the book spelled out Pell's beliefs in how the world could move beyond an age when nuclear weapons threatened the planet with destruction, and pollution of the environment, particularly of the oceans and the air, threatened it with a slower, though also eventually catastrophic, end. And while all nations should cooperate in the effort for peace and protection, the United States was destined to play the decisive role, Pell argued in the book — in an echo of John F. Kennedy.

The concluding pages to *Power and Policy* constituted a sort of Pell manifesto on how America could, in essence, save the world — and the grim consequences for the planet and all its peoples if America failed.

"The true course of international diplomacy is to direct itself to the overriding problems created by the world's multiplying population and the starvation, deprivation and world-wide pollution of the environment that goes with it," Pell wrote. "The quantum leap in technology, and in the sheer numbers of human beings sharing the same planet, has in our lifetime overturned virtually all the old philosophies for the conduct of affairs among nations. If we are to survive, we must recognize that it will make no difference whether the last man to survive on an uninhabited planet happens to be a communist or a capitalist." It was a world that Pell's father Herbert, his most important influence, would scarcely have recognized. Pell went on:

We must bear in mind that international agreements, in order to last, must be of mutual advantage, must be voluntary, and must contain sanctions sufficiently severe to ensure a better chance of not being broken. We must bear in mind the interdependence of the world's people, an interdependence that increases with the raising of the technology of the various nations. We must bear in mind that the greatest natural resource is technological ability and education. As [French journalist and founder of *L'Express*] Jean-Jacques Servan-Schreiber puts it, "the one really important natural resource is gray matter." We must bear in mind that while technology and the means of production, of travel and communication and of war and destruction are enlarging at a geometric rate, human nature and desires are constant. Man today is drawn by pretty much the same basic desires as he was two thousand years ago. And these desires are pretty much the same throughout our world. That is why true communism, which runs against so many of man's basic desires, contains the seeds of its own destruction within itself . . .

We cannot decide for other nations; we can only hope. But for ourselves, we can determine that America's voice in the world will be raised on behalf of the real problems of the last third of the twentieth century and not used in querulous debate and continuous conflict with the ghosts of people who never saw an airplane or envisioned a world where two powerful nations on opposite sides of the globe could in half an hour obliterate the human race.

Our technical problems can be met, but not without quantum leaps in our thinking. Peace is the single most important problem confronting us. But a nation's foreign policy grows out of its own internal situation and men cannot be at peace with their neighbors unless they are at peace with themselves. It is quite true that there are many people in the world who do not wish us well, and it is also true that there are a few citizens of our own country who feel the same way. The gravest threat to our well being, however, comes not from outside or from any international or even internal conspiracy but from ourselves, those of us whose ideas and ways of life fall within the mainstream of American society.

As inheritors of the New World, we are still the last best hope of man-kind. If we cannot make the changes in our institutions and ways of thought that are required to cope with change, no one will do it for us. We will have the thanks of our descendents if we succeed. If we fail, we may not have descendents.

The Cold War and the lessons of Vietnam had tempered Pell's innate opti-mism, but not quashed it; he intended his conclusion in *Power and Policy* to be a warning Americans would heed as they built a better future, not a prediction of inevitable doom.

From his seat on the Senate Foreign Relations Committee during the 1970s and early 1980s, Pell advocated measures to achieve the outcome: wise steward-ship of the environment, arms control, human rights, and a strong American military without a threatening presence abroad, all achieved through negotia-tion and not conflict, with the United Nations as the globe's central diplomatic body. He still carried a copy of the United Nations charter with him everywhere for a reason.

Pell intended to play a leading role in that future; he intended to chair the Foreign Relations Committee and was willing to campaign for the job. In late 1980, when chairman Frank Church lost reelection and Pell was under consid-eration to succeed him, Pell issued a three-page "Foreign Policy Profile" stating his credentials and philosophies.

"An early opponent of Vietnam War, Pell is wary of sizable U.S. presence abroad," he wrote, in third-person. "Takes optimistic view of U.S. ability to meet Soviet threat worldwide . . . advocate of relations with all countries, including adversaries." Pell listed attributes that he believed would best serve the commit-tee chairman. "Accustomed to consensus approach in other committees; would strive for same approach in Foreign Relations. As former diplomat, Pell would seek to avoid confrontation either within committee or in relations with execu-tive. Emphasis on quiet, behind-the-scenes approach."

Noble in principle, these were the very gentlemanly virtues that would work against him when he finally did assume the chairmanship, in 1987, after twenty-two years on the committee.

▫ ▫ ▫ The spring of 1973 brought bad news for the Rhode Island economy.

As part of a reorganization of the nation's military capabilities as the Vietnam War disappeared into history, the Pentagon announced that it was closing the Navy base at Quonset Point and reducing the massive Navy presence in New-port. Nearly 21,000 military and civilian jobs with a combined annual payroll of almost $250 million would vanish, with an impact that would severely threaten wholesalers, retailers, and the hospitality industry. Pell joined the rest of the state's Congressional delegation and state and local leaders in denouncing the cuts, which many believed were politically motivated, though precisely how and to what end was never clearly articulated. Observers were hard-pressed to unearth a Nixonian grudge: the president had carried Rhode Island in the 1972 presidential election, and Chafee, former Navy Secretary, was widely expected to run again for the Senate in 1976, when senior Senator John Pastore would likely retire after twenty-six years. It would do the Republicans little good to saddle him with blame for ruining the local economy.

But Pell saw political opportunity. In a speech in Middletown, where much of the Newport Navy base was actually located, he linked the Navy cutbacks to the unfolding Watergate scandal, what he called "the almost daily revelations of dishonesty or misconduct in the executive branch of the federal government."

Both Watergate and the Pentagon's decision had a "common element," Pell asserted. "In both cases," he said, "there is a sense that the people's reasonable expectations have not been fulfilled, and a deep sense that the people's trust has been betrayed. The people's trust and confidence in their government has been seriously damaged." Evidence of the depth of this betrayal, Pell maintained, came when the cutbacks were announced "suddenly, precipitously, with little warning, and absolutely no [local] consultation after a partnership of many years between the state and the Navy."

It was a thin argument, but so was Republican Chafee's.

Former Navy Secretary Chafee suggested that the closings were the fault of Democrats—especially Pell and Pastore, who, he alleged, had rarely visited Quonset (he left untouched the fact that Pell lived in Newport).

"Senators Pastore and Pell are blaming everyone from President Nixon on down for Rhode Island's plight," Chafee said, "but the fact is their inattention to duty is the direct cause." Chafee did propose an economic plan to help fill the vacuum left by the Navy's cutbacks with measures designed to encourage private development, and from this and other plans would come the transition of Quonset to a center of industry and the emergence of Newport as a popular tourist attraction—efforts that Pell supported.

In the end, Rhode Islanders would see the villain in a remote federal bureaucracy, if they saw any villain at all.

▫ ▫ ▫ In Washington, Pell at the start of his third term continued to be known for the lunches and dinner parties he and Nuala hosted in their Georgetown home for politicians and distinguished thinkers in many fields. One frequent guest was the young Joe Biden, new senator from Delaware, who years later would recall the gatherings: "Claiborne would put together occasional dinners and lunches with really the outside experts, the equivalent of and sometimes including the Nobel laureates, the people who really were not in government but who knew a great deal about [issues,] whether it was high-speed ground transportation or sea-grant colleges or the nuclearization of the ocean's floor. He would bring all these people together and I became sort of an acolyte. I'd be invited to these lunches and dinners. The relationship just sort of morphed into something more than him helping this young senator."

Biden had come to Pell's attention in 1972, when the young lawyer, twenty-nine and a political unknown, was running for Senate on issues that Pell was emphasizing in his own reelection campaign: among them the environment, mass transit, civil rights, and opposition to Vietnam.

"The issues that I was running on," Biden said, "related to Vietnam, arms control, the B-1 bomber—all those things also were issues that were at the core of what Claiborne was concerned about. And in the process of this and coming and getting advice [in Washington], I met Claiborne. Claiborne was a terrible fundraiser but Claiborne used to direct me to people who would be helpful to me in my campaign."

Six weeks after Biden narrowly won, his wife and one-year-old daughter were killed in a car accident, leaving Biden with two young sons. Pell and Nuala were among those who offered comfort to Biden—opening their residence to them on those nights when the Senate met late into the night and Biden could not make the hour-and-a-half daily commute by Amtrak to his home in Delaware. Biden remembered this period of his life: "After I got elected and the accident happened involving my family, Claiborne was among a key group of senior, quote, 'powerful' senators who took an interest in me personally and politically. What Claiborne would always do, knowing I went home every night to see my children, on the nights we were very late in session would always insist that I come and stay at his home in Georgetown rather than sleep in my office, or sleep in the gymnasium and/or rent a room at Hyatt which was at the bottom of the hill . . . I did it a number of times, but it was more the exception more than the rule. But his was the only person's house that I stayed at of all of the senators who were generous and said, 'Joe, why don't you stay with us?'—everyone from Fritz Hollings to Tom Eagelton to Hubert Humphrey. He was the only one that I did that with."

Pell's intellectual curiosity impressed Biden, whose passions were similarly diverse, as did Pell's empathies, which, despite his class background, were for the common man. "His interest in education and the Pell Grants," Biden said.

"His interest in transportation. He was the guy who actually came up with Megalopolis. It really intrigued me that here was this guy who was from the oldest of old money was writing about the transportation net in the East Coast from Boston to Washington. It fascinated me."

And yet, as Biden soon learned, Pell's personality and his odd and old-fashioned ways could overshadow his accomplishments.

"Sometimes people looked at him and they sort of marginalized him because he was sort of eclectic," Biden said. "I thought he was really in every sense — I'll use the phrase 'value-added.' I realized he was ahead of the curve on a lot of things. I don't think most people thought in those terms about him."

▫ ▫ ▫ The Pell who took Biden under his wing began 1973 with his new moustache. The general public first saw it on February 24, when *The Providence Journal* published a photograph on the front page, accompanied by this account:

> Rhode Island now sports two mustaches in the U.S. Senate. The one with seniority — John O. Pastore's — is a familiar landmark. The latest outcropping — Sen. Claiborne Pell's — has yet to become full established. "I grew it really because my children all wanted me to grow a beard after the election and this is a really feeble compromise," Pell explained apologetically when he was caught in the act. "I'm not sure how long it's going to survive. I'm not really sold on it."
>
> Would he allow a press photographer to take his picture?
>
> "Unfortunately, my face — like so much of my life — has to be public property," the senator lamented, agreeing to pose. "I'm not sure yet that it should be called a mustache," he added. "I look as if I haven't shaved."
>
> Does she approve of the new décor, Mrs. Pell was asked.
>
> "Uh, let me look at it again (long pause). I have not made up my mind yet," she said. "I'm going to give it a little bit longer chance."

Pell was a handsome man, but the addition of a moustache combined with his offbeat attire lent him more easily to caricature. His wardrobe still included the same eclectic mix of custom-tailored suits and suits he bought at church sales or had inherited from his father. He wore shirts until the collars frayed. He always wore Herbert's belt, which nearly looped around him twice, and often his father's shoes, which he retired from use only when the leather had literally worn out — and even then he didn't throw them away.

On his daily jogs, he wore what was surely the most distinctive attire of any U.S. Senator: running shoes, white socks and shorts, topped with a suit jacket (often one from his Princeton days), shirt and tie, and sweater when it was cold.

A stranger viewing him might wonder where he slept at night. His pinkie ring and watch chain might have provided clues to his wealth—but even glimpsing those, one would have wondered what world he really came from. Both his ring and watch had the image of a pelican, the bird on the family coat of arms and an old Christian symbol of piety. And this was a U.S. Senator?

"I used to get such a kick out of Claiborne's lack of self-awareness," Biden said. "He was, like, 'why would [anyone] think this was unusual?' And I was young enough that I could be irreverent with him. When he told me about his father's belt, genuine rawhide, I said, 'Claiborne, you've got to be kidding me!' All the money! He'd say, 'This is my father's suit—it's tweed,' or whatever the hell it was. And I'd say, 'Claiborne, you cheap s-o-b, what the hell's the matter with you!' And he'd just laugh, that laugh of his."

Pell's peculiar fashion became fodder for the national press in the winter of 1973–1974 when Knight-Ridder syndicated columnist Vera Glaser, whose crusading journalism for women's causes won serious accolades, published a whimsical piece naming the ten best-dressed and the ten worst-dressed senators.

Texas Republican John Tower led the list of best-dressed. Pell was named worst—the leading "slob," Glaser called him.

"Socially prominent Democrat Claiborne Pell tops the frump list," she wrote. "He once wore the same seersucker suit five days running and according to a colleague, 'looked like he was born in it.'"

Asked about the allegation, Pell told a *Journal* reporter that in fact, he had never worn the same suit for so long; he owned three identical seersucker suits with two pairs of trousers each, and that had surely led to confusion. Pell said he had "not lost a minute's sleep" over the publicity, and he cared not how people might judge him based on such a frivolous matter as his attire. When he had arrived in the Senate in 1961, Pell said, Democratic senator Carl Hayden had told him that two types of people worked there: show horses and work horses. He put himself in the latter category.

"I think he's rather proud of it," Nuala told the reporter. "I would rather see him listed as the worst-dressed senator than the best-dressed. It means he's working." Still, she said, "it does backfire on me. After all, I'm the one who sends him off to work looking a little rumpled. I can't help feeling it's my fault."

More than anyone, Nuala was familiar with another of Pell's quirks, this one lesser known and constituting a true threat. It was his driving.

Pell's first experiences behind the wheel as a teenager in the 1930s had been fraught with difficulty—and after decades of holding a license, the middle-aged senator still had a tortured relationship with motor vehicles. His head was often somewhere else when he was driving—in his own thoughts, or in conversation with people riding with him. He rubbernecked and sometimes ignored stop signs and red lights, if he indeed he even saw them. He sometimes drove erratically, veering into the wrong lane, as if highway lines were symbols to be ignored — or were symbols that had been wrongly designed. Staff members told of the day he demonstrated how "logically" they should have been designed: as markers from which a motorist would guide a vehicle from its middle, not markers containing it on the sides.

"Oblivious, a great deal of the time," Nuala would recall. "His driving was appalling. *The* worst driver I ever knew."

It sometimes led to arguments between the two.

"When I'd get mad about his driving," Nuala said, "he'd stop the car and say, 'Don't complain about it, you drive.' I would."

Even starting his car could spell trouble. One morning, with the standard transmission still in gear, he turned the ignition key — and his car leapt into reverse, taking down a piece of cast-iron fence at the Pells' Georgetown residence. Age would not improve Pell's skills. And an automobile accident in the early 1990s — when, ironically, Pell was a passenger, in the back seat of a New York City taxi — would cause a severe head injury that may have precipitated his Parkinson's disease.

Along with Pell's questionable driving skills came frugal taste in vehicles. Pell could have afforded any brand or model, but he preferred cheap American cars — which he drove until they rusted and his efforts to keep them serviceable with touch-up paint and duct tape became futile. One car he drove for years was a 1973 stickshift Ford Mustang convertible. It had a pelican as a hood ornament — and a roll bar, which had not been installed for protection but to placate him after he was led to believe he had been cheated of a deal when purchasing the car. This senator who legislated treaties and Acts of Congress knew nothing of the negotiation that went into buying a car.

David Evans, who headed Pell's Education Subcommittee staff, would later tell the story of the Mustang. "You got into the back of this car and you could hardly sit in it because of this roll bar," Evans recalled. "I said to somebody one day, 'What is it with the roll bar in this convertible?' The story was he went to a Ford dealer and he bought the car and paid sticker price on it. He went back to the dealership because somebody told him, 'well, they didn't give you a deal? They didn't give you anything for it?' He said, 'no.' So he went back to the dealership and said, 'You know, you didn't give me a deal on this.' They said, 'OK, we'll put in a roll bar.' So the roll bar was his deal."

With cars, an Einstein Pell was not.

Pell's personal eccentricities alone would have supported the growing body of stories circulating in Washington and Rhode Island; combined with his more esoteric Senate initiatives, they guaranteed an offbeat lore that would follow him into retirement and survive his death. Here was a man who had shepherded one of the nation's most significant education reforms ever into law—and who, in 1974, introduced legislation to require all federally financed buildings be built with windows that could open. True, fresh air was beneficial to health and open windows would save some energy costs from unneeded heating and air-conditioning—but didn't the senator have more pressing issues? To Pell, windows *were* a pressing issue. "Increasingly, we in the United States have been shutting ourselves into these airtight, air-conditioned, tomblike buildings that use up and waste immense amounts of energy," Pell was quoted in the April 23, 1974, *Providence Journal*. "Think how often we have been in airtight buildings in which we sweltered or shivered."

In May 1976, with Pastore having confirmed his intention to retire at year's end, *The Sunday Journal Magazine* published a lengthy feature on Pell entitled "Our Next Senior Senator Goes His Own Way." The reporter C. Fraser Smith spent a day with Pell in Washington shadowing this senator he described as "a political legend in his own time." Pell, Smith observed, was a "somewhat awkward, somewhat enigmatic and more than somewhat wealthy" politician—one who could not, perhaps, be fully appreciated in his own time.

"He thinks of himself as a Far Thinker, a futurist and planner in the midst of men who often have no time for the future. Such a man always risks ridicule."

To buttress that conclusion, Smith wrote of the "laughing, loving folklore that chronicles his encounters with the real world." Smith cited stories that were making the rounds. One involved Pell's ignorance of the previous fall's World Series, in which the Cincinnati Reds defeated the Boston Red Sox, New England's oldest and most revered professional sports team.

"He is a man who often seems to be visiting from another world," Smith wrote, "discovering, as he did last fall, that the World Series is an event involving two *baseball* teams. 'I never watch football on TV,' he told a political reporter who was enlisting him in a prayer for the Red Sox."

A related but lesser-known story was told by Thomas G. Hughes, Pell's chief of staff from 1971 until Pell's retirement. During a reelection campaign, Pell agreed to throw out the first pitch at a Pawtucket Red Sox game; it was, Hughes said, "in the interests of making him sort of an ordinary guy," not always the easiest of tasks. Arriving early at Pawtucket's McCoy Stadium, home to Boston's triple-A farm team, Pell, accompanied by Hughes, went onto the field, where players were warming up.

"In much the same way as he always felt the need to go back in the kitchen at any banquet and shake hands with all the servers," Hughes said, "so, too, he felt the need to shake hands with all the ballplayers." He engaged some of them in conversation.

What do you do for a living? Pell asked.

I play ball, the players said.

Oh, yes, I know that must be great fun, Pell said. *But what do you really do? Do you teach school? Are you a plumber?*

No, no, I play ball!

"He had not the faintest idea that any 22-year-old kid would make a living playing baseball," Hughes said, "He figured it was like after school. It was an absolutely wonderful insight into his total obliviousness about professional sports and that whole world."

The quintessential quirky Pell story involved brand recognition and was told and retold in Washington and Rhode Island endlessly. The story grew over time, so embellished in the retellings that eventually it was impossible to confirm its every detail or original source. In Biden's version, the story emerged from the 1972 campaign against Chafee, when Mike McAdams, a political consultant who was nicknamed "Goose," accompanied Pell on a campaign stop.

"As he walked out," Biden said, "it was pouring rain. And he said, 'Goose, I'm going to ruin my shoes. I don't have galoshes.' And he said, 'You wait here, Senator, campaign a little more and I'll take care of that.' There was a Thom McAn shoe store across the street." In 1972, the Thom McAn chain had hundreds of stores.

"Goose went and bought this — he swore this to be true — this pair of slip-on rubbers that you can put on over your shoes. He got them and Claiborne was very pleased. He put them on, walked out to the car in this driving rain with an umbrella, and was driven home with Goose in the back seat. As Claiborne was getting out of the car he took out the rubbers and he said, 'where'd you get these, Goose?'

"And Goose said, 'Thom McAn, sir.'

"Claiborne said, 'Well, you thank Tom for me.'"

Although Pell was sometimes depicted as unaware of his own image, his behaviors were not so easily explained.

"The thing that always struck me about Pell," Hughes said, "was how many layers there were to his consciousness. By the time I got to know him, he had already perfected the art of his fixation on his father — the belt and all that — and making it into a little bit of a joke. He constructed some of these eccentricities almost consciously because he saw the eccentricities as somehow a valuable part of his persona. They came naturally, of course, but he saw benefits sometimes from magnifying them — benefits that we didn't always see, but he saw them. These eccentricities were worn on his sleeve with considerable knowledge. He wasn't some dumb fool . . . His mind worked that way. He had many layers to him and this eccentricity thing was one of the layers."

John E. Mulligan, who as *Providence Journal* Washington Bureau Chief covered Pell more closely than any journalist for the last two decades of Pell's career, saw glimpses of self-perception behind the oddball persona. During one of Pell's reelection bids, Mulligan followed the senator on the campaign trail, including his appearance in a parade.

"I like parades," Pell told Mulligan. "It's a cheap and easy way of showing that you're alive and well, that you don't have a terminal disease."

"The rumors of illness," Mulligan wrote in his story, "of impending retirement, have followed him for 20 years, he said, perhaps 'because I'm very thin.'

"At one point in the interview the reporter, trying not to give offense in the presence of the senator's wife, groped haltingly for a way to describe the enduring caricature of the wifty Claiborne Pell. The senator interrupted to offer the description himself. 'Head-in-the-sky?' he asked. 'Mr. Magoo?'

"Pell said he didn't mind. 'As long as you feel you're doing what's basically right, the short-term criticisms really don't faze me all that much.' Besides, he suggested, after the amusement is over, the Mr. Magoo issues get results. In the early 1970s, for example, Pell pushed through a package of low-interest loans and grants to poor students [the Pell Grants], based on his somewhat lonely belief that higher education should be 'a matter of right.' Millions of students have benefited from the results."

Mulligan later reflected on Pell's image:

"The same reporter — me — came to believe during more than 20 years of observation, that Pell's embrace of his inner Mr. Magoo was related to a strain of stubbornness and, perhaps, vanity beneath his exterior," Mulligan said. "Pell indulged all these traits — sometimes to his political benefit, but not always. Certainly there was no political profit, for example, in Pell's dogged advocacy of conversion to the metric system, or in his liking — decades after it fell out of fashion even in elite circles — for the 'One World' view of the onetime Republican presidential nominee, Wendell Willkie.

"On the other hand, if you want to change the world, it can be very helpful to have an ally who refuses to listen to reason."

Pell possessed an appealing smile, but he was not prone to laughter; the laughter he generated was mostly from the many Pell stories. Still, he did have a sense of humor, which the public occasionally glimpsed. Pell regularly attended The Follies, the annual late-winter satirical review sponsored by the Providence

Newspaper Guild, which represented most of the editorial staff of *The Providence Journal*. For Rhode Island's political establishment, attendance was all but mandatory. Reporters and editors wrote and acted in the skits, and in many years Pell was a target — an easy one. The appearance of a "mystery guest" at the end of each show was a Follies tradition. Each Guest was secretly invited, and given time to prepare his or her comments, in the spirit of stand-up comedy. Pell was the pick for the 1975 Follies.

The main performance that year included a spoof of his unofficial visit with Senator Jacob Javits to Cuba, the country Pell had first seen at the age of nine on one of the seminal foreign trips that would influence him for life. With Javits, Pell met Premier Fidel Castro, returning to America with the hope that their visit might prompt a thaw in U.S.-Cuba relations. Predictably, given his Vietnam War views, Pell was labeled a traitor by some. "Seeking out friendship with that godless Commie bum is an insult to the American people," one man wrote to Pell. Wrote a woman: "If you like being so buddy-buddy with Castro, why don't you just move there and keep your cotton pickin' hands off trying to run this free country." *The Journal* covered the story exhaustively.

The 1975 Follies ended and the mystery guest was announced.

Pell took the stage.

"We take *The Journal* very seriously in Washington, you know," he deadpanned. "I assign one staff member to read it cover to cover every day. That's done between 8:37 and 8:38 a.m." The audience of nearly 800 roared.

"I was going to take the train up here tonight," Pell continued, "but Amtrak said I wouldn't make it in time for the show. After seeing the show, I'm sorry I didn't take the train, after all."

◻ ◻ ◻ Chafee was elected to the Senate on his second try, in 1976. His win effectively removed Pell's most formidable competitor from the political equation for 1978, when Pell would seek his fourth term.

But a young and potentially powerful challenger had emerged: the colorful Republican Vincent A. "Buddy" Cianci, Jr., who was in his first term as mayor of Providence in the spring of 1977 when he hinted he might challenge Pell. An April poll privately commissioned by Cianci gave him a 71-percent approval rating among Providence residents. That was the only number the mayor released to the press, but he told *Journal* political writer Bakst that he had run second in a trial heat against Pell, a sufficiently encouraging result for him to declare: "Senator Pell would be a formidable man to beat, although he's not unbeatable."

In the end, Cianci decided to seek reelection to City Hall. With no prominent

Democrat willing to challenge Pell in a primary, a Republican attempting to unseat the incumbent would face a candidate able to devote most of his considerable resources to the general election. It would be a difficult battle, at best. As 1978 began and Pell's reelection funds topped $135,000 (with his personal wealth untapped), it seemed only a foolish or naively ambitious candidate would declare. One came forward.

Republican James G. Reynolds, 34, was the vice president of a bakery when he announced his candidacy against Pell in March. Reynolds received high marks for his intelligence when Bakst profiled him a short while later, and he presented himself as someone qualified to do a better job than Pell on the economic issues of taxes and jobs that would be at the heart of his campaign.

"I have no question in my mind that I could be a very good U.S. Senator," Reynolds said, citing his University of Chicago Law School degree. "I'm not in any kind of awe or anything of that job. You have to be able to write and read legislation, articulate yourself, be able to get along with people of all different backgrounds and educations. I can handle that. You do have to be someone with very sound judgment. You should have a humanity about yourself—see beyond yourself, that it's not an extension of your ego." But ego was certainly required to take on Pell, who had recently made headlines when President Jimmy Carter came to Rhode Island to show his support for the senator, and whose campaign war chest by April had swelled to almost $200,000.

"Reynolds' is one of the great long-shot candidacies of 1978," Bakst wrote. "For him to try to upset Pell, an eighteen-year Senate veteran, an apparently popular pro-labor Democrat in a pro-labor Democratic state—well, it takes a lot of imagination to visualize it."

Lacking a record, Reynolds offered his fiscally conservative ideas—and pointed criticism of Pell. He tried, as had Chafee in 1972, to depict his opponent as a man out-of-touch with the average Rhode Islander: a "dilettante," as he described him on May 24, who was more interested in the arts and humanities and conversion to the metric system (which Reynolds called "hogwash") than the bread-and-butter concerns of working-class people. He tried, as had Raul Archambault, Jr., in the 1960 general election, to depict Pell as a man born with a silver spoon—a "millionaire from birth who has never had to compete," Reynolds said. "He's never known the tough realities of life that most of us face every day. He's always been able to buy whatever he wanted."

Over the course of the campaign, he called Pell a succession of unflattering names: "ineffective" (June 18), "loaded" (August 19), "arrogant" (October 12), and "Stillborn Pell" (October 23), among others. The "loaded" label, at least, was not entirely off base: new Senate rules required release of senators' finances, and

Claiborne and Nuala in May reported assets of between $4.6 million and $7.2 million ($15.9 million and $24.8 million, respectively, in 2011 dollars) despite a loss of some $400,000 in securities holdings during the previous five years. ("I'm sorry that they went down," Pell told Bakst. "The people who handled my affairs did not do very well.")

But Reynolds' attacks and his issues did not gain traction with voters, as polls demonstrated. Nor did they bring him the money he needed against his better-financed opponent: by the end of October, he had raised only $72,047 to Pell's $353,639, a five-to-one disadvantage.

Declining to counterattack, which had never tempted him, Pell ran on his accomplishments, reemphasizing many of the themes from his 1972 effort: education, the environment, the Arts and Humanities Endowments, the Sea-bed Treaty, and the Sea Grant College program, which had so benefited the University of Rhode Island. He emphasized the virtues of his seniority, which now included chairmanship of the Rules and Administration Committee, and of two major subcommittees: Education, Arts, and Humanities; and Arms Control, Oceans and International Environment, which gave him responsibility for overseeing the Strategic Arms Limitation Talks between the United States and the Soviet Union, continuing negotiations that carried the hope for an end to the Cold War.

And he spoke of accomplishments since his last run, including one that began in tragedy.

Stephen Wexler was chief legal counsel for Pell's Education Subcommittee when he was struck and killed by a drunk driver as he was riding a motorcycle in September 1975 in Annapolis, Maryland; credited with a key role in Senate legislation since Pell assumed his chairmanship in 1969, including the Pell Grants, Wexler left a wife and a ten-month-old son. And he was not the first of Pell's staff to die at the hands of a drunk driver: press assistant Elizabeth Powell was also killed by one, in November 1974.

Citing both cases, Pell in June 1976 introduced legislation that would deny states federal highway assistance unless they passed laws requiring ten-day jail sentences for people convicted of drunk driving—and also "alcohol safety programs in which convicted drunk drivers must participate." Those convicted could serve alternate sentences in community service, according to the legislation.

"Are we powerless in this mighty nation to confront a problem that in a decade wipes out more than 500,000 of our fellow citizens? I hope not," Pell said in announcing his legislation, which he would continue to reintroduce until it finally passed. Recognizing the pathology behind many of those who drive drunk, Pell urged private hospitals to admit and treat alcoholics, rather than send them to second-rate state facilities or release them to the streets. "Our hospitals must be willing to provide the care and services needed by persons who are intoxicated as they are willing to treat manifestations of other diseases," he told a Rhode Island health-services group in November 1976.

The senator had found a new cause — at a time when the general public had yet to fully recognize drunk driving as the public-safety menace that it was (Mothers Against Drunk Driving, the prominent awareness group, was not founded until 1980).

In the nominal Democratic primary on Sept. 12, Pell, recovering from pneumonia he said he contracted while in Rome to attend the installation of Pope John Paul I, trounced his two marginal opponents: one a forty-eight-year-old political novice and the other a sixty-eight-year-old Newport resident who had failed twice before in primaries against Rep. Fernand J. St. Germain. Pell took nearly 90 percent of the vote and every city and town. He had campaigned over the summer, but with an eye toward the general election.

The final two months of the 1978 election season generated little fire in the Senate contest.

Reynolds and Pell met only once in debate: a televised event at the end of October. The incumbent stuck to his issues, repeating what was becoming his legislative mantra: "Translate ideas into action and help people." Reynolds focused on the economy — and tried unsuccessfully to "goad Pell into an outburst," as one reporter put it.

Something more the opposite happened: Pell caught Reynolds in a trap. Asked by the moderator what he could hope to accomplish as a freshman senator, Reynolds said that some of the most "aggressive" forces in the Senate were senators in their first or second year. Reynolds named a few. He turned to his opponent and said:

"Senator Pell, I don't think you've been aggressive at all."

Pell replied that the senators Reynolds had cited may have been vocal in debate, but had sponsored very little legislation that had actually passed. What mattered, Pell said, were results. With that, he lifted onto the debate desk a ten-inch stack of bills and reports for which he said he had been responsible. Then he smiled. Point made.

Days before the election, *The Providence Journal*'s editorial board urged voters to reelect Pell. "For three terms, Claiborne Pell has represented Rhode Island with energy, distinction and honor," the paper wrote in its endorsement. "He remains vigorous and his influence within the Senate can only increase. On the strength of his record, Mr. Pell clearly merits another term, and these newspapers so recommend."

Voters agreed. On November 7, Pell buried Reynolds with a better than three-to-one margin, 221,936 votes to 73,006. Pell took every city and town — even Reynolds's hometown of Barrington, overwhelmingly, 3,756 votes to 2,695.

It seemed no Republican would ever stand a chance against Pell.

But one would: Claudine Schneider, a 34-year-old environmentalist and lawyer who was on the ballot with Pell that November. In that first bid for Congress, she nearly unseated Rep. Edward P. Beard. In the rematch two years later, she would prevail, but her House seat would not satisfy her.

PELLIANA

The four Pell children came of age in the 1960s and early 1970s, the era when the Vietnam War and the youth revolution personified by Woodstock transformed America, leaving it a different world than the one into which Claiborne and Nuala had been born. Pell opposed the Vietnam War, which made him a political progressive, but his parenting was grounded in the upper-class mores of a bygone age, which, together with his quirks and career, made him a most uncommon father.

When his children were young, Pell insisted they eat separately from the adults, the cook serving their meals through a porthole from the kitchen; when they were allowed to join grownups at the dinner table, at about the age of ten, small-talk was forbidden. "Father always tried to elevate discussion at the dinner table," recalled Toby. "Always about politics. Never gossip." As teenagers, the Pell children, like Europeans their age, were allowed a glass of wine with dinner. Pell himself rarely drank hard liquor and he did not drink anything to excess, though he had proved his capacity in college: "He had a hollow leg when it came to wine, but he was never a drinker," Toby said. Pell loved beer, as had his father, but he was allergic to it and had to abstain. He ate in moderation, with health, not pleasure, being the goal: "Food is fuel," he liked to say. He exercised regularly, most commonly by jogging. Sometimes, his children went along.

Pell exposed Bertie, Toby, Dallas, and Julie to his frugal ways — the tattered clothes, the beat-up cars, the money he was delighted to save by scrounging appetizers at social functions — but he was generous in his support of their education, their travels, and their leisure. He insisted they learn to sail and play tennis, but not get jobs that would provide lessons they might need later in life. "Enjoy your childhood," Claiborne and Nuala would say, "because you're never going to have this kind of free time again." There nonetheless were cardinal rules: always do good, be kind, and be honest. One sibling calling another a liar or cheat, even in jest, was a punishable offense. It was simply unimaginable to

Pell that one of his children could engage in such dishonorable behavior; they were, after all, Pells.

As they grew toward adulthood, Pell expected that his children, like him, would embrace the philosophy incorporated into the Pell family crest, which asked allegiance to "God, our friends and ourselves." He expected they would be accomplished, in ways that would do the family and himself proud (though he did not share his own underlying doubts that he had failed to meet the expectations of his father, doubts that lay behind the quest he took to learn what comes after death).

"He always had an agenda for the family," Toby recalled. "To follow in his footsteps. He was very clear that anything that would bring credit to the family would be good, in business or in politics." This was the kind of upbringing and pressure that, in Toby's word, was "tough" on the children, who responded in various ways.

At his father's insistence, Bertie, who bore his grandfather's name, attended St. George's, Claiborne's alma mater. He enrolled at Princeton, also Claiborne's alma mater—only after Pell overruled the teenager's choice, Stanford. Artistically inclined, Bertie disliked Princeton, and he left after junior year, during which he had submitted a "junior thesis" which was actually a one-page essay explaining why he disliked his major—essentially a ploy to escape the Ivy League school. After a summer in Canada and time as a Fort Ticonderoga tour guide, Bertie entered the Rhode Island School of Design, where he met a fellow artist, Eugenia Diehl. They married in September, 1969, after graduating from RISD. After three years in the Coast Guard, Bertie moved to Arizona, where he became a loan officer at a bank and then a car dealer. He and Eugenia had two children: Christina and Herbert Claiborne Pell IV, Clay, named for Bertie's father and grandfather, whose sudden death on the streets of Munich he had witnessed as a teenager. Bertie would die young: at age 54, of cancer.

Dallas, named for Pell's maternal great-great granduncle, George M. Dallas, U.S. vice president from 1845 to 1849, was a debutante while at Madeira School in Mclean, Virginia. After graduating from Boston University, she worked variously as a research assistant to a professor at Harvard, an emergency medical technician, and a literary agent. She married and had a son, Eames Yates. She later would become a leader in a campaign, through New York's College and Community Fellowship, a women's convict rehabilitation organization, to restore Pell Grant assistance to prisoners. Prisoners were excluded from Pell Grants in 1994, in a move by a Republican-controlled Senate.

Like Dallas, Julie, youngest of the Pell children, attended Madeira School until she was expelled for refusing to implicate a schoolmate in an infraction involving marijuana. Furious at his daughter, Pell, who at the time was being mentioned as a vice-presidential candidate, sent her to a finishing school in Switzerland. She was miserable there — but it was in Switzerland that she discovered she was a lesbian. After dropping out of the University of Denver and Boston University, she enrolled in the University of Rhode Island, where she earned a bachelor's degree. Julie would struggle with mental health issues her whole life, but she would manage to live independently. She would become the only child of Pell who undertook a political career. As president of the Rhode Island Alliance for Lesbian and Gay Civil Rights, she would be one of the state's foremost gay-rights advocates, a familiar presence at the State House and on the op-ed pages of newspapers. Like her brother Bertie, Julie would die young: at 52, also of cancer.

Second child Toby attended St. George's and graduated from Brown University. In January 1971, he married Janet Alexander, a Madeira School classmate of Dallas, and daughter of a late chairman of Morgan Guaranty Trust. Toby enrolled in Georgetown University Law School but soon left for New Hampshire, where he took work as a carpenter and then as executive director of a financial research corporation. In 1976, he returned to his home state, where he earned a master's degree in marine affairs from the University of Rhode Island; became a partner in an investment firm; became executive director of the Preservation Society of Newport County, whose headquarters were in his grandfather's former estate on Bellevue Avenue; and served on a number of arts, humanities, and community boards. He and Janet had two children: Tripler, the Pell's first grandchild, and Nick.

Janet's early impressions of her father-in-law were of "a very self-focused" man whose passions were politics and Pells.

"He wasn't interested in anything beyond his interests," she said. "The same at the dinner table, you know — he had his subjects that he liked to talk about. And then he'd expound. But outside of that, I don't know whether it was a slight case of OCD or something. Outside those subjects, he really wasn't interested in table conversation."

Janet could see how Pell worshipped his dead father, even though Herbert with his great intellectual curiosity and indulgence in life's pleasures — in good food, drink and company — stood in contrast to the son who seemed incapable of joy. Ancestors obsessed her father-in-law, Janet believed, more than politics.

"He was totally interested in his forbears," she said. "I think one of his — I'm using his word here — forbears — invented the division sign or something and my god, my god, we all had to hear that a thousand times. And he was very interested in his bloodlines. If you mentioned one of his relatives and what they were doing, he perked right up and entered the conversation. And he might tell you he was related to this person and that person . . . This was an obsession. He was so obsessed with it that when Bertie had a little girl about a year after my son was born, he wanted them to marry. He told me that. And I said, 'Claiborne, they are first cousins, that's not a good idea,' and he was horrified that I didn't think it was a good idea.'"

Pell told Janet: "It keeps the bloodlines going."

ɑ ɑ ɑ Pell's children grew up, as did their father and his father, surrounded by the presence of dead people, mostly on Claiborne's side of the family. Nuala acknowledged her heritage, her Hartford A&P forbears, but she was not obsessive about ancestors, as her husband. He was fascinated with Pells especially, but also with Bigelows, deBordas, Kernochans, Lorillards, and Dallases — and even stepfather Commander Koehler, whose mysterious life before meeting Matilda fascinated Claiborne.

Pell decorated his Newport home with mementoes of ancestors, but the comfortable design of the house lent itself to more contemporary sentiments — paintings and photographs of his wife and children, and of people and events from his unfolding political career. In Washington, the past seemed to weigh more heavily. It simultaneously tugged at Pell and brought him pride, as guests to his home discovered.

"Claiborne Pell was a man intrigued by the notion of a subtle byplay in the crosscurrents of family and history and fate and, well, something else," said the *Journal*'s Mulligan.

"He delighted in acquainting visitors with the touchstones of a legacy borne not through mere decades or generations but through centuries. Imagine yourself a guest at the big house on Prospect Street in Georgetown in the middle years of his long sojourn in the United States Senate. It was almost as if the standard Pell tour was staged for dramatic effect and surprise.

"Mount the stair, round the banister, climb again to the landing and hark: this full suit of armor that was handed down from times when Pell forbears crested at well under six feet in height. In a hallway upon a wall, the image of a bewigged ancestor who devised the dash-and-dots arithmetic symbol for division. More tokens and oddments in the senator's cluttered study and more gleanings from his patter. The family-held fortress at Ticonderoga. The forefathers who fought on both sides of the Revolutionary War.

"Downstairs again and in to the front room that faces the Potomac and rounds out the tour. Here above the fireplace, a portrait in vibrant oils: a blonde schoolgirl with her father, the Hartfords of The Great Atlantic & Pacific Tea

Company. And now as you exit the room, a genealogical parlor trick on the opposite wall: a slender boy and his father, the Pells of New York and Newport, on a canvas of jarringly similar composition. The senator registers the click of recognition in the visitor's eye. 'Oh, yes,' Pell says in a seemingly unpracticed way, 'Nuala and I come from very similar backgrounds.'"

They did, indeed, in the shorter term of history. But Nuala could not claim lineage to a Lord of the Manor or other shapers of America, save in business.

Another immersion in Pelliana greeted those invited into Pell's beloved hideaway office along the north wall of the first floor of the Capitol. Here, as in his Newport and Washington homes, Pell chronicled milestones in his life and career — and paid homage to predecessors, notably his father, whose suits, shoes and belt he wore. Among the dozens of items that decorated the wall were a poster from Pell's 1960 campaign; an oil painting of Pell and Nuala; prints of vice president George M. Dallas, and forbears William Charles and Nathaniel Herbert Claiborne, nineteenth-century southern politicians; photographs of Pell with several presidents, and with Teddy Kennedy; and many photographs of Herbert. His books were mostly historical volumes, but also an Olive Pell Bible and, increasingly as the 1980s unfolded, explorations of near-death experiences and life after death.

"If there was a top personal favorite icon," Mulligan recalled, "it must have been the black-and-white photograph of three rising stars of New York State politics in the early part of the twentieth century: Al Smith, Franklin Roosevelt, and Herbert Pell. Rarely would the son of the long-ago Democratic chairman's son fail to point out that right here, wrapped twice around his own slender waist, was the very same length of scarred leather that had once held up the senior Pell's trousers. Stoutness ran in the family, the senator would explain, and heart maladies, too. Hence his lifelong regimen of eating in moderation and exercising often."

Encouraged by his father, Pell had begun to amass Pelliana as a child, and as he moved through middle age, his collection swelled through inheritance, donation, and purchase. Incapable of discarding any of it, he placed what didn't fit on Newport and Washington walls and desktops in storage. Most eventually was shipped to the University of Rhode Island Library. There among the approximately half-mile of linear shelf space that constituted the Pell personal and political archives were dozens of boxes filled with ancestral photographs, prints, engravings, locks of hair, seals, coats of arms, birth and death certificates, last wills and testaments, passports, social security cards, charts, poems, place cards, postcards, stamps, foreign currency, and bank ledgers. Pell's schoolboy papers, report cards and drawings were there. Thousands of letters from and to friends and relatives, notably his father and mother, were there. Home movies were there.

A similar, if smaller, archive existed at the Franklin D. Roosevelt Presidential Library and Museum in Hyde Park, N.Y., where Herbert's papers were kept. Still more Pelliana was found at the Fort Ticonderoga Library & Archives.

◻ ◻ ◻ Pell pursued his family obsessions mostly out of view of the media.

Like his father before his death, Pell remained quietly involved in the administration of Fort Ticonderoga and in the activities of The Pell Family Association, which sporadically published the journal *Pelliana* and tracked far-flung relatives across America and abroad. He attended Pell family reunions. He was a Pell by paternity, but he carried his mother's genes as well, and that led him to the Bigelows, deBordas, and Dallases.

An early reader of the classics, Pell understood, as had his father, the power of books to immortalize. He was in his second term when he hired the future Pulitzer Prize–winning author Leonard S. Baker to write a biography of his father. Pell gave Baker, who had written books about Franklin Roosevelt and Lyndon Johnson, access to Herbert's papers and to his own. Doubleday published the resulting 350-page volume, *Brahmin in Revolt: A Biography of Herbert C. Pell* in 1972. It attracted little critical attention, but it preserved Herbert's story — and provided clues into the father-son relationship, which continued so powerfully after Herbert had died. One of the most revealing, if understated, clues was a photo, selected by Pell, of the son sitting on his father's lap when Claiborne was about eight or nine. Claiborne looks adoringly at his father, whose expression is one of studied intellect. "Herbert Pell took great interest in his son's upbringing, even after he and Matilda were divorced in 1927," the caption reads.

Herbert's story was readily told: Baker had only to comb the archives, read the newspapers, and interview the senator and other Pells and friends of Herbert to capture the man. The story of Commander Koehler was something else. Pell had lived with him for many years, but important chapters of his past had always been secretive. A boy would have been fascinated by the tales the former Navy officer told of his escapades as an American spy in post–Bolshevik Revolution Russia — but an adult could not but wonder who Koehler really was and whether the tales he told had been true. There were too many missing pages.

According to U.S. Navy records, Koehler was born in St. Louis on July 19, 1886, the son of Oscar Carl and Mathilda (Lange) Koehler, a brewer and his wife. But Koehler came to think that they were not his biological parents, though they had indeed raised him. He strongly suspected — and occasionally hinted to others, including, perhaps, his young stepson — that he was actually the illegitimate son of the Archduke Rudolf, Crown Prince of Austria, and his mistress, the Baroness Marie Alexandrine von Vestera. The two established a trust fund for their love child, the theory went, and they arranged for his adoption. The archduke and baroness died in early 1889 at Mayerling, the hunting lodge of Rudolf's father, Emperor Franz Joseph. Their deaths, never properly investigated but widely publicized, spawned a multitude of theories that played out in articles, books, plays, and movies. Perhaps Rudolf had killed his lover and then himself. Perhaps both had committed suicide, after the baroness had become pregnant. Perhaps both had been murdered. What was uncontested was that the Vatican granted a special dispensation so that Rudolf could be buried in Vienna's sacred Imperial Crypt, where members of the Catholic Habsburg dynasty had been interred since the 1600s.

By early 1974, Pell was actively investigating Koehler. He was cooperating with New York journalist Guy Richards, who was writing a book destined for publication the next year, *Rescue of the Romanovs: Newly Discovered Documents Reveal How Czar Nicholas II and the Russian Imperial Family Escaped*. Despite convincing evidence that the last czar and empress of Russia and their children were murdered by the Bolsheviks (notably in the 1967 *Nicholas and Alexandra*, by future Pulitzer Prize–winning historian Robert K. Massie), Richards theorized that the Romanovs had been secretly smuggled from prison to safety in 1918, a year after the revolution — and that one of the principal participants in the plot was Koehler. Richards would cite unsubstantiated "secret" U.S. government files in his book, but little that constituted independently verifiable proof.

Pell's cooperation with Richards and his wild theories alarmed a staff member, who wrote on October 4 to his boss: "I have a bit of an uneasy feeling about this book Guy is writing." The staff member told Pell that Richards' book would mostly present speculation, not verified fact. "Therefore it occurs to me," he wrote, "that it could be subject to scholarly ridicule and perhaps controversy and I wouldn't want to see you mixed up indirectly with this."

But on this, Pell listened to himself, not staff. He helped to pry loose government files for Richards, and he gave him a quote about his stepfather.

"From the time I was nine years old," Pell wrote, "I lived most of the time, for ten months of each year, in the same house as my stepfather, Commander Koehler. I loved the man. He was a very gifted, very unusual person. On many occasions, I have met people who knew something about his exploits and from them, as well as from my mother and from what I could note myself, I have been convinced that a fine book could be — and should be — written about him. Whoever wrote it, however, would have to dig into areas where the facts are not easy to come by."

Richards' book was in stores in the summer of 1975 and Pell inevitably was questioned about it. "It certainly raises a lot of very valid questions," he told the *Providence Journal* in a story published on July 20. "A lot of the pieces fall together in a remarkable way." Pell acknowledged that Richards had not decisively proved the Romanovs had survived, but he said he the author was a man of integrity. "I do not believe it's a hoax by Richards," he told *The Journal*. "I spent several hours with him and have acquired quite a respect for him."

Pell's quest that summer of 1975 had also led him to the Archdiocese of Vienna, where, he hoped, archival records would at least reveal details of Koehler's trust—if it existed. Pell suspected proceeds of the trust had been paid to the adult Koehler through Leopoldinenstiftung, a missionary society established in 1829 to channel Austrian donations to Catholics in America. Pell received early encouragement: on October 22, 1975, an archdiocesan archivist wrote that he "knew" that "remittances have been sent to Mr. Hugo Koehler" and that he would undertake additional inquiry.

"I am deeply grateful to you and the cardinal for your willingness to organize further research into this problem," Pell wrote back. "As you know, it is of great personal interest to me and its resolution would answer a question for which I have searched for many years." But the search would reach a dead end four years later when another person Pell enlisted in his quest, Brigitte Hamann, an Austrian author who had written a biography of Rudolph, determined (after an audience with Archbishop Franz Jachym) that no records of the trust existed. Perhaps, Hamann speculated, such records—if they had ever existed—had been destroyed by the Nazis.

By 1977, Pell had found two other people he hoped would help him: American broadcast journalist David Osterlund, who had partnered with Richards as he pursued a television piece on the Romanovs; and Peter J. Bessell, a former British Member of Parliament who had fled to the United States in debt and under fear of prosecution for fraud, and who claimed inside knowledge of the Romanov's demise. Pell opened government doors to Osterlund and Bessell, as he had with Richards—but one door seemed to close that year, when Pell asked President Carter's National Security Advisor Zbigniew Brzezinski to assist Osterlund. Brzezinski assigned Gregory F. Treverton, a European specialist on his staff, to look into it. Treverton came up empty-handed.

"I have talked several times with Mr. Osterlund and have asked various agencies of the government for their assistance," Treverton wrote to Pell on November 16, 1977. "Unfortunately—or perhaps fortunately—the trail has not led very far. I passed to Mr. Osterlund an unclassified report done several years ago by the Central Intelligence Agency which cast considerable doubt on several elements of the story that Mr. Peter Bessell outlines in his affidavit."

Pell was not easily discouraged; it was both the key to his success in his greatest legislative accomplishments, and a frustration to people around him. "Very persistent, focused, never gave up," son Toby would recall. "To the point where it could drive some people crazy."

A decade after the U.S. intelligence establishment told him their efforts to shed more light on Koehler were futile, the obsessive Pell was back on the quest, enlisting an Austrian researcher. Writing from her office in Vienna on February 27, 1987, Hildegard Weidinger wrote what she called her "final report on my research concerning Mr. Hugo Koehler." She confirmed that banking records of the Hapsburgs prior to World War I had been destroyed in a July 1927 fire at Vienna's Palace of Justice. She interviewed a member of Habsburg royalty, who told her that the time-honored practice was to grant stipends to mothers of illegitimate offspring — not establish trusts. "Therefore, I guess, the regular income of Mr. K. must have come from another source." She conveyed to Pell her contacts with the Vatican, where she said she had learned nothing new.

"I have to inform you that I consider my assignment at an end," Weidinger wrote. "I am very sorry that I could not be of more assistance."

▫ ▫ ▫ Pell's involvement in *Rescue of the Romanovs* also brought him to someone else who was sharing information with Richards: Margaretta Wood Potter, an elderly woman living in Jamestown, Rhode Island, who had met Koehler in 1921, the same year the commander met the then-married Matilda and Herbert Pell. Like other women, Potter had become romantically involved with Koehler, and she maintained her affections for him even after he married Pell's mother, with whom she eventually became friends. Whether still carrying a romantic flame or merely intrigued by Koehler's cryptic past, as was Pell, Potter remained in Koehler's spell long after he had died.

"I think I knew him better and saw him more truly than did most of his other friends," Potter wrote in *Rescue of the Romanovs*. "He was a puzzle for two reasons: his brain was vastly superior to our brains, and he simply did not fit into the American scene. Physically he was tall, but squarely built and very strong. When he walked, with rather short steps, he carried his head high, slightly thrown back, and he never watched his feet, as Americans invariably do. He was strikingly handsome, even in his last years, when he was not well and his hair had turned white and his waist had thickened. He spoke English in his deeply pitched voice with a faint Germanic accent. He was one of the best raconteurs and conversationalists I have ever listened to, although this excellence led him to the sin of pontificating, and when there was no one well-informed enough for him to sharpen his wits against, he could be really insufferable."

One could picture the nine-year-old Pell, spellbound by the swashbuckling stories told by this outsized man who had married his recently divorced mother.

Richards unveiled nothing about the true circumstances of Koehler's activities in the Russian Civil War nor of his birth. He had not undertaken Koehler's full life story — but Potter was capable of researching it, Pell concluded, and in the early 1980s, she agreed to write a memoir. She died at the age of 85 in 1985 without publishing it, but from letters Koehler had written to her, her memories, and other sources, she had produced a typewritten manuscript that provided more details of Koehler's life — and also her own, an early chapter of which illustrated the hold the commander could have on people he met.

She met Koehler, she wrote, in April 1921 — the same year Koehler met Matilda and Herbert Pell — at a Washington dinner hosted by her father, a Navy officer. Potter was twenty-one; the commander thirty-five, and greatly experienced in the ways of the world.

"I fell madly in love with him," Potter wrote,

and I think that he loved me as much as I loved him. We had a wonderful three-month interlude. In early August, he was ordered to Warsaw as Naval Attaché. On his return from Poland, we were to be married. I do not know what happened in Poland. All I know is that I received a terrible letter from him, telling me that he could not marry me and that I must "forget" him. I loved him so much that whatever he wanted was my law, so I tried to obey, even though the resulting anguish nearly caused me a breakdown. Years later, we became friends, but even then I did not ask, and so never learned what had changed his mind.

But Potter had a theory.

Koehler later told her that on this European trip, he had met several times with Archbishop Ambrogio Damiano Achille Ratti, papal nuncio to Poland, who became Pope Pius XI the next year, and with Archbishop Eugenio Maria Giuseppe Giovanni Pacelli, the German nuncio, elected Pope Pius XII on Ratti's death in 1939. Koehler's claim of these meetings was not independently verified, but Richards accepted it, speculating that Koehler met with Ratti to discuss the Romanovs. Potter saw something more scheming.

"I feel more urgently that they had to do with Hugo's possible future," she wrote in her memoir. "[Pell's mother] Matilda once said to me, 'I think it was a shame how they got his hopes up,' and I was a little too diffident to press her as to exactly what she meant by that. Now I suspect that Pacelli or Ratti had some plan for Hugo which did not include his marriage with the daughter of an unpretentious American naval officer." Potter did not speculate about the supposed plan, but a reader with a conspiratorial bent might have wondered if it had been to use Koehler to help restore the Habsburg monarchy.

Potter was a widow, mother, and grandmother who was remembered for her involvement in civic-charitable and historic-preservation causes when she died in May 1985. Pell passed her unpublished memoir and notes to a postgraduate history student at the University of Rhode Island, P. J. Capelotti, who would devote three years to researching and writing Koehler's biography. A credible scholar who would go on to a successful academic career, Capelotti turned his doctoral thesis into the first of his many books.

Our Man in the Crimea: Commander Hugo Koehler and the Russian Civil War, published in 1991 by the University of South Carolina Press, was a meticulously researched and documented account of Koehler's life. Among others, Capelotti interviewed Pell and Koehler's son, Pell's half-brother, Hugh Koehler, who died on the eve of publication. He received access to Pell's archives and letters that Hugh had kept. He searched the National Archives and other sources. Capelloti found no hard evidence of Koehler's involvement with the Romanovs. Nor did he discover hard evidence of any relation to the Habsburgs, only unexplained statements and circumstances that together could make a circumstantial case, if one were so inclined, for what Koehler suspected.

Citing what Koehler had told Potter in an episode she wrote in her memoir, Capelotti recounted what the commander claimed his Missouri grandfather told him as a young man: that his supposed father, Oscar Carl, who had died in 1901, was really someone else. His real father, the old man told his grandson, was Archduke Rudolph.

"There is no record extant of how Koehler responded to this," Capelotti wrote,

> though it is not difficult to imagine the swirling thoughts of a man suddenly ripped forever from familiar moorings. Neither is it difficult to imagine that he must have been both stunned and yet somehow unsurprised; unsurprised, possibly, because he recalled the extreme deferential treatment his supposed parents had extended to him as a child. Further, there were the strange visitors from Austria and the trip to Vienna, where his grandfather had introduced him to the emperor, and the trip to England, where he met Empress Elizabeth. Why, Koehler must have wondered, why was I the only one to accompany him, on these travels? Why did he never take either my brother or sister on these important journeys?

Capelotti wrote of Koehler's own search "after this supposed extraordinary revelation" for proof of his origins, an exercise in futility that "yielded only conflicting opinions and speculation . . ."

Capelotti noted, as Potter had, the physical resemblance of Koehler's chin to the distinctive chins of Habsburgs. He mentioned the alleged trust fund, which, he wrote, Pell believed had existed:

> He bases this belief on otherwise unexplained income and on the fact [as presented by Pell in a 1988 interview] that Koehler had to go to Vienna at the time of his marriage to Matilda Bigelow (Pell's mother) to seek termination of the trust because Hugo, a Roman Catholic, in marrying a divorced Protestant, was no longer eligible to receive it. Senator Pell at one point asked Mrs. Oscar Koehler—the only woman Hugo ever knew as his mother—point-blank, was the story that Hugo was Rudolph's son true? The woman only laughed and, while certainly not confirming the story, did not directly deny it then, and her later demise preserved this silence.

Koehler died in 1941, while Pell, a year out of Princeton, was trying to get into the Navy. "Here, as in so many other parts of Commander Koehler's unrecorded past," Capelotti wrote, "a melancholy silence closes over him like the depths of the sea." In this quest, Pell had failed to find the truth.

▫ ▫ ▫ The Coast Guard mandated retirement at age sixty, and as that birthday approached, Pell decided to leave the reserve officer corps with a public ceremony. He chose the cutter *Vigilant*, which was docked in Newport on August 28, 1978, when Captain Pell, in the company of his family, approached the podium for his farewell remarks.

A wasp stung Pell, giving him a metaphor.

"I feel there must be some significance," he told *Journal* reporter Brian C. Jones after the ceremony. "This is a sad occasion."

The next year, his friend Javits was diagnosed with amyotrophic lateral sclerosis, a fatal disease that progressively destroys a person's body, though not the mind. Despite it, Javits would seek reelection in 1980, losing to Alfonse D'Amato in the Republican primary. Olive Pell, Pell's stepmother, was near death. At sixty-two, Pell was no young man. He was contemplating a biography of himself—if not to immortalize him, then perhaps to contribute to the public discourse, and to preserve his own role in the Pell story. He wrote a seven-page "outline of a biography or autobiography of Claborne deB. Pell" that began with John Pell, the seventeenth-century mathematician.

The senator approached Jackie Kennedy Onassis, who had established herself as a leading editor at Doubleday. Onassis provided encouragement to Pell, but no offer of a contract for an autobiography or biography by another writer. Pell turned to his cousin John Pell Train, author and co-founder of *The Paris Review*. Train found a writer he deemed suitable to write a Pell biography and an agent, to whom Pell wrote an introductory letter on December 10, 1980, two days after his stepmother died at age 94.

"My thought is that an interesting, salable biography could be written," Pell wrote to the agent, Gerard McCauley, "perhaps with some reverse of the Horatio Alger 'born in a log cabin' theme. My personality and approach are a bit oddball but nevertheless have survived in this very real rough-and-tumble world of politics for four Senate terms, the last of which I won by 75 percent of the vote."

The next year, Pell's proposal reached several publishers, including William Morrow and Harper and Row. All declined. More than a decade and a half would pass before Pell tried seriously again, a time during which his mortality increasingly weighed on him.

THE NEW RIGHT

The year 1980 brought honor for Pell. At the suggestion of Senator Thomas F. Eagleton, a member of Pell's education subcommittee and a conferee during the decisive 1972 House-Senate negotiations that led to Pell's crowning achievement, the Basic Educational Opportunity Grants were formally christened "Pell Grants" during that year's reauthorization of the Higher Education Act.

The year also brought change to Washington.

That November, Ronald Reagan defeated Carter and the Republicans won a majority of the seats in the Senate, the first chamber of Congress that they had controlled in more than a quarter of a century (Democrats kept a majority in the House). Pell for the first time was a member of the minority party, his chairmanships lost and his influence on committees diminished. But he would not go away: as ranking Democrat on the Senate Foreign Relations Committee, he would serve as a counterpoint to Reagan's hard-line stand against the Soviet Union, a policy, incorporated under the President's March 1983 "Evil Empire speech," that included revival of the B-1 bomber program, NATO deployment in Europe of nuclear-armed missiles, and an overall buildup of the American military (what he called "peace through strength") that followed Carter's post-Vietnam drawdown of forces. In his votes and public statements, Pell would oppose Reagan's fiscally conservative economic policies, Reaganomics, and the president's conservative social policies.

But Pell would not personalize his opposition. He would not lose his patrician manners, or his desire to always seek consensus. He remained a senator who asked "Who's the Republican we can work with on this?" when a staff member brought an issue to his attention. He remained true to a philosophy that had become his legislative mantra: "I always try to let the other fellow have my way."

"When the Republicans assumed the Presidency and control of the Senate in the 1980 elections, the shift in power was a dramatic one," recalled Education Subcommittee staff chief Evans. "It was the first time that Senator Pell would find himself in the minority. I remember vividly his reaction to a House-Senate conference meeting on changes in the student loan program. He told me he was literally amazed that no one looked at our side when making decisions. He felt left out and had a difficult time believing it was happening. The interesting thing is that he took this to heart and instead of becoming an opponent of the Administration, he sought to stake out positions where he could work with the Republican majority. This was especially easy because Senator [Robert] Stafford [moderate Republican from Vermont], as Chairman of the Education Subcommittee, valued Senator Pell's input."

In nearly two decades of working for Pell, Evans only once heard him use a derogatory word about a Congressman — and the word was "jerk," which, Evans said, he used to explain why this particular senator was so difficult to work with (out of respect for his former boss, Evans would not name the senator). Pell's manners held universally, staff said.

"I cannot say that I ever heard him utter a bad word [personally] about President Reagan or the Republican leadership in Congress, the White House and the Administration, especially the Department of Education, with which I was most familiar," Evans said. "He opposed their policies, but he was part of the loyal opposition, and 'loyal' is the controlling word."

Pell would not verbally disparage a colleague, but those who knew him best could sense his displeasure, and few things displeased him more than disrespect. Biden said:

"One of the things that I admired most about him, which my father shared without any of the patrician background, was this sense of honor: your word was your bond. I was raised in a household where my dad would say 'you're a man of your word; without your word, you're not a man.' Well, Claiborne lived that. Claiborne was the embodiment of rectitude. And I really always genuinely admired him for it.

"Claiborne was an absolute gentleman. But Claiborne had difficulty—he would never say it, but you could feel it in his body language. Claiborne just absolutely abhorred prejudice, at least that's my experience with him. Claiborne abhorred those who didn't play and fight by the rules of the Marquis of Queensbury. Claiborne continued to have an expectation that people that he dealt with, his colleagues, might rise above their self-interest or their prejudice or their smallness. It was like, 'gentlemen don't do that. Gentlemen don't do that!' Whatever that was. It could have been anything. It could have been disrespecting one of the women in the Senate who worked in the cafeteria who delivered the coffee to the office. It could have been a harsh or mocking statement made on the Senate floor or in a press release.

"He wasn't naïve, which I think everyone made the mistake of thinking. But he was a graceful man. I think his observation of lack of grace disappointed him repeatedly. He didn't think that grace flowed from your manners, knowing which fork to use. It flowed from the way you treated other people, the way he thought you thought of them."

◻ ◻ ◻ Lost in the 1980 election headlines, save in Rhode Island, was Claudine Schneider's success in her rematch against Representative Beard for the U.S. House.

A moderate Republican, like junior Senator Chafee, Schneider, the first woman elected to Congress from Rhode Island, quickly established a reputation in Washington as a national environmental advocate and friend of the Northeast economy, her home state especially — and an independent-minded voice who was not afraid to criticize Reagan's social policies. Schneider was one of just two House Republicans who voted against Regan's 1982 budget, with its deep cuts in human services. She was working-class Rhode Island's kind of Republican, and, with 56 percent of the vote, she easily defeated Democrat state representative James V. Aukerman in the 1982 election.

Talk of a 1984 Schneider challenge to Pell began almost immediately.

"I'd love for her to be the candidate," Rhode Island state Republican chairman John A. Holmes, Jr., told *Journal* political reporter Bakst, who described Holmes as "euphoric" over the possibility. "People respect and admire her."

Over the next year, the talk built — and not just in Rhode Island.

"Claudine," as many called her, had appeal that her national party leaders believed could finally topple Pell, who would be nearing seventy when he sought a fifth term in 1984. She was young, progressive, popular, and a proven fundraiser, and despite her disagreement with some of the administration's policies, Reagan and Vice President George H. W. Bush could support her candidacy.

Landing at Quonset State Airport on his way to a private GOP fundraiser in Newport, Bush on August 12, 1983, told reporters of his enthusiasm for Schneider.

"Next year is an important year and, without being subtle about it, I know what I'd like to see Claudine Schneider do," the vice president said. "She's made a tremendous record nationally and a most impressive record in the state of Rhode Island, which is not known as a Republican stronghold . . . I'd love to see her join a most distinguished senator, my friend of long standing, John Chafee." Bush said he could "guarantee" that Reagan would be "pleased" if she took on Pell.

The president himself confirmed Bush's assessment on October 8 in a speech in Lexington, Kentucky, to the National Federation of Republican Women. Noting that the only two women Senators were Republicans (Nancy Kassebaum Baker of Kansas and Florida's Paula Hawkins), Reagan said his party should "at least double" its number of women in both houses in the next year's election. Reagan turned to Schneider, who was with him on the stage, and said: "Claudine Schneider, I hope you're listening, because I'd like to think that one of those new Senators will be you."

Schneider said she was flattered by the president's attention, but undecided about a Pell challenge. A telephone poll taken the same day as Reagan's endorsement showed her trailing Pell in a trial heat, 33 percent to 24 percent — but with 43 percent undecided and the election more than a year away, Schneider had significant opportunity. She told Bakst that she would "cautiously analyze the pros and cons," and that her final decision "really comes down to how I can best serve Rhode Island."

A poll conducted for a Providence television station the first week of November 1983 showed a statistical dead heat between Pell and Schneider, with the Republican favored by 36.6 percent of respondents and Pell by 36.1 percent; asked regardless of their leanings whether they wanted to see Schneider run, 49 percent said yes, with only a third saying no. And so anticipation built in the hours approaching the press conference Schneider called for the afternoon of November 7.

In a statement prepared for the conference and released to the press in advance, Schneider said she would seek reelection to the House, not challenge Pell. She repeated her intentions in an interview with Bakst at 7 a.m. the morning of November 7. Stating her belief that she could beat Pell, Schneider said that a strenuous campaign would interfere with her Congressional initiatives: among them, cleaning up toxic waste, achieving equal educational opportunities for women, and cutting unnecessary government.

"I am reluctant to interrupt my work toward these goals to devote the time and resources required to successfully seek the office of U.S. Senator under the present circumstances," Schneider said in her prepared remarks. "While it is clear that I can succeed, too much ground stands to be lost in the trying."

But Schneider did not take herself out of contention for the Senate forever.

"For those many who have urged me to seek the position of Senator," she declared, "I can only say, 'Keep your powder dry, for the day will surely come.'"

It came, potentially, mere hours later, at her 12:30 p.m. press conference.

"In a move that stunned even some of her top staffers," wrote Bakst in the next morning's *Journal*, "she left open, and underlined, the possibility that she may decide to go for the Senate after all."

Deviating from her prepared remarks pertaining to her House initiatives, Schneider had ad-libbed: "I will underline 'under the present circumstances' and 'at this time.' That is not to say that I might not be of the opinion perhaps three months from now that the circumstances may change. Who knows? I may be able to pass my Title IX [women's equality in education] resolution next week, and a number of other projects I'm working on may come to fruition earlier than I expect."

Bakst, whose reputation as a fair but tenacious reporter was well deserved, didn't let Schneider off with that. What might change her mind? he asked.

"I don't know," Schneider said.

All right, then, what had changed since 7 a.m.?

"Just as I was walking in the door now," Schneider said, "a constituent walked by and he yelled, 'Go for it.' A number of people who I had spoken with both last night and this morning said, 'Well, Claudine, don't cut off the opportunity of maybe changing your mind a little way down the line.' And I guess these people felt the same way I did: At this moment, today, they were saying, 'You know, well, maybe you're making the right decision, but I'm not sure that it's the right decision.'"

Wouldn't an opponent, in whichever race, seize on this as waffling?

"Well, they can call it whatever they like," Schneider said, "but I'm saying today that I am not inclined to announce for the U.S. Senate, and it wouldn't be the first time that people change their minds on political offices."

But didn't this now discourage other potential Republicans, who could not be sure which seat would open?

"Well, skip the three months, then. I won't put a time limit on it. But the point is that the door is not closed to my running at some point in the future . . . Other qualified candidates certainly have the opportunity and the option to decide to run . . . And somebody terrifically qualified may decide to run, and I may decide, 'Well, that's fine, let them run, and I won't.' So, you know, the ball game is wide open."

Schneider's performance suggested she shared a degree of Pell's quirkiness. It suggested that if the two indeed confronted each other, a memorable campaign would result — as it would, when the long-awaited race materialized, in 1990.

It suggested, correctly, that in certain ways, Pell and Schneider were cut from the same cloth in more ways than one.

□ □ □ Schneider's flirtation with a 1984 challenge to Pell ended on January 6, 1984, when Republican businesswoman Barbara Leonard announced, with the support of her party, her candidacy against the Democrat incumbent. Leonard had never sought political office, but the disastrous experience of the last political novice to take Pell on did not dissuade her.

"I'm running to win," said Leonard, fifty-nine.

On learning his likely opponent in the general election, Pell was typically courteous, describing her to Bakst as "a very nice person." Saying that any opponent was "potentially dangerous," Pell promised a vigorous campaign. "I've always run as hard as I possibly could," he said, "and intend to keep doing so."

In the weeks leading up to Leonard's formal announcement, on May 23, press accounts depicted her candidacy as an "uphill battle" and the candidate herself as "a distinct underdog," among other discouraging descriptions. With her own fundraising just getting underway, the national Republican Party had pledged $100,000 to her effort — but that was less than a third of the more than $350,116 Pell had on hand in the middle of February, with many donors yet to contribute.

Leonard on May 23 spelled out the major issue she would emphasize until November: eliminating the approximately $180-billion federal deficit, a task to which she said she would bring skills she had learned as chairman of H & H Screw Products Mfg. Co., an electronics manufacturer she took over when her husband died seven years earlier. Leonard said she would achieve a balanced budget through a combination of spending cuts, greater government efficiencies, and $44 billion in increased taxes. Leonard acknowledged that tackling the debt would be "politically dangerous," given her call for higher taxes, but that the country's financial stability required pluck.

"I'm a nice lady," Leonard said, "but someone has to make a stand on these deficits, and I think it's going to take someone with courage and common sense, which is my definition of tough."

The 1984 elections saw the return of the National Conservative Political Action Committee, or NCPAC (pronounced "nick-pack"), the New Right group founded in the 1970s that had played an instrumental role in bringing Republicans the White House and control of the Senate. NCPAC's stock-in-trade was the personal attack ad. Leonard declined to use such tactics against Pell — and he, in this campaign as in all of his earlier ones, declined to target Leonard, even though some advisers believed he should have.

Pell and Biden were on the same election cycle, and early in their 1984 campaigns, both attended a Democratic strategy retreat. Senators who had won and lost in earlier years spoke to the current candidates, along with outside consultants.

"They were telling us how we had to run negative campaigns, because negative campaigns worked and these [NCPAC] guys were going to come after us," Biden recalled. "And they predicted exactly how they were going to come after Claiborne and me. I remember us sitting there together and he said:

"'I will not run a negative campaign.'

"And I said, 'I'm not going to do it, either.'

"He just had a big grin on his face and he said, 'that's good, Joe. I never ran a negative campaign.'

"Nor did he. I'm not comparing—I'm not putting myself in the same class as Claiborne Pell—but we shared this notion that if in order to win, you have to run down the very institutions that you work in, it makes it harder for the institutions to work."

So Pell, yet again, ran on his record.

He had few of the headline-making achievements that had characterized his first three terms to show; his fourth term had been one of more modest successes, of initiatives that he had long pursued that were finally coming to fruition or moving forward. Among them were his principal authorship of the Foreign Service Act of 1980, which overhauled an antiquated system that dated to 1946; authorship of a section of the 1982 Foreign Assistance Act that protected threatened plant and animal species; and several initiatives that culminated in the 1983 groundbreaking on a $100-million revival of downtown Providence, including a new railroad station that would be an asset to the Northeast rail service high-speed rail system that Pell had championed since his first term decades before (his vision would move yet closer to reality with the advent, in late 2000, of 150-mph Acela service on the Boston-to-Washington line).

But arguably his most significant success was a bill Reagan signed into law on October 25, 1982. Public Law 97–364, which provided federal funds to states establishing programs discouraging drunk driving, capped six years of Pell's dogged efforts. The law also established a computerized federal driver register to track offenses nationwide, reducing the chances of a chronic offender crossing state lines to get a new license.

"We can never hope to end all the accidents that result from drunk driving," Pell said in late September, when the House embraced its version of his bill, then returned it to the Senate, which voted approval and sent it to the president. "But I believe that this legislation will go a long way toward reducing the needless slaughter that has occurred on our highways day after day."

Pell was not in Washington when Reagan signed the measure. He was at a press conference in Rhode Island heralding the new law, and he was joined by the mother of Elizabeth Powell, one of two Pell aides whose 1970s deaths caused by drunk drivers had sparked his crusade. "It's just a beginning," Powell's mother said, but a "good beginning that may saves the lives of many young people."

Her words were prophetic: Pell's impact would be enduring, as states increasingly passed laws requiring suspensions for first offenses and jail sentences for repeat offenders. What some had once dismissed as bad judgment — or fodder for jokes and tales of drunken swagger — would eventually be seen as criminally dangerous behavior that society would not tolerate.

"To be sure," journalist Mulligan said many years later, "nobody would argue as a matter of political mechanics that the campaign against drunk driving could ever have prospered without the gradual spread of the grassroots movement that fought under such banners as MADD. And nobody, least of all Claiborne Pell, would argue that he was responsible for a sea-change in American culture that ranks right up there with the decline of smoking — the popular intolerance of drunk driving that today is almost taken for granted.

"All the same, Pell made a contribution to the change by his willingness to fail for so many years at so many variations of the anti-drunk-driving legislation. By the time the MADD movement and others had mustered sufficient support to prod Congress for action, Pell and other legislators had fashioned legislative models to fit the popular mood: essentially to withhold federal money from states that did not enact their own sanctions against drunk driving."

▫ ▫ ▫ The 1984 Rhode Island senatorial campaign would not be remembered for its excitement. There was virtually none.

In the first of two debates, on September 30, Leonard attempted to portray Pell as out of touch with his constituents; Pell, in turn, implied that her understanding of foreign affairs was naïve, gently correcting her when she implied that Czechoslovakia was in Western Europe (in fact, it was part of Eastern Europe).

Along with economic policy, foreign policy dominated the second debate, on October 12. Listing his top priorities for a fifth term as world peace, employment, and education, in that order, Pell told the TV cameras that "we both live on the same planet, and we must talk to each other." Leonard said she would welcome an end to the arms race, an aim long supported by her opponent, but that the U.S. "must be realistic."

It was not the most memorable evening in Rhode Island's political annals, but the candidates did inject a degree of drama into the campaign during its closing weeks. In an address on October 19 to a teachers' union in his old haunt, the Providence Biltmore hotel, Pell accused Reagan of attempting to "slash, cut and maim" federal aid for schools. Reagan had "failed the test of leadership in education," the senator said.

"To my mind, it is an unrightable wrong that we have had to spend almost the entire first half of this decade fighting to keep the doors of educational opportunity from slamming shut on millions of deserving young Americans," Pell said. "It is deplorable that while the costs of a college education have increased 37 percent over the past four years, the value of student aid has declined by 20 percent."

Four days later, Leonard fired back, accusing Pell himself of having failed the education leadership test. "Although we have poured millions of dollars into federal education programs, test scores have declined and illiteracy has increased," Leonard said. "Obviously, the problem is not a lack of money. It is a failure of leadership in Congress and in Senator Pell." She urged programs to reward teacher excellence and schools that stressed the Three Rs: the basic skills of reading, writing, and arithmetic.

But Leonard was not getting through.

On November 6, Rhode Island humiliated her: Pell took every city and town, with nearly 73 percent of the vote. Asked if he had felt threatened by his opponent, Pell said, not tongue-in-check, "Absolutely. I always run scared to the last possible moment."

Leonard was also gracious.

"I knew when I entered this race that he would be a difficult man to beat and the prognosis was not of the best," she said. "I'm not sour-graping and am not a sore loser, but I'm just disappointed the issues were not brought out more."

The Republican told reporters she had not yet considered whether to run again for elective office. She would not. Like all but one of Pell's opponents, her political career was over for good.

THE COSMOS

One evening during the winter of 1977–78, Pell met a medical researcher for dinner in a Washington restaurant. Pell had learned about Dr. Robert A. Hallowitz from an acquaintance that the doctor had successfully treated for a severe hormone-related medical condition that had defied conventional therapies. His success intrigued the Senator, who was obsessive about his own health.

A scientist who also had a private practice, Hallowitz, thirty-four, had distinguished himself for his work in the Laboratory of Brain, Evolution, and Behavior at the National Institute of Mental Health, where his mentor had been Dr. Paul D. Maclean, a pioneer in the study of the ancient roots of certain human behaviors. Hallowitz specialized in the relationships between mind and body, and the often debilitating disorder that would become known as Chronic Fatigue Syndrome. He saw connections among a person's mental and physical health and nutrition, environmental toxins, and the stresses of modern life. A believer in improving health by meditation and other measures, Hallowitz was something of a doctor celebrity. *Rolling Stone Magazine* (March 14, 1974) and *The New York Times* (December 9, 1973) were among the publications that had profiled him.

In its story titled "Oz in the Astrodome," *The Times* wrote about the impression that fifteen-year-old Divine Light Mission leader Prem Pal Singh Rawat, the Indian guru Maharaj Ji, had made on Hallowitz. The doctor told the paper that he had been skeptical at first of the guru and the supposed changes his followers, who were called "premies," experienced—but that his skepticism had become acceptance after months of discovery.

"It was visible on the faces of these premies that they were experiencing a radiant and intense peace," Hallowitz said. "And it was infectious; I began experiencing the same thing. I felt marvelous. I said, I don't know who Guru Maharaj Ji is, but he's giving a valid experience and I want it. Since then, I've had experience so intense as to be beyond my capacity to imagine, and if that's suggestion, it's very strong. I've come to the point where I know there is a Supreme Being and He is one with that 15-year-old boy."

Hallowitz, *The Times* reported, believed that the guru's teachings were consistent with credible scientific brain research such as his own. He believed, according to the paper's reporter, that meditation techniques "provide a way for man to control an imperfectly designed brain away from fear and stress and toward pure thought and inner peace. Because of his evolutionary inheritance, Hallowitz says, man is burdened with a primitive orientation towards fear and survival, which sets the tone of individual and institutional behavior, starts wars, and destroys civilizations."

This was a theory with great appeal to Pell, whose ultimate foreign-policy objective could be summarized in a single word: peace. Peace that so far, with the ordinary mechanisms of diplomacy, continued to elude humanity.

Hallowitz, *The Times* continued, explained that

> scientists are already studying the physiological effects of meditation as a way out of this bind. They have found decreased heart rates and oxygen consumption, increased galvanic skin response and low-frequency alpha activity that may be correlated with states of subjective relaxation.

Hallowitz believes that receiving knowledge from the guru "involves a lowering of response to stressful situations, a heightening of capacity for pure thought, a scaling down of body processes, libido, appetites and sleep requirements — it changes the organism's perspective of the environment; we no longer view the environment as stressful, we are no longer draining our vitality. What I'm saying is that meditation brings about physiological transformations that have tremendous implications for our physical and emotional well-being."

Over dinner on that winter evening, Hallowitz and Pell discussed theories of what happens after death. Pell's curiosity was already taking him on a journey of discovery in which he (with the assistance of a staff member) investigated stories of near-death experiences, of lights in tunnels, of angels or Jesus greeting the newly dead, of ancestors appearing to help smooth the passage over, of reaching beyond the grave to contact deceased loved ones. Pell wanted to answer, if he could, the ancient question: What is the essence of life?

It was an intensely spiritual and intellectual quest for Pell — and a primary objective would be to determine if he might be able to contact his father.

That evening, Pell asked Hallowitz if he were afraid of dying.

The doctor said he was not. He related to Pell an experience that had convinced him that there was, indeed, life after death. It began, he told the senator, on an occasion when he fell asleep and drifted into what a layman would call a "lucid dream." Many years after his dinner with Pell, Hallowitz recounted it again:

"I go to sleep. The lucid dream begins with me in a very white pajama-like outfit in a room with no furniture, with white padded walls. I am immediately aware of my sense of constant anxiety to the point of almost pain. I recognize that I am a prisoner. I don't know who I am — I'm recognizing that I am a prisoner. I'm in this costume, this white pajama thing in this room with no windows. It's diffusely illuminated; I don't see an incandescent bulb or anything, it's just diffusely lit. And then suddenly, a door opens where I couldn't see a door before.

"And in come three people, one of whom is carrying a weapon of some sort. It looks like a gun, but it doesn't look like a gun; I don't really recognize it from my worldly experience. Immediately, they push me to the floor. I'm on my knees. One of the men has got my hands behind my back holding me like that, and the other dude with the weapon has put it to my head and is screaming at me in a language I couldn't even begin to comprehend or even recognize, obviously wanting me to provide information. I am getting more and more terrified with each passing second: I know I am going to die because I can't answer his questions.

"Just before this crash there's a recollection that I do know how to meditate — but I hadn't been doing it. Immediately I started following the force behind my breath. A peace came over. Then there was the crash. Suddenly, there was the appearance of like an ocean coming at me — of light, sound, I can't even put it into words — just a force. There was a moment when I had to make a choice: to either turn from it or accept it. But because I had been in meditation, I had no problem accepting it. And I was suddenly engulfed in this ocean of bliss, of joy — whatever you want to call it — love, peace, you can't even comprehend it in worldly terms. I stayed there for, I don't know — I have no idea whether it was a whole night or a minute or a second.

"But when I awoke, I realized this is what happens after death. You have a choice: if you are familiar with the ocean that comes at you, you'll merge with it. If you're not, I don't know what will happen. I only know that I am familiar with it so I will merge."

Dinner ended and Pell, who was interested in having Hallowitz become his personal physician, asked him to visit him in his hideaway office. A short while later, the doctor did. Pell served sherry while Hallowitz took in the photographs and mementoes that covered the walls. Hallowitz felt the weight of history.

Pell asked Hallowitz to set him on a journey.

He wanted to find his father, if he were out there.

OK, Bob, the Senator said. *Can you take me across the universe? Can you take me to god? Can you show me what you talked about in the restaurant?*

I don't know that we can do it with so little preparation, Hallowitz replied.

Pell was insistent.

Hallowitz told him to look into his eyes and, following his own breathing, to slip into a meditative state.

But Pell did not go away. He was severely disappointed.

Hallowitz tried to soothe him: There was a silver lining, he told Pell, in not being able to achieve something that could, for lack of a better word, become addictive.

"Senator," Hallowitz would recall saying, "this experience is so profound and potentially disorienting because of the fact that you could then become singularly focused on realizing what you just experienced on a regular basis. Your service right now, Senator, is very, very important to our nation, to the world. And as a statesman right now, you have to be very grounded.

"Perhaps in God's own way, this is not a failure but a message that you're fine where you are right now. You're very grounded, you're very practical, you're very detail-oriented. What would happen to you if, all of a sudden, you became so distracted by wanting to dissolve yourself into the light that you couldn't do your job? I don't know that that would happen, but maybe that will assuage some of your feelings of inadequacy for not being able to get there with me."

Pell never again asked Hallowitz to help him meditate. But he did ask him to be his personal health and wellness adviser, a role that Hallowitz played for many years. Confidentiality concerns would prevent the doctor from disclosing details of the relationship, though Hallowitz would say that generally he counseled his patients on such matters as exercise, nutrition, and dietary supplements as he to sought to utilize the mind-body connection to improve living in a stress-filled world.

◻ ◻ ◻ One day in the summer of 1983, Pell placed a telephone call to a former Navy officer whose recent investigations of paranormal phenomena and their possible military and Secret Service applications had come to his attention. The following week, C. B. Scott Jones met Pell in the Senate Dining Room. An exchange of letters followed, and Jones invited the senator to the Symposium on Applications of Anomalous Phenomena he was sponsoring on Thursday, November 30, and Friday, December 1, 1983, in Leesburg, Virginia.

"I didn't think that he would show up," Jones would later recall. "He spent all day Friday at the symposium. His appearance surprised and impressed the government attendees. While this was an unclassified event, I only invited government scientists and intelligence personnel. By the end of 1984, our personal relationship had matured, and he offered me a job during a dinner at his Georgetown home."

Jones officially joined Pell's staff in January 1985.

Some other staff members were not sure what to make of him. Nor did they quite understand why their boss, quirky though he could be, would pay him — through the public payroll — an annual salary of nearly $50,000, plus reimbursement for what would become considerable travel and related expenses for the six years he would remain on the payroll.

Certainly, Jones had an impressive military background, with extensive overseas service that had exposed him to the kinds of foreign-policy issues that had concerned Pell since coming of age with his diplomat father. A fighter pilot early in his career, Jones spent much of his time in the Navy in intelligence, where he specialized in missiles and astronautics operations. Jones retired with the rank of commander. He had become intrigued with anomalous phenomena, a loosely related category of claimed experiences such as ESP, near-death experiences, ghosts, and UFOs that cannot be readily explained by traditional science. He was, like Pell, an unconventional thinker.

Jones would later tell a reporter that his paranormal interests were rooted in an incident in the 1960s, when he was a Naval attaché, based in India, with intelligence responsibilities for North Africa, the Middle East, and Southeast Asia. Saying that the incident "might embarrass the government," Jones declined to give specific details to *Providence Journal* reporter C. Eugene Emery, Jr., who wrote about Jones in July 1988. Whatever it was, the experience "enabled me to do my intelligence assignment with much greater speed than one ordinarily expected," Jones said. "It left me wondering." Jones also told Emery of the origin of his belief in UFOs. "I was flying actively when all the big sightings were taking place in the '50s and '60s," he said. "I've seen many UFOs. But when I got close enough to them, they were no longer unidentified." They were, he said, extraterrestrial vehicles.

By 1984, the year Reagan was reelected, Jones was working for a civilian think tank, Kaman Tempo, headquartered in Santa Barbara, California, with an office in Virginia. Interest in psychic research, Jones said, had reached high levels of government—and led to the symposium he convened that Pell attended late that year.

"I cannot provide detail about the work I did with the Secret Service and the Intel Community," Jones would later declare, "except to say that the Secret Service came to me with a very serious problem—a threat to President Reagan. From the letters being sent to the president, they concluded that the writer was willing to sacrifice his life in order to kill the president. In my office, they said, 'We have tried everything to identify this guy, without success, we are willing to try a damn psychic.' I told them that I did not work with 'damn' psychics, and suggested that they try to find someone who did if that was a requirement.

"After they apologized, we got down to business. I briefed my team and we started providing them with details that were helpful in making an arrest of a person who was seriously mentally ill. Among other procedures, my team worked over the letters, and guided the Secret Service artist to create a sketch of the person that the Secret Service printed up and distributed. My assessment of this case was that the Secret Service and others solved the case by effective police work using every input they could get. Yes, the guy looked like the sketch. This was known as the C.A.T. case, as the letters were signed by these initials. It will be a waste of time to try to get this confirmed by the Secret Service, as their official position is that they do not use psychics."

But Pell was not averse to psychic possibilities. There might be government use for such powers, he believed—and even if not, inquiry into unconventional possibilities of the human mind appealed to his intellectual curiosity and to the longing he still felt for his father.

◻ ◻ ◻ Pell wrote an internal mission statement for Jones after he came on staff.

"To acquire as wide and deep a knowledge as possible of all parapsychological and exceptional ability programs and results in both our own country and abroad," was the senator's first objective. Second, Pell wanted "on the basis of this knowledge, to bring together the results of what is being done in our government and outside our government." And finally, Pell hoped "to use these skills for the enhancement of human beings and human lives to insure that both government and private industry engage in the greatest possible utilization of this knowledge."

Jones himself spelled out his interests in another document, "Sighing a Bit about Psi," a common abbreviation for psychic research.

"The first observation," he wrote, "is that it is far from a unified and well-defined field. Indeed, the 'psychic pot' holds a most wondrous collection of phenomena, claims and artifacts. In addition to the standard list of phenomena historically associated with psi, e.g., telepathy, remote viewing, clairvoyance, precognition/retro cognitions, psychokinesis, out-of-body experiences, mediumship, channeling [and] apparitions, it has become an unfortunate habit to label as 'psi' many other phenomena and reported events, I have yet to talk to a reporter about psi without the conversation at some point being shifted to Big Foot " and other such subjects. "Clearly, considerable sorting out needs to be done. Until this is accomplished, notice how those fearful of psi routinely provoke the 'giggle factor' . . ."

Jones wrote that he hoped that psychic inquiry could be legitimized for the "anticipated value the results of such research would have for our society," a view Pell shared. But Jones acknowledged the military interest in it during this second term of the Reagan presidency, when the Soviet Union remained America's Cold War enemy — and when, some believed, the Soviet KGB was developing psychic weapons. "If we have good intelligence about Soviet activity in this area and it is assessed as threatening to U.S. interests," Jones wrote, "I assume that the government would not be shy in supporting efforts to counter the perceived threat."

His mission identified, Jones went to work. On his own time, he continued his research through the private Center for Applied Anomalous Phenomena, which he founded in 1985 and operated from his suburban Washington home.

Like his new boss, Jones possessed an uncircumscribed curiosity. Pell's support opened doors that might ordinarily have been closed to an ex-fighter pilot who claimed to have encountered UFOs, a man some would not take seriously on his own — and there were many doors to open. This was a decade when the New Age movement matured and found both wide acceptance and skepticism, a decade of angels and Shirley MacLaine and Harmonic Convergence.

During his years on Pell's staff, Jones investigated alleged instances of dolphins communicating with autistic children, UFO sightings and abductions, and spoons being bent. He looked into reincarnation, metaphysics, Andean spirituality, Area 51 in Nevada, crop circles, the mind-body connection espoused by Hallowitz, the claims of a man professing to have found "evidence for the interaction of consciousness with microorganisms," cyberphysiology (the role of the mind in healing), psychotronics (defined by the U.S. Psychotronics Association as "the science of mind-body-environment relationships, an interdisciplinary science concerned with the interactions of matter, energy, and consciousness"), and Austrian-American psychiatrist Wilhelm Reich's concept of orgone, a sort of primordial cosmic energy that Reich believed could be found in St. Elmo's fire and the testicles and ovaries of mammals.

Jones traveled around America, and to Scotland, England, Germany, Canada, Mexico, France, Peru, and Moscow, in September 1988, for a conference titled "Hidden Reserves of the Human Psyche." He met with astrologers, astronomers, professors, the Dalai Lama, authors, Ufologists, active and retired military officers, and self-proclaimed psychics, self-healers, remote-healers, hypnotherapists, and shamans. He met with present and former members of the CIA, NASA, the National Institutes of Health, the National Institute of Mental Health, the National Academy of Sciences, the National Science Foundation, the Arms Control and Disarmament Agency, the White House Office of Science and Technology Policy, the Oak Ridge National Laboratory, and the Office of Technology Assessment. He reached out to private groups, including the International Survival Research Foundation, the Parapsychological Association, Society for Scientific Exploration, the Fetzer Foundation, the American Society for Psychical Research, the Mankind Research Foundation, and the National Spiritualist Association. His quest knew no limits.

Jones also reached out to other Congressional staff members. Some became interested, including aides to Maryland Senator Barbara Mikulski, Ohio Senator John Glenn, California Representatives Henry A. Waxman and Meldon E. Levine — and Rhode Island's Claudine Schneider.

Jones's enthusiasm was grand.

"A few days ago," he wrote in one of his early weekly reports to Pell, "I was reminded by a friend that the Chinese character for 'crisis' (wei-ji) is made up of 'danger' and 'opportunity.' The point is that it is impossible to make a significant forward move without meeting danger. The scent of danger alerts us to the fact that we may be heading in the right direction."

And that direction, he often told Pell, was nothing less than the betterment of mankind.

"Our work will make a critical difference," he wrote in a card to Pell on the senator's sixty-eighth birthday, November 22, 1986. "Man is capable of solving all of the problems we currently recognize and the new ones to come along, but only if the full potential of man is recognized and actualized. That is the business we are in."

▫ ▫ ▫ The Democrats regained control of the Senate in the 1986 midterm elections, and the following January, Pell realized his longtime ambition of becoming chairman of the Foreign Relations Committee. He took command of the committee with arms control topping his agenda. It would remain there for the rest of his tenure.

Out of public view, Jones continued his research. Pell particularly encouraged the former Navy officer's investigations of weapons that might be developed from mind control and other unconventional means. These pursuits, former chief of staff Hughes recalled, received the quiet support of several in Washington, including some fellow senators.

"Pell was interested in whether there were any superhuman, some kind of capacity for communications, viewing, extra-human talents that people might have that would be useful in a national security sense," Hughes said. "There were a number of reputable people, including a few colleagues, that had a similar interest. I was always astonished that when Pell's interests became known sort of by word of mouth around the Senate there were more than a few colleagues who sidled up to him and said, 'You know, Claiborne, you're awfully gutsy to be going out and doing this. I just want you to know that I'm interested in this, too, or I've read this, too.'"

Jones met regularly with John B. Alexander, a retired Army colonel whose advocacy of unconventional weapons would become the basis of the best-selling book *The Men Who Stare at Goats*—and whose ideas, as the book (and movie made from it) would document, received a hearing at high levels of the Pentagon. After one meeting with Alexander, Jones sent Pell a memo outlining some of the ex-colonel's interests.

"A major project he is working on is non-lethal weapon systems," Jones wrote:

> Some of the systems being considered are novel and while they may be 98 percent non-lethal, they will require some selling before their use would be sanctioned. For example, it may be possible to focus specific electromagnetic energy on a hostage situation and cause everyone targeted to become grossly nauseous and to vomit uncontrollably. Another idea is to use certain chemical

agents causing a "slime" that normally cannot be negotiated by walking or crawling. Another consideration is spraying the area with very quick-acting "super glue."

There is another class of non-lethal weapons being considered. These are mind control and mind-influencing systems. All weapons have more than one edge, more than one use. Development of mind-control systems would have to be carefully considered. There would be some temptation to use such systems in the marketplace, in politics, hospitals, prisons, schools, and on production lines.

Perhaps inevitably, Jones's explorations brought him to the Israeli-born Uri Geller, whose claims of psychic powers had made him an international celebrity.

Geller's signature claim, of being able to use his mind to bend spoons, had been dismissed by skeptics as a clever stage trick—but his followers believed he possessed paranormal abilities. They believed he could communicate through telepathy and even use his mind to influence the thoughts of others—an ability that, if true, would have enormous potential for the Pentagon and State Department.

Pell had already privately met Geller, who would later describe (on his website) the Senator as receptive to his ideas.

"We got along very well from the start," Geller said.

I found Senator Pell to be a man of great dignity and wisdom, and although he could be described as a member of the old school of politics, he also struck me as one of the most forward-looking and open-minded statesmen I had ever met. What especially impressed me was that he wanted above all to know if I thought psychic power could be used for peaceful purposes. We had a very pleasant meeting. I bent a spoon for him and reproduced a drawing he had made out of my sight, of a smiling face.

More publicly, Geller had encountered Pell on February 27, 1987, at a reception and dinner in Geneva, Switzerland, for American and Soviet delegates involved in nuclear arms-reduction negotiations that President Reagan and Soviet President Mikhail Gorbachev had revived in 1985. Geller would later say that he had been invited by an aide to diplomat Max M. Kampelman, who headed the American delegation—and that he had been told to present himself as an "entertainer." He would say that spent an evening with American and Soviet officials, including Pell, Senator Al Gore, and high-ranking Soviet diplomat Yuly M. Vorontsov, among others.

A photograph of him with Pell, Gore, and Voronstov taken by the U.S. mission and later released to the press would substantiate his claim.

"Vorontsov knew who I was," Geller would write,

> and since I had been brought along as an entertainer, I thought I had better do some entertaining. I began by making a seed sprout, and then picked up a spoon and began to bend it in my usual way, handing it to Vorontsov and telling him it would go on bending while he was holding it. To his delight, and my great relief, it did. His manner towards me after my little show became even more cordial. He smiled, and said, "I know these powers are real," then went on to tell me about the Soviet healer Dzhuna Davitashvili, who is thought to have treated the late Mr. Brezhnev . . .
>
> After the reception, I was invited to join a group for dinner at Roberto's restaurant, where I was seated opposite Vorontsov at the table that also included Kampelman, Pell and two other senators. Like the reception, the dinner was more than a purely social affair, and I will not repeat any of the dialogue that buzzed around my ears during the meal. It soon became clear to me — by perfectly normal means — that both sides had come to Geneva to bargain, negotiate and discuss, not to present previously established fixed positions, as might have been the case under earlier Soviet administrations. History was being made all around me, and the well-being of tens of millions of people would depend on how well my fellow-diners got along with each other. Throughout the meal, I kept up a steady bombardment of my own form of negotiation: intense images of peace.

With Pell's support, Jones arranged for Geller to travel to Washington to brief the Senator, other Congressmen and staff, and representatives of military and intelligence agencies. Speaking on April 24, 1987, in a bug-proof room in the Capitol not far from Pell's hideaway office, Geller told a gathering of about three dozen officials of his belief that the Soviet Union had developed mind-control techniques with strategic implications — and that the U.S. should invest in similar psychic research. To encourage it, Geller tried to guess the shapes that those in the room had drawn on pieces of paper — but failed.

"I just had a bad day as far as telepathy was concerned," Geller would later assert. "I was really worn out after barnstorming around the country. I had been on [a book] promotion bandwagon since October, with very few rest breaks . . . All I could concentrate on by then was getting back to my wife, my children and my home."

Word of the meeting leaked to the press, and reporters in America and abroad began calling Jones and Pell's office. *Newsweek*, *U.S. News & World Report*, and

The Sunday Times of London were among the publications that ran stories. Once only whispered, Pell's interest in the paranormal was now public record.

◻ ◻ ◻ If there was any doubt that New Age philosophies had arrived in Washington, it was dispelled in the spring of 1988 with the publication of former top presidential aide Donald Regan's book *For The Record*.

Regan confirmed in print what had been whispered around the Beltway: First Lady Nancy Reagan regularly consulted with an astrologer before the president scheduled important events, including his reelection announcement and the 1986 bombing of Libya. "Virtually every major move and decision the Reagans made during my time as White House Chief of Staff was cleared in advance with a woman in San Francisco who drew up horoscopes to make certain that the planets were in a favorable alignment for the enterprise," Regan wrote. The woman was Vassar-educated astrologer Joan Quigley.

At *The Providence Journal*, reporter Emery, who with a skeptical eye often examined paranormal and supernatural claims, began looking into Pell's interests and Jones's employment. His resulting story, published on July 18, 1988, confirmed in detail the investigations into paranormal phenomena that the senator and his aide had been conducting—and included Pell's first expansive public comments on his personal beliefs about such matters.

"I do think some people start out with certain abilities that can be improved, and I think that what is currently accepted as intuition can be enlarged," Pell told Emery. "I would like to see more emphasis made on developing human intuition and developing human potential, because many times theories that seem ridiculous at the time produce greater areas of knowledge." Pell said that his interest in the paranormal dated to early in the decade and had naturally flowed from his personality. "I've always been intellectually curious, and I think these things should be examined," he said.

The senator told Emery he believed that Geller was probably something more than a magician: "I sort of feel that he's for real," he said. And whether or not Geller specifically was credible, the senator argued for government funding of paranormal activities.

The *Journal* wrote:

Ray Hyman, a University of Oregon psychologist who recently evaluated the military applications of psychic research at the Army's behest, said that Pell "has been arguing very forcefully for our getting into something like a Manhattan Project-style effort to catch up with the Russians, who are supposedly 25 years ahead of us in so-called psychic warfare." The top-secret Manhattan

Project concentrated the efforts of the country's top scientists on development of the atom bomb.

Pell at first declined to say whether he had tried to influence the Pentagon to spend more money in the field. But, when told of Hyman's assessment, he characterized it as "correct but vastly exaggerated." He said he favors a modest increase in financial support for "intelligent, skeptical" research into psychic phenomena.

"I think we should expand our program, but not with a Manhattan-type project at all," he said. "You couldn't spend that kind of money in this field."

In a sidebar story, Emery wrote of the Pentagon's interest in "the idea of using paranormal and other unorthodox techniques to enhance the performance of its soldiers," an interest that led the Army Research Institute in 1984 to ask the National Academy of Sciences to examine possibilities. The NAS study found no hard evidence of psychic powers with military application, though it did not decisively dismiss such potential.

In a second sidebar, Emery profiled Jones. "It's my observation that there's a great deal of personal interest [in psychic powers], but that's not shared generally in our culture and, specifically, not in the federal government," Jones told the reporter. "And if they have a career to nurture, they cannot appear to be weird at all." Emery noted Jones's seemingly obsessive interest in UFOs, quoting his suggestion that the National Institute of Mental Health "be directed and funded to investigate the psychological consequences of encounters with extraterrestrials."

For Pell's staff, this was a big problem: UFOs and extraterrestrials, in which Pell himself had only passing interest, projected a more bizarre and potentially politically damaging image than an interest in bending spoons, a feat that fascinated many, as Geller's popularity demonstrated. Hughes internally had cautioned Pell, writing in a memo: "Senator, I do not understand why Scott devotes so much of his time and energy to UFO abductions, etc.! I thought you long ago asked him to limit his work for you, at least in this field."

Hughes believed that Jones explored areas beyond Pell's interest. "I don't think that Pell really was remotely anywhere near where Scott was in terms of theories and ideas and areas of pursuit," he later said. But there were no clearly specified distinctions, and Hughes walked a fine line. "My position was sort of tricky," Hughes said, "because my role was to, on the one hand, try and protect [Pell] politically and reputation-wise, and on the other hand to let him be him — in part because he was going to be him anyway."

So Hughes could only advise Pell, in essence: *Please do what you want and pursue it — but try to be cool, calm and sensible.*

The "guffaw factor," as some called it, cemented Pell's image as the Senate's leading nonconformist — but politically, it exacted only a small price in the 1980s, when Pell seemed untouchable at the ballot box and Rhode Islanders took a certain pride in his quirkiness. "It hurt his reputation," Hughes said, "but by that time his reputation as an eccentric was well established. And he had been reelected again and he was pretty senior. It's very hard to quantify what kind of harm it did. I think it was just frosting on the cake." Pell's interest in the paranormal would become an issue in his final campaign, but his opponent, Claudine Schneider, would not be able to turn it to her advantage.

Emery closed his main story with Pell's preoccupation with death:

Pell is also interested in near-death experiences, which are the visions some people see when they are on the verge of dying. Because those visions often include images of Jesus or deceased loved ones, many people believe that near-death experiences offer a preview of a life after death. There is a scientific debate over the source of such visions, but few disagree that they do occur.

Two years ago, Pell helped organize a symposium in Washington on the topic, and, according to a transcript of the meeting, he expressed the hope that the session would "build support and respectability for the subject" so the government would support research in the area.

Pell said he is curious about the phenomenon because "there seems to be validity" to it, and because, "obviously, as you get older, you get more interested in those subjects."

He will be 70 Nov. 22.

Pell did not reveal the true core of his interest, which was his father.

◫ ◫ ◫ Herbert Pell had been dead more than a quarter of a century in 1988, the year that Pell turned seventy. But time had not dimmed the memory. The senator still missed his dad. He still sought his approval, those who knew him intimately believed.

"As long as I had known him," Nuala would say, "he wanted to do what his father had done. He wanted either to be an ambassador or a member of Congress. He looked up to his father and wanted to measure up to him." But for many years, Nuala said, he never thought he did measure up — though in reality, he had greatly surpassed Herbert as both a legislator and a foreign-policy force. "I think Claiborne was always trying to 'catch up,' never quite sure that he'd gone way beyond what his father had ever done," Nuala said. "I think he realized he had at the end — but he didn't think so at first."

Pell's desire in his later years to connect with his dead father combined with his own advancing age encouraged him to discover, if he could, what happens when the heart stops beating for good. With Jones also intent on the issue, Pell read extensively and joined or closely followed several organizations, including the International Survival Research Foundation, a California-based group that was interested in apparitions, mediums, poltergeists, near-death experiences and reincarnation; the International Institute for the Study of Death, founded by Arthur S. Berger, author of several books on thanatology, including 1987's *Aristocracy of the Dead: New Findings in Postmodern Survival*; and the Institute of Noetic Sciences, another California-headquartered organization that describes itself as a sponsor and conductor of "leading-edge research into the potentials and powers of consciousness — including perceptions, beliefs, attention, intention, and intuition." Pell became a permanent board member of the Noetics Institute, and he gave the introductory address at its first major conference into the possibility of life beyond biological death, in Washington in October 1985, the year he hired Jones.

The address is the most extensive public record of Pell's thinking on the question that obsessed him in his later years. "Does Consciousness Survive Physical Death? Is the Question Important?" began with an insight into Pell's frame of mind.

"These are vital questions," he said. "As one grows older and physical death becomes more imminent, the question of survival is of increasing actual importance, rather than theoretical relevance. Thus, it is a question I have asked myself with increasing seriousness." He did not mention his father.

"Death and taxes are traditionally the two immutables of our life," Pell continued. "Taxes are specific, predictable, and part of the government process with which I have been concerned as a senator for the past 25 years. Death, on the other hand, is the ultimate mystery, meaning different things and providing differing images to a multi-faceted humanity. What does death mean? What happens? I don't pretend to know. I suspect no living being knows."

Nonetheless, Pell said that he had concluded that there were five possibilities.

The first was reincarnation, in which, he said, "the soul embarks on a long pilgrimage, perhaps involving many lives, hoping to achieve Nirvana." The second, Pell said, was the concept of the Great One: "Here, death means that the soul and its accompanying memory join the Great One, or Cosmos. And a particular soul's memory simply is an add-on to the sum total of memory, or knowledge." A third possibility was "the idea that the individual soul with its accompanying memory lives on eternally. Some variation of this view has been historically identified with Christianity. It is the view to which many of us incline, and certainly the view we hope is correct." A fourth possibility, Pell said, had been proposed by Nuala: "That is, whenever you die, what will happen is what you believe will happen."

Pell maintained that "positive knowledge" — proof — of survival after death could affect "the affairs of individuals in the balance of peacefulness and violence." He implied that such proof would have an impact on individuals and therefore on society in other ways. "How additionally responsible would any of us be if we had full scientific knowledge of immortality and the reasonably assured karmic consequences that would go with immortality?" he asked. "Is it an important question? Would knowing the answer make a difference? In my view, the answers to both these questions are yes."

If the answers were yes, his father might be reachable. Hallowitz several years before had failed to make the connection. Pell would try again, with the use of psychic mediums — but again, he would fail. If Pell ever believed he had succeeded in contacting Herbert, he would keep it a secret, one he would take with him to his own grave.

"He was fascinated by anything of the occult that could take you to the other side," daughter-in-law Janet would recall. "He never had an out-of-body experience. I told him once that my brother had an out-of-body experience. My brother is a doctor and a scientist — not the weird type at all — and he had an experience: he rose up and walked through the house out-of-body. Claiborne was riveted. He said, 'that's what I always wanted. And I don't know how to do it.'"

Those who knew Pell best suspect that he never reached a conclusion on death. "It bugged him," Janet said, "because there's no answer to it. You can read all those books and you can meet the Dalai Lama, you can meet an African chieftain, a witch doctor — and you're never going to know."

The fifth of the five possibilities Pell enunciated at the 1985 Noetics symposium disturbed him deeply, as he implied in his address.

"Perhaps the most disagreeable alternative," Pell said, "is oblivion."

The senator did not share publicly his feelings about nothingness being the final destination, but privately, he wanted to forestall his own death as long as possible — perhaps with the notion that in the meanwhile, science would find the path to biological immortality, the dream held by those in the emerging field of life extension. Pell remained fanatic about diet and exercise, keys to longevity. He heeded Hallowitz. He was fascinated by reports of peoples such as the Azerbaijan villagers who claimed to live longer than anyone on earth, supposedly with the help of a diet rich in yogurt. He refused to sign a Do Not Resuscitate order, or DNR, which instructs family, caregivers, and professionals to forgo medical intervention in the case of respiratory or cardiac arrest; he wanted extreme measures to be used in an attempt to keep him alive.

"He was really scared of dying, so he wanted to do anything to keep from dying," son Toby said. "He wanted to live until he was 120."

And if he couldn't, perhaps he could put his faith in cryonics, the use of extreme cold to preserve a body until the day when a person can be revived—potentially decades or centuries away. The basic premise of cryonics has been discredited by scientists, but Pell late in life told his son Toby of his interest. Toby responded with a reference to Alcor, the Scottsdale, Arizona, company that preserves either whole bodies or heads—the heads taking less space and thus being cheaper. Red Sox great Ted Williams, according to reports, supposedly chose the head treatment before dying in 2002.

"Do you want the full body or do you want the Ted Williams whack job?" Toby asked his father. Pell made no arrangements for cryonic preservation.

ﾛ ﾛ ﾛ In 1987, Jones wrote a speech for Pell to deliver at a meeting of the International Survival Research Foundation. The speech called for the establishment of an endowed university chair for "interdisciplinary survival research" that would combine biology, psychology, physics, chemistry, psychology, and other hard sciences. The arts would have had a place as well. "Indeed, up to this point they have had more involvement on the issues of death and survival than have all the sciences combined," the Jones-written speech declared. "In song, literature and art, the hopes, fears and wonderment of the transition we call death, and the disposition of whatever may survive, has been a rich and important part of every culture."

The endowed chair was one of several ideas influenced by Jones that were never realized. A more public failure was the proposed National Commission on Human Potential, which would formalize paranormal and related research, seek greater funding, and "advise the Congress, the president and the American public on policies and programs designed to facilitate the attainment of fuller human potential," according to Jones's draft of legislation. "It is a normal aspiration of each citizen to achieve fuller potential in body, mind and spirit," the draft legislation stated. "Tools and techniques for attaining fuller potential can be identified. . . . Success in maximizing individual human potential is directly related to freedom of choice from a broad selection of approaches and techniques of human technologies."

Pell introduced a Senate bill to establish the commission in August 1988, and a joint resolution sponsored by Waxman, Levine, and Claudine Schneider was introduced into the House. The commission never cleared Congress.

In 1989, two years before he left Pell's staff, Jones began work on founding the Human Potential Foundation, an outgrowth of his private Center for Applied

Anomalous Phenomena, which he had been operating on his own time. Late that year, Jones opened a bank account and prepared articles of organization. Originally called the Claiborne Pell Foundation of Human Potential, the Human Potential Foundation attracted financial support from Laurance Rockefeller, whose late-in-life obsession with UFOs was well-known, and Hans-Adam II, Prince of Liechtenstein. Both were friends of Pell.

Backed by Rockefeller's money, the Human Potential Foundation would become preoccupied with UFOs. But it, too, would eventually fade into irrelevance. In November 1998, after Pell retired from the Senate, the organization was officially dissolved; one of its central initiatives, a student-based effort to bring world peace, was transferred to a new group Jones founded and ran from his new home in Tennessee, the Peace and Emergency Action Coalition for Earth, Inc., or P.E.A.C.E.

Jones would have one last burst of national publicity before he left Pell's staff (in 1991). It would involve the Gulf War and then Secretary of Defense Dick Cheney — and it would surface during Pell's final reelection campaign, in 1990, against Schneider.

"Claiborne was one of the few futurists on the Hill, and recruited me to find out what other countries were discovering in consciousness research," Jones would write after Pell's death. "He recognized that discoveries in the physics of consciousness would be a key to the expansion of knowledge that we needed to save civilization."

In the end, Jones had expanded Pell's interests but brought no independently verifiable proof of what he had pursued during six years on the senator's staff. Like Pell in his paranormal quest into the realm beyond death, Jones was left with more questions than answers.

SEVEN □ FOREIGN RELATIONS

THE SPREAD OF FREEDOM

When he finally realized his longtime goal of chairing the Senate Foreign Relations Committee, in January 1987, after Democrats had resumed control of the Senate following the 1986 midterm elections, Pell took charge with a record of helping to ease global tensions and encourage responsible stewardship of the planet.

The Vietnam War that he had so strongly opposed was long over. His Seabed Treaty had been international law since 1972. The Law of the Sea, which he had also tirelessly pursued, had been accepted by most nations, although the U.S. Senate was yet to ratify it. Pell hoped to lead the ratification effort. He hoped for continued progress on nuclear arms control. He hoped to advance the spirit of cooperation between America and the Soviet Union that had emerged from the October 1986 meeting, in Iceland, of Reagan and Gorbachev, whose perestroika policies had brought new freedoms to his countrymen and helped move the American president beyond his early 1980s declaration that the old Cold War enemy was an Evil Empire.

This senator who still carried a copy of the United Nations charter in a pocket of his ill-fitting suits hoped to further the cause of world peace.

Whether he could achieve this ambitious goal was an open question. In contentious Washington, where Pell's personal quirks and noncombative legislative style were by now legendary — and where Republicans felt empowered by their success in Reagan's final midterm election — many people, on both sides of the political aisle, harbored doubts.

They surfaced almost immediately after the 1986 elections, when Pell's chairmanship was assured. In a story whose headline described Pell as "unaggressive," *Providence Journal* Washington Bureau Chief Mulligan wrote:

After a career in the background of the Senate Foreign Relations Committee, Sen. Claiborne Pell is about to become chairman and could be a key Democratic leader on global affairs — but the question is whether he is the sort of person to seize that role. The popular wisdom on Pell is that he tends by instinct to hang back from the fray rather than stake out the risky, controversial stand on an issue. And as a liberal in a moderate-to-conservative new Senate, he will be hard-pressed to make his panel a firm ground for bipartisan consensus.

Mulligan quoted a scholar with the conservative American Enterprise Institute who predicted that Pell's nonconfrontational ways spelled trouble — and not only with Republicans, but with strong-minded members of his own party who served on the committee, including Christopher Dodd of Connecticut and John Kerry of Massachusetts. "He's going to preside much more than he'll lead," said the Enterprise Institute's Norman Ornstein. "He's going to get caught in a crossfire between his very strong liberals and his moderates and the ultra conservatives, who will try and tie the place up in knots."

And there was no more conservative — and confrontational — member of Pell's committee than North Carolina's Jesse Helms, the ranking Republican, who stood in stark ideological opposition to Pell, and not only on foreign-policy issues. Two more different men could hardly be found.

Pell himself acknowledged the potential difficulties ahead, saying he saw "merit" in the description someone had made of him as "thoughtful but not dynamic." Pell also acknowledged that his belief in the power of ideas differed from some other senators who placed political expediency over long-term nurturing of noble goals. Nonetheless, Mulligan saw strengths: Pell's background as a Foreign Service officer, he wrote, had long kept him in good standing with the State Department, where "Pell is widely viewed as a known and welcome presence because of his foreign service background and inclination to practice compromise." Pell told the reporter that he was less than keen on television coverage of hearings, since TV could be an impediment to his longstanding philosophy of "letting the other man have your way."

"That approach," Mulligan concluded, "may be a hidden source of strength, particularly on Pell's premier goal of 'nudging' the administration along on a variety of arms control areas."

But "nudging" was not in evidence during the first hearings that Pell called, during the second full week of January 1987, to consider two test-ban treaties that two presidents had signed more than a decade before but which the Senate had never ratified. The Threshold Test Ban Treaty (TTBT), signed by Nixon in 1974, and the Peaceful Nuclear Explosions Treaty (PNET), which Gerald Ford signed two years later, limited underground tests to a yield of 150 kilotons, the equivalent of about 150,000 tons of TNT — an important threshold, since it prevented testing of new, vastly more powerful weapons whose force was measured in megatons (the most powerful nuclear weapon ever tested, the Soviet "Tsar Bomba" AN602 hydrogen bomb, exploded with a force of 50 megatons, in 1961).

Shortly before the hearings opened, on January 13, Reagan had asked the Senate to delay ratification of TTBT and PNET until the U.S. and the USSR could agree on "direct, accurate" means of verification.

With uncharacteristically caustic language, Pell on the first day of hearings rebuked the president, calling Reagan's request "little more than a charade, and really a waste of the committee's time." It was, Pell said, "DOA—dead on arrival." The new chairman was more conciliatory the next day, when, in acknowledgment of an upcoming meeting in Geneva of Soviet and American representatives—and of strident Republican opposition on his own committee led by the cantankerous Helms—he said that swift ratification might elude him. "I also recognize, from a political viewpoint, that it may not be feasible," Pell remarked after a session that included testimony by William E. Colby, former director of the Central Intelligence Agency.

But Pell had set a new tone of public criticism of the administration that would continue throughout much of Reagan's next-to-last year in office. In a February 19 address to the national Women's Democratic Club in Washington, his first major outside foreign-policy speech since becoming chairman, Pell called the president's arms control policies "a charade." Reagan's support for the Contra rebels seeking to overthrow the Nicaraguan government was, Pell added, "dirty" and "repugnant." And the administration-approved sale of arms to Iran for fund the rebels, the Iran-Contra affair, was "hypocrisy," Pell said.

"I believe this nation can learn from recent foreign policy blunders," Pell told the gathering. "And it now falls to a Democratic Congress to act decisively in pushing toward an American foreign policy based on American values . . . Democrats must take the lead in bringing a sense of direction to an entire American foreign policy in disarray." Foreign policy should be conducted by the State Department, Pell said, not by the sort of shadowy White House groups that had engineered Iran-Contra. One could hear echoes of his long-ago Foreign Service days in his remarks.

As the year progressed, Pell would sharply criticize the administration for other policies, notably its approach to the strategically important Persian Gulf region, where the ongoing conflict between Iraq and Iran had jeopardized oil shipments. The Tanker War, as the maritime battle between the two nations was called, had killed civilians and damaged oil-carrying vessels. In March, Reagan offered Navy protection of Kuwaiti ships (carrying Iraqi oil) that flew the American flag—an intervention that some feared would draw America directly into the Iraq-Iran conflict. Pell reacted with a blistering criticism of Reagan's approach to the volatile region, calling it in one Senate speech "ill conceived and dangerous," and in another, "hastily conceived, ill considered and lacking in essential public support." Pell asked Reagan to seek a United Nations Security Council meeting to consider an American Peace Keeping Force in the Gulf, a proposal that found no favor with the president.

Reagan's negotiators, however, were making progress in arms-control talks with Gorbachev's representatives — and Pell was optimistic, if cautiously. The talks, aimed at an agreement to eliminate intermediate-range nuclear and conventional ballistic and cruise missiles, had started in Geneva before Reagan took office and continued with periodic interruptions. During the seven years of sessions, Pell had visited the American delegation several times for updates, notably in February, when he posed with Geller, Gore, and delegation chief Max M. Kampelman. In late June, Pell returned to the Swiss capitol for another briefing.

Back in the U.S., he told reporters that he believed the superpowers were "on the threshold" of concluding terms of a treaty to limit the intermediate-range weapons. "I came back the last time, feeling that Max Kampelman and his team really wanted to move ahead — and that the president really wants to move ahead," Pell said, "and I came back this time, feeling the same way." His feelings were true.

An Intermediate-Range Nuclear Forces Treaty (INF as it would be called) would be a step toward a larger agreement to limit long-range strategic weapons, Pell declared, in reference to the Strategic Arms Reduction Treaty, first proposed in 1982. But another factor, Regan's proposed Strategic Defense Initiative, nicknamed "Star Wars," would impede progress on that front, Pell said.

"If things move fast with the INF it is also conceivable we could move ahead on a strategic weapons treaty — conceivable, but not likely," he said. "We're dancing around on a pin on this point, because if we build up a good space defensive weapons system that means that the strategic weapons systems — in order to overwhelm it — would have to be doubled or tripled . . . I just don't see how you can fully separate the strategic weapons system from the defensive space system."

Three weeks after Pell returned from Geneva, on July 22, 1987, Gorbachev removed one of the last obstacles to an INF treaty by dropping an insistence on retaining the Soviet Union's last 100 medium-range missiles (in Asian territory of the USSR). In a Senate speech, Pell greeted the announcement that both sides now supported a complete global ban with cautious optimism — and with the hope, again, that an intermediate-range treaty would be a step toward the larger goal of reducing more dangerous long-range ballistic missiles, whose collective megatonnage was frighteningly greater.

Negotiations continued in Geneva, and on September 18, the White House and Kremlin announced they had reached agreement in principle for the treaty. Pledging to continue discussions toward broader reductions of nuclear weapons, Reagan and Gorbachev signed the INF treaty in the White House on December 8.

Ratification was now in the hands of the Senate, starting with Pell's committee.

"When the ink dried on the Intermediate Nuclear Forces treaty yesterday, it became Sen. Claiborne Pell's baby," *The Providence Journal* wrote. "It's a job he's been preparing for during most of his career. Critics say he may not be equal to it."

There were many critics.

In a scathing commentary, *New York Times* writer Jonathan Fuerbringer doubted Pell could manage his twenty-member committee, which was deeply divided along liberal/conservative lines, and lead it and then the full Senate to ratification.

"Many Democrats and some Republicans, while loath to criticize Mr. Pell on the record, question whether he has the stature to carry the debate, and their concerns have already led other Senate leaders to step in to help him," Fuerbringer wrote. "Mr. Pell himself has little presence in the Senate and a deferential style that Democrats worry will assure that the ranking Republican on the committee, Senator Jesse Helms of North Carolina, will run roughshod over him in the treaty debate."

Helms had already publicly committed to fighting for a more conservative foreign policy—and was staunchly opposed to the treaty his president had signed—telling *The Times* that Pell's committee "lost favor in past years because the committee was totally liberal, and that did not reflect the American people."

"Politically, he is tougher," Washington Republican Daniel J. Evans, another member, said of the ranking Republican. "Pell doesn't stand up to that."

Even Pell's friend Biden, also a committeeman, suggested that Helms, a master of parliamentary procedure, could paralyze the committee.

"If Claiborne has any weakness, he is too much a gentleman," Biden said. "He doesn't like confrontation and he tends to accommodate people, and around here sometimes you have to be confrontational."

To which Pell himself publicly agreed.

"I am not confrontational by nature," he told *The Times*. "I've never enjoyed confrontation."

As Congress recessed for the Christmas holiday, Pell would not predict the fate of the INF treaty. His only strategy, he told *The Providence Journal*, was "to meet in the morning, meet at night, try to keep [reservations or amendments] to a minimum, and let each person have his day in court." In the end, he said,

"I think you have to be judged by your life and your results. I would hope we'd come out of this with a good treaty."

□ □ □ Pell opened what was expected to be weeks of hearings on January 25, 1988, by calling Secretary of State George P. Schultz, who declared that the INF treaty would make the world safer.

"President Reagan knows the only way to deal with the Soviet Union, on arms control as on other areas of our agenda, is to return to first principles — strength and realism," Shultz said. "Patience, or, if you prefer, the ability to hang tough" — not weakness, as Helms maintained — had led to the agreement, the secretary of state said. "We got this treaty because we were persistent at the bargaining table."

A strong bipartisan majority of the committee supported ratification, but the strongest opponent was not impressed.

Predictably — and flamboyantly — Helms used the first day to continue his efforts to sabotage the pact. He began with a stunt, staged to take advantage of national media coverage. Partway through the hearing, he had an aide present Shultz with a document labeled "Top Secret" in large red letters: it contained, he said, details of alleged Soviet cheating already on the treaty. Shultz was taken aback. "I have a hard time with this," said. "There are cameras all around and people can take pictures. And I just don't think this is the place to open this document up for, in effect, public inspection." The document contained nothing of substance, but Helms had taken control of the spin.

Helms went to lengths to keep control as the hearings continued and Pell moved toward a vote on the Senate floor. With bluster and his signature theatrics, Helm accused the CIA of dangerous failures. He introduced three dozen amendments he hoped would delay, if not derail, approval. He ridiculed witnesses. His eye on his own future, he parted company with a lame-duck president. He played the brat, consummately.

Pell's challenge was not swaying his committee, since most of its members had pledged their support before the hearings began. Isolating Helms was.

Characteristically, Pell declined to personalize his disagreement with his obnoxious colleague, even privately.

"He should have come home and said that 'that damn Jesse Helms is driving me crazy,'" daughter-in-law Janet said. "He never did. Never said bad things about anybody. Someone would say 'Oh, Jesse did this or that today,' and he would just shake his head."

To counter Helms, Pell called leaders from both parties to his committee hearing room.

After Shultz came Reagan's Secretary of Defense, Frank Carlucci, who in his appearance on February 1 said the treaty "demonstrated to the Soviets that our [NATO] nations have the political resolve to make—and stand by—the tough decisions to ensure our security." Pell called five former secretaries of defense, including Caspar W. Weinberger, who served during Reagan's first seven years, and James Schlesinger, secretary for Nixon and Ford. He called two former secretaries of state: William P. Rogers, who served under Nixon; Cyrus Vance, who served under Carter. He called Elliot Richardson, the only person in history to serve in four Cabinet-level positions.

After Senate Majority Leader Robert C. Byrd announced his support for the treaty, Pell joined Byrd, Armed Services Committee chairman Sam Nunn, Defense Secretary Carlucci, and other Reagan officials on a trip to Europe to brief NATO leaders.

On March 30, the Senate Foreign Relations Committee voted overwhelmingly to send the treaty to the full Senate, where a two-thirds majority would be required for final passage. Helms was one of only two committee members to vote against approval.

Six weeks later, on May 17, Pell opened full Senate debate by declaring that "a journey of a thousand miles begins with a single step." Although passage was all but assured, Helms remained belligerent, declaring that ratification would abandon Europe to domination by the Soviets. "I'm going to oppose it if I'm the only senator who does so," he vowed. A long delay would thwart plans by Reagan to bring the pact to Moscow for his next summit with Gorbachev, set for May 29.

By now, Helms's intransigence had become an embarrassment to his party's leaders. In a public rebuke of Helms, Senate Minority Leader Bob Dole named Indiana Senator Richard Lugar, former Foreign Relations chairman, to manage Republican floor debate on the treaty. With Lugar in charge of his party, the Senate on May 18 voted ninety-one to six to reject a bid by Helms to stop debate on the specious charge that Gorbachev was not authorized to sign the treaty. Nine days later, the Senate voted ninety-three to five to approve.

"As the tally was announced," The New York Times reported, "the crowded chamber was momentarily silent before spectators in the gallery broke into applause that quickly spread to the Senate floor—something not only unusual, but against the rules. Lawmakers who had been shouting at each other in the final debate only hours before grinned broadly and congratulated each other. Off the Senate floor, administration officials celebrated with champagne."

The first major Senate-approved Soviet-American arms accord since the 1972 Strategic Arms Limitation, the INF treaty resulted in the destruction of nearly

2,700 nuclear weapons: 846 from the American arsenal and 1,846 by the Soviet Union. Verification was confirmed by a provision allowing each side to inspect the other's installations where the weapons had been deployed. Although the weapons represented only a small percentage of the superpowers' destructive nuclear power, Reagan on his arrival in Moscow joined Gorbachev in hailing the treaty as an advance toward a more comprehensive accord.

"We have taken our work step by step, and I have come here to continue that work," the President said. "We both know it will not be easy. We both know there are tremendous hurdles yet to be overcome. But we also know that it can be done because we share a common goal, strengthening the framework we have already begun to build for a relationship that we can sustain over the long term, a relationship that will bring genuine benefits to our own peoples and to the world."

Shortly after the Senate vote, Pell shared his thoughts with *Providence Journal* reporter Jody McPhillips in his hideaway office. He seemed tired, McPhillips wrote, after two weeks of floor debate and "collegial arm-twisting sessions" that took place beyond public view.

"I'm exhilarated and relieved," Pell said. "But I am glad these last three or four days are over."

Pell noted that never before had an arms-control treaty called for the destruction of existing nuclear weapons; even the landmark Seabed Treaty that he had championed many years before was prospective.

"For the first time, however modestly, we are reducing nuclear weapons," Pell said. "It is an essential first step. The escalator is going down. That is a truly remarkable achievement."

Pell had proved his critics wrong — this time. He had neutralized Helms. He had put aside his philosophical differences with Reagan and worked with the President toward a noble ambition. But he would never again experience such triumph in foreign affairs. His inability to manage the growing conflicts inside his committee would frustrate and depress him, and his tenure as chairman would end in disappointment.

▫ ▫ ▫ For Pell, the second half of 1988 passed in relative anticlimax. Completing a genuine contribution to world peace was a difficult act to follow.

But there were moments when Pell used his Foreign Relations chairmanship to further the cause. In September, Pell led the Senate in passing economic sanctions against Iraq for its use of poison gas against Kurdish civilians living in the Gulf nation (sanctions that the House then also overwhelmingly approved, but which died in October, the victim of a House-Senate power struggle). "This is truly a crime against humanity," Pell said. "It is genocide, in fact." In late November, after George H. W. Bush had been elected president but Democrats had kept control of the Senate, Pell made his third visit as Senator to Cuba, where he met with Castro to again discuss ways to ease tensions. On his return, Pell told reporters that he hoped the incoming President would continue momentum toward restoration of full relations with Cuba, much as Nixon had opened the door to renewed relations with China; as a Republican president, Pell said, Bush would find the job easier than if a member of his own party tried. "If we Democrats had done what Nixon did in China, we'd have been impeached," Pell said. "Moves in this direction are easier for Republicans to make," he argued, since conservative opposition would be diminished if not neutralized, as ratification of the INF treaty had demonstrated. Pell said he conveyed this message to Secretary of State-designate James A. Baker III, who would soon be confirmed in Foreign Relations Committee hearings.

In 1989, Pell would not achieve anything on the order of INF treaty ratification, but he would finally witness a geopolitical event that he had long predicted: the demise of the Soviet Union and the advent of Western-style democratic governments in Russia and Soviet-bloc nations. The Iron Curtain would fall.

Spurred by the freedoms Gorbachev had encouraged and the example of Poland's Solidarity Movement, led by future Polish President Lech Walesa, the end came fast.

In March, under Gorbachev's democratic glasnost policies, Soviets voted representatives to a new Congress of People's Deputies in the first truly free election since the 1917 Bolshevik Revolution. Pell hailed the elections, in which many old-guard Communists were defeated, as "mind-boggling" and "the beginning of a second Russian Revolution in the making," a description that would prove accurate when the Soviet Union was finally dissolved in December 1991. "The Soviet people have made it clear that they want change — and fast — and that should strengthen Gorbachev's hand with the conservatives who oppose him," Pell said in a statement.

In April, Poland legalized Solidarity, and two months later the party won a stunning 99 of 100 seats in the newly created Senate of Poland. In a speech to graduates of St. Andrew's School in Barrington, Pell hailed the emerging freedoms overseas — and, striking a theme that hearkened to the Vietnam War, said that the costs of America's defense during the decades of confrontation with Soviet-bloc nations had been an obstacle to full development of America's resources.

"Our Cold War military and defense expenditures have seriously handicapped the United States in the intense competition of the new global economy," Pell said. But, as always, he was optimistic, telling the young high school graduates that they and their generation were on the threshold of a "great era of peace, progress and improved living conditions for Americans."

Autumn brought the spread of freedom to Hungary, Bulgaria, Romania, and Czechoslovakia, where decades before Pell had experienced at first hand the oppression of Communism. The Berlin Wall fell in November. Accompanied by Nuala, Pell after Thanksgiving joined John Chafee and other senators on a ten-day trip through Europe that brought them to soon-to-be-reunited Germany, Czechoslovakia, Vienna, and Geneva, where the senators met with arms-control negotiators.

On his return, Pell sat in his hideaway office and shared his reflections with the *Journal*'s Mulligan. Particularly strong, he said, was his memory of being forced to leave Prague in 1948 when the Communists seized power—but even then, he said, he had had confidence that Communism could not endure.

"Communism contained the seeds of its own destruction," he said, "going against normal human desires to work freely, travel freely, worship freely, try to pile up a little money for one's children." Nonetheless, Pell said, events had unfolded "much more quickly than many of us expected. Freedom proved much more contagious than we realized it would." And, he predicted, it eventually would spread across the planet.

"Thirty years from now," Pell said, "I doubt if we'll see a Communist government anywhere, a totalitarian government."

In one of his last interviews while still Senator, Pell in 1996 was asked if the Cold War could have been avoided.

Yes, Pell answered—by a worse alternative, a hot war.

"By keeping the Cold War," Pell told the TV interviewer, Truman Taylor of Providence station ABC-6, "it did not escalate. My view has always been—I used to be called impolitic for saying this—but that Communism is such a dreadful system, that the cure for it is to surround it, isolate it and then let it die of its own ineptitude and that's just what we did . . . Communism in direct competition with democracy can never win."

CLAUDINE

As the summer of 1989 had wound down, Pell had pondered his future. In 1990, he would turn seventy-two. With three decades in the Senate, he was undecided about wanting a sixth term—which, if he won reelection, would end when he was almost eighty.

"My health—I have my fingers crossed—is pretty good," he told *The Journal* in a story published on September 24, 1989. "Mentally, I feel fine." And the Senate, he said, remained captivating. But he was no longer the young politician with a driving ambition. He had accomplished many things in Washington, but at a personal cost.

"You can do so much good work on the job," Pell said. "It's a wonderful job. On the other hand, I have interests outside."

Pell counted his family among those interests. He wanted to write a book and he remained intrigued with the paranormal. "I'm very interested in the development of human potential," he said "If I did quit, I'd stay busy." Nuala was prepared to support whatever he did, but she expressed frustration with his indecision, saying, "I just wish he'd make up his mind." It was hardly the first time her husband had prevaricated with a major career choice.

With the formidable Schneider likely to seek Pell's seat, national Democratic Party leaders worried that they would lose it if anyone but the still popular Pell were on the ballot on November 1990. Biden was among Pell's close friends who were enlisted in encouraging him to run. Years later, Biden would recall the effort.

"I remember walking over to the Senate after three of us were assigned [by party leadership] to get Claiborne to run again the last time," Biden said. "Looking back on it, I wish I hadn't: He may have been happier, I don't know. I'm walking over with him from his office to the floor to vote . . . and I said, 'What else would you do, Claiborne?'

"He said, 'I have mountains to climb, Joe.'

"I thought it was a euphemism. I said, 'What do you mean?'

"He said, 'I have mountains to climb.'

"I said, 'Claiborne, this is Joe. What the hell are you talking about?'

"He said, 'Joe, I want to climb . . .' and he named three mountains. He was serious — it wasn't a joke. He had mountains to climb! I was like, give me a break, Claiborne.

"Most people who have mountains to climb — it's 'I want to write that book.' He literally meant mountains, in Lichtenstein."

On the morning of November 14, eight days before his seventy-first birthday, Pell placed telephone calls to *The Providence Journal* and to several fellow senators and friends elsewhere in government. After months of the same sort of indecision that had beset him during the 1950s, when he could not settle on a course to elective office — and after changing and rechanging his mind a half dozen times, son Toby said — Pell was ready to announce his intentions.

He had finally decided, just the day before, to seek reelection.

In the end, Pell told reporters, the renewed realization that he had the "best job" possible had trumped the outside interests tempting him to leave office.

The rapid advancement of freedom in Eastern Europe and the Cold War's passing excited him, he said. So, still, did his work in the arts and education. And more work remained — another treaty to be ratified, the environment in need of further protection.

Pell told *The Journal* that his announcement "was a culmination of a lot of thinking and discussions with various members of the family." Nuala expressed relief that her husband had finally moved off the fence. "Whew. And how," she told reporters.

In Washington and in Rhode Island, where Pell's name on the ticket had proved gold in past elections, Democrats were similarly relieved.

"This is welcome news," said Kerry, junior senator from Massachusetts. "Senator Pell is a gentleman who has shown tremendous sensitivity to the needs of Rhode Islanders and to world concerns." Senate Majority Leader George Mitchell of Maine professed himself "happy that he will continue to serve with distinction." Ted Kennedy, senior senator from Massachusetts, said he was not surprised. "I never really doubted he would run again," said Kennedy. "He's too valuable in the Senate."

Pell as yet had no opponent — not one who had formally announced, that is. But an official declaration was all that Claudine Schneider lacked to launch a campaign that had been widely anticipated since 1983.

□ □ □ Since Barbara Leonard's humiliating loss to Pell in 1984, the National Republican Party had targeted Pell's seat for the 1990 election — with Schneider the candidate deemed as having the best chance at winning it. By early 1989, planning and fundraising were seriously underway. Republican strategists were not naïve: they believed that Pell's strong favorability and scandal-free professional life presented Schneider with large obstacles. But they also believed they could be overcome: Pell, they maintained, could be depicted as a senator past his prime, a politician who had always been eccentric and now was alarmingly distant from the real concerns of his constituents.

A confidential June 1989 "Pell Vulnerability Study" prepared by the National Republican Senatorial Committee outlined areas where Schneider might find advantage in what the authors described as "a unique political situation in which two of the most popular, well-liked and hard-working politicians are matched against one another."

The study's overall conclusion, underlined in the introduction, was that "Pell is out of touch with the future needs of Rhode Island. While in the past, Pell has played some part in significant accomplishments, Pell is no longer able to meet the new challenges that the future brings as Rhode Island moves forward. The same old answers used in 1970 will no longer adequately address the problems of the 1990s."

Pell, the study asserted, was just too old.

Under "the age issue," the authors noted that were Pell reelected, he would be seventy-eight when his term ended in 1996. "Only seven senators are older than Pell; only one of them is standing for reelection. Senator Proxmire, who retired last Congress, outlined his thoughts on being 'too old' for the Senate when he announced he would not seek another term. 'I am 71 years old. I'd be 73 when I took office [for another term]. I'd be almost 80 years old when I retired. That's too old.'" But Republican strategists would have to be careful, for there was potential peril in exploiting the age difference between Pell and Schneider, who turned forty-two on March 25, 1989 — especially in Rhode Island, a state with one of the largest percentages of senior citizens in America. One of Pell's core constituencies was the elderly, many of whom saw the senator as a trusted friend.

The study also found vulnerability in Pell's taxation and spending policies, his Foreign Relations Committee chairmanship ("he supports funding for countries who constantly oppose us in the United Nations"), his legislative record ("given his seniority and chairmanships, Pell has not been effective at passing legislation"), and what it called his "record of flip-flopping on issues." Perhaps failing to fully comprehend how Rhode Islanders accepted Pell's personality, it saw potential in exploiting the senator's many quirks. "Stories resound around Rhode Island regarding Pell's unusual lifestyle and his lack of understanding of the average person's life. Although these stories may, in part, endear him to the Rhode Island voters as a loveable eccentric, these anecdotes — combined with a legislative record that is equally out-of-touch with reality — can be a powerful tool against Pell's re-election."

The study cited several quintessential Pell stories, including his Red Sox World Series faux pas and the all-time favorite, "McAn Shoes." It noted Pell's inquiries into the afterlife, citing a December 5, 1988, *U.S. News & World Report* piece that quoted Pell on his unsuccessful efforts to reach his dead father by means of séance. It emphasized Pell's interest in the paranormal, citing his relationship with Uri Geller and quoting him as favoring a "Manhattan Project-style effort to catch up with the Russians," and stating that Pell's bill to establish a National Commission on Human Potential was ridiculed on Capitol Hill as "the spoon-benders' bill."

It seemed the authors were unaware of Schneider's own paranormal interests, which would effectively negate the issue in the campaign. It seemed they failed to see that Schneider herself was so quirky.

◻ ◻ ◻ Seven days after Pell announced his decision, on November 20, 1989 — two days before his seventy-first birthday — what would be the final test in Pell's long elective career began, with a visit to Rhode Island by President Bush, who came with a message to elect the still-undeclared Schneider.

It was not the first time a member of the First Family had traveled north to praise the Congresswoman: wife Barbara had visited on June 13, hosting Republicans at two Schneider fundraisers, a $1,000-a-person reception followed by a $150-a-head luncheon. The First Lady had trumpeted Schneider's "enormous leadership and energy, vitality and compassion," saying that "I've heard George say over and over, 'We need Claudine, and we need her energy and innovative ideas.'"

In his November visit, a $250-a-ticket fundraiser at Warwick's popular Rocky Point Park Palladium that raised nearly $200,000, the president struck the same theme.

Schneider, Bush said, possessed "indefatigable energy," which struck him when he landed in Rhode Island. "When I got off the plane, I felt tired just being around her." Like Barbara's comments, the president's were a barely veiled reference to the age issue. The Bushes apparently had read the June Vulnerability Study, which had quoted Pell in a 1981 UPI interview describing his job as senator. "By the end of the day," Pell had told UPI, "you're a limp rag, and you still have to work at home or go to those dreadful receptions where you have to show your face to show you're interested in a particular cause." It was, at the time, simply a candid assessment of any senator's life. Out of context, the study's authors believed, it would be another weapon against Pell.

On January 9, 1990, Schneider called a press conference to describe her recent visit to Panama, which the U.S. had invaded in December, resulting in the capture of dictator Manuel Noriega. Her trip conveyed not only a youthful image, Schneider hoped, but also expertise in foreign policy. Not to be outdone, Pell traveled to Moscow to speak at an international environmental conference, which Gorbachev also attended. Pell urged nations to invest their defense savings — the so-called "peace dividend" — in protecting the environment and developing alternatives to fossil fuels. "We have successfully met the challenge of the Cold War," Pell said. "The question now is how we will meet the challenge of peace."

On his return, Pell cosponsored a $511-million package of aid for Eastern Europe, a supplement to a similar aid bill he introduced and steered to approval in November. Pell's so-called SEED II bill (Support for Eastern European Democracy) included a provision for assistance to the Soviet Union, with the president's consent. "This kind of action," he said, "is clearly our most cost-effective form of defense spending."

With Schneider soon to formally declare her candidacy, the 1990 campaign was about to intensify. And it was about to take the first of several strange twists that would make the race one of the more unusual in Senate-election history.

◻ ◻ ◻ Although the authors of the Pell Vulnerability Study seemed to have underestimated the potential impact of Schneider's own interests in the paranormal when they suggested that Pell's better-known interests could be exploited to their candidate's benefit, Washington insiders were well aware of Schneider's fascination. The general public was brought in with a series of stories that made headlines in the first months of 1990.

"Lotsa rumors on Capitol Hill about Rhode Island Rep. Claudine Schneider's dabbling in astrology," a *Washington Times* columnist wrote in the "Charlotte's Web" column on January 5. "Someone just told the Web the one about the job applicant who was told he'd passed the first interview and now it was time to talk to the astrologer." A spokesman for Schneider confirmed that she found astrology "personally interesting." But unlike the Reagans, the spokesman said, she did not use astrology in hiring or political decisions.

It was a distinction the authoritative *Roll Call* daily newspaper chose not to emphasize when it christened the Pell-Schneider contest the "Psychic Senate Race," a title *The Providence Journal* brought to the attention of Rhode Islanders in its popular Political Scene column of February 3:

> The "campaign could be the first psychic showdown in congressional history," according to the [*Roll Call*], which covers Capitol Hill. Some of the travel will be familiar to Rhode Island followers of matters political and paranormal: Pell has been to mediums ("Nothing happened," as *Roll Call* recalls Pell's recollection) and he has a full-time aide who does some research in the field.
>
> Miss Schneider's belief in ESP has also been noted. A new — but disputed — wrinkle is what the paper calls her "fascination with astrology." *Roll Call* quoted a Schneider spokeswoman to the effect that her association with an old friend who is an astrologer shows Miss Schneider's "high tolerance for other people's intellectual curiosities." But Miss Schneider said recently that she doesn't have "any interest in astrology." She said she knows her sign (Aries) "and that's about it."

Clearly, neither candidate would find political gain in the other's unconventional interests. Nor would they be able to create another kind of scandal, since both Pell and his opponent had already publicly admitted that they had tried marijuana. Schneider had revealed her history with the drug in 1988, when she said she "experimented" with it while in college in the 1960s. "It didn't interest me or excite me at all," she said, "because, quite frankly, I'm into natural highs, and, in addition to that, I am not at all involved in any kind of substance abuse — or participation, for that matter." Pell revealed his own history in 1987, when he said he had taken "several puffs of a marijuana cigarette" several years before. "I didn't like it," he said, "and never tried it again."

On February 14 Schneider formally announced her candidacy in a speech at Providence's Roger Williams Park Casino.

"Most of my life — like Rhode Island — I've fought the odds, and won," she said. "Now it's time to challenge the odds again."

She referred to her 1980 upset of representative Edward Beard, and to her battle against Pell, whom many Rhode Islanders now called an "institution" — an institution who led her in a recent television poll, 52 to 41 percent.

She referred, also, to her diagnosis at age 25 of Hodgkin's disease.

"My world turned upside down," she said. "Doctors said I had a fifty-fifty chance to beat cancer. Like other survivors, I was able to fight, able to live. We survivors beat the odds. We won. My parents were right: no obstacle is insurmountable and the future depends on the choices we make today. Beating cancer felt like a new life, a second chance. From this experience came a personal commitment to share every ounce of energy to serve the people and place who had helped me live."

In her speech, Schneider did not mention Pell. Nor did she reveal her decision to ignore much of the previous June's Vulnerability Study and run a positive campaign, though she would make that point publicly later. She spoke, instead, of the causes she had pursued in the House and her plans for the Senate. Schneider said she would be a champion of the environment. She would address global warming. She would be a friend of the elderly, an advocate for better health care, and a worker for a better economy.

These were noble ambitions. They were also Pell's issues. Strip away the party affiliation, and on many issues it was difficult to discern much of a difference between the two. Schneider's task was a formidable one, especially with her vow not to go negative.

□ □ □ The spring and early summer passed with little visible drama in the race between the liberal Democrat and the moderate Republican.

Schneider in April proposed nine live televised debates on the three major Rhode Island stations, arguing in letters to station managers that this would be an appealing alternative to the negative campaigning that characterized many campaigns.

"My opponent, Claiborne Pell and I have already agreed to run positive, issue-oriented campaigns," she wrote. "I believe this year Rhode Island has an unprecedented opportunity to send a signal to the nation to show that in this age, a campaign still can be conducted on serious issues, not sensational sound bites." The stations were willing, but Pell declined to participate in nine debates. He saw no advantage.

In May, a poll by Providence's Alpha Research Associates confirmed the wisdom of Pell's refusal: leading Schneider 49 to 38 percent, there was no benefit to him from so many debates, since the chances of a gaffe would increase simply by being live on-air for all that time. Both candidates put a spin on the poll results, with a Schneider spokesman saying the results were "well beyond our expectations" at this stage of the race and Pell campaign manager Mary Beth Cahill saying it confirmed their assessment of "a very tight race." Cahill expressed pleasure with another poll finding: only three percent of respondents believed age was an issue.

In late June, Pell formally kicked off the final stage of his campaign with a vow to be more aggressive. Speaking at the old State House in Newport, a short drive from his home, Pell acknowledged that until now, he had devoted most of his time to quiet fundraising and Senate business. "As a result," he said, "we are a little behind."

But the polls still had him ahead of Schneider, if only by single-digit margins, and he had more than a million dollars of unspent campaign funds, double his opponent's war chest. For campaign director, he had hired Bob Squier, a top consultant whose previous clients had included Hubert Humphrey and Jimmy Carter. He had settled on the issues he would stress. Education, the environment, and global harmony had served him well before and to this standard list he added a new one: a pledge to continue exploiting the peace dividend, using money not spent on a Cold War military for domestic programs as the nation moved into a "new golden age," as he called it.

"The collapse of communism and the apparent coming end of the Cold War open the prospect of an unparalleled era of peace and opportunity," Pell said. "Peace and jobs. Two of the most central issues we face today. And I am in the unique position in the United States Senate to see that on both of these critical issues, Rhode Island's interests are heard." Schneider shared the peace dividend ambition, but Pell pointed to his Foreign Relations chairmanship and seniority as third-ranking Senate Democrat overall to make the case that he was better suited to achieve results than a freshman senator.

By the middle of the summer, what had been a mostly sleepy race had appeared on the national radar. Democrats controlled the Senate, with fifty-five members to the Republicans' forty-five; gaining five seats would give Schneider's party de facto control, since Vice President Dan Quayle could break any tie. With a gain of six seats, the Republicans would have a majority. It was an unlikely, but not impossible development: the Democrats themselves had won back control of the Senate in the last midterm election, 1986, when they picked up nine seats, changing the dynamic in Washington for Reagan's last two years. And so in 1990, the national Republican party targeted Pell's seat as one they had to win in order to have a chance at regaining control of the Senate.

The president rejoined the battle in July, when he hosted a breakfast fundraiser at Washington's Mayflower Hotel that raised about $150,000 for Schneider. The same month, Mulligan's story about the national importance of the Pell-Schneider contest led the Sunday edition of *The Providence Journal*.

The story began by recounting a C-Span program the week before that had featured the heads of the Democratic and Republican senatorial committees discussing what Mulligan termed "one of the more peculiar pairings on the nation's political score sheet," a race that both heads agreed was one of the three or four top battles of the thirty-five Senate campaigns that year. Noting what one analyst described as the candidates' ideological similarities, Mulligan suggested that for some voters, the race could come down to personality, especially since the approval ratings for both Schneider and Pell were high. Shared interests in the paranormal aside, their styles were markedly different: Pell the low-key, patrician Washington institution whose mannerisms and speech seemed to have come from an earlier century; Schneider the vivacious, progressive thinker who seemed to overflow with energy and ideas.

"Finally, of course," Mulligan wrote, "are the touchy numbers that can only be read subjectively: Pell is 71, Miss Schneider 43. No one can prove that Pell's legendary Mr. Magoo-ishness has gone foggier with age. No one can prove that Miss Schneider remains more a striver than a doer after a dozen years in politics."

On August 1, Pell himself seemed to provide proof of having gone foggy.

Appearing with Schneider on a special edition of Providence station WJAR's popular 10 News Conference program, Pell was asked to name a specific bill he had personally championed that had directly helped his constituents.

"I couldn't give you a specific answer," Pell said. "My memory's not as good as it should be, but if any of the people out watching us, I would be delighted if you sent me a postcard to do it."

Pell then mentioned Pell Grants and the Sea Grant program, initiatives that were some two decades old.

"But you can't remember the last bill you sponsored?" the host asked.

"That directly hits Rhode Island?" Pell said. "No."

The next morning's *Journal* headline proclaimed: *A forgetful Pell trips in 1st debate with Schneider.* More than a year after the Vulnerability Study, here was the age issue, front and center, courtesy of Pell himself.

The next day, August 2, Iraq invaded Kuwait.

Pell's embarrassment disappeared in a deluge of news coverage of Saddam Hussein's attack, which would prompt America to retaliate, in the 1991 Gulf War. Pell returned to Washington, where he immediately introduced a resolution condemning the invasion and calling for a United Nations-coordinated effort to restore peace to the region. In his speech, Pell condemned Hussein as "the Hitler of the Middle East," a quote that showed up in coverage by *The New York Times* and other outlets. The resolution passed, 97 to 0. These were the kind of numbers voters were paying attention to, not the 71–43 age difference between the senator and his challenger.

Schneider broke through unrelenting news of the growing Gulf tensions in mid-August, when Bush stumped for her in Rhode Island again, but Pell continued to draw greater coverage for his role in Persian Gulf diplomacy. On August 16, he welcomed Kurdish opposition leader Jalal Talabani his Senate office: "Senator Pell is an old friend of the Iraqi people," Talabani told reporters. "Bush — we don't know him, unfortunately." Ten days later, Pell made headlines for his support of a United Nations resolution allowing military force in the naval blockade of Iraq.

More dominating coverage attended Pell's late-summer visit to Saudi Arabia, which had sought and received U.S. military protection under Operation Desert Shield. Pell's tour, chronicled by journalists and a Senate-paid cameraman who were invited to accompany him and several other senators, led the broadcasts and front page for days beginning with his August 31 departure — and the attention continued when he returned to Washington, where he briefed the president and then presided over a Foreign Relations Committee hearing featuring Secretary of State Baker. No ad campaign or debate could bring the sort of positive publicity Pell was receiving. Here, at a time of crisis, was a man of action. Fate had handed Pell a gift. The age issue returned to the background.

Leading Schneider by just six points in two midsummer polls, Pell had widened his margin to twelve points in a poll taken after his return from the Middle East. "It reminded people of his stature in foreign affairs," said pollster Jana Hesser, of Alpha Research Associates. "People are likely to fall back on sort of the tried and the true in times of crisis." Schneider's much-publicized visit to Panama earlier in the year seemed insignificant by comparison.

In their only formal debate of the campaign, on September 23, Pell and Schneider politely discussed issues — and Pell made a joke at his own expense. Asked by the moderator the same question that led to his August 1 gaffe, Pell quipped, "I forgot, what was it?" He then named several bills recently benefiting Rhode Islanders that he had sponsored, including oceanography grants for the University of Rhode Island and legislation establishing a national park along the Blackstone River, birthplace of the American industrial revolution. *Civility, not hostility, marks face-off*, read the headline in the next day's paper. Neither Schneider nor Pell had gained any advantage.

But Schneider had tried, by attempting to portray her opponent as an ineffective Foreign Relations chairman, a charge he refuted by saying "You have to judge a committee not by the amount of television, but by what it produces." Three days after the debate, Pell steered the Senate to unanimous ratification of the INF Treaty. It had taken a long while, but Pell had produced.

Schneider's vow to refrain from negative campaigning was getting her no traction, as a Brown University poll released in the last week of September demonstrated. The survey found Pell leading Schneider among likely voters by 23 percent, 58 to 35 — a prohibitive deficit for the Congresswoman, with just six weeks left until Election Day.

"When you're challenging a popular incumbent," said Brown pollster professor Darrell West, "you have to give voters a reason to unseat him. Many citizens do not yet believe that Representative Schneider has done that."

An encounter on the campaign trail recounted in *The Providence Journal* illustrated Schneider's predicament. Stopping by a church bazaar in Bristol, Schneider told a voter, Karen Nygaard, that the election was not a referendum on her decade in the House, or Pell's three decades in the Senate.

"This vote is not a thank you for the past 10 years or 30 years," Schneider said, hoping for a favorable reaction.

"I love Senator Pell; I love Claudine," Nygaard told reporter Scott MacKay when Schneider was out of earshot. "Senator Pell has done so much for this state. As long as he wants to run, we should let him have what he wants."

Pollster Brown predicted that Schneider would become more aggressive, if not go negative, during the few weeks left. And she did, to an extent. In an interview published in the Washington Post, Schneider repeated an assertion she had made earlier in the year to USA *Today*: Pell, she said, sometimes slept in committee meetings. "I hear it from colleagues," she told *The Providence Journal*. "Maybe they wouldn't tell you." But Schneider could provide no proof, and the paper's Washington bureau reporters, who had covered him most closely over the years, could not recall a single incident when he had dozed off.

And once again, events beyond Schneider's control thwarted her: On October 5, a federal budget negotiated over two months of talks between the administration and Congressional leaders was rejected by the House, forcing a weekend shutdown of the government. The impasse would preoccupy legislators until a final settlement on October 27, only ten days before the election. Like fellow legislators, Schneider would lose valuable time in Washington when she could have been campaigning in her state. It was a predicament that worked in a popular incumbent's favor and Pell surely benefitted.

◻ ◻ ◻ If not for Schneider's own interest in the paranormal, Pell aide Scott Jones's decision to send a bizarre letter on Senate stationery to Defense Secretary Dick Cheney might have become the issue she needed to help overcome her twenty-three-point deficit.

Acting on his own, Jones on October 3, 1990, wrote to Cheney of his discovery that when tape of the secretary's speeches were played backwards, the word "Simone" could be heard; the same word, Jones said, could be heard when tapes of speeches by Bush and Baker were played that way.

"I mention this situation," Jones wrote to the secretary, "in case it is a code word that would not be in the national interest to be known." The implication was that such a word might tip Saddam Hussein to some impending U.S. military operation.

Years later, in a letter to *The Washington Post* that the paper never published, Jones elaborated. "I knew that there was something important to learn from 'Simone,'" he wrote, "and visited the Middle East Desk in the Library of Congress to follow a hunch. I told the 'Simone' story to an Arabic-speaking staff person. His immediate response was that the word we heard was probably, 'simoom, a hot desert storm.' I suspect that even *The Washington Post* remembers that Desert Storm was the forty-three-day first Gulf War following the five-month Desert Shield."

Journalists besieged Pell, who told them that Jones had not informed him of writing the letter, which had been leaked to the press, perhaps by Cheney himself. Jones had erred in sending the letter on Senate letterhead, Pell told reporters. But he did not disavow Jones or his explorations over the past several years into the paranormal — nor specifically into what was called reverse speech therapy, the pseudo-science of divining hidden meaning from tapes of speech played backwards.

The theory, never generally accepted or proved, holds that a person can unwittingly reveal unconscious thoughts when speaking — unconscious thoughts the brain mysteriously encodes in words that make sense only when heard backwards. Jones had learned of reverse speech from an Australian named David John Oates, whose later web site would describe his concept:

> Language is bi-level, forward and reverse. As the human brain constructs the sounds of speech, it forms those sounds in such a way that two messages are delivered simultaneously. One forwards, which is the conscious mind speaking, and the other in reverse, which is the unconscious mind speaking. The applications of this discovery are exciting. On the surface level, it can act as a sort of Truth Detector as Reverse Speech will usually correct the inconsistencies of forward speech. If a lie is spoken forwards, the truth may be communicated in reverse. If pertinent facts are left out of forward speech these may also be spoken in reverse. It can reveal hidden motive and agenda and other conscious thought processes. At deeper levels, Reverse Speech can reveal thought patterns that are unconscious, including reasons behind behavior and disease.

To most people, this was gibberish.

Pell told a reporter that while he had never heard of reverse speech therapy before the Cheney letter, he was intrigued. "While it sounds wacky, there may be some merit to it," he said. He compared the theory to television, a fact of life in 1990. But 100 years ago, anyone predicting it "would have been told they were crazy," Pell said.

The senator did not disavow Jones — but chief of staff Hughes reprimanded him for violating a policy against sending letters on Senate stationery without his or Pell's approval. Jones, said Hughes in an interview, was "saddened and . . . chastened."

On October 20, as Congress continued wrestling with the federal budget, *The Providence Journal* published a front-page story examining the impact of this latest offbeat revelation on the Pell–Schneider race.

"Their interest in certain unconventional fields of inquiry — meditation, ESP, human potential, New Age-ism, call-it-what-you-will — also puts Pell and Schneider in a class they hold uniquely among rivals for federal office this year, or maybe any year," wrote Mulligan.

The bureau chief recapped Pell's long interest in these matters, which was well-known to voters. Schneider's, he noted, was less so. "Miss Schneider's interest in untapped human potential sprang literally from a life-or-death issue," Mulligan wrote,

> her bout in her mid-20s with a form of cancer that attacks the lymphatic system. While she accepted conventional therapies such as radiation treat-

ment, Miss Schneider also practiced a self-healing technique — imaging or visualizing — and has since counseled others to train it on their illnesses. She described imaging this way: "You visualize the cancerous cells" and focus on them, "imagining them going out of your body with your breaths."

Miss Schneider still practices meditation and is a believer, she said, in the power of positive thinking and positive action. She has written and given interviews on the subject in a number of forums. The editor of one such publication, Jonathan Adolph of *New Age* magazine in Boston, described the New Age movement as a set of "emerging ideas, thoughts and values in a number of different fields — environmentalism, health, politics and other fields." Miss Schneider believes imaging helped cure her. Adolph said, "When someone experiences that, it opens their mind to other things."

Miss Schneider was once asked in a television interview whether she believed in ESP and replied without hesitation, 'Yes I do. Are you reading my mind?' But lately, she has downplayed that, saying, for example, that she has never read any books about ESP. She has had the experience of thinking of certain people just before getting a phone call from them but said that's probably coincidence.

This close examination of Schneider's own interests ended, once and for all, the paranormal as an issue in the race for Senate. And the Cheney letter that prompted it was the last straw for Hughes and other staff members, who for six years had tolerated Jones out of deference to their boss. Pell did not move immediately, but when the election was over, he let Jones go. He was still pursuing the paranormal after Pell died, when he wrote his unpublished letter to *The Washington Post*.

"Claiborne was one of the few futurists on the Hill," Jones wrote,

and recruited me to find out what other countries were discovering in consciousness research. He recognized that discoveries in the physics of consciousness would be a key to the expansion of knowledge that we needed to save civilization. In six years of inquiry at research facilities around the world, we learned some rather important things that the *Washington Post*, [the Committee for Skeptical Inquiry, an organization devoted to debunking paranormal and fringe-science claims], and most of academe find fearful and avoid with nervous giggles . . .

It will probably upset you to learn that a common thread appeared through my six years of listening to what researchers were discovering about two of the "forbidden" subjects in U.S. academe and most of the media. Before the Soviet Union imploded, leading research institutes there viewed psychic phenomena and UFO/Extraterrestrial phenomena together. One lab director told me, "So much of what we see in ET research is psychic in nature. We must look at them together." China made this discovery, and of course the same discovery was made in the United States years ago. But we don't talk about that . . . The price tag of secrecy in this area has become a threat to civilization.

Jones was in his eighties when he penned his letter to *The Post*, a true believer still.

□ □ □ On October 27, 1990, Congress finally broke the federal budget impasse. With only ten days until the election, Schneider and Pell returned to Rhode Island for the final campaign push. Both planned to blanket the state with appearances.

For Schneider, who had far less money left for TV advertising than Pell, overcoming her double-digit deficit in the polls would prove an impossible task. A last-minute boost came on the Sunday before Election Tuesday, when *The Providence Journal* endorsed the Republican. "In his five terms in Washington, Senator Pell has served the people of Rhode Island with efficiency, candor, wisdom and courtesy," the paper wrote. "Of course, his achievements speak for themselves — Pell Grants, the National Endowments for the Arts and Humanities, the Sea Grant College Program — and his tenure as chairman of the Foreign Relations Committee has added new luster to Rhode Island's reputation. But after nearly 30 years in the Senate, Claiborne Pell's significant accomplishments are now largely behind him. It is time for a new political generation to take office." Here, in veiled form, was the age factor.

But the backing of *The Journal's* editorial board, of questionable value at a time when newspaper endorsements mattered less to voters than TV advertising, was about the only good news for Schneider.

"He's an institution, they'll never knock him out," said a voter watching Pell campaign on the final weekend.

Voters did not: With nearly 62 percent of the vote to Schneider's 38 percent, Pell was an easy victor. Pell won a great majority of Rhode Island's cities and towns, including Schneider's hometown of Narragansett.

"People decided to cast their vote as a thank you for the past, as opposed to an investment in the future," Schneider said.

"My opponent was dogged by bad luck," said Pell, graciously.

With the exception of Chafee, who had come back from his 1972 defeat, Pell now had politically buried every opponent he had faced in an election. Schneider was out of politics, too, never to return. On the eve of his sixth term, Pell could legitimately claim the title of Senator for Life. He could be excused if, in six years, he would be tempted to run again—to seek membership in the rarefied club of senators who had served into their 80s and 90s, among them the man he had succeeded, Theodore Francis Green, who was 94 when he finally retired.

Pell would be tempted, despite the onset of a terrible disease.

SOFT AND DISTANT

The Iraq crisis dominated Washington's attention as Pell's sixth term began. In late November, the United Nations had passed Resolution 678, which gave Hussein until January 15, 1991, to withdraw from Kuwait or face certain attack from a coalition of nearly three dozen nations led by the United States. On January 8, Bush asked Congress to adopt its own resolution supporting military action.

In advance of full Senate and House votes, Pell called a hearing of his Foreign Relations Committee — a hearing marked by sharp disagreement that reflected divided popular opinion. Some who testified urged more diplomatic efforts; others said the time for diplomacy had passed. Predictably, Pell placed himself in the former camp, urging a strategy of United Nations-ordered sanctions that, he said, could eventually force Hussein to retreat.

"With sanctions," he said, "time is on our side, because Iraq's machines, its weapons, are being degraded."

But arguments like Pell's did not prevail on January 12, when, after three days of debate, the full Senate voted 52 to 47—and the House concurred, 250 to 183 — to give Bush authority to wage the war that had become all but inevitable since the August invasion of Kuwait.

On January 16, the Gulf War began with air strikes against Iraq. Pell was at his desk in his main office when a staff member delivered the news.

"These are particularly sad days," the Senator told reporters, but now that war had started, he said "I pray for all those endangered, courageous servicemen and women and innocent civilians in Kuwait and Iraq." Speaking somberly, Pell expressed his hope that "our armed forces and those of our United Nations allies will bring [the war] to a speedy and successful conclusion." Less than a month and a half later, when allied forces had driven Iraq from Kuwait and Bush declared a ceasefire, Pell welcomed the news.

Spring came, and other concerns preoccupied Pell.

He continued his efforts to secure federal help in resolving a financial crisis that had prompted Governor Bruce Sundlun, a longtime Pell friend and political ally, to close the state's credit unions. As chairman of the Education Subcommittee, he introduced a bill to widen eligibility for Pell Grants so that more students of middle-income families would benefit. He traveled to Czechoslovakia to join in a ceremony reopening his old office in Bratislava. After cosponsoring, with Helms and other senators from both parties, the Chemical and Biological Weapons Control and Warfare Elimination Act of 1991 — a law providing sanctions against countries using such weapons in violation of international law — he continued to build support for the measure, which Congress would enact that October. In June, he hosted Boris Yeltsin, Soviet president-elect, at a Foreign Relations Committee reception that drew seventy-two senators — and headlines. Pell praised Yeltsin, who was embarking on a four-day tour of the U.S., for what he described as the soon-to-be-president's policy of "turning swords into plowshares."

And in late July, he greeted the Moscow signing of the historic Strategic Arms Reduction Treaty, which cut American and Soviet long-range nuclear arsenals, by Bush and outgoing Soviet President Gorbachev.

Pell seemed in his element: presiding over new developments on the road to world peace. But out of public view, Pell had accepted that he lacked the political mettle — and desire — to effectively lead the Foreign Relations Committee. His continuing battles with Helms and others had finally worn him out.

"His lifelong goal was to become chairman of the Foreign Relations Committee," son Toby said. "But when he became chairman, he hated it. He found it really difficult — almost impossible — to deal with Jesse Helms. Complete obstructionist. Never any room to compromise and he found that just distasteful." Rancor had never been Pell's style and he found nationally televised confrontation distasteful. He did not play to the cameras.

The conservative Republican had not been Pell's only frustration: some junior Democratic committee members, notably John Kerry and Biden, who chaired subcommittees, had sought greater influence and that had caused further tensions. After the fall midterm elections, Hughes and Geryld B. Christianson, director of the committee's Democratic staff, had approached Pell and proposed a new committee structure in which the subcommittees would handle the day-to-day work of legislating in their areas of expertise and Pell would manage those major issues that most appealed to him. "It's time to start a new way of doing business," Christianson told his boss. Relegating substantial power to subcommittees would also have the practical value of neutralizing Helms, since each subcommittee had its own different ranking Republican.

Pell was relieved at relinquishing power, he told *The Providence Journal* in an August 11 story. "The system was not working before," Pell said. "I've been miserable."

And while he claimed not to have been in "over [his] head," as some believed, Pell did concede that his "very heavy load" had discouraged him. As evidence of the newly restructured committee's improved effectiveness, *Journal* reporter Mulligan pointed to a foreign-aid bill, a State Department funding bill, and an authorization for the Arms Control and Disarmament Agency that had all recently cleared the Senate with ease — under the management of Kerry, Biden, and Delaware's Paul Sarbanes.

Mulligan portrayed Pell's more than four years as chairman as characterized by an unwillingness, or perhaps inability, to strongly lead on foreign policy.

"The Berlin Wall has been smashed; the U.S. has gone to war against Iraq; the great Soviet republics and satellites have strained at the limits of their independence," Mulligan wrote.

Pell has visited the sites of global ferment. He viewed the Brandenburg gate; he placed a memorial wreath at a public square in Prague; he flew to the Persian Gulf with about a dozen other senators during the buildup to the war last August.

But Pell's role has been more as a witness to history than as an actor on the world stage. He has passed up even the second-banana role in which foreign-policy-minded senators are typically cast, in the shadow of the President, his generals and his envoys. Even though Rep. Claudine Schneider, his GOP challenger, failed to make a hot issue of it last year, Pell's doggedly bland style and his committee's record of frustration had long made him a favorite target of wags and critics, particularly in the close community of Washington policy-makers and watchers.

Why did Pell wait so long to change the panel's way of business? he was asked recently. He put his answer in the context of his long indecision about running for office: "I had really not made up my mind. In fact at one point, I had made up my mind not to run. I had no great passion or desire."

On December 8, 1991, leaders of the Russian, Ukrainian, and Belarussian republics signed the Belavezha Accords, which signaled the official end of the Soviet Union. Yeltsin sent formal notice to the United Nations on the day before Christmas, and two days later, the Supreme Soviet of the Soviet Union dissolved itself, the final step in the collapse of America's old Cold War nemesis. That New Year's Eve, Pell was in Moscow during an eleven-day tour of Russia, Ukraine, Belarus, and Kazakhstan.

After attending a party hosted by Moscow's mayor during which the Russian Army Choir sang *God Bless America* for hundreds of Russians and their cheering foreign guests, Pell reported feeling "exhilaration and zest" at witnessing the dawn of a new age he had long predicted, but never was sure he would live to see.

"I love it," he said, a statement that for him passed as jubilation.

□ □ □ Back in the U.S. two weeks later, Pell was injured in a car crash. The accident would prove to be prelude to the final, increasingly tragic, chapter of his life.

Pell was with Nuala in New York City on January 15, 1992, to visit Nuala's mother, Josephine Hartford Bryce, who was ailing and bedridden at her Upper East Side home (she would die on June 8). Nuala had left for Washington and Pell was enroute to LaGuardia Airport for a flight to Rhode Island when the taxi in which he was riding rear-ended a Honda that had stopped in rush-hour traffic in the northbound lanes of FDR Drive. Pell was catapulted into the Plexiglass partition dividing the cab's front and back seats. Only Pell sustained serious injury.

"I had observed the approaching taxicab in my rear mirror," the driver of the Honda later wrote in a statement. "Apparently the driver only made efforts to stop his car in the last few yards . . . Upon checking the cars involved for possible injured passengers, I found Senator Pell on the passenger seat of the taxicab, profusely bleeding." His eyeglasses had been broken and he was momentarily unconscious.

Pell was taken by ambulance to Cabrini Medical Center, a few blocks from the accident, where he was treated for a possible concussion and facial cuts, mostly around his right eye, that required some seventy stitches to close. An unpublished photograph taken shortly after the accident showed ugly bruising over much of the top of his face. He looked like an aging boxer who had gone down in the ring.

From his hospital bed the night of the accident, Pell described the accident by telephone to a *Journal* reporter.

"I was pretty badly knocked around," he said, but he expected to be released after being held overnight for observation. "I'm alive and reasonably well and ready to come back [to Rhode Island] tomorrow." In a brief phone interview with an Associated Press reporter, Pell made a joke: "Winston Churchill got hit by a New York City taxicab, so I guess I'm in good company."

□ □ □ Pell, seventy-three now, seemed to recover as the year wore on.

He resumed his normal schedule almost immediately, joining colleagues in sponsoring alternative-energy legislation and partnering with Chafee in a successful effort to save funding for construction of two new Seawolf submarines, parts of which were built in Rhode Island, from defense cuts proposed by Bush. In April, he tried, without initial success, to get Chinese permission to visit occupied Tibet, birthplace of the exiled Dalai Lama, where human-rights violations were alleged. Over Memorial Day weekend, he joined Chafee at an international-policy conference in Geneva. In July, he was honored when Governor Sundlun signed into law a Rhode Island bill renaming the Newport Bridge, which connects Jamestown to Newport, the Claiborne Pell Bridge. In August, he supported Senate legislation to electrify Amtrak lines between Boston and New Haven (where diesel locomotives switched to electric power for the remainder of the trip to New York); coupled with earlier improvements, the $1.2-billion project would eventually cut an hour from the four-hour Boston-to-New York trip, another step toward Pell's decades-old ambition of high-speed rail transportation along the Northeast Corridor.

Late September found Pell on the major foreign-policy stage again when his committee opened hearings into the Strategic Arms Reduction Treaty, or START.

The thousand-page START removed thousands of American and Russian nuclear warheads, on missiles and on bombers, from their arsenals (with the breakup of the Soviet Union, warheads from Ukraine, Belarus and Kazakhstan were also destroyed). First proposed by Reagan in 1982, START had been signed by Bush and Gorbachev in Moscow on July 31, 1991, but the U.S. had never ratified it. Opposed by only a handful of the most strident conservatives, the treaty easily cleared Pell's panel and encountered little opposition in the full Senate.

"In this post-Cold War environment," Pell said on the Senate floor, "START will provide regulation of the arsenals, a regime of ensuing inspections and opportunities for cooperation that will be of value in ensuring that old threats do not return in any significant fashion."

On October 1, the Senate voted 93 to 6 to ratify. The Cold War really was over, as further evidenced by another measure the Senate approved that early-autumn day: a foreign aid bill giving nearly a half-billion dollars in aid to the former Soviet republics, provided they met human-rights standards and enacted economic and democratic reforms.

As Congress prepared to recess for the 1992 elections, Pell, now the second-ranking Senate Democrat, acknowledged a year of minor accomplishment. He had managed renewal of the Higher Education Act and finally succeeded in broadening middle-class access to Pell Grants, although he had failed — again — to make the grants a federal entitlement, similar to Social Security.

"Not much innovation, no new concepts," he said of his Pell Grants, a description that suited the entire year and all of the 102nd Congress, now drawing to a close. "It's been humdrum, not exciting," Pell said.

One last foreign-policy mission awaited Pell in 1992. Shortly after his seventy-fourth birthday, he left for a seventeen-day fact-finding trip to war-torn Somalia, India, Pakistan, Israel and Syria, Russia, China, and Tibet, which the Chinese had finally allowed him and the two senators traveling with him to visit. Pell met with Jiang Zemin, general secretary of the Communist Party (and soon to be Chinese president) and Israeli Prime Minister Yitzhak Rabin, but the highlight of the trip, he said on his return, was his stop in Tibet. Long an admirer and casual acquaintance of the Dalai Lama, Pell for years had hoped to set foot on Tibetan soil.

"Oh, it was unbelievable," he said on his return. "The snow and ice, the great, huge mountains. You felt like you were on top of the Earth."

His enthusiasm evoked the boy Pell, traveling the world with his father or mother.

▫ ▫ ▫ Democrats retained control of the Senate in the 1992 elections, which brought Bill Clinton to the White House. Pell remained chairman of Foreign Relations as 1993 began, and during the year, the committee would confirm members of the Clinton administration and conduct hearings on the war in Bosnia and the failed "Blackhawk Down" raid on Somalia that left eighteen Americans dead and dozens wounded in early October. It would consider the "Star Wars" missile-defense system, human-rights violations in China and East Timor, Middle East peace talks, and more.

But Pell was rarely at center stage. His greatest moment of enthusiasm seemed to be the day in April that he hosted the Dalai Lama for a committee lunch. Pell called the Buddhist "a man of humor, calm, physical courage and simplicity," a result, the senator said, of his "great interest in things intangible, things of the soul."

Pell's retreat from prominence was the subject of a *Providence Journal* analysis that Mulligan wrote in May, after Biden commanded headlines for his criticism of America's European allies in the Bosnian war. Testifying at a Foreign Relations hearing, Secretary of State Warren Christopher recounted his recent European trip, prompting Biden to declare: "What you've encountered, it seems to me, was a discouraging mosaic of indifference, timidity, self-delusion and hypocrisy." But Biden, Mulligan reported, was alone at the impromptu press conference that followed the hearing; committee chairman Pell, he wrote, had slipped away, unnoticed.

"Later on," Mulligan wrote,

he would speak his mind on intervention in Bosnia — although, unlike Biden, he's really of two minds — in a speech to a near-empty Senate that might almost have been planned for maximum invisibility. Not that Pell needs to plan for invisibility. Especially in moments of potential warfare and other high drama, it naturally comes his way . . .

The Bosnia debate offers the latest example of Pell's lack of flashiness and of his hands-off style of chairmanship that Senate Democratic leaders actually institutionalized as his condition for seeking a sixth Senate term in 1990. Pell gave much of the panel's power to his subcommittee chairmen. This week, the *National Journal*, a magazine well-respected in Washington circles, reported that recently, "Senate gossip has boiled over with scenarios that would relieve Pell of his post." When pressed to respond to the *National Journal*'s comparison of his chairmanship to that of Rhode Islander Theodore Francis Green — incompetent by all accounts when he was eased out of the Foreign Relations chair — Pell demurred. "He was a very dear friend," said Pell, who succeeded Green 32 years ago, "and I won't get into that." After a long pause, however, Pell added: "I feel I do the job just as well as I did 20 years ago or 30 years ago or 32 years ago."

Pell remained as chairman, albeit quietly. As the year wore on, he even hinted that he might seek a seventh Senate term two years later.

The hint came in late September, when Pell joined the popular Democratic Representative Jack Reed, elected to Congress in 1990 and presumed by many to be Pell's successor, at a live radio talk-show broadcast from the White House lawn. With a bit of a wink and a nod, the host asked Pell if he had anyone in mind for the senator who would follow him.

"No," Pell said, "just myself."

The remark drew laughter and a follow-up question by a *Journal* reporter, who reminded Pell that during the Schneider race, the senator had said the campaign was "definitely" his last.

"At that time," Pell told the reporter, "that was how I felt. How I feel now may not necessarily be the same."

The reporter pressed on: So he might, indeed, be a candidate in 1996, when he would turn seventy-eight years old?

"I wouldn't rule it out, and I wouldn't rule it in," Pell said. "I haven't made a final decision."

◻ ◻ ◻ The year 1993 brought personal tragedy for the Pells: oldest child Bertie, named for Pell's father, was diagnosed with non-Hodgkin's lymphoma, a fatal disease of the lymphatic system. It was the latest blow to Bertie, his wife Eugenia, and two young children, Christina and Clay, who were living in Arizona: Bertie had lost nearly everything in the savings and loan crisis of the late 1980s and early 1990s, including the car dealerships he had opened and run profitably until the crash.

Pell and Nuala took the news of Bertie's disease hard; Nuala especially could empathize with their son, as she herself had been diagnosed with breast cancer in 1980 (her successful treatment included a mastectomy). As Bertie's lymphoma progressed, the Pells would move, for a while, to Arizona to be with their son.

And it wasn't the only health problem facing the family.

Something was afflicting Pell himself.

The symptoms had advanced gradually, and were barely perceptible at first: an occasional drooling, a voice sometimes so soft that staff had to prompt him to speak louder, an unusually stiff facial expression, an overall aura of unhealthiness that prompted others to whisper that he was beginning to look "frail" beyond his years. Cognitively, Pell was unchanged; his mind remained sharp. He kept his ordinary full schedule and continued his regular jogs. He seemed, to casual observers, the same old Pell.

But he and those closest to him could not but think that he was unwell. They began to suspect he had Parkinson's disease — perhaps precipitated, as Nuala and others came to believe, by the head trauma he sustained during his 1992 taxi accident.

▫ ▫ ▫ As 1994 began, Pell had several ambitions, including reauthorization of the Elementary and Secondary Educational Act to include a new formula providing more federal aid to poorer urban schools — an ambition that was achieved that fall, when the Senate passed the bill. But he held no ambition higher than long-overdue Senate ratification of the Law of the Sea Treaty, whose roots lay in the first year of his second term, 1967, when he introduced the resolution that became the Seabed Treaty. A companion to the Seabed pact, the broader Law of the Sea Treaty, so strongly advocated by Pell, establishes international ocean boundaries and protects international maritime resources. The treaty was concluded by 1982, but Reagan had refused to sign it, and conservative opposition had continued into Clinton's presidency.

Clinton embraced the treaty, and on July 29, U.N. ambassador Madeleine K. Albright signed it. Pell joined her on the United Nations floor.

"I'm tickled pink," said Pell, with uncharacteristic exuberance. "This issue interests me more than any single topic since I've been in the Senate . . . It's something I've worked on all my life." He spoke literally: since his Newport childhood, since summer days of sailboats and Bailey's Beach, the ocean had cast a spell.

On August 11, Pell held a hearing on Law of the Sea, but it was for the purpose of drawing attention to the languishing treaty, not to seek a formal committee vote; Clinton had not yet formally submitted the treaty to the Senate, and the committee could not take formal action until after he did. The approaching midterm elections, in which Democrats were predicted to lose Senate seats and possibly control of the body, further complicated the issue.

"Senator Pell was eager to get the process started, if for no other reason than that he didn't know how the election would turn out and whether he would still be Chairman in January of 1995," committee Democratic staff director Christianson later recalled. "The August 11 hearing was Senator Pell's way of putting his personal stamp on the process even though he was not sure whether he would be in a position to complete the process."

He was not: the Republicans indeed regained a Senate majority in the midterm elections and Helms stood in line to replace Pell as chairman of the Foreign Relations Committee when the new Congress convened in January 1995. In a CNN interview on November 18, Helms vowed a combative relationship with Clinton, whom he bluntly declared was not "up to the job" as Commander in Chief. He vowed to continue his opposition to Law of the Sea.

Helms would succeed, and Pell would leave office without realizing the treaty's ratification.

▫ ▫ ▫ By the end of 1994, even casual observers suspected something was seriously wrong with Pell.

His driving, never exemplary, had dangerously worsened. In October, he was fined $25 for making an illegal turn that resulted in a collision between his Mustang convertible and a taxicab in a busy downtown Washington intersection; shortly after, staff took his car keys away. Ordinarily impeccably groomed, he would sometimes leave home with his shirt partly unbuttoned or his face partly unshaved. On the eve of the November elections, Pell joined Clinton at a Rhode Island rally—but he did not speak. He looked so unhealthy that a *Journal* reporter was obligated to take notice, albeit delicately: "Mr. Clinton acknowledged Pell, who appeared a bit frail," the reporter wrote.

Pell heard the whisperings. "Do I look frail?" he began to ask those who knew him best.

"Frankly, yes," Hughes and others answered.

During a routine checkup, a Senate doctor diagnosed no disorder. Pell proclaimed that seemingly clean bill to doubters as evidence of his good health—

but he was in denial. He was remembering, perhaps, his friend Javits, who with the onset of ALS had begun a slow decline into mute paralysis and eventual death that had horrified Pell.

Rhode Island governor Sundlun, a friend for decades, was among those increasingly concerned—but he, like others, kept silent as his last term as governor wound down in 1994. "I thought he looked terrible but didn't have the guts to say anything," Sundlun later said.

But at a post-election lunch Sundlun hosted for several politicians at Providence's Hope Club, Pell appeared so disheveled and disoriented that Sundlun finally decided he had to do something. He called a doctor, who said that while he could not make an accurate diagnosis without examining Pell, the symptoms suggested Parkinson's disease. Sundlun brought that word quietly to Nuala, who gave her blessing to Sundlun meeting privately with her husband to discuss his condition. They spoke at Pelican Ledge, in Pell's study, which overlooked the Atlantic Ocean.

"He listened," Sundlun said. "He thanked me and he gave me no reason to believe he was going to do anything about it."

But Nuala now was insistent that Claiborne visit a neurologist, which Sundlun's doctor acquaintance had suggested. During the Christmas holiday, Dr. Jonathan H. Pincus, chief of neurology at Georgetown University Hospital in Washington, examined Pell. He concluded that Pell was indeed in the early stages of Parkinson's, with typical symptoms but a mind that was unaffected. Pincus said that with medication, Pell might forestall more serious complications for five or more years.

Mulligan broke the story in the April 9, 1995, *Sunday Providence Journal.*

In an extensive interview that Mulligan conducted in Pell's hideaway office, the senator said that he had not believed Pincus when the neurologist told him in December, "You seem to have a touch of Parkinson's." Pell told Mulligan that he remained in denial, refusing to accept what Nuala and others had all been saying. "I don't see in myself what others see in me," Pell declared. He said he had declined to take the drug Sinemet, which Pincus had prescribed. At one point in the interview, he said that friends told him that when he walked, he was noticeably hunched-over. He got to his feet and paced back and forth across his hideaway office floor.

"Do I seem hunched over when I walk?" he asked the reporter.

Mulligan did not think that he did.

"But his speech, truth be told," Mulligan wrote, "did seem soft and hesitant that day as he said: 'I accept that I may have the disease. But I don't accept that it's 100-percent certain.'"

Asked his political intentions by Mulligan, Pell said the diagnosis had not changed anything; a reelection bid, he suggested, remained a possibility. Just days before news of his diagnosis broke, Pell in a separate *Journal* story had said: "I've not made up my mind. I'm not playing games, but I don't want to make up my mind at this time."

Pell held to that position as spring turned to summer. Only he could decide whether to seek a seventh term in 1996, but as the speculation grew that he wouldn't — or physically couldn't — it seemed to some that his long public service career was already ending, a perception that was reinforced in late June when he joined the president in San Francisco for ceremonies marking the fiftieth anniversary of the signing of the charter of the United Nations. "Some of those who worked at that historic conference are still here today," Clinton said on June 26, "including our own Senator Claiborne Pell, who to this very day, every day, carries a copy of the U.N. Charter in his pocket." Fifty years was a long time, and Pell at seventy-seven was an old man.

Before leaving Washington, Pell had shared his recollections of his role in the founding, as an assistant secretary to the United Nations Conference on International Organization. "It started out just right," Pell said. "Instead of flying us to San Francisco, they chartered a train across the United States. You could see the eyes of all those people who had been in war-torn Europe boggle as we passed the wheat fields, the factories. You could feel the richness, the clean air of the United States. It was a wonderful image. We shared a spirit, a belief, that we would never make the same mistakes; everything would now be done differently. We had a sense of creation and exhilaration." He had been young then: a twenty-six-year-old with a sense of wonder and his life still ahead of him.

More somber sentiments accompanied the question still facing Pell as Labor Day neared and Rhode Island's political establishment looked increasingly to 1996, a presidential election year. Pell's decision would affect not only him, but anyone who ran for his seat — and also those with an interest in the positions held by any such potential Senate candidates, notably Jack Reed, deemed Pell's heir apparent.

"I'm satisfied with my health. I'm confident and satisfied, too, that it won't be a factor in my decision," is all Pell would say when asked, yet again, in August what he intended. In an interview, neurologist Pincus continued the suspense, confirming that Pell was following doctor's orders — with promising results.

"He's taking the medicine, his gait is improved, his turning is improved, his posture is improved," the neurologist said. "If he's going to run or not going to run, he's going to have to make up his mind on some other basis than this."

Privately, Nuala and his closest staff wanted him to retire. Pell himself was torn. With yet another momentous decision, he characteristically could not make up his mind.

On the Saturday of Labor Day weekend, chief of staff Hughes and top aides Jack Cummings, Bill Bryant, and Dennis Riley drove to Pelican Ledge. Sitting with Nuala in Pell's office overlooking the Atlantic Ocean, they addressed the issue at hand. Hughes presented the issues making the case for Pell to announce that he would not seek reelection: his Parkinson's, the negative impact his continuing indecision was having on his party, the fact that Reed would be a worthy successor, the notion that now just seemed the right time. Pell listened, and then he wanted to hear the arguments again.

By evening, Pell remained undecided.

The staff returned the next day for more discussion.

"OK," Pell finally said. "All right." He would retire.

The announcement was set for Tuesday, September 5, the day after Labor Day, in Pell's office in Providence's Federal Building, across Kennedy Plaza from the Biltmore Hotel, nerve center for so many Pell campaigns. An alert was sent to reporters and Hughes wrote Pell's two-page statement. At seven o'clock that morning, Riley drove to Pelican Ledge to pick up his boss.

"OK, senator, are you ready?" Riley said.

"I'm not committed to this yet," Pell said. "I don't know if this is the right decision."

Riley was dumbfounded. He and Pell talked on the forty-five-minute drive to Providence, but they arrived with Pell still seemingly, again, undecided.

When Cummings saw Riley's face, he said: "What's wrong?"

"I don't think he's going to do it," Riley said.

Cummings and Hughes brought Pell into a private room.

When they returned, more than fifty journalists, staff members, and well-wishers had filled the office. Some wore buttons from his first election year, 1960, when he was an improbable candidate no one predicted would become a Rhode Island political institution overshadowing even Senator Green. Some told stories of his many reelection campaigns, when Republicans with more ambition than political savvy dared to believe that they could topple the quirky patrician millionaire.

Pell began to speak, his voice barely audible, reading from his prepared statement.

I am here this morning to announce my intentions regarding reelection to the United States Senate. This has been a most difficult decision for me. It is fashionable today to malign the Congress, the federal government and those who serve the public in elective office.

I, however, consider the United States Senate a marvelous institution full of talented and committed men and women who — contrary to popular belief — are dedicated to serving their constituents and to improving the quality of our national life. And I continue to believe that government, and the federal government in particular, can, should and does make a positive impact on the lives of most Americans. Federal programs and agencies do not always work perfectly, and many need reform, but they were conceived to help people and I believe most continue to do so.

When you believe as strongly as I do in the value of good government and see so many of its virtues under attack, there is a great temptation to continue to serve and to fight for the values and the programs that I consider vital. As to my health, I have been assured that there is no medical barrier to my seeking reelection and to serving another six-year term. I feel strong and healthy and sharp.

However, I have decided not to be a candidate for reelection.

There is a natural time for all life's adventures to come to an end and this period of thirty-six years would seem to me about the right time for my service in the Senate to end. I know I will miss more than anything the people of Rhode Island, whom it has been my very real pleasure to serve all these years. They are a fine, caring people who put their trust in me all these years, tolerated my eccentricity and gave me great affection. I pray that I repaid their trust and served them faithfully. And I will particularly miss the Senate and the men and women who serve there. Let me say again, almost without exception each of them believe he or she can make a positive difference to our nation's well-being.

This Senate seat from our state has been held for six decades by a forward-thinking Democrat, first Theodore Francis Green and then me. I want to make it clear today that I am intent on doing all I can to insure that another progressive Democrat is elected to fill this seat. And I also plan to do all I can to assist in the reelection of President Clinton, whom I consider a sadly underrated and really quite successful President. He has served this country with intelligence and vision and passion and I fully believe he deserves another term.

Beyond that, I have no concrete plans. I will stay active, I will stay engaged in public service and I will continue to cherish my associations with Rhode Island and its wonderful people.

Word of Pell's decision traveled swiftly, eliciting tribute from Rhode Island politicians, Democrat and Republican. That afternoon, Pell flew to Washington, where he read his statement on the Senate floor. An hour of praise from colleagues on both sides of the aisle followed. Many noted Pell's long unbroken record, in the Capitol and in campaigns, of refusing to speak negatively of an opponent, an increasing rarity in the new political order. "In the end," *The Providence Journal* wrote the next morning, "Claiborne deB. Pell exited with a grace rare in politics today."

Three weeks later, Reed announced his candidacy for Pell's seat: a liberal Democrat who shared Pell's philosophies on most issues, he had Pell's blessing. A torch first lit with the 1936 election of Green, who had led the transformation of previously Republican Rhode Island into a Democratic state, was soon to be passed.

TRANSCENDING DIFFERENCES

Pell began his final year in office with his last major official foreign-policy tour: a weekend visit to Croatia, Hungary, Italy, and Bosnia, with President Clinton, Reed, and other lawmakers. The group visited American peacekeeping troops, and Pell spoke to *Journal* reporter Karen Lee Ziner from Air Force One on the flight home. Pell said he had slept but a few hours in two days, and that the Bosnia stop had not been without risk, notably from land mines. "We were given strict orders just to walk on the cement sidewalks, or cement streets— not to go off in the fields," Pell said.

Back home, Pell continued with the routines established over nearly thirty-six years, but they were to little legislative end. The last months would be mostly a time of honors, memories, and bittersweet closing rituals. Reed, meanwhile, launched his Senate campaign with a commanding lead in the polls and the mantle of a political legacy that portended well for victory in November.

Save the Bay, Rhode Island's leading environmental group, honored Pell on March 3 at its annual meeting. The next month, the Rhode Island Historical Society recognized his creation of the National Endowments for the Arts and the Humanities at a benefit gala that drew more than 300 people. On May 18, Pell received the first Lifetime Achievement Award from Bryant University, which had awarded him the first of his nearly fifty honorary degrees in 1962. A month later, New York Senator Daniel Patrick Moynihan quoted Yeats in describing Pell as a man "who is blessed and has the power to bless" in bestowing the Hebrew Day School Amudim Award, given to a recognized pillar of society. On July 3, his 1960s vision for high-speed rail was celebrated in Providence, when U.S. Department of Transportation secretary Federico Pena formally launched the final phase of Amtrak's Boston-to-New Haven electrification project.

"Today we are writing a new chapter in transportation history," said Pena, at the downtown Providence station. "We are all here for one reason, that is, to construct our rail link with the twenty-first century."

Electrification would complete preparations on the Boston-to-New York line for 150-mile-per-hour Acela service, expected to begin by the end of the decade. In his remarks at the electrification ceremony, New Jersey Senator Frank Lautenberg, another longtime champion of high-speed passenger-rail service on the Northeast Corridor, credited Pell and his 1966 book *Megalopolis Unbound* with the vision that was soon to be realized. Pell received a standing ovation, and spoke a few words when the applause had subsided.

"Being here is an emotional experience," Pell said, "because it is a dream come true."

The next day, Pell, wearing a linen suit, marched alongside Reed in his final appearance at the Bristol, Rhode Island, Fourth of July parade, oldest in the country and a mandatory tradition for Rhode Island politicians. Pell vacationed at home for part of the summer, entertained the Prince and Princess Michael of Kent as houseguests, attended charity events, welcomed the return of cutters to the Newport Coast Guard base, and campaigned for Democratic candidates, including Reed and Rhode Island Representative Patrick Kennedy, son of Ted.

Back in Washington, the Pells on September 16 hosted the last of their annual cookouts for college students at their Georgetown residence, which they would soon sell.

In the Senate, the end neared.

◻ ◻ ◻ The tributes began on September 25, when Robert Byrd of West Virginia, Tom Daschle of South Dakota, Kent Conrad of North Dakota, J. James Exon of Nebraska, and Biden took the Senate floor to speak of Pell's contributions during thirty-six years, one of the longest tenures of any senator in history. More tributes from many other senators from both parties followed in the days ahead. Even Helms would speak admiringly.

Biden recalled his early days in Washington, when Claiborne and Nuala took him under their wing in the wake of the accident that had claimed his wife and daughter. He spoke, as others would, of Pell's unflagging civility, in Washington and on the campaign trail — a diminishing trait in a public discourse increasingly characterized by anger and ill manners, as the bombastic Helms so eloquently illustrated.

"The presence of Claiborne Pell on the floor of the U.S. Senate — just, literally, his physical presence on the floor — inhibits members from yielding to the temptation of engaging in uncivil conduct, in conduct that, quite frankly, we should all realize is beneath us and demeans the public debate and demeans this institution," Biden said. "And I can say, without reservation, that in the twenty-four years I have served here there is not a single, solitary person whose mere physical presence in a committee, in a caucus room, on the floor of the U.S. Senate — just his presence inhibits negative behavior on the part of all of us. He is a man of such character, such gentility, such class, and such persuasion by his actions. I mean it. Think about it."

Biden closed with praise for the forward-looking ideas Pell had slowly nurtured to fruition, despite skepticism and, sometimes, ridicule as Senator Oddball, as *Time* magazine had dubbed him many years before.

"This man is a man who is, to use a trite-sounding phrase, a quiet visionary," Biden said. "This is a fellow who wrote about the transportation system in the Northeast and predicted what would be needed and used a word I learned as an undergraduate that no one had ever heard of — 'megalopolis' — and he talked about Richmond to Boston and what would have to be done to accommodate the needs of this area of the country.

"He is the guy who came up with the notion of [the Arms Control and Disarmanent Agency]. He has been the single most consistent, persistent spearheader of the notion of bringing about the diminution of the number of nuclear weapons that exist in this world. He is the man who has been devoted to the notions and concepts embodied in the United Nations. He is a man who has been the leader in education and learning, a man who comes from considerable standing in terms of his own personal wealth and education but has bent down to make sure that people of competence, regardless of their economic status, would be able to achieve the same intellectual competence, capability, and background as he has achieved.

"This is a wonderful man, I say to my friends. You all know it. But not many have passed this way who have his personal characteristics and capabilities, and I doubt whether very many will come this way again. I will truly miss his presence in the Senate."

In his farewell remarks, Pell took credit for nothing he had achieved, not even the federal-assistance program that bore his name that by then had enabled tens of millions of Americans to realize a college education. He spoke, instead, of a philosophy that he said had guided him in his thirty-six years in Congress, a philosophy passed on to him from his father: that the ultimate ambition of public servants should be to advance America toward a modern-day Athens, noted for its civilized culture, and not a Sparta, remembered for its militarism and wars.

He spoke, too, of his hopes that rapidly evolving communications technology, which by 1996 included the Internet, would not so distort the democratic process that consensus needed for progress was imperiled, as his time before the television cameras at committee hearings had led him to fear. Years later, at a time when a member of Congress felt free to publicly call the president a liar, a national debate over health care degenerated into threats of physical harm, and bloggers routinely used the ugliest language to demean their elected leaders and fellow citizens, his words would resonate.

"In retrospect," Pell said, "it may well have been the widespread disillusionment with foreign policy in the Vietnam era which sowed the seeds of a broader cynicism which seems to be abroad in the land today. And with it came an end to that sense of unlimited possibilities that many of us brought to public life. Many other factors have contributed to that current of cynicism, but primary among them, in my view, is the impact of the electronic media, particularly in its treatment of politics and public affairs. At its worst, it glorifies sensationalism, thrives on superficiality and raises false expectations, often by holding people in public life accountable to standards which are frequently unrealistic or simply not relevant.

"The result has been a climate which exploits the natural confrontational atmosphere of the democratic process by accentuating extremes without elaborating on the less exciting details. It is a climate which encourages pandering to the lowest levels of public and private greed, a prime example of which is the almost universal defamation of the taxing power which makes it virtually impossible to conduct a rational public debate over revenue policy."

With language that could have been borrowed from diplomat Herbert or one of Pell's political-science professors at 1930s Princeton, Pell offered his colleagues gentle guidance for the new era.

"Comity and civility, transcending differences of party and ideology, have always been crucial elements in making Government an effective and constructive instrument of public will. But in times such as these, when there is fundamental disagreement about the role of Government, it is all the more essential that we preserve the spirit of civil discourse . . . The fact is that the democratic process depends on respectful disagreement. As soon as we confuse civil debate with reckless disparagement, we have crippled the process. A breakdown of civility reinforces extremism and discourages the hard process of negotiating across party lines to reach a broad-based consensus.

"The Founding Fathers who prescribed the ground rules for debate in Congress certainly had all these considerations in mind. We address each other in the third person with what seems like elaborate courtesy. The purpose, of course, is to remind us constantly that whatever the depth of our disagreements, we are all common instruments of the democratic process. Some of that spirit, I believe, needs to be infused into the continuing national debate that takes place outside the Halls of Congress. It should be absorbed by our political parties and it should be respected by the media, particularly in this era of electronic information. The democratic process is not well served by spin doctors and sound bites."

He had chosen not to note that some of the Founding Fathers themselves had resorted to slander in their early debates over the size and role of government — and then sanctioned a freewheeling public discourse in adopting the First Amendment, with its free-speech and assembly rights. But surely, they had not envisioned the outcome two centuries later.

"I would only add my own prescription for comity," Pell continued, "which can be summarized in three simple rules:

"First, never respond to an adversary in ad hominem terms. In my six campaigns for the Senate, I have never resorted to negative advertising. The electorate seems to have liked that approach, since they have given me an average margin of victory of 64 percent.

"Second, always let the other fellow have your way. I have always found that winning an ally is far more important than getting exclusive credit. In politics, the best way to convince someone is to lead him or her to discover what you already know.

"Third, sometimes, half a loaf can feed an army. The democratic process is meant to be slow and deliberate, and change is hard to achieve. Very often, achievement of half of an objective is just as significant as achievement of 100 percent. And it may make it easier to achieve the rest later. In Government, as in all endeavors, it is the end result that counts — whether that result is half a loaf or more. Hopefully, an increase in comity and civility, together with renewed emphasis on moral responsibility, will result in a qualitative improvement in end results. In that regard, I have been guided throughout my Senate career by a simple motto and statement of purpose. It is a mantra of just seven words: translate ideas into action and help people."

Pell closed with his vision for his country, still idealistic after nearly four decades in the bruising world of national politics.

"Over the years, I have thought time and again of the historical comparison between Sparta and Athens. Sparta is known historically for its ability to wage war, and little more. Athens, however, is known for its immense contributions to culture and civilization. In all that I have done over the past 36 years in the U.S. Senate, I have had that comparison uppermost in mind. I believe deeply that when the full history of our Nation is recorded, it is critical that we be known as an Athens, and not a Sparta.

"My efforts in foreign relations have been guided accordingly. I believe that instead of our ability to wage war, we should be known for our ability to bring peace. Having been the first and only nation to use a nuclear weapon, we should be known as the nation that brought an end to the spread of nuclear weapons. We should be known as the nation that went the extra mile to bring peace among warring nations. We should be known as the nation that made both land and sea safe for all. In particular, I believe that we should seize every opportunity to engage in multilateral efforts to preserve world peace. We should redouble our support for the United Nations, and not diminish it as some propose. We should not lose sight of the UN's solid record of brokering peace — actions that have consistently served U.S. interests and spared us the costly alternatives that might have otherwise resulted.

"In education, I want us to be known as the nation that continually expanded educational opportunities — that brought every child into the educational mainstream, and that brought the dream of a college education within the reach of every student who has the drive, talent, and desire. We should always remember that public support for education is the best possible investment we can make in our nation's future. It should be accorded the highest priority.

"In the arts and humanities, I want us to be known for our contributions, and for the encouragement we give to young and old alike to pursue their God-given talents. I want us to be recognized as a nation that opened the arts to everyone, and brought the humanities into every home. And here too, I believe government has a proper role in strengthening and preserving our national cultural heritage.

"Pursuing these objectives is not an endeavor that ends with the retirement of one person. It is a lifetime pursuit of a nation, and not an individual. It is always a work of art in progress, and always one subject to temporary lapses and setbacks. My hope, however, is that it is our ongoing mission to become, like Athens, a nation that is known for its civility and its civilization."

□ □ □ The 104th Congress, Pell's last, adjourned on October 3. The final bill to bear Pell's name, Senate Resolution 311, designating November 1996 as "National American Indian Heritage Month," a resolution he cosponsored, was approved on that day. Pell cast his final Senate vote: a "yea" on a 1997 transportation appropriation. It was his 13, 213th vote since his first, in early 1961, when newly inaugurated John F. Kennedy, the president he admired most, brought Americans a message of hope.

Pell's career was almost over. Pell allowed Mulligan, who knew him best of all journalists, to chronicle the closing minutes. Mulligan wrote a lyrical account:

The last vote and the closing conversations lingered on the Senate floor. Pell moved from colleague to colleague, not neglecting doorkeepers and staff, his bony right hand proffered at half-clasp. He slipped unannounced into the cloakroom, past the giant urn that guards the entrance. The last farewell was to Sen. Howell Heflin, another retiring Democrat. The bearish old judge from Alabama and the crane-like Rhode Island patrician clasped hands and parted ways.

Pell descended the marble staircase slowly, his hand riding the brass rail over a wrought-iron balustrade. He crossed the hall under the painted murals of Early American sowing and tilling instruments and of gentry in knee-breeches pondering maps of the Louisiana Purchase. He entered his hideaway for a last round of photos with staff and a last couple of hours of precious routine amid his cluttered hillocks of paper.

There lies ahead for Pell his stumping in the coming weeks for Senate candidate Jack Reed and other Rhode Island Democrats, his work in the coming months as a delegate to the United Nations, his varied social life . . . But there will be an emptiness in the day, Pell confessed as he walked his last walk of his last voting day through the hallways, gripping his bag of papers and books and medicines.

"I've thought about it but I haven't allowed myself to complete the thought," he said of the empty place where the Senate will no longer fill his day. "I may just decide to enjoy myself. Not to fill it."

Pell emerged with his small entourage into daylight shadowed by the Capitol dome. A chill northerly wind blew the season's first clatter of brown oak leaves away from the building. The battered white sedan whined alive at the foot of the granite stair to the Senate chamber. The old man ducked into the front seat. The car wheeled around for the final run to the airport. It was time to go home.

◻ ◻ ◻ In his earlier television interview with ABC-6 television journalist Truman Taylor, Pell had reflected on his career. He acknowledged the influence of his father, saying, "My own interest in politics is in a great deal derived from my father's ideas." Asked what legislation had given him the most satisfaction, he listed the Pell Grants and the Seabed Treaty.

Asked what had disappointed him, Pell answered: "I've one particular regret:

The Law of the Sea Treaty, which I've worked on for many, many years and have not succeeded [in getting ratified]."

On November 5, Reed won election to the Senate with almost 63 percent of the vote, a nearly two-to-one landslide that Pell could well appreciate.

Seventeen days later, the departing senator marked his seventy-eighth birthday.

His disease was gaining on him.

Twilight was gathering.

EIGHT · LIFE AFTER

FAVORITE STORIES

Pell kept a prominent profile and an active but not overburdened schedule in his first year out of office. He spent time in his new office at Salve Regina University's Pell Center for International Relations and Public Policy, in Newport, which had been established with a $3-million U.S. Department of Education grant the previous fall. In January, he dressed in black tie and joined Nuala at the first annual Pell Awards for Excellence in the Arts, a fundraiser honoring actor Jason Robards that raised more than $100,000 for Providence's Trinity Repertory Company. A month later, educators honored him at a Brown University symposium that drew more than 600 people.

"As you can imagine, I'm quite overwhelmed," he said in a two-minute speech, one of the last he would give. "Thank you for an evening I will never forget."

The spring and summer found Pell at several fundraisers, including a ball benefiting a children's cause and the Ben & Jerry's Octopus Garden Party, a benefit for Save the Bay that he and Nuala hosted at Pelican Ledge. By autumn, his legacy preoccupied him. He had arranged for the University of Rhode Island to house his personal, ancestral, and Senate archives, and he spent time there with the collection. He began to work with a new writer on the biography he wanted to see to publication — but that effort, like earlier ones, would not reach fruition.

In the election year of 1998, Pell appeared — but did not speak — at political fundraisers featuring appearances by Vice President Al Gore and First Lady Hillary Clinton. He greeted, from afar, the Reauthorization of the Higher Education Act that nearly doubled the maximum Pell Grant from $3,000 annually to $5,800 annually (an increase phased in over four years).

And he turned eighty.

Pell had not celebrated his birthday since Kennedy was killed on that day, and Pell had additional reasons not to observe this one: he did not like turning eighty, he said, and his Parkinson's left him less than festive. But Nuala persuaded him to have a dinner party.

Daughter Dallas came with her young teenage son, Eames Yates. The Pells' other daughter, Julie, came with her partner, Julie Smith. Toby and Janet were there with their children, Tripler, a teaching assistant at Harvard, and Nick, an undergraduate student at Duke. Son Bertie, who was in Arizona being treated for the cancer that was now in its final stages, could not come, nor could his wife — but one of their children, Christina, a student at Rhode Island School of Design, Bertie's alma mater, was there (brother Clay, Claiborne's namesake, was spending his high school junior year abroad in Spain). Sister M. Therese Antone, president of Salve Regina, and a small group of close friends rounded out the group. The party ended a period of well-wishing that began on his birthday morning with telephone congratulations from Jesse Helms, of all people.

In an op-ed piece, former governor Sundlun recounted the party, to which no press had been invited: the evening was, he said, one of toasts and reminiscing. Asked his favorite of the eight men who had been president while he was in Washington, Pell told Sundlun: "I put Kennedy at the top because he had the greatest vision." Carter, Pell said, had been the most difficult. And he described the late Javits as his best Senate friend.

"As the party drew to a close," Sundlun wrote, "Senator Pell walked himself to the fireplace and made a short speech. He thanked everyone for being present, and in particular he thanked Nuala as his wife for 54 years. He said that she was in his dreams practically every night. He acknowledged the love and support she had given him throughout their lives together, and he thanked her for being the most important influence in his life. Everybody present realized the emotion with which the senator made his short speech. After the speech, grandson Eames went off to bed, but before he left he said:

"'Grandpa, can we take a long walk tomorrow morning?'"

◻ ◻ ◻ The memories Pell's grandchildren would keep would be of an eccentric Grandpa who could be affectionate but was rarely emotional. They would remember a man of stature who possessed an odd tender side: calling seaweed "sea plants," never seaweed, for example. They would remember a man who was obsessive about his ancestry and was insistent, to the point of annoyance, that all of his progeny do their part to further the family legacy. Their later memories would be of an elderly man who did not bring up the topic of his disease, but when asked, would concede frustration — yet declare that it was better than another affliction of old age, Alzheimer's.

"It could be worse," Pell would say.

"When I walked into the room, even when he was extremely frail and sick with Parkinson's, his whole face would light up," said Christina, Bertie's first child. "I remember he would look at my dad that way often, and I always knew that he really loved my father. When my father died too early, I remember being in his hospital room, and watching my grandfather, the most important man that I had ever known, walk in and kneel down to pray by the hospital bed and say goodbye to his first child. My grandfather was the kind of man who had indescribable passion buried underneath a reserved outward persona. When I was with him, I could feel his intensity."

Tripler, the Pell's oldest grandchild, would recall her travels with her grandparents, notably to Paris, where Pell preferred to stay at cheap hotels. "I was with Grandpa several times in Paris over the course of fifteen years and every time there were three requisite stops that say a lot about him," she said. One was The American Church in Paris, where Pell's father worshipped, and where a plaque commemorated Herbert. The second was Agry, the Parisian establishment, dating to 1825, that maintains and sells royal family crests — and where Pell ordered a family ring for his granddaughter. The third was the restaurant Fouquet's, on the Champs-Elysees. "We went to Fouquet's because that is where apparently Grandpa's father had a dish on the menu named especially after him, 'Oeufs Pell.' Of course, that was ages ago and every time we went, Grandpa caused a big commotion in asking for Oeufs Pell. Inevitably, some chef would come out and regret that he could not recall the exact recipe."

And Tripler would recall the times in high school and college that she spent time in Washington, interning on the Foreign Relations Committee while living with her grandparents in Georgetown. "I remember the morning ritual. Grandpa would come down and have a bowl of prunes, freshly squeezed orange juice, toast and coffee. He and my grandmother would read through the papers together. Then Grandpa would make the harrowing drive to work. Grandpa was wonderful in many ways, but he was not a good driver." Tripler soon decided to walk. "The days were busy, we would say 'hi' and touch base at his hideaway. Then, we would either join Mimi or I would get to be his date at the circuit of cocktail party events that he would have to attend after work. He was very good at getting in and out of an event. The three of us also saw many shows together, which was great fun. My grandmother and I in particular loved ballet — I had been a dancer — and Broadway shows. Grandpa would go and was a great supporter, but viscerally it is my grandmother who genuinely loves and truly appreciates the arts."

Clay would remember especially his grandfather's love of reading and, before his disease overtook him, his love of walking — his love of "shuffles," as Pell termed them to his grandchildren.

"One of the treasures in my life," Clay said, "is to open a book margined with Grandpa's scratchy handwriting annotating various facts, often curiously obscure, that would be entirely forgotten but for Grandpa's underline or scrawl. They often were nuggets he hoped to use in his own projects but just as often seem intended for a reader who might pick up the volume a generation or two later. Grandpa loved books — to mark them, to collect them, and to read them.

He was the longest-serving member of the Committee on the Library of Congress, an adored institution not really known, at least not deeply, by many of his colleagues.

"A favorite experience visiting Washington as a little boy, apart from the glee of meeting Senators and Members of Congress engaged in the nation's business, was to walk with Grandpa out his hideaway office in the U.S. Capitol and across to the Library of Congress at midday. Like D.C.'s other world-class museums, the Library is free, open to the public, and a gilded expanse of awe and marble. But the books make it so much more familiar and warm. There is a room in one part of the Library for "Members," i.e., Members of Congress, but it appeared no one other than Grandpa took advantage of this privilege. Below the stacks, Grandpa would point me to a sofa and himself to another, and we would take an intraday nap."

Pell's "shuffles" were the family version of the walkabouts that he took in his capacity as senator, during campaigns and after election.

"Over the years," Clay said, "Grandpa would often come by looking for company on a parade, a shuffle, a visit to the Coast Guard station or a festival in Woonsocket. Maybe I didn't have as much to do as the others or maybe I was so young that the novelty never wore off, but I would usually be the person to go. I reveled in these interludes with Grandpa, being outdoors, learning from him, and getting to know people of all kinds. I remember Grandpa pointing out the buildings of historical interest and asking the questions that interested him, and me: 'Is there an afterlife?' 'What are you reading?' 'What are your plans and dreams?'

"I'd ask my concerns and insecurities, too: 'Grandpa, I get very nervous when I speak — how can I become a better public speaker?'

" 'Practice,' he would say, 'and over time you will not be nervous. But I have never been a good public speaker, and haven't found it to have held me back. The important thing is just to speak, even if you don't sound very good.' "

The grandfather's frugality and idiosyncratic relationship with food — and the interaction of the two — would figure in the stories the grandchildren would tell. They would recall his cheap cars, his simple meals, the brown-bag lunches he ate in his cabana at Bailey's Beach, in violation of club policy, much as his mother in her leaner years had done. They would recall his seat always at the head of the dinner table, where he presided over discussions of politics, history, current events, and foreign affairs — but never gossip, which he found distasteful, or the popular culture, which was alien to him.

"He didn't focus on the equivalent of Paris Hilton because it was not a relevant issue in his life," recalled grandson Nick. "He wouldn't care about fashion or fancy food or these other things. He felt like those are not important things in the grand scheme of things."

Nick, an investment banker, would tell of the occasion that he, his parents, sister and grandparents dined at a sushi restaurant near Newport.

"I don't really think he had ever had sushi before," Nick said. "Could have, but it seemed reasonably foreign to him while we were there. He was eating the sushi and put a huge amount of wasabi onto his plate. And I don't really think he understood what wasabi was. No one was paying attention until all of a sudden he threw the whole thing in at once, as if it was a vegetable. He just sort of seizes up — but just takes it in and never says anything about it. It was all sort of internalized, like the bomb squad: the bomb goes in. There was no external [reaction]. It must have been painful, but he didn't really show it. Not a guy you would want to play cards against."

A favorite story told by grandchildren and Nuala alike concerned an expensive suit Pell found at a church yard sale. Delighted at its cost, which was pennies on the dollar, Pell purchased it. He was wearing it one day when the donor, a wealthy friend who had not been present at the sale, recognized it. Nuala was mortified — but not Pell, who could afford the finest clothes.

In part, this was another of Pell's quirks, in which he took a measure of pride. But it was also a lesson he had learned from his father, who had carried on the Pell tradition of public service while protecting the financial base that allowed freedom for that service while leaving something for future generations. Working-class people seeking to serve faced different challenges.

Like Clay, Nick would have an interest in someday seeking elective office. He had been influenced by his grandfather's philosophy.

"'I inherited some money and it allows me to live a life of service,'" is how Nick summarized his grandfather's relationship to his wealth. "'I'm not going waste money on buying a Ferrari or something: I'm going to hand it down to my children and grandchildren so that they can live lives of public service and do good things with their time and not have to occupy their time with things that aren't service-related. Because the world needs people who are giving back. Not like I need to get the new boat next year when the new Hinckley [luxury yacht] comes out; I need to save it and invest it wisely and take only what I need to live my life and then be able to hand it down.'"

▫ ▫ ▫ As 1999 unfolded, Pell was walking with increasing difficulty, but he resisted using a wheelchair. He could still get out, and he and Nuala continued a busy social life that brought them to parties and, during the good weather, lunch and dinner at Bailey's Beach. They continued entertaining and hosting house guests, including Ted and Vicki Kennedy, whose summertime cruises aboard their sailing yacht Maya and stopovers at Pelican Ledge had been a summer tradition for years. They continued spending time with their children and grandchildren.

With son Bertie that year, it was a lot of time.

Doctors in Arizona had failed in their efforts to stop the progression of his lymphoma, and he had returned to the place where he had grown up; living in the garage apartment at Pelican Ledge, he began treatment at Rhode Island Hospital, where he was under the care of the same doctor who had cured Nuala of her breast cancer. Radiation treatments prolonged his life, but he died at the hospital on September 24, 1999. A memorial service was held at St. George's School, from which he, his brother, his father and a nephew had all graduated. He was buried at St. Columba's Chapel cemetery in Middletown, near the grave of his paternal grandmother, Matilda, and his maternal grandfather, Charles Oliver O'Donnell, who had died before he was born.

Pell was crushed, those closest to him said, but, typically, he contained his feelings. "He was devastated when his son died," said Jan Demers, his longtime Senate aide who remained his assistant after leaving Washington. "But he controlled it. He never showed his emotions — never on anything."

Another reminder of mortality came that October, when John Chafee, who became Rhode Island's senior senator after Pell's retirement, died suddenly while in office of heart failure. And there would be yet another reminder of what was ahead the following July, when John Pastore, senior senator for much of Pell's tenure, died at the age of ninety-three.

Like Pell, Pastore suffered from Parkinson's. Reading what Pastore's son had declared about his father in his obituary, one could not but think of Pell himself. "He never complained," said Dr. John O. Pastore, Jr. "He was a very stoical guy, and I have to think that is one of the reasons he lived as long as he did."

The year 2000 marked a transition in Pell's life. He returned to Washington for President Clinton's final State of the Union Address on January 27 — but he arrived at the Capitol in a wheelchair, which he was using regularly now. He could still speak, but slowly, and in fewer sentences. When asked in a *Providence Journal* telephone interview for his reaction to Clinton, Pell parsed his words. "I thought his speech was long," he said. "It covered the waterfront, and it was exceptionally well delivered." This was one of the last spoken public comments Pell would make. When Pastore died, only released a written statement.

Amtrak began Acela service late in 2000, but Pell, who had traveled on the high-speed Metroliner, did not ever ride on this faster train; he experienced the

Acela only vicariously, watching from the Kingston, Rhode Island, station one day as it sped by.

By year's end, the Pells reluctantly decided to sell their Georgetown house, the closing of another chapter. "I'm heartbroken," Nuala said. But Claiborne could no longer climb the three-story home's stairs. His voice was muting, his face devolving into the expressionless Parkinson's mask. He was requiring daily assistance beyond what Nuala could provide, and aides were hired. He was becoming like Javits.

"My father was absolutely terrified of getting ALS," Toby said. "The thought of ending up like that was the worst thing in the world."

"And he ended up with something worse that didn't last a year, it lasted ten," said Janet.

Pell did not seek pity. He did not acknowledge to others that he was receding.

"He would never talk about it," Toby said. "He never complained. He had a high threshold of pain."

And still, he did not want to die.

SILENCE AT THE END

In early 2005, Claiborne and Nuala welcomed a *Providence Journal* writer into their home for a series of interviews, the last Pell would grant. Pell required assistance now in virtually everything. He could still speak, but only in a slow whisper, and no more than three or four words at a time. His face was frozen, no longer registering anything.

"Claiborne deBorda Pell sits in a wheelchair at a table in his seaside home, eating a lunch of lasagna cut into small pieces," the writer's story began.

> Nuala, Pell's wife of sixty years, is seated to his left. She is telling the story of their early days together, when they lived with the first two of their four children in the chaos of postwar Europe.
>
> It is a dreary day in late winter: the sky threatens snow, and the ocean, south of the living room, is an angry gray. To the west, the cabanas at Bailey's Beach Club are all shuttered. The waves roll onto lonely sand, playground for the old-money set on summer days. Inside the Pell residence, a single-story house so unlike the gilded mansions on nearby Bellevue Avenue, the atmosphere is inviting. The living room is furnished with upholstered sofas and chairs, and salmon-colored drapes frame the windows. Paintings of relatives and ancestors — including great-grandfather Eugene deBorda, a Paris-born Basque — cover the walls. And there is a fireplace, lit every night in cold weather, next to the reclining chair where Claiborne takes his long, daily

naps. A nineteenth-century clock that he inherited from his father chimes on the quarter hour. Nuala winds it once a week.

In 1948, Nuala says, Claiborne was an officer in the U.S. Foreign Service. After spending many months in Prague, he had been assigned to Bratislava, the capital of Slovakia. The Pells were there when the Communists took control of the government. "A lot of our friends were put in prison, and a lot of our friends were tortured," Nuala says. One was Claiborne's interpreter, Andrew Spiro. "One day they kidnapped him and put him in prison and asked him to report on us, and we assumed he would be doing that, so we were very careful. He didn't get out for three months, and he had a terrible time. Am I correct so far, Claiborne?"

Once, Pell possessed a distinctive aristocratic voice — a voice heard in Washington and many overseas capitals during the thirty-six years he was a U.S. senator, longer than any other Rhode Islander. For more than a decade, Pell chaired the Senate Foreign Relations Committee.

But Pell, eighty-six, suffers from Parkinson's disease now, and while his mind remains firm, his memories clear, he can barely whisper.

"Yes," he tells his wife, who is eighty.

"You stop me if I'm not," she says.

"Nuala continues as Claiborne finishes his lunch assisted by an attendant; with effort, Pell can still get a fork or a glass to his mouth, but the attendant's help is appreciated. Someone is on duty twenty-four hours a day for the former senator, whose many legislative accomplishments include the Pell Grant college aid program, which has helped millions of needy students.

Nuala finishes her Bratislava tale: in the fall of 1948, they and their two young children departed for a new assignment in Genoa, Italy.

"When we were leaving," Nuala says, "Spiro, who by that time had been released from prison, asked Claiborne if he would take him out of the country. Claiborne said no, he couldn't. However, Claiborne said, 'The trunk of my car will be unlocked.'" Pell succeeded in smuggling his interpreter to freedom.

Lunch ends. An attendant wipes Pell's mouth and straightens his tie, worn with a button-down shirt. Pell stares across the room, his eyes focused on a small painted altar, one of several pieces of furniture — including the dinner table, with its exquisite inlaid Japanese figures — that the Pells bought in postwar Europe.

"That was from Romania," Claiborne whispers. It is one of the longest sentences I will hear him say in several visits.

"Wood?" I ask.

"Yes," he says.

"Poor Claiborne," Nuala says. "He's so good about it. He never complains. But it's such a shock if you run all your life — and he was constantly working and constantly doing things, he never stopped. And to be suddenly trapped in your body. It's horrible."

But she is accepting.

"We've had a remarkable life, really. I must say I was looking forward to even more trips after we got out of the Senate and doing a lot of things, but be that as it may; it doesn't matter. We're really lucky because all our children live around here, or basically around here, and most of our grandchildren, too. We have a lot of family around."

I notice Nuala's wedding ring, a thin gold band that her husband placed on her finger in a New York church so long ago. Claiborne is not wearing his: he was never big on jewelry, and for more than sixty years, Nuala has kept his ring in her jewelry box.

"He said he'd be willing to wear it now," Nuala says.

She takes her husband's hand and holds it gently.

"But I wouldn't do that to your fingers. They're all curled up."

▫ ▫ ▫ The next year, the Pells lost their second child: Julie, who had become a prominent gay-rights advocate in Rhode Island, a familiar presence every year when the General Assembly met at the Rhode Island State House, died of lung cancer. She was memorialized at a service under a tent on the grounds of Pelican Ledge, scene of so many more joyous occasions, and buried next to her older brother in Middletown.

By then, Parkinson's had silenced Pell completely. Never one to vent inner emotions, the possibility that he might ever share his feelings was gone.

But family members continued to believe he wanted to keep living, regardless of his condition. They believed that desire kept him alive past the stage where many Parkinson's patients finally succumb. They pointed to his insistence on never having a Do Not Resuscitate order — of wanting the opposite, all possible measures to keep his heart beating. "He was caught in his own body," Janet said, but "I think he wanted to live that way rather than die." Perhaps, if he survived long enough, science might find something to save him.

"He thought that there was always a chance," Toby said.

Until his final months, Pell continued to attend parties, movies, and political events with Nuala. He followed the news, and voted, by absentee ballot, for Hillary Clinton in the March 2008 Rhode Island Democratic Primary.

"He can't get to the polls," Nuala, a Barack Obama backer, told *The Providence Journal*. "But he worked with Bill Clinton and he really likes Hillary Clinton."

▢ ▢ ▢ On November 22, 2008, Pell turned ninety. Salve Regina's Pell Center for International Relations and Public Policy marked the occasion with an online video retrospective of his life, but the family held no celebration. Pell was sleeping much of the time now; sometimes they or the staff had to confirm that he was breathing. But on most days, they still dressed him and placed him in his favorite living-room armchair, where he dozed by the fireplace in the company of paintings of his ancestors, his family, and himself.

Christmas passed and Pell's condition worsened. By New Year's Eve, Nuala's premonition that he would not last the winter seemed soon to be realized.

The family gathered with Nuala at Pelican Ledge.

Minutes past midnight, Pell joined his father, mother, Bertie, and Julie in death.

EPILOGUE ▫ THE SHADE OF A COPPER BEECH

The sun was breaking through an overcast sky as Nuala Pell left her home and rode down Bellevue Avenue past her father-in-law's former estate, now the headquarters of the Preservation Society of Newport County. A writer was at the wheel.

It was Veterans Day, 2009.

The car passed the Tennis Hall of Fame and First Beach and continued into Middletown. St. George's School came into view as the car traveled past Hanging Rock, a massive outcropping of ledgerock in the woods below the school that has been a favorite destination for generations of young lovers. A memory brought a smile to Nuala's face. In the summer of 1944, not long after they met, Claiborne took her on a date here, Nuala said.

The writer suggested that perhaps the twenty-five-year-old suitor spoke about his alma mater.

Nuala laughed.

"He wasn't talking about St. George's," she said.

North on Indian Avenue the car continued, past Eastover, where Claiborne spent part of his childhood with his mother and stepfather. The car turned off at Saint Columba's Chapel, a stone church built during the nineteenth century in old-English style.

Ten months before, Pell's worldly journey had ended here. His family had gathered around a freshly opened grave beneath a grand old copper beech tree as Episcopal Bishop Geralyn Wolf led them in the Lord's Prayer. Coast Guardsmen fired a twenty-one-gun salute, a bugler played taps, and the American flag that draped the mahogany casket was folded and handed to Vice Admiral Clifford I. Pearson, Coast Guard chief of staff, whose father served with Pell on a cutter. Pearson gave the flag to Nuala. The casket was lowered, and Nuala and her family threw spades of earth on it. All was silent for a moment, and then the Pells disappeared inside black funeral-home limousines.

Snow had frosted the cemetery grounds on that cold January day — but now it was covered with fallen leaves, a blanket of yellow and gold that reached up the chapel steps. Nuala pointed out her husband's tombstone, recently erected. It was a simple gray tablet, like the stones marking the graves of Bertie and Julie, who lie next to their father. Inscribed on it were Pell's name; dates of birth, death, and Senate service; and the epitaph he had written.

"Statesman, legislator, champion of education and the arts," it read.

Nuala walked through the churchyard, pointing out other graves she knew. There was Ollie O'Donnell, her father, who had found little time for Nuala and her brother after his divorce from their mother. There side-by-side were Claiborne's mother, Matilda, who died in 1972 at Pelican Ledge, and Matilda's husband, the mysterious Commander Koehler, whose death in 1941 had left Matilda in financial difficulty. There in front of the Koehlers was their only child together: Hugh Gladstone Koehler, who passed in 1990 at the age of 60. His premature death had moved stepbrother Pell to tears, one of the few times in his life that he cried.

On the drive home, Nuala talked of Claiborne's obsession with what lay after death.

"He couldn't accept the fact that there wasn't anything," she said. "I told him it was what you believed it to be — but you had to believe strongly that it would happen. But if you were doubtful, there was nothing."

Claiborne, Nuala said, went to his grave without ever revealing if he had reached any conclusion in his quest. No one would ever know if this man who had worked so long for peace had found it for himself.

ACKNOWLEDGMENTS

This book began one day in June 2009 with a phone call. It was Nuala Pell, who I had last seen at her husband's funeral, on January 5 of that year. I covered Pell's funeral for *The Providence Journal*, where I have been a staff writer for most of my long career as a journalist.

"Have you ever thought of writing a biography of Claiborne?" Nuala asked on that early-summer day.

In fact, I had not. I had written about Claiborne Pell several times over the years, most notably in the early spring of 2005, when *The Journal* published "A Remarkable Life," the last substantial profile of Pell before he died. I had spent several days with Nuala and Claiborne for that piece, and when Nuala called, I remembered a comment that longtime Pell aide Jan Demers had made during that time: she, too, had asked if I might consider a biography. I had other preoccupations and the idea passed.

But this time, having covered Pell's funeral and having had time to reflect on his long career, accomplishments, and distinctive personality, I was intrigued. Over lunch at Bailey's Beach, Nuala and I discussed the idea. She offered to open her archives to me and enlist the cooperation of her family and former Pell staff and friends, which meant a book would be an authorized biography, and we agreed that I would retain editorial control, which meant the book would be mine. And so began more than a year of work leading to *An Uncommon Man: The Life and Times of Senator Claiborne Pell*.

My thanks first to Nuala, who has been candid, open, gracious, sharing of both memories and access—and often a humorous voice in her recollections of her late husband. A writer could not ask for more. Thanks also to other Pells who were equally helpful: Claiborne's daughter Dallas and her son, Eames Yates; son Toby and his wife Janet, and their children, Tripler and Nick; and daughter-in-law Eugenia Stillman Diehl Pell and her children Clay Pell and Christina Pell. All were as gracious as Nuala in my in-person interviews and endless pestering questions via phone, email, and Facebook. Thanks also to Columbus O'Donnell, Nuala's brother.

Gratitude to several former Pell staff members, starting with Jan Demers, who remains a family assistant, and who has been an invaluable resource on this book. Gratitude to Thomas G. Hughes, Pell's chief of staff from 1971 through Pell's 1996 retirement; staff member David Evans; staff member Dennis P. Riley; staff member Geryld B. Christianson; and the late John L. Lewis, who joined Pell in his first campaign, and remained with Pell for many years.

The Pell archives at the University of Rhode Island were my primary source for many passages of this book (along with other collections, including those of John Chafee and Claudine Schneider). Pell archivist Mark Dionne was, quite simply, the best: without his organizational skills and knowledge of the vast archives, some of which remains formally uncatalogued, I would have been in deep trouble. Thanks also to David Maslyn, dean of URI Libraries, and Sarina Wyant, special collections librarian. And a nod to Linda Acciardo, director of URI communications and marketing.

I spent two days at the Franklin D. Roosevelt Presidential Library in Hyde Park, N.Y., where Herbert Pell's papers reside (along with many of his son's letters); thanks to Bob Clark, Supervisory Archivist, and archivists Virginia Lewick and Alycia Vivona. Malcolm Mills, of the East Fishkill Historical Society, assisted me with research into Herbert's Hudson Valley estate Pellbridge, which I visited on my trip to Hyde Park. Another trip brought me to Fort Ticonderoga, where distant Pell cousin Robert Pell-deChame was especially helpful both during a guided tour and with genealogy research he provided me by phone and email. Also, thanks to another cousin, Eve Pell, author of *We Used to Own the Bronx: Memoirs of a Former Debutante*. And thanks to Kip Greenthal, daughter of the late Anne Grosvenor, who was a friend of Pell in childhood and as an adult.

Rhode Island senator Jack Reed, who succeeded Pell, granted me important interviews. Thanks to Jack's press secretary Chip Unruh who helped arrange them — and who also connected me to AnnMarie Tomasini, former deputy press secretary to Vice President Joe Biden, whom I interviewed on December 14, 2009, by telephone from the White House.

A special note of thanks to Linda Henderson, former library director of *The Providence Journal*, who conducted significant archival research, and also transcribed several tapes; this is the seventh nonfiction book of mine to which she has contributed, and I cannot thank her enough. Other *Journal* people, past and present, helped, none more than current Washington bureau chief John Mulligan, who knew Pell better than any other journalist (including me); John's observations and quick response to my endless questions were invaluable, as were the many stories I quoted or references in this book. M. Charles Bakst, the *Journal's* former longtime political columnist and writer, belongs in John's league: his influence is also seen on many pages of this book.

Thanks to current *Journal* publisher Howard G. Sutton and executive editor Thomas E. Heslin, who approved the leave of absence I needed to write *An Uncommon Man*, and who have both been supportive of my work for a very long time. Thanks to Michael Delaney, the *Journal's* Managing Editor, Visuals; editor Dave Reid; and staff photographers Connie Grosch and Bob Breidenbach, who took some of the *Journal* photos used in the book. And thanks to Gene Emery and Karen Lee Ziner, still at the paper; and Brian C. Jones, Jodie McPhillips, Scott MacKay, and C. Fraser Smith, former writers.

At Salve Regina University, gratitude to Kristine Hendrickson, director of communications, and to Peter Liotta, former director of the Pell Center for International Relations and Public Policy. Thanks to Elyse Katz and Steven Feinberg, who are making a documentary movie about the Pell Grants.

Thanks to Bruce Sundlun, former governor of Rhode Island; John Winslow, a childhood (and lifelong) friend of Pell, and former president of the Spouting Rock Beach Association, more commonly known as Bailey's Beach; Ellen Koehler Kiley, granddaughter of Commander Hugo Koehler; Tom Erb, artistic director of Trinity Church, Newport; Scott Tirocchi, grandson of John Lewis; Gregory F. Treverton, of the Rand Corporation; Thomas R. Wolanin, senior associate at the Institute for Higher Education Policy; and Darrell West, formerly at Brown University and now vice president and director of Governance Studies and director of the Center for Technology Innovation at The Brookings Institution.

Also, Stephanie Babyak and John White, of the U.S. Department of Education; Sheri M. Whitley and David M. Stone, Columbia University; Kristen Ulrich, Archives Technician, Ronald Reagan Presidential Library; Anne Wheeler, Claudia Anderson and John Wilson, of the LBJ Library and Museum; Judith Havemann and Noel J. Milan of the National Endowment for the Humanities; and Jamie Bennett, Don Ball, and Michael Faubion of the National Endowment for the Arts.

Also, Sharon Kelly, Reference Technician, John F. Kennedy Presidential Library; Chandra Taylor Smith and Abby Miller of the Pell Institute for the Study of Opportunity in Higher Education; Bennett Kelley; Dick Farley; Paul Hacker, author of *Slovakia on the Road to Independence: An American Diplomat's Eyewitness Account*; Rochelle Denisha Gregory; and Dale Collett, Bruce Crooks, Don Fowler, Jim Clarke, Ana Rocha, Cory Howland, Tim Saucier, Frank J. Soares, Norman Lincoln, and Jason Paskowitz, who all shared their stories about Claiborne Pell.

Kind permission to use the photographs in this book was granted by: Howard Sutton, of *The Providence Journal*; Special Collections, University of Rhode Island Library; Nuala Pell and the Pell family; and Dennis P. Riley.

Gratitude to the good people at University Press of New England, who saw the promise in this book and steered it with enthusiasm and skill to publication: Editor-in-Chief Phyllis D. Deutsch, Design and Production Director Eric. M. Brooks, Marketing and Sales Director David P. Corey, copyeditor Ann Klefstad, Publicity and Subsidiary Rights manager Barbara L. Briggs, Marketing and Publicity Coordinator Katy Grabill, and Editorial Assistant Lori A. Miller. Thanks to indexer Joanne Sprott.

Thanks to my longtime agent, Kay McCauley, who sold my first book in 1988 and has been with me on this writing journey ever since.

And finally, a word about Yolanda Gabrielle, to whom this book is dedicated. Yolanda endured the 4:30 a.m. alarms, the long days at this desk, the periodic crankiness and the obsessive mentality that accompanied the writing of this book (it always happens) — and yet was pleased to offer ongoing support and expert critiques.

Thank you, honey, for everything. I love you!

AUTHOR'S NOTES

A PREFATORY NOTE

My ambition in writing this book was to strike a balance between Claiborne Pell, the person, and Senator Claiborne Pell, one of the most prominent senators of the second half of the twentieth century — a politician who came almost literally from nowhere to defeat his party's entrenched establishment and go on to thirty-six years in the Senate, never once losing an election. In those thirty-six years, his achievements were considerable. It is not hyperbole to state that his greatest contribution, the Pell Grants, has truly changed the lives of millions.

From the start, I knew that the political story would be the easier one to tell. Most, if not all, of Pell's Senatorial papers survived, and his long career had been masterfully and exhaustively covered from its earliest days by *The Providence Journal*, where I have been a staff writer since 1981. I mean "easy" in the sense that the raw material of the political half of the book was all there, just awaiting an investment of time to weave it into a narrative.

Telling the personal story of Pell was more difficult, for many reasons. Pell did not keep a diary as such, though I suppose his thousands of letters to and from his father technically constitute one. He was an emotionally closed man, not given to sharing his inner thoughts or feelings. He had thousands of acquaintances and others in his life, but no truly close friends or confidantes that I could find except for his wife, Nuala, who was a tremendous resource in this regard. The man who perhaps knew him best from birth to middle age — and who was certainly the greatest influence on Pell, from birth to death — was his father, who died in 1961. Pell himself was dead by the time I began this book, but even had he been alive, his Parkinson's had long since silenced him. And so, for this part of the story, I relied on the memories of Nuala and her two living children; on Pell's letters to his father and to his mother; and on my own experiences in writing about similarly seemingly inscrutable men, notably surgical pioneer Dr. C. Walton Lillehei, protagonist of my fifth book, *King of Hearts*. And I have to think that growing up with my own (late) father Roger L. Miller, an old Yankee like Pell, provided me with insights.

My work at *The Journal* brought me into periodic contact with Claiborne Pell during the latter years of his Senate service. I met him at news events and at the Providence Newspaper Guild's Follies, an annual satirical review of the news and newsmakers. A search of *The Journal*'s electronic library shows my byline on thirty-three stories in which I interviewed, quoted, or cited Pell. From my arrival in Providence in 1981 until his 1996 retirement, I read about him almost daily in my paper.

Ironically, perhaps, I came to know Pell better after he left the Senate and returned to living full-time in Newport. He was a prominent figure in my six-part *Journal* series about Newport society, "A Nearly Perfect Summer," published July 2–7, 2000. During and after that series, I encountered him regularly at Newport parties and other events. I spent several days with him and Nuala at a point in his life when his Parkinson's disease had greatly advanced for an extensive *Journal* profile, "A Remarkable Life," published on April 10, 2005. And I covered his funeral, writing "A Senator for all times: A fond farewell for a man with a common touch," published January 6, 2009.

The Journal is now simply *The Providence Journal*, but for many years prior to 1995 The Journal Company also published the *Evening Bulletin*. The news staffs were integrated, and for the sake of simplicity in most cases I cite only *The Journal* for both *Journal* and *Evening Bulletin* stories, and what for a time were *Journal-Bulletin* stories (and also for *Sunday Journal* stories). I have included, whenever possible, dates of publication for stories: the newspaper's electronic library dates to 1981, and thus precise references from that year to the present are easily confirmed. Stories prior to that were, of course, hand-clipped and also recorded on microfilm — and this preservation was subject to the dictates and habits of the different news librarians over time. The specific Pell biographical microfilm reels from his young adulthood through the 1970s contain many stories that are dated only by month and year. For major stories during this timeframe, I also pulled the main microfilm to determine precise dates (and play within the paper). But the sheer volume of stories prevented me from precisely dating some smaller stories; the time required would have been prohibitive, and so no precise dates are listed for those lsser references, only month or season. Otherwise, I would still be at the microfilm reader now!

I relied extensively on stories from *The New York Times*, whose online archives is wonderfully organized and easily searched. I also accessed other newspapers' archives, as noted in the book, and digital versions of stories in *Time* magazine and other publications. Many clips were found in Pell's personal scrapbooks, to which I had access.

For biographical information on members of Congress, I relied on the Biographical Directory of the United States Congress: 1774–Present, http://bioguide.congress.gov, which is maintained by the Office of History and Preservation (under the jurisdiction of the Clerk of the U.S. House of Representatives) and the Historian of the United States Senate.

I relied extensively on The Congressional Record, in print form before 1994, and online from 1994 to the present at www.gpoaccess.gov/crecord/index.html

Also of great use as an initial guide, subject to second-source confirmation, was Wikipedia's list of federal legislation, with links to significant measures, http://en.wikipedia.org/wiki/List_of_United_States_federal_legislation

I conducted more than a dozen lengthy, in-person interviews of Nuala Pell; Toby and Janet Pell; Dallas Pell; Eugenia Stillman Diehl Pell; and all five of Claiborne and Nuala's grandchildren, listed in the Acknowledgments. I maintained an email (and Facebook) correspondence with all of these Pells but Nuala, who prefers the telephone and personal contact. During the last nearly two years, I was a frequent visitor to Pelican Ledge, the Pell family home, mostly to tape-record Nuala and sift through family mementoes. I relied on the recollections, photographs, and papers of several Pell aides, as described in the Acknowledgments. Others who provided recollections, photographs, and other information are also listed in the Acknowledgments.

A NOTE ON THE PROLOGUE

I attended Pell's funeral and burial, and the reception at the Pell Center for International Relations and Public Policy. I also relied on recorded television coverage of the funeral and published (and unpublished) photographs of the burial by *Journal* photographer Bob Breidenbach; he and I were the only journalists allowed to attend the burial.

NOTES ON CHAPTER ONE

Here, as in every chapter, I relied extensively on the Pell archives at the University of Rhode Island Library, formally known as the Senatorial Papers of Claiborne Pell. The approximately half-mile of linear space that comprises this collection does indeed hold his Senate papers — but also nearly two centuries' worth of Pell family photographs, prints, engravings, locks of hair, seals, coats of arms, birth and death certificates, last wills and testaments, passports, social security cards, charts, poems, place cards, postcards, stamps, foreign currency, and bank ledgers. Pell's schoolboy papers, report cards, and drawings are there. Thousands of letters from and to friends and relatives, notably his father and mother, are there, along with home movies. The media sub-collection — audio and video tapes, mostly during his political career, some digitized and some not — was also helpful to me. *An Uncommon Man* is a general biography, but the Pell Collection is a priceless archive for historians, scholars, and others with more specific interests in Pell and the many issues that intersected with his career.

The personal papers of the late John L. Lewis were helpful, as was a University of Rhode Island dissertation on the 1960 Rhode Island Primary by Ann Schulz, March 1961, found in URI's Pell collection. Pell's analysis of his 1960 primary and general-election victories was given in "Remarks of Senator Claiborne Pell (D-R.I.) before the Princeton Club of Washington, D.C., June 7, 1961," a copy of which was provided by Lewis's grandson, Scott Tirocchi, who also provided me with other 1960 campaign material.

Pell's recollections of meeting members of the Kennedy family are contained in "Oral History Interview with Senator Claiborne Pell," conducted February 6, 1967, in Washington by John F. Stewart for the John F. Kennedy Library, Boston, from which I obtained a copy.

Here and elsewhere, I used the U.S. Bureau of Labor Statistics' Inflation Calculator to convert dollars in earlier years to their value in 2011.

NOTES ON CHAPTER TWO

I pieced together the story of Pell family genealogy from many sources, including a lineage found in the URI archives and the many documents Pell himself kept of the various branches of his family; unofficial Pell family historian Robert Pell-deChame was also very helpful.

Blake A. Bell, *Thomas Pell and the Legend of the Pell Treaty Oak* (New York: iUniverse, 2004) was a useful source on Pell family history. I found other background on the Pell family on www.historicpelham.com, a web site maintained by Bell, who is on the Board of the Pelham Preservation & Garden Society and the Westchester County Historical Society.

Information on Pell's family was found in Leonard Baker, *Brahmin in Revolt: A Biography of Herbert C. Pell* (Garden City, New York: Doubleday, 1972); and in Olive Pell, *Olive Pell Bible: Condensed from the King James Version*. New York, Crown: 1952.

Some of the letters of Pell's mother, born Matilda Bigelow, and of Matilda's mother, Sophia Dallas deBorda, are found in the Pell archives; before she died, Matilda destroyed letters written to and received from her second husband, Commander Hugo Koehler. Information on Koehler was found in P. J. Capelotti, *Our Man in the Crimea: Commander Hugo Koehler and the Russian Civil War* (Columbia: University of South Carolina Press, 1991), and in Margaretta Wood Potter, "Memoir of Hugo," an unpublished partial collection of letters, dispatches, and personal reminiscences of Cmdr. Hugo W. Koehler (Special Collections, URI Library). This collection was a helpful supplement to Capelotti's book.

Many of Pell's letters to and from his father are archived at the University of Rhode Island, and also at the Franklin D. Roosevelt Presidential Library in Hyde Park, N.Y., where I found material from Pell's Princeton years.

Pell's St. George's School classmate John Winslow, perhaps the only member of their class still living as I was writing this book, was an invaluable resource, granting me an interview and access to their 1936 yearbook.

A NOTE ON CHAPTER THREE
The engagement and wedding of Claiborne and Nuala Pell was covered in several newspapers, cited in the text; I also relied on Nuala's tape-recorded recollections and the family scrapbooks that she keeps at Pelican Ledge. These scrapbooks, maintained by her husband from his youth, were an invaluable complement to the URI archives — in this chapter and throughout the book.

NOTES ON CHAPTER FOUR
President John F. Kennedy's February 20, 1961, remarks supporting his $5.2-billion proposed aid to education are found in their entirety at The American Presidency Project, www.presidency.ucsb.edu, maintained by political science professors John T. Woolley and Gerhard Peters at the University of California, Santa Barbara. Complete versions of addresses, messages to Congress and other communications by Kennedy and other presidents whom I have quoted throughout the book are also found here.

Pell's October 24, 1962, letter to Jacqueline Kennedy on the subject of an arts advisor is appended to the 1967 "Oral History Interview with Senator Claiborne Pell," John F. Kennedy Library.

More background on the creation of the National Endowment for the Arts and the National Endowment for the Humanities is found in Mark Bauerlein and Ellen Grantham, eds., *National Endowment for the Arts: A History, 1965–2008* (Washington, D.C.: National Endowment for the Arts, 1998), and in Roger L. Stevens, *The First Annual Report of the National Council on the Arts, 1964–1965* (Washington, D.C.: National Council on the Arts, September 28, 1965).

Also, histories and timelines on the Endowments' websites were helpful: www.neh .gov/whoweare/timeline.html and www.nea.gov/about/Chronology/Chronology.html

Pell's ideas about high-speed rail and other urban issues are incorporated in Claiborne Pell, *Megalopolis Unbound: The Supercity and the Transportation of Tomorrow* (New York: Frederick A. Praeger, 1966).

Two special collections at the University of Rhode Island Library were useful in writing about John Chafee in this and subsequent chapters: *John H. Chafee, Governor of Rhode Island, United States Secretary of the Navy, 1962–1976*; and *The Senatorial Papers of John H. Chafee, 1976–1999*.

NOTES ON CHAPTER FIVE

Pell's ideas about how the world's oceans should be managed are found in Claiborne Pell, with Harold Leland Goodwin, *Challenge of the Seven Seas* (New York: William Morrow, 1966).

Three written sources were crucial to my writing the story of the Pell Grants: Angelica Cervantes, et al., *Higher Education Act, Forty Years of Opportunity: Open the Doors to Higher Education, Perspectives on the Higher Education Act 40 Years Later* (Round Rock, Texas: TG Research and Analytical Services, 2005) and Lawrence E. Gladieux and Thomas R. Wolanin, *Congress and the Colleges: The National Policies of Higher Education* (Lexington, Mass.: Lexington Books, 1976), as well as Lawrence E. Gladieux, Bart Astor, and Watson Scott Swail, eds., *Memory, Reason, Imagination: A Quarter Century of Pell Grants* (New York: College Entrance Examination Board, 1998).

The role that administrative assistant Ray Nelson played in influencing Pell's vision of the Pell Grants was related to me by two of his children: David C. Nelson and Rebecca Nelson, who also provided me with news clippings and a copy of the June 2, 1981, Congressional Record, which commemorated Nelson after he was found murdered in his Washington home. The murder remains unsolved.

NOTES ON CHAPTER SIX

Part of the story of these years was found in Pell's *Power and Policy: America's Role in World Affairs, a Clear Analysis of National Self-Interest* (New York: W.W. Norton & Company, 1972); another source on Pell's family researches was Guy Richards, *The Rescue of the Romanovs: Newly Discovered Documents Reveal How Czar Nicholas II and the Russian Imperial Family Escaped* (Old Greenwich, Conn.: The Devin-Adair Company, 1975).

A special collection at the University of Rhode Island Library was useful in writing about Claudine Schneider here and in the next chapter: *Claudine Schneider, United States Representative, 1975–1990*.

I interviewed Dr. Robert A. Hallowitz by telephone, and engaged in an extensive email correspondence; similarly, I interviewed C.B. Scott Jones by email. Jones provided me a copy of Pell's address at the Noetics Institute's October 1985 conference into the possibility of life beyond biological death. I learned more about the Institute through an email correspondence with president Marilyn Mandala Schlitz and the Noetics website, www.noetic.org

I found information about Uri Geller on Geller's website, www.uri-geller.com, and confirmed pertinent details through other sources, including *Newsweek, U.S. News & World Report,* and *The Sunday Times* of London.

NOTES ON CHAPTER SEVEN

I reconstructed the story of Pell's Parkinson's Disease from a variety of published and unpublished sources. Thomas G. Hughes, Pell's chief of staff from 1971 through Pell's 1996 retirement, and staff members Dennis P. Riley and Jan Demers; former Rhode Island governor Bruce Sundlun; *The Providence Journal*'s Mulligan; and family members were especially helpful.

Pell expressed his thoughts about the end of the Cold War and his regret about not achieving ratification of the Law of the Sea Treaty in an interview with ABC-6's Truman Taylor that was broadcast on July 7, 1996.

A NOTE ON CHAPTER EIGHT

I wrote "A Remarkable Life," published in *The Providence Journal* on April 10, 2005, edited passages of which are included in this chapter.

A NOTE ON THE EPILOGUE

I am the writer in this chapter.

FINAL NOTES

This book, more than a year in the making, was possible only with the leave of absence I took from *The Providence Journal* for the months of research that went into it. A grant from the Pell family was required to make this economically feasible for me, but it was accepted only on the condition that it be paid back in full from royalties, and that I retain editorial control of everything within these pages. It will be, and I did.

An Uncommon Man is biography, not manifesto, but I feel compelled to imagine what Claiborne Pell would say if he were here to observe the politicking surrounding his lifetime achievement, the Pell Grants, which have given a college education to so many who otherwise could not have afforded one. As of this writing, proposals to significantly cut Grant assistance have won support in Congress.

In his farewell Senate address fifteen years ago, Pell said: "We should always remember that public support for education is the best possible investment we can make in our nation's future. It should be accorded the highest priority."

Cutting Pell Grants, I can hear Pell saying today, would be penny wise and pound foolish — not just for the individuals who would suffer, but for our nation as a whole. And while he never swore, I can imagine that this time, he might. I can hear him calling any proposal to dash so many dreams damn stupid and damn wrong.

G. Wayne Miller
Providence, Rhode Island
June 12, 2011

INDEX

Briggs, 125–27; 1972 vs. Chafee, 148, 167, 172–77, 180–87; 1978 vs. Reynolds, 200, 201–2; 1984 vs. Leonard, 22–223, 217–21; 1990 vs. Schneider, 250–65; 1996 debate and decision not to run, 271, 275–78; campaigning style and strategy, 13–20, 23–25, 32, 126, 174, 182, 201, 220–21; Herbert's observations of first campaign, 22–23, 27; personal wealth issue, 11, 14, 15–16, 20–24, 29

elections, presidential. *See* presidential elections

electronic media, Pell on dangers of, 281

Emery, C. Eugene, Jr., 234

End the War resolution, 147–48

environmentalism, 2, 139, 188, 241, 272–73, 285

EOG (Basic Educational Opportunity Grant) program. *See* Pell Grants

Ervin, Sam J., Jr., 166

Evans, Daniel J., 245

Evans, David, 195, 216

Exon, J. James, 279

face-to-face campaigning, Pell's talent for, 15, 19, 174, 182

Filo, John, 146

financial investment ideas, 64, 92, 93–94

fisheries legislation, 103

Flynn, Raymond P., 135–36

Fogerty, John E., 10, 13

Forand, Aime J., 12

foreign language facility, Pell's, 13, 14, 28, 94, 182

foreign policy: Bosnia conflict, 270–71, 278; chemical and biological arms control, 266; Cuba, 101, 199, 249; Czechoslovakia, 89, 90–91, 266; Eastern European aid bill, 254–55; focus on in first term, 104–5, 108–10; Gulf War position (1991), 259, 265; Iraq, 243, 248–49, 259, 265; last

fact-finding mission (1992), 270; Law of the Sea Treaty, 2, 241, 272–73, 285; Mexico-United States Interparlia-mentary Conference, 104; *Pacem in Terris* International Convocation, 136; P.E.A.C.E., 240; Pell's election cam-paign positions, 16–17; Pell's summary of philosophy on, 282–83; *Power and Policy: America's Role in World Affairs*, 188–90; roots of Pell's, 99; Russia in post-Soviet era, 265–66, 267–68. *See also* Cold War; peace initiatives; Vietnam War

Foreign Relations Committee: appoint-ment to, 125; Gulf War (1991), 265; Pell's ambitions for, 112, 115, 190; Pell's chairmanship of, 190, 231, 241, 266–67; Pell's gradual withdrawal during sixth term, 270–71; restructuring in 1990s, 266–67; Seabed Treaty, 141–42. *See also* peace initiatives

Foreign Service career, 11, 86, 87–89, 90–92, 93

Forrestal, James V., 85

Fort Adams, 103

For the Record (Regan), 234

Fort Ticonderoga, 8, 36, 208

Franklin D. Roosevelt Presidential Library and Museum, 208

Fuerbringer, Jonathan, 245

Fulbright, J. William, 134

Gamble, Millard G., 99

Gardner, John W., 153

Geller, Uri, 232–33, 234

Genoa, Italy, 92–93

Gerry, Peter, 66–67

Giamo, Robert N., 113

Gibbs, Charles Herbert, 45–46

Gibbs School, London, 45–46

G.I. Bill, 152, 156

Gladieux, Lawrence E., 168

O'Donnell, Nuala (wife). *See* Pell, Nuala (née O'Donnell)

Onassis, Jacqueline Kennedy (née Bouvier), 14, 24, 101, 118, 214–15

"An Open Letter to the People of Rhode Island" (Pell), 13

Ornstein, Norman, 242

Osterlund, David, 210

Oswald, Lee Harvey, 117

Our Man in the Crimea (Capelotti), 213

Outer Space Treaty, 138–39

Pacelli, Archbishop Eugenio Maria Giuseppe Giovanni, 212

Pacem in Terris International Convocation, 136

Padelford, Sophia Dallas (née deBorda) (grandmother), 34, 41, 69, 177–78

Palermo, Sicily, WWII, 76–77

paranormal phenomena: Jones and, 227–40, 261–62, 263–64; life after death, 7–8, 225–27, 236–39; mind-body relationship and world peace, 223–25; Pell's interest in, 7–8, 223–40, 251, 253, 261–62; psychic (psi) powers, 228, 229, 231–33, 234–35; Schneider's interest in, 253, 255–56, 261, 262–63; UFOs, 228, 235, 240

Pardo, Arvid, 140, 141

Parkinson's disease, 195, 272, 273–75, 291–94

Pastore, John, 101, 196, 291

Pauling, Linus, 136

Peace and Emergency Action Coalition for Earth, Inc. (P.E.A.C.E.), 240

Peaceful Nuclear Explosions Treaty (PNET), 242

peace initiatives: criticism of Pell's leadership, 245–46; mind-body relationship, 223–25; Outer Space Treaty, 138–39; Pell on demise of Soviet Union and the Cold War, 250; Pell's criticism of

Reagan, 243; Pell's diplomatic leadership approach, 241–42; Russia in post-Soviet era, 265–66, 267–68; sanctions against Iraq for chemical weapons use, 248–49; United Nations seabed committee, 160; WWII experiences as impetus for, 80. *See also* nuclear arms control agreements

Pearson, Clifford I., 296

Pelican Ledge, 22, 177

Pell, Anna (Native American ancestor), 36

Pell, Benjamin (ancestor), 36

Pell, Christina (granddaughter), 204, 272, 287–88

Pell, Christopher Thomas Hartford "Toby" (son): biographical sketch, 205; birth of, 91; on father's dislike of Foreign Relations Committee chairmanship, 266; at father's eightieth, 286; on father's expectations, 204; on father's fear of death, 239; on father's grief over his mother's death, 180; on father's intellectual discussions, 203; on father's persistence, 211; on father's struggle with Parkinson's, 292; name origin, 24

Pell, Claiborne deBorda: ancestry obsession of, 7, 13, 96–97, 205–8; ancestry overview, 35–36; appreciation for those not in his economic class, 52, 73, 152; Biden and, 191–93; biography project, 214; birth of, 39; businesses and investments, 64, 92, 93–94; campaigning style, 13–20, 23–25, 32, 126, 174, 182, 201, 220–21; car accident (1992), 268; cemetery visit (2009 — epilogue), 296–97; character of, 2–9, 25, 45–46, 49, 107–8, 193–99, 203–6, 216–17, 280–83; childhood and early education of, 39–52, 54; college education of, 52–65; courtship